In Nomine Patris et Filii et Spiritus Sancti, amen. Benedic Sancte Pater

Protestation

In all that I shall say in this book I submit to what is taught by Our mother, the Holy Roman Church; if there is anything in it contrary to this, it will be without my knowledge. Therefore, for the love of Our Lord, I beg the learned men who are to read it to look at it very carefully and to make known to me any faults of this nature which there may be in it and the many others which it will have of other kinds.

If there is anything good in it, let this be to the glory and honor of God in the service of His most sacred Mother, our Patroness and Lady.[1]

Matthew R. Plese
meaningofcatholic.com/contact

---

[1] Adapted from the protestation given by St. Teresa of Avila in *Way of Perfection*

The Roman Catechism has been a trusted source of Catholic doctrine for centuries. Mr. Plese has done a great service in transmitting this classic catechism for the modern world.
– *Bishop Athanasius Schneider, Auxiliary Bishop of Astana*

Our age is almost unique in its lack of sound catechesis. Matthew Plese's work fills an enormous need by making better known the clarity of the Roman Catechism. Given that many people today lack a foundation in basic religious concepts, Plese's explanation of the Roman Catechism will make this treasure more accessible and useful to a contemporary audience. Mr. Plese has performed a great work for the Church by completing this detailed and deep explanation of this treasure of the Church.
– *Dr. Brian McCall, editor-in-chief, Catholic Family News*

The *Roman Catechism,* commonly known as The Catechism of Trent, is the most important catechism in the history of the Catholic Church. It was composed by order of an Ecumenical Council, at the height of the Protestant Revolution, to give pastors precise, succinct definitions of the dogmas of the Faith, and it became the gold standard for teaching and preaching the dogmas of the Faith for 350 years. It is still authoritative, and it is the only catechism quoted in the 1992 Catechism—it is quoted 20 times—because it gives such beautiful, clear definitions of the dogmas of the Faith. *The Roman Catechism Explained for the Modern World* gives an excellent introductory commentary on the Catechism of Trent, so that contemporary Catholic readers will hopefully be motivated to appreciate and make use of this great treasure.
– *Hugh Owen, Director, Kolbe Center for the Study of Creation*

"Many Catholics today are confused about the teachings of their faith." This is troubling and not something a faithful Catholic would expect to hear 20 centuries after Christ "dwelt among us." It is probably more accurate to say "most *prelates* ordained and charged with *teaching* the Catholic faith are confused about it." This little book on catechism aims to address this confusion with four simple implements of teaching whose beauty and simplicity I would be wrong to reveal; rather that you should take up this book and become immersed in them and turn that neon light out yourself.
– *Mike Church, Radio & TV Presenter on The CRUSADE Channel*

The Roman Catechism Explained for the Modern World

By Matthew R. Plese

THE ROMAN CATECHISM EXPLAINED

FOR THE MODERN WORLD

Matthew R. Plese

OUR LADY OF VICTORY PRESS

© Our Lady of Victory Press, MMXXII

ISBN 979-8-218-10412-2

2ND PRINTING: NOVEMBER 2023

Our Lady of Victory Press is an imprint of The Meaning of Catholic, a lay apostolate dedicated to uniting Catholics against the enemies of Holy Church.

MeaningofCatholic.com

Design and layout by W. Flanders.

Our Lady of Victory, pray for us!

This text was originally published in 41 parts at *Catholic Family News* and is published here with permission.

Table of Contents

The Ten Commandments

The Lord's Prayer

FOREWORD

In his 1905 Encyclical *Acerbo Nimis*, on the teaching of Christian doctrine, Pope St. Pius X lamented the "decline in religion" — that is, the "indifference" to Catholic faith and morals — he saw spreading in his day (one can only imagine what he would say about our times!). He said that, although "we should not overlook other considerations, We are forced to agree with those who hold that the chief cause of the present indifference and, as it were, infirmity of soul, and the serious evils that result from it, is to be found above all in ignorance of things divine. This," he said, "is fully in accord with what God Himself declared through the Prophet Osee: 'And there is no knowledge of God in the land. Cursing and lying and killing and theft and adultery have overflowed: and blood hath touched blood. Thereafter shall the land mourn, and everyone that dwelleth in it shall languish'" (1).

In order to remedy this "ignorance of divine things," St. Pius X reminded "all parish priests and in general all those having the care of souls" of their solemn duty to instruct both children and adults "on those things they must believe and do in order to attain salvation" (19). And he specified that the "catechetical instruction" they provide "shall be based on the Catechism of the Council of Trent," that is, the Roman Catechism. He further directed that the contents of the Catechism should be "divided in such a way that in the space of four or five years, treatment will be given to the Apostles' Creed, the Sacraments, the Ten Commandments, the Lord's Prayer, and the Precepts of the Church" (24).

The book you now hold is a concrete and timely response to St. Pius X's call to base catechetical instruction on the Roman Catechism, the renowned compendium of Catholic faith and morals produced under the watchful eye of St. Charles Borromeo (1538-1584) and published by decree of Pope St. Pius V (r. 1566-1572). The author of the present work, Matthew Plese, originally composed the contents of this book as a series of articles for *Catholic Family News*, a monthly journal and online media apostolate which has always held sound catechesis as central to its mission.[2]

While St. Pius X rightly observes that parish priests are responsible for the religious instruction of their parishioners, he does not neglect to mention the importance of lay catechists, who are needed "especially in places where there is a scarcity of priests...." (22). He explains:

---

[2] For more information, visit https://catholicfamilynews.com.

The task of the catechist is to take up one or other of the truths of faith or of Christian morality and then explain it in all its parts; and since amendment of life is the chief aim of his instruction, the catechist must needs make a comparison between what God commands us to do and what is our actual conduct. After this, he will use examples appropriately taken from the Holy Scriptures, Church history, and the lives of the Saints — thus moving his hearers and clearly pointing out to them how they are to regulate their own conduct. He should, in conclusion, earnestly exhort all present to dread and avoid vice and to practice virtue (13).

Throughout this book, Mr. Plese does all of the above with commendable clarity and charity. In addition to quoting extensively from the Roman Catechism itself, he also draws from other trusted sources and provides his own commentary to round out each topic in the "plain and simple style" called for by St. Pius X (24).

My hope is that Mr. Plese's book will find a wide readership among Catholic fathers and mothers, who, as the Roman Catechism recalls, "are obliged to bring up their children in the knowledge and practice of religion, and to give them the best rules for the regulation of their lives; so that, instructed and trained in religion, they may serve God holily and constantly." As Archbishop Marcel Lefebvre (1905-1991) counsels parents in his *Open Letter to Confused Catholics*, "Read and reread as a family the Catechism of Trent, the finest, the soundest and most complete."[3] I would humbly add that parents and catechists should read and reread Mr. Plese's book as a means of deepening their own understanding of the Roman Catechism and of the Catholic Faith, in general.

Matt Gaspers
Managing Editor, *Catholic Family News*

July 7, 2022
Sts. Cyril and Methodius

---

[3] Archbishop Marcel Lefebvre, *Open Letter to Confused Catholics* (Kansas City: Angelus Press, 1986), 186.

The Roman Catechism

Studying Our Faith from a Trusted Source
An Indulged Practice, Vital for Our Times

Learning our Religion: A Commandment for the Modern Catholic

For there is no other Name under heaven given to men, whereby we must be saved (Act iv. 12), and yet, how many of us feel a pull on our hearts because of it? How about when we hear St. Paul remind us elsewhere: *How then shall they call on Him, in whom they have not believed? Or how shall they believe Him, of whom they have not heard? And how shall they hear, without a preacher?* (Rom. x. 14). How often do we think about the vast numbers of souls who die each day? How many go to hell? Do we ever think to ourselves, "Is there anything that I can do to stop it?"

We live in a state of complete moral collapse and deterioration in Catholic belief. Rather than opening the Church up to better confront and guide the modern Catholic, Vatican II and its aftermath have led to a continual downward spiral in Catholic belief. Average Catholics should feel grief in their own souls as they see more Catholics fall away from the Faith and reject the one means given to us to be saved – Holy Mother Church.

Since 1970, according to data analyzed from USCCB records, the number of students in religious education has decreased by 60%, adult baptisms have fallen by 68%, and the annual number of infant baptisms has fallen by 18%. Furthermore, according to Sherry Weddell's research published in *Forming Intentional Disciples* (Our Sunday Visitor, 2012), only 30% of Americans who were raised Catholic still practice the Faith, and 10% of all adults in the United States are fallen-away Catholics.

In our modern age, it is easy to become distracted with the use of technology, the day-to-day responsibilities of life, and the physical demands placed on us each day. How often do we step back and *actually* pray? Do we truly try to go to daily Mass, recite part of the Divine Office, get in our daily Rosary, or practice thirty minutes of mental prayer a day?

Do we at least keep all things in perspective and ensure that we are spending adequate time each day in practicing the Catholic Faith? Our Lord Himself affirmed, "Heaven and earth shall pass, but My words shall not pass" (Mt. xxiv. 35), yet modern man acts as if religion is a fable or at best something that, while true for some, applies to others and not himself. We will all die. We will all be judged on our Faith. And unbeknownst to the modern Catholic is the reality that neglecting the Sacraments and neglecting our faith formation and that of our children is a serious sin.

Religious education is not an obligation for children alone. It is our responsibility as adults to continue learning our Faith in order to live it out and spread it. Our Lord Himself observed the Jewish law to the letter and affirmed that He had come to perfect, not abolish, the law (cf. Mt. v. 17). And the law of charity imposes on us who have been given the grace to be Catholic the responsibility to spread the Faith, to admonish sinners, to instruct the ignorant, to raise children in the Catholic Faith, and to be a role model to others. As King David exclaimed in the Psalms, *O how have I loved Thy law, O Lord! it is my meditation all the day* (Ps. cxviii. 97). But, do we *really* love the Lord's law? Do we love it enough to set down the television remote, the football, and our other comforts in order to pick up a copy of the Roman Catechism or the Lives of the Saints?

The world and the Church herself are in a state of unprecedented crisis, a crisis that is greatly exacerbated by the average lay Catholic failing to understand his religion. It was only a few decades ago that the illustrious Archbishop Fulton Sheen remarked: "Who is going to save the Church? Not our Bishops, our priests and religious. It is up to the laity. You have the minds, the eyes, the ears to save the Church. Your mission is to see that your priests act like priests, your bishops act like bishops and your religious act like religious."[4] But if he were on this earth today, I suspect he would weep for how little those in the Church seem to care about true doctrine.

The Divine Remedy of Christian Doctrine

Despite modern man's propensity to forget the souls in purgatory and the reality of our certain death and our encounter with Our Lord as Judge, these truths exist independent of our awareness of them. In fact, if modern man were to step back and examine the amount of time he puts into mundane (or even commendable) earthly endeavors that pass away, he would weep. Why do we place so much time into thinking of tomorrow, or our next vacation, or our future jobs, or our retirement plans? And yet, all of us will one day stand before the Just Judge Who knows the hidden sins of our life

---

[4] Archbishop Fulton J. Sheen's Address to the Supreme Convention of the Knights of Columbus, June 1972.

and will judge us for every last omission and action. Why do we resist planning for a certain death and ensuring that we are prepared to stand before the Supreme Arbiter of our eternal destiny?

Despite Protestant attacks on purgatory and indulgences, both the former and the latter are real and should thus be taken seriously. Specifically regarding indulgences, the traditional indulgence is this: "The faithful who devote twenty minutes to a half hour to teaching or studying Christian Doctrine may gain: an indulgence of 3 years. The indulgence is plenary on the usual conditions twice a month, if the above practice is carried out at least twice a month." *The Enchiridion of Indulgences* maintained this Raccolta indulgence as meriting a partial indulgence.

The Church not only bestows upon parents the responsibility to educate their children, but She offers all the faithful involved in learning and teaching religious doctrine the remission of temporal punishment due to sins. How truly generous Holy Mother Church is! Many times, when we are given an obligation and we perform it, we do not receive a great reward for doing our duty. But in this instance, we are given, for the performance of this duty, the partial remission of the temporal punishment due to our sins.

Teaching Christian Doctrine is also a forgotten spiritual work of mercy. Indeed, the first three of the seven spiritual works of mercy have at their core the transmission of true doctrine: instructing the ignorant, counseling the doubtful, and admonishing the sinner. Not everyone is considered capable or obligated to perform the first three spiritual works of mercy if they do not have proper tact, knowledge or training to do so. Yet, in our crisis, Holy Church is calling to arms those Catholics who are committed to learning and defending her teachings.

Far from being a novelty, the responsibility of all the Church's members to teach the Sacred Deposit of the Faith dates to the very beginning of the Church, far before the time of either Vatican II or Pope John Paul II. His Holiness Pope Leo XIII's *Sapientiae Christianae* (Jan. 10, 1890) explained the necessity of all Catholics to help spread the Faith quite clearly:

> Now, faith, as a virtue, is a great boon of divine grace and goodness; nevertheless, the objects themselves to which faith is to be applied are scarcely known in any other way than through the hearing. 'How shall they believe Him of whom they have not heard? and how shall they hear without a preacher? Faith then cometh by hearing, and hearing by the word of Christ.' [Rom. x. 14] Since, then, faith is necessary for salvation, it follows

that the word of Christ must be preached. The office, indeed, of preaching, that is, of teaching, lies by divine right in the province of the pastors, namely, of the bishops whom 'the Holy Spirit has placed to rule the Church of God.' [Acts xx. 28] It belongs, above all, to the Roman Pontiff, Vicar of Jesus Christ, established as head of the universal Church, teacher of all that pertains to morals and faith.

No one, however, must entertain the notion that private individuals are prevented from taking some active part in this duty of teaching, especially those on whom God has bestowed gifts of mind with the strong wish of rendering themselves useful. These, so often as circumstances demand, may take upon themselves, not, indeed, the office of the pastor, but the task of communicating to others what they have themselves received, becoming, as it were, living echoes of their masters in the faith. *Such co-operation on the part of the laity has seemed to the Fathers of the [First] Vatican Council so opportune and fruitful of good that they thought well to invite it.* 'All faithful Christians, but those chiefly who are in a prominent position, or engaged in teaching, we entreat, by the compassion of Jesus Christ, and enjoin by the authority of the same God and Savior, that they bring aid to ward off and eliminate these errors from holy Church, and contribute their zealous help in spreading abroad the light of undefiled faith.' [Const. *Dei Filius*] *Let each one, therefore, bear in mind that he both can and should, so far as may be, preach the Catholic faith by the authority of his example, and by open and constant profession of the obligations it imposes.* In respect, consequently, to the duties that bind us to God and the Church, it should be borne earnestly in mind that in propagating Christian truth and warding off errors the zeal of the laity should, as far as possible, be brought actively into play. (nn. 15-16, emphasis added)

In fact, the Blessed Mother's apparition to Adele Brise in Champion, Wisconsin in 1859 further affirmed the need to teach the Catechism.[5] Under the title of Our Lady of Good Help, the Blessed Virgin said to Adele, "Gather the children in this wild country and teach them what they should

---

[5] This apparition has been approved by ecclesiastical authority. See championshrine.org.

know for salvation. Teach them their catechism, how to sign themselves with the Sign of the Cross, and how to approach the Sacraments; that is what I wish you to do. Go and fear nothing. I will help you."

The Church needs us. We are being called to live radically Catholic lives grounded in the eternal truths of the Faith. The idea that Catholic dogma can change and that what was once true is no longer true is entirely and unequivocally false. *Jesus Christ is the same yesterday, today, and forever* (cf. Heb. xiii. 8). If the Church believed in the unity of the Trinity, the sinlessness of Mary, the necessity of Baptism, the evil of divorce, and more in times past, those truths remain valid today. While certain disciplines can change like the exact date of feast days or the color of vestments, dogmas of faith and morals cannot change by definition.

Pope St. Pius X upheld the immutability of the Deposit of Faith by including the following in his list of condemned propositions (July 3, 1907): "Christ did not teach a determined body of doctrine applicable to all times and all men, but rather inaugurated a religious movement adapted or to be adapted to different times and places" (*Lamentabili Sane*, n. 59). Some months later, he promulgated his encyclical *Pascendi Dominici Gregis* against the heresy of Modernism (Sept. 8, 1907), providing a more thorough exposition and refutation of what he defined as "the synthesis of all heresies" (n. 39). And finally, on Sept. 1, 1910, St. Pius X instituted the Oath Against Modernism, requiring every bishop, priest, religious superior, seminarian, and professor of Theology or Philosophy to publicly and solemnly affirm, among other vital points, "I entirely reject the heretical misrepresentation that dogmas evolve and change from one meaning to another different from the one which the Church held previously."

In our doctrinal confusion today, clarity is desperately needed. What exactly is the Faith? What is the true doctrine of Christ? Thankfully, there is a resource for us and that resource is none other than the Roman Catechism.

The Roman Catechism, A Trusted Source

Known as the "Roman Catechism," the "Catechism of St. Pius V," and also the "Catechism of the Council of Trent," this book has fallen into extreme disuse. In fact, the word "catechism" today is often used only in reference to the post-conciliar *Catechism of the Catholic Church*, originally published by Pope John Paul II in 1992. Sadly, however, this modern catechism fails in many respects: its verbose language, its frequent references to the novelties of Vatican II as opposed to actual dogmatic works, and the recent errors promulgated by Pope Francis in regard to capital punishment. In fact, the number of religious education programs that feel they must teach children from this catechism is frightening – no young child could attempt to learn from a text that is best suited for an undergraduate or master's course. So why do we either water down the Faith or teach children that the only true source of doctrine is the 1992 text?

Unbeknownst to many, the new catechism is far from the only catechism. St. Peter Canisius, who was instrumental in fighting Protestantism in Germany, wrote the first catechism in 1555 known as the "Catechism of St. Peter Canisius." Less than a decade later in 1562, the Roman Catechism was commissioned by the Fathers of the Council of Trent, who saw the need for an authoritative explanation of the Faith for the universal Church. Prepared under St. Charles Borromeo's supervision and issued by Pope St. Pius V in 1566, it remains the most authoritative catechism in print.

The notion that the title "Catechism" belongs exclusively to the 1992 text promulgated by Pope John Paul II is absurd. In fact, as the crisis in the Church deepened, Cardinal Joseph Ratzinger (the future Pope Benedict XVI) commented on the failure of modern catechesis in the Church when he said in 2003, "It is evident that today religious ignorance is enormous; suffice it to speak with the new generations. Evidently, in the post-conciliar period the concrete transmission of the contents of the Christian faith was not achieved."[6] This echoed his previous sentiments published before the New Catechism was written: "The catastrophic failure of modern catechesis is all too obvious."[7]

For the present-day Catholic who wishes to heed the call of Pope Leo XIII to engage in true apostolic work and win souls, the New Catechism with its ambiguities and verbosity is certainly ill suited for the job. Instead, I wish to refer readers to the timeless and enduring Roman Catechism. Unless otherwise noted, all quotations from "the Catechism" are from this trusted source.[8]

The Catechism itself is divided into four principal parts as stated in the introductory section of the work:

> The truths revealed by Almighty God are so many and
> so various that it is no easy task to acquire a knowledge
> of them, or, having done so, to remember them so well

---

[6] "Cardinal Ratzinger on the Abridged Version of the Catechism," *Zenit.org* (May 2, 2003) <https://zenit.org/articles/cardinal-ratzinger-on-the-abridged-version-of-catechism/>, accessed August 3, 2022.

[7] Joseph Ratzinger, *The Yes of Jesus Christ* (New York, 1991), 35.

[8] *Roman Catechism* (TAN Books and Publishers, Inc., 1982).

as to be able to explain them with ease and readiness when occasion requires. Hence our predecessors in the faith have very wisely reduced all the doctrines of salvation to these four heads: The Apostles' Creed, the Sacraments, the Ten Commandments, and the Lord's Prayer.

The part on the Creed contains all that is to be held according to Christian faith, whether in regard to the knowledge of God, the creation and government of the world, or the redemption of man, the rewards of the good and the punishments of the wicked. The part devoted to the Seven Sacraments teaches us what are the signs, and, as it were, the instruments of grace. In the part on the Decalogue is described whatever has reference to the law, whose end is charity [I Tim. i. 5]. Finally, the Lord's Prayer contains whatever can be the object of the Christian's desires, or hopes, or prayers. The exposition, therefore, of these four parts, which are, as it were, the general heads of Sacred Scripture, includes almost everything that a Christian should learn.

The Necessity of Faith
and Apostolic Origin of the Creed

The Necessity of Faith

"O my God, I firmly believe that You are one God in three divine Persons, Father, Son, and Holy Ghost. I believe that Your divine Son became man and died for our sins, and that He will come to judge the living and the dead. I believe these and *all the truths* which the holy Catholic Church teaches, because in revealing them You can neither deceive nor be deceived."

This short but powerful Act of Faith is a prayer that all young Catholics learn. But how often do we reflect on it in our daily life? Do we make this Act of Faith along with an Act of Hope and Act of Charity each morning with our morning prayers? Or has it fallen by the wayside amidst the busyness of life? Do we even know what "faith" means?

The Roman Catechism begins with an overview of Faith, its necessity, and the origins of the Apostles' Creed. The Roman Catechism plainly asserts in this first section: "In preparing and instructing men in the teachings of Christ the Lord, the Fathers began by explaining the meaning of faith. Following their example, we have thought it well to treat first what pertains to that virtue... we here speak only of that faith by which we yield our entire assent to whatever has been divinely revealed."

According to the *Modern Catholic Dictionary* by Fr. John Hardon, S.J., faith is "the acceptance of the word of another, trusting that one knows what the other is saying and is honest in telling the truth. The basic motive of all faith is the authority (or right to be believed) of someone who is speaking. This authority is an adequate knowledge of what he or she is talking about, and integrity in not wanting to deceive. It is called divine faith when the One believed is God, and human faith when the persons believed are human beings."[9] Thus, when we speak of faith in God or faith in the teachings of the Catholic Church, it is not a mere aspiration or dream; rather, it is a sure and firm belief in something objectively true. Although we cannot scientifically demonstrate all the dogmas of Faith, our belief is not based on emotions or convictions; rather, in the words of Pope St. Pius X, "faith is a genuine assent of the intellect to truth received by hearing from an external source" – namely, from God (Oath Against Modernism).

Concerning the virtue of Faith, the *Catechism of St. Thomas Aquinas*, composed by the Angelic Doctor himself, expounds on this notion when he writes, "The first thing that is necessary for every Christian is faith, without which no one is truly called a faithful Christian." To be a Christian it is necessary to possess faith – faith in God and in all that His Holy Church teaches. Those who reject certain dogmatic teachings (e.g. Purgatory, the necessity of confessing one's sins to a priest, Transubstantiation, etc.) reject the entirety of the Faith since to reject part of what is necessary for salvation is to reject it wholly. To be a Catholic, one must profess faith in *all* that the Church teaches, as St. Thomas explains: "...a heretic with regard to one article has no faith in the other articles, but only a kind of opinion in accordance with his own will" (II-II q5 a3).

According to the Church's Code of Canon Law:

> A person must believe with divine and Catholic faith *all those things* contained in the word of God, written or handed on, that is, in the one deposit of faith entrusted to the Church, and at the same time proposed as divinely revealed either by the solemn magisterium of the Church or by its ordinary and universal magisterium which is manifested by the common adherence of the Christian faithful under the leadership of the sacred magisterium; therefore all are bound to avoid any doctrines whatsoever contrary to them... therefore, one who rejects those propositions which are to be held definitively is opposed to the doctrine of the Catholic Church.[10]

To obstinately deny or doubt even one divinely revealed truth is to fall into the mortal sin of *heresy* – a sin that requires not only sacramental Confession but also a repudiation of the false teaching and a return to harmony of belief with the truth as taught by Holy Mother Church.

---

[9] Fr. Hardon's entire *Modern Catholic Dictionary* is available online at <http://www.thercalpresence.org/dictionary/adict.htm>.

[10] 1983 Code of Canon Law, Can. 750 §1-2.

St. Thomas continues his discussion on Faith by pointing out its four effects:

> The first is that through faith the soul is united to God, and by it there is between the soul and God a union akin to marriage... The second effect of faith is that eternal life is already begun in us; for eternal life is nothing else than knowing God... The third good that comes from faith is that right direction which it gives to our present life. Now, in order that one live a good life, it is necessary that he know what is necessary to live rightly; and if he depends for all this required knowledge on his own efforts alone, either he will never attain such knowledge, or if so, only after a long time. But faith teaches us all that is necessary to live a good life... The fourth effect of faith is that by it we overcome temptations: the devil would have us disobey God and not be subject to Him. This is removed by faith, since through it we know that He is the Lord of all things and must therefore be obeyed.[11]

Faith is necessary for salvation, for it is by faith that we attach ourselves to all that God has revealed for our salvation. The Roman Catechism continues by its succinct but clear affirmation: "That faith thus understood is necessary to salvation no man can reasonably doubt, particularly since it is written: Without faith it is impossible to please God [Heb. xi. 6]."

Faith Alone is Insufficient

While faith is necessary for salvation, the intellectual assent to God's existence and revelation is not enough, in and of itself, to save a man. *Thou believest that there is one God. Thou dost well: the devils also believe and tremble*, says St. James in his Epistle (Ja. ii. 19). A man could certainly believe in God, be baptized, and then live a life of sin which would condemn his soul to hell. A man could also live a holy life for many years, but then give in to temptation, commit a mortal sin, and die separated from God. Those who claim otherwise fail to understand the malice of sin and forget that Our Lord will condemn those who merely give Him lip service (cf. Mt. vii. 21). More than mere belief in our Divine Redeemer is necessary to save our souls, once again, as St. James testifies: *For even as the body without the spirit is dead, so also faith without works is dead* (Ja.

---

[11] Thomas Aquinas, *Expositio in Symbolum Apostolorum*, trans. Joseph B. Collins (New York, 1939).

ii. 26). Catholics would do well to familiarize themselves with the Church's timeless teachings on this matter.

When speaking of the Redemption, we begin with *objective* redemption, which deals with Christ. Objective redemption began when Christ was conceived and completed in His Resurrection. During that period, He fulfilled the prophecies of long ago and *was offered once to exhaust the sins of many*, that is, *for the destruction of sin by the sacrifice of Himself* (Heb. ix. 28, 26). Three days later, He rose from the dead, and we, too, believe that if we die in Christ, we also will rise with Him (cf. II Tim. ii. 11). This is a central truth of the Faith, one that is expressed in the Creed.

Subjective redemption, however, is also vitally important to the Christian faithful in reaching Heaven because even though Christ died for all, not everyone chooses to cooperate with God's salvific will and thus be saved. In other words, there are people who reject Jesus and the Redemption He merited for us. Our Lord Himself alluded to this truth when He instituted the words of consecration for His Precious Blood, saying, *Take this, all of you, and drink from it, for this is the chalice of My Blood, the Blood of the new and eternal covenant, which will be poured out for you and* for many *for the forgiveness of sins*. Concerning this reality, St. Thomas comments: "The Blood of Christ has been shed for all concerning its sufficient power (*quem ad sufficientam*), but only for the elect as regards to its efficacy (*quo ad efficiam*)."

Christians have an obligation to grow in the Faith by following Christ in obtaining their salvation. We believe that salvation cannot be earned, but we do believe, as Catholics, that we have a responsibility to live a life of *faith that worketh by charity* (Gal. v. 6).

Our Lord instructed the Apostles shortly before His Ascension, *Going therefore, teach ye all nations, baptizing them in the Name of the Father, and of the Son, and of the Holy Ghost. Teaching them to observe all things whatsoever I have commanded you: and behold I am with you all days, even to the consummation of the world* (Mt. xxviii. 19-20). He never told His followers to merely believe, teach others to accept Him as their "personal Lord and Savior," then return to their previous ways of life.

By God's grace, we receive the gift of faith that allows us to believe. The works that we do, in turn, demonstrate our faith. Thus, we are saved by God's grace (cf. Eph. ii. 8), but His grace in us must not be void (cf. I Cor. xv. 10).

Everyone, from the highest kings to the lowest servants, must put their faith into action in order to obtain salvation, as St. Paul says (Philip. ii. 12-13).

Some Protestants will counter with Romans: *For we account a man to be justified by faith without the works of the law* (iii. 28). Notice, however, that St. Paul did not say faith *alone*. In his German translation of the New Testament, Martin Luther added the word "alone" to the above verse in a shameful attempt to legitimize his heresy of *sola fide*. Ironically, the only verse in Scripture that features the phrase *sola fide* ("faith alone" or "faith only") *categorically rejects* Luther's heresy: *Do you see that by works a man is justified, and* not by faith only? (Ja. ii. 24). This is why Luther contemptuously referred to the Epistle of St. James as the "epistle of straw."

Faith and Works: Harmonizing Paul and James

To account for the apparent (not real) contradiction between St. Paul's Epistle to the Romans and the Epistle of St. James, we must understand that St. Paul, in Romans, is talking about the works of the law required by the Jewish faith. In addition to the Ten Commandments, the Jews were required to follow hundreds of other legal prescripts ranging from liturgical and dietary laws to the wearing of tassels on their cloaks. According to a strict interpretation of the Mosaic law, something as small as lighting a fire in one's home on the Sabbath would break the law (cf. Ex. xxxv. 3). For St. Paul, the former Pharisee, the debate is obviously not about Catholic versus Protestant, but about Jewish versus Gentile and the requirements under the New Covenant, which has replaced the Old Covenant.

Remember the words that Christ spoke during His Sermon on the Mount: *So let your light shine before men, that they may see your good works, and glorify your Father Who is in heaven* (Matt. v. 16). So must we, with a sincere heart, have works that glorify God. Our works will be an outward expression of our Faith, for faith without works is indeed dead. Long before the Protestant revolt, St. Anthony of Padua (1195-1231) asserted inspired words which surely apply to us in the 21st century: "Actions speak louder than words; let your words teach and your actions speak. We are full of words but empty of actions, and therefore are cursed by the Lord, since He Himself cursed the fig tree when He found no fruit but only leaves. It is useless for a man to flaunt his knowledge of the law if he undermines its teaching by his actions."[12]

---

[12] June 13th entry in *Catholic Mom's Cafe: 5-Minute Retreats for Every Day of the Year* by Donna-Marie Cooper O'Boyle.

The Creed

After establishing the necessity of faith and its unity, the Roman Catechism continues with an overview of the Apostles' Creed. A creed is a summary or statement of what one believes. "Creed" comes from the Latin *credo*, which means *I believe*; that is, I accept or hold true something on the word of another. A creed, in the Catholic sense, is not a product of human wisdom expressing subjective opinions. It is a systematic statement of divinely revealed truths.

The Apostles' Creed is a series of twelve truths about God, the Trinity, and the Catholic Church that He founded. The Roman Catechism summarizes for us the origin of the Creed in its introduction: "Now the chief truths which Christians ought to hold are those which the holy Apostles, the leaders and teachers of the faith, inspired by the Holy Ghost, have divided into the twelve Articles of the Creed. For having received a command from the Lord to go forth into the whole world, as His ambassadors, and preach the Gospel to every creature, they thought it advisable to draw up a formula of Christian faith, that all might think and speak the same thing, and that among those whom they should have called to the unity of the faith no schisms would exist, but that they should be perfect in the same mind, and in the same judgment."

The Apostles' Creed sums up in one prayer all that we believe as Catholics. The Creed has come down to us from apostolic times and contains a summary of the principal truths taught by the Apostles. All the truths of our Faith are contained in the Creed, albeit in a compressed and reduced form. To memorize, study, and internalize the Creed is to intellectually and spiritually unite ourselves to the mission of the Church.

We begin the prayers of the Holy Rosary with the Apostles' Creed. We also commit to the content of the Creed when we are baptized, whether personally (if above the age of reason) or through the promises that our godparents make on our behalf.

The Creed gives us a breakdown of all that we believe, and by studying it line by line we gain insight into Who God is and what He expects from us, His creatures. When we say the Apostles' Creed, we are making an Act of Faith. We are professing to hold as true the words that we recite. And just as we should start each day with such an Act of Faith, we confirm our Act of Faith in our daily actions by living in conformity with the commandments and with the conscious awareness that we are missionaries in our world today. We are the hands and feet of Our Lord. If people see our actions, would they be inspired to join or re-join the Catholic Faith?

I

Credo in Unum Deum

First Article of the Creed

I Believe in One God

The five simple words, "I believe in One God," by which we start the recitation of the Creed are incredibly powerful and worthy of sufficient reflection word-by-word. Even the Roman Catechism, in its first paragraph on the start of this first article of the Creed, notes that "since great mysteries lie concealed under almost every word, the pastor must now give them a more careful consideration, in order that, as far as God has permitted, the faithful may approach, with fear and trembling, to contemplate the glory of His majesty."

Taken from the first-person *Credo* ("I believe") in Latin, the "I" in the Creed requires that we speak for ourselves. Each individual person must declare his faith publicly and individually, not allowing his statement to be absorbed into the collective "We" of the assembly. Just as we must all individually stand accountable before God, while here on this earth we must individually live a life of grace and individually assert our faith. This is not something that our families, our parents, our priests, or anyone else can do for us. With personal conviction, each of us must boldly and unhesitatingly begin the Creed in the first person: *Credo*.

What It Means to Believe

When we look up the word "believe" in the dictionary, we find it has five definitions: "to accept as true, to judge or regard or look upon as reliable, to be very confident of, to follow a creed or have a faith, to credit with veracity." When we use the word "believe" in the Catholic Church, we mean all of those things. Our Faith is a supernatural gift of God which enables us to believe all that God has revealed, not based on our understanding, but on the authority of God revealing. We believe in God, even though we cannot see Him. We believe in the Trinity, although it is beyond our understanding.

The Roman Catechism explains, "The word *believe* does not here mean *to think, to suppose, to be of opinion*; but, as the Sacred Scriptures teach, it expresses the deepest conviction, by which the mind gives a firm and unhesitating assent to God revealing His mysterious truths. As far, therefore, as regards use of the word here, he who firmly and without hesitation is convinced of anything is said to believe."

Rather than merely reciting the Creed without considering the meaning behind its words individually, the Roman Catechism further extorts us, the faithful, to utter our *Credo* with the same conviction that spurred on the Apostles to proclaim the truths of God despite certain persecution:

> [H]e who says, *I believe*, besides declaring the inward assent of the mind, which is an internal act of faith, should also openly profess and with alacrity acknowledge and proclaim what he inwardly and in his heart believes. For the faithful should be animated by the same spirit that spoke by the lips of the Prophet when he said: *I believe, and therefore did I speak* [Ps. cxv. 10], and should follow the example of the Apostles who replied to the princes of the people: *We cannot but speak the things which we have seen and heard* [Acts iv. 20]. They should be encouraged by these noble words of St. Paul: *I am not ashamed of the gospel. For it is the power of God unto salvation to everyone that believeth* [Rom. i. 16]; and likewise, by those other words; in which the truth of this doctrine is expressly confirmed: *With the heart we believe unto justice; but with the mouth confession is made unto salvation* [Rom. x. 10].

To assert belief in one God rather than many was an irreconcilable rupture with the pagan world to which Our Lord came. Aside from the Jewish people of the time, the peoples of the entire world were given to polytheism almost entirely. In the Catholic Church, the true *Israel of God* (Gal. vi. 16), there is likewise only one God – a single Divine Nature. We do not worship many gods or even several gods or even a few gods; we worship one God alone, that is, the one true God.

And it was the oneness of God that brought about the persecution of the early Christians. Unknown to many, the Romans at first were accepting of the Christians and even invited them to display a statue to Christ in the Pantheon, the pagan temple dedicated to all gods. But the Christians refused to do so, and they refused to accept any pagan deity as real. It was this refusal to accept false gods that brought about the persecution of the early Church.

For us present-day Christians who are told, "Keep your religion to yourself and all will be fine," we can see a parallel between our need to speak out against error and publicly defend the truth that spurred on the early martyrs, even when threatened with torture. Do we have the conviction to utter our *Credo* in one God in the face of social persecution, the threat of losing our jobs or being ostracized? Do we have the same conviction to persevere that we can speak the words of King David: *I spoke of Thy testimonies before kings: and I was not ashamed* (Ps. cxviii. 46)?

Monotheism Alone Is Rational

The Roman Catechism appeals to our ability to reason to illustrate that there can only be one God: "From what is said it must also be confessed that there is but one God, not many gods. For we attribute to God supreme goodness and infinite perfection, and it is impossible that what is supreme and most perfect could be common to many. If a being lack anything that constitutes supreme perfection, it is therefore imperfect and cannot have the nature of God."

The Angelic Doctor summarizes this point in his *Summa Theologiae* when he writes that "God comprehends in Himself the whole perfection of being. If then many gods existed, they would necessarily differ from each other. Something therefore would belong to one which did not belong to another. And if this were a privation, one of them would not be absolutely perfect; but if a perfection, one of them would be without it. So, it is impossible for many gods to exist" (I q11 a3).

God Himself possesses the epitome of all virtues. We say that He is the most perfect, most benign, most generous, most loving, etc. We also assert that God knows all things, sees all things, directs all things, etc. So, if there was more than one God, then God would be lacking. There would be a different entity that was perhaps more loving or more knowledgeable or more generous.

Regarding the certainty of our faith in God, the Catechism explains, "The knowledge derived through faith must not be considered less certain because its objects are not seen." Our belief in one God is not a mere opinion. It is the profession of an objective, metaphysical truth.

The Father Almighty, Creator of Heaven and of Earth

Why do we call God "Father" in the Creed? The Catechism expounds:

> Even some on whose darkness the light of faith never shone conceived God to be an eternal substance from whom all things have their beginning, and by whose Providence they are governed and preserved in their order and state of existence. Since, therefore, he to whom a family owes its origin and by whose wisdom and authority it is governed is called *father*, so by an analogy derived from human things these persons gave the name *Father* to God, whom they acknowledge to be the Creator and Governor of the universe.

What does it mean to create? To create means to bring something out of nothing. Only God has the capacity to produce things from no-things. What did God create? Everything. Creation is the mirror through which God shows us His Divine reflection. God created Heaven and all of what is contained in Heaven. We know that the greatest benefit of being accepted into Heaven is encountering the "Beatific Vision," which is the ability to see the face of God and live. Seeing God produces the greatest joy, happiness, peace, and love that are beyond imaginable to the human mind. In fact, the definition of being a saint is to possess the ability to see God and not to die from it, a gift which no man earns but which God Himself gratuitously gives (cf. Ex. xxxiii. 20).

The Church teaches dogmatically that Heaven is the state of everlasting happiness. It is a dogma of Faith that the happiness of the blessed is everlasting. This truth has been repeatedly defined by the Church, because if it was not everlasting then it would not truly be a place of "happiness."

Jesus called Heaven the "Kingdom." We understand that in this Kingdom there are Angels and Saints, the throne of God, and above all the Blessed Trinity. Jesus reigns in Heaven, along with His Blessed Mother who is Queen of Heaven and earth. It is a Kingdom that makes even the most luxurious of earthly kingdoms pale in comparison. In this Kingdom, Christ is the Head of His Church, in Heaven and on earth. We recognize the Pope as the visible head of the Church on earth, that is, the earthly representative (i.e., vicar) of Christ Himself, the invisible Head.

The Pope works to help the Church on earth obtain salvation in Heaven by bringing as many people into the Church as possible. The only sure way to gain Heaven is through the Catholic Church, because the Catholic Church alone was founded by Christ as the guardian of Divine Revelation and dispenser of the saving grace He won for us. Through the Sacraments, which Christ Himself instituted and entrusted to His Church, we receive sanctifying grace – the very life of Christ within us – which is necessary for salvation. As Pope Pius XII articulated so well in his encyclical on the Church, *Mystici Corporis Christi*:

> … We have committed to the protection and guidance of heaven those who do not belong to the visible Body of the Catholic Church, solemnly declaring that after the example of the Good Shepherd We desire nothing more ardently than that they may have life and have it more abundantly [Jn. x. 10]. …We ask each and every one of them to correspond to the interior movements of grace, and to seek to withdraw from that state in which they cannot be sure of their salvation. For even though by an unconscious desire and longing they have a certain relationship with the Mystical Body of the Redeemer, they still remain deprived of those many heavenly gifts and helps which can only be enjoyed in the Catholic Church. Therefore, may they enter into Catholic unity (103).

It is often said that the Mass is Heaven on earth. During the celebration of the Mass, all the Saints and Angels are present and praising God along with us. As you sing the Gloria, the Angels who originally sung this hymn of praise at the birth of Christ are there at the Mass proclaiming these words again.

During the Holy Sacrifice, we are united mystically to the perpetual Eucharistic Liturgy that is celebrated in Heaven. We do not actually walk into Heaven, but we are taken to the threshold of Heaven, into the vestibule of the gates of Heaven. Although physically in church, we are spiritually at the gates of Heaven, on Calvary at the Crucifixion, peering into the empty tomb, and participating in the celestial *marriage supper of the Lamb* (Apoc. xix. 9). The Book of the Apocalypse, written by St. John the Apostle, describes in Heaven the presence of an altar (cf. Apoc. viii. 3), the same altar to which our prayers ascend from our altars here on earth. This is why the Canon of the Mass includes the following prayer after the Consecration: "We most humbly beseech Thee, almighty God, command these offerings to be borne by the hands of Thy holy Angel to Thine altar on high, in the sight of Thy divine Majesty, that as many as shall partake of the most holy Body and Blood of Thy Son at this altar, may be filled with every heavenly grace and blessing."

Creator of All Things Visible and Invisible

In addition to Heaven, God created all of what is contained in Heaven. The Angels are diaphanous beings, meaning they are pure spirits without bodies. They were created to praise God, manifesting a state of perpetual adoration of the Most Holy Trinity. They are the attendants of God, *mighty in strength,* who *execute His word, hearkening to the voice of His orders* (Ps. cii. 20). They act as messengers and are sent to communicate with humans what God's Will is in a given situation.

All of the Angels were created by God prior to His creation of man. In Hebrews we read, *Are they not all ministering spirits, sent to minister to them who shall receive the inheritance of salvation?* (Heb. i. 14). Like humans, Angels have intelligence and free will, the ability to either obey God or rebel against Him. Unlike humans, however, the Angels were given a much greater infused knowledge of God and His mysteries due to their more exalted nature as pure spirits. As such, shortly after He created them, they were given one opportunity by God to either choose Him or not. Sadly, as we read in Scripture, many chose to rebel:

> And there was a great battle in heaven, Michael and his angels fought with the dragon, and the dragon fought and his angels: And they prevailed not, neither was their place found any more in heaven. And that great dragon was cast out, that old serpent, who is called the devil and Satan, who seduceth the whole world; and he was cast unto the earth, and his angels were thrown down with him (Apoc. xii. 7-9).

Commenting on this episode, the Roman Catechism explains that "although they were all endowed with celestial gifts, very many, having rebelled against God, their Father and Creator, were hurled from those high mansions of bliss, and shut up in the darkest dungeon of earth, there to suffer for eternity the punishment of their pride."

Scripture and Tradition indicate that there are various Choirs of Angels. These levels or orders have distinct qualities and have identifiable roles in the Angelic world. St. Gregory the Great (Homily 34, *In Evang.*) gives us a clear idea of the view of the Church's doctors on the point:

> We know on the authority of Scripture that there are nine orders of angels, viz., Angels, Archangels, Virtues, Powers, Principalities, Dominations, Throne, Cherubim and Seraphim. That there are Angels and Archangels nearly every page of the Bible tells us, and the books of the Prophets talk of Cherubim and Seraphim. St. Paul,

too, writing to the Ephesians enumerates four orders when he says: 'above all Principality, and Power, and Virtue, and Domination' [Eph. i. 21]; and again, writing to the Colossians he says: 'whether Thrones, or Dominations, or Principalities, or Powers' [Col. i. 16]. If we now join these two lists together, we have five Orders, and adding Angels and Archangels, Cherubim and Seraphim, we find nine Orders of Angels.

St. Thomas divides the Angels into three hierarchies, each of which contains three orders, with their proximity to God serving as the basis of this division. In the first hierarchy, he places the Seraphim, Cherubim, and Thrones; in the second, the Dominations, Virtues, and Powers; in the third, the Principalities, Archangels, and Angels (I q108 a1-7).

In addition to creating Heaven and the Angels, God created all of this world as well. It would take an unimaginable amount of space to describe all that God has created. Every galaxy, solar system, planet, and star has been created by God. Likewise, every blade of grass, fruit fly, and microscopic gnat were created by Him. And He created them all from nothing. Whereas some have falsely claimed God used raw matter or pre-existing matter, God Himself is the one substance without a beginning in time. All matter or things were begun by His unique and sole power to bring something into existence out of non-existence. This fact is affirmed in the Catechism: "For God formed the world *not* from materials of any sort, but created it from *nothing*, and that not by constraint or necessity, but spontaneously, and of His own free will."

The Old Testament opens with the verse, *In the beginning, God created the Heavens and the earth* (Gen. i. 1), and when He had completed His creation of the universe, He *saw everything that He had made, and, behold, it was very good* (Gen. i. 31). On the sixth day, He created *man in His own image, in the image of God created He him, male and female created He them* (Gen. i. 27). Thus, from the furthest galaxies to the smallest atoms, God is the Creator. And unlike the Deists, who thought of God as a clockmaker who created the clock, wound it up, and left it to itself, God governs all things and preserves them all. "For as all things derive existence from the Creator's supreme power, wisdom, and goodness, so unless preserved continually by His Providence, and by the same power which produced them, they would instantly return into their nothingness," says the Catechism.

The Purpose of Creation

Yet, most profoundly, do we ever consider *why* God created all things? God has no need of earthly goods or companions as He is infinitely sufficient and happy in and of Himself. And yet, He did. In an immense act of generosity and love, God has brought all of us into existence. He has brought every mountain and every lake and every cloud into being. The Catechism explains, "Nor was He impelled to create by any other cause than a desire to communicate His goodness to creatures."

In one particularly powerful homily I heard a few years ago, while speaking on the topic of the reason for the world's existence, the priest said the following: "Why Did God create the world? He did so for one reason and one reason alone – for His Son. He created the blades of grasses since His Son would one day walk on this earth. He created the water since His Son would one day use it. He created the creatures of this world since His Son would one day see them on this earth." The creation of the world was an outpouring of God's love. And even as immense and powerful as the act of creation was, it pales in comparison to the central mystery of the Christian Faith – the Incarnation of His Son, Our Lord Jesus Christ, to Whom we now turn.

II

I Believe in Jesus Christ, His Only Son, Our Lord

Second Article of the Creed

The Core of Christianity is the Person of Jesus Christ

The Roman Catechism begins this article with a concise and essential statement: "For this Article is the most firm basis of our salvation and redemption." To believe in Jesus Christ and Who He really is – namely, *the Son of the living God* (Mt. xvi. 16) – is one of the unmistakable marks of a Christian. To deny the nature and role of Christ is to deny Christianity entirely, for it is not possible to profess to be a Christian and at the same time deny the role of the Christ Himself.

Unfortunately, in the modern era man has become inclined to portray the Lord in his own image. He is portrayed to some as a liberator, to others as a merciful Savior who would never condemn anyone for any reason, and to others as a wise teacher no different than Plato and Socrates of old. But what do we as Christians know of Jesus Christ? Who was He *really*?

God's Name: Jesus

First and foremost, Jesus Christ, the Son of the Blessed Virgin Mary, is God Almighty. He is the Second Person of the Blessed Trinity. He is not merely a wise teacher or a lawgiver or even the Savior; He is God. There exists only one God Who has created the world, guides it, judges it, and by Whose care all things come to be. He is the only substance that was never created. God has always existed and will always exist without beginning or end. And this omnipotent, omniscient God chose to become a man, as we read in the beautiful Prologue of St. John's Gospel:

> In the beginning was the Word, and the Word was with God, and the Word was God. The same was in the beginning with God. All things were made by Him: and

> without Him was made nothing that was made. ... And
> the Word was made flesh, and dwelt among us, (and we
> saw His glory, the glory as it were of the Only Begotten
> of the Father,) full of grace and truth (Jn. i. 1-3, 14).

God Himself, *the Only Begotten of the Father*, the Second Person of the Blessed Trinity, assumed a human nature from the Immaculate Virgin Mary and was born in the most destitute of circumstances – even to the point of being laid in a feeding trough for animals. Concerning this awesome mystery of our Faith, Saint Peter Chrysologus (d. 450), Bishop and Doctor of the Church, wrote: "Our God chose to be born this way because He wanted to be loved." And yet, when "the Word was made flesh and dwelt among us," for the most part He was met with coldness of heart, neglect, and indifference to His teachings. Sadly, the same is true today of many who are exposed to the traditional teachings of the Faith. They prefer to neglect them, act indifferently to them, and fashion a religion to their liking.

Nevertheless, the truth remains that God Himself became man. And why did He become man? In order to *save His people from their sins* (Mt. i. 21), a mission that is summed up by His very Name.

The Roman Catechism explains, "*Jesus* is the proper name of the God-man and signifies Saviour: a name given Him not accidentally, or by the judgment or will of man, but by the counsel and command of God." As St. Alphonsus Liguori relates, "This great name of Jesus was not given by man, but by God Himself."[13] The Baltimore Catechism summarizes the meaning of Our Lord's Name when it states, "The name 'Jesus' signifies Savior or Redeemer, and this name was given to Our Lord by an Angel who appeared to Joseph and said: 'Mary shall bring forth a Son; and thou shalt call His name Jesus' [Mt. i. 21]."[14]

As we advance in years and fight illness, busyness, and sloth, there is one prayer that we should always have at our forefront: The Holy Name of Jesus. We do not always need to remember the most elaborate prayers, nor do we always need to feel God's inspirations during prayer. Amidst trying or difficult times, we may be unable to do anything more than pray the Name "Jesus" over and over. And yet, such a simple prayer of a single word is nevertheless of immense value.

Richard Rolle (d. 1349), a hermit, mystic, and writer of devotional works and Biblical translations succinctly summarized the power of the Holy

---

[13] *Discourse on the Name of Jesus* by St. Alphonsus Liguori.
[14] *Baltimore Catechism* No. 3, Q. 322.

Name of our Redeemer: "If you think the Name 'Jesus' continually, and hold it firmly, it purges your sin, and kindles your heart; it clarifies your soul, it removes anger and does away with slowness. It wounds in love and fulfills charity. It chases the devil and puts out dread. It opens heaven and makes a contemplative man. Have Jesus in mind, for that puts all vices and phantoms out from the lover."[15] May we always have recourse each and every day – even, or perhaps especially, in sickness and anxiety – to the Name of so sweet and holy a Redeemer, Who chose to save us while we were still sinners (cf. Rom. v. 8).

Christ: The Title for the Redeemer

Regarding the name "Christ," the Roman Catechism explains why it is part of the Name of Jesus: "To the name *Jesus* is added that of *Christ*, which signifies *the anointed*. This name is expressive of honour and office, and is not peculiar to one thing only, but common to many; for in the Old Law priests and kings, whom God, on account of the dignity of their office, commanded to be anointed, were called christs... When Jesus Christ our Saviour came into the world, He assumed these three characters of Prophet, Priest and King, and was therefore called *Christ*, having been anointed for the discharge of these functions, not by mortal hand or with earthly ointment, but by the power of His heavenly Father and with a spiritual oil; for the plentitude of the Holy Spirit and a more copious effusion of all gifts than any other created being is capable of receiving were poured into His soul."

As a result, the name "Christ" is a title which applies so intricately to Our Lord's work and mission that it has become a part of the Name of the Son of God made man. The Baltimore Catechism summarizes this teaching as follows: "The name 'Christ' means the same as Messiah, and signifies Anointed; because, as in the Old Law, Prophets, High Priests and Kings were anointed with oil; so Jesus, the Great Prophet, High Priest and King of the New Law, was anointed as man with the fullness of divine power."[16]

Who Is Jesus Christ?

The Name of Jesus Christ is truly unique, *a name which is above all names* (Philip. ii. 9)! This is the Name of the Savior of the world, the Redeemer, the Anointed One par excellence, and the Second Person of the Blessed Trinity made flesh. As St. Peter the Apostle boldly proclaimed shortly after the outpouring of the Holy Ghost on Pentecost, *Neither is there salvation*

---

[15] *The Form of Perfect Living and Other Prose Treatises* (Thomas Baker, 1910 London).
[16] *Baltimore Catechism* No. 3, Q. 323.

in any other. For there is no other name under heaven given to men, whereby we must be saved (Acts iv. 12). Jesus Christ was not merely a new Aristotle, nor was He a marauder who conquered villages and subdued peoples like Mohammed to advance a religion. He was not a new Buddha who taught a "way of life" without a road to salvation. Rather, the religion inaugurated on Mount Calvary by Jesus Christ was revolutionary! Never before or since has a religion been founded on a man who claimed to be God Himself and by whose death salvation would abound. Simply put, Jesus Christ did not merely claim to be a prophet, a military leader, a teacher, or someone sent by God. He claimed to be God. And it was for this reason that the Jews brought about His death (cf. Mt. xxvi. 59-66).

The Roman Catechism expounds on this awe-inspiring reality, which we as Christians too often take for granted: "But when we are told that Jesus is the Son of God, we are not to understand anything earthly or mortal in His birth; but are firmly to believe and piously to adore that birth by which, from all eternity, the Father begot the Son, a mystery which reason cannot fully conceive or comprehend, and at the contemplation of which, overwhelmed, as it were, with admiration, we should exclaim with the Prophet: *Who shall declare his generation?* [Is. liii. 8] On this point, then, we are to believe that the Son is of the same nature, of the same power and wisdom, with the Father, as we more fully profess in these words of the Nicene Creed: *And in one Lord Jesus Christ, His Only-begotten Son, born of the Father before all ages, God of God, light of light, true God of true God, begotten, not made, consubstantial to the Father, by whom all things were made.*"

True God and True Man: The Hypostatic Union

How, we might rightly ask, did the Son of God take on a human nature? This mystery is so far beyond our mind's ability to understand that we can only begin to grasp the very basics of it as defined by the Council of Chalcedon (A.D. 451):

> Following therefore the holy Fathers, we unanimously teach to confess one and the same Son, our Lord Jesus Christ, the same perfect in divinity and perfect in humanity, the same truly God and truly man composed of rational soul and body, the same one in being [Greek *homooúsion*] with the Father as to the divinity and one in being with us as to the humanity, like unto us in all things but sin [cf. Heb. iv. 15]. The same was begotten from the Father before the ages as to the divinity and in the latter days for us and our salvation was born to His humanity from Mary the Virgin Mother of God.

> We confess that one and the same Lord Jesus Christ, the only begotten Son, must be acknowledged in two natures, without confusion or change, without division or separation. Their union never abolished the distinction between the natures but rather the character proper to each of the two natures was preserved as they came together in one Person and one hypostasis. He is not split or divided into two Persons, but He is one and the same only-begotten, God the Word, the Lord Jesus Christ, as formerly the prophets and later Jesus Christ Himself have taught us about Him and as has been handed down to us by the creed of the Fathers.[17]

Simply put, Jesus Christ is one Divine Person with two natures, divine and human. To help make clear the distinction between *person* and *nature*, the *Baltimore Catechism* (specifically, the *New Saint Joseph* illustrated edition) explains that the term "nature" refers to *what* someone or something is, whereas "person" refers to *who* someone is. One illustration in this children's catechism shows a boy asking Our Lord, "Who are You?", with Our Lord answering, "I am Jesus Christ." The boy then asks Him, "What are You?" and Our Lord replies, "I am God and man."[18]

As a result of the Incarnation (the Word becoming flesh), there is a union of the Divine Nature and our human nature in the one Divine Person of Our Lord, "without confusion or change, without division or separation" (Council of Chalcedon). This marvelous union is called the Hypostatic Union because the Greek term *hypostasis* (literally "substance", cf. Heb. i. 3) is similar to "person," as in the definition of Chalcedon that "the two natures… came together in one Person and one hypostasis." Jesus is not a human person, for He is not a finite creature (as the Arian and Nestorian heretics falsely claimed) but rather the infinite Creator. He does, however, have a human soul with its natural faculties (intellect and will), but those faculties are wholly *informed by* and *conformed to* the Divine intellect and will.[19]

The dogma of the Hypostatic Union reminds us that while Jesus is fully God, "consubstantial with the Father" (Nicene Creed), He is also fully

---

[17] Denzinger-Hünermann, *Enchiridion Symbolorum*, 43rd ed. (San Francisco: Ignatius Press, 2012), nn. 301-302.
[18] *New Saint Joseph Baltimore Catechism No. 2* (New York: Catholic Book Publishing Corp., 1969-1962), 22, 47.
[19] For a more detailed discussion of the Hypostatic Union, see the *Summa Theologiae* III q9 and q19 a1.

human, and we see His humanity portrayed so beautifully all throughout the Gospel accounts. Jesus had emotions, He felt hunger, He slept, He worked, and He was even subject to cold and heat and pain and death. That is how much God humbled Himself in becoming human.

At the same time, once again, Jesus is fully God. As the Roman Catechism teaches, "we say in truth that Christ is Almighty, Eternal, Infinite, and [that] these attributes He has from His Divine Nature," that is, the one Divine Nature He shares with the Father and the Holy Ghost. He never stopped being God, and never stopped relating to the Father precisely as the Son: *I and the Father are one* (Jn. x. 30), He testified. This means that whatever pertains to the God the Father (e.g. omnipotence, omniscience, infinite goodness, etc.) pertains also to Jesus of Nazareth, the Son of Mary, because He is God the Son Incarnate.

Putting Faith Into Practice: Honor the Holy Name

Truly, no name deserves more respect than the Redeemer's own Name. Catholics are bound to bow their heads at the Holy Name of Jesus. The practice of bowing the head at the mention of His Name was formally written into the law of the Church at the Second Council of Lyons in 1274:

> Those who assemble in church should extol with an act of special reverence that Name which is above every Name, than which no other under Heaven has been given to people, in which believers must be saved, the Name, that is, of Jesus Christ, Who will save His people from their sins. Each should fulfil in himself that which is written for all, that at the Name of Jesus every knee should bow; whenever that glorious Name is recalled, especially during the sacred Mysteries of the Mass, everyone should bow the knees of his heart, which he can do even by a bow of his head.[20]

Additionally, the bow of the head is also to be made at the mention of the Holy Name of Mary as well as when the name of the saint in whose honor the Mass is being said is mentioned. And additionally, when the Holy Trinity is mentioned by name (Father, Son, and Holy Ghost), a bow of the head is also required. Therefore, we should bow our heads during the *Gloria Patri* prayer whether during Mass, while saying the Rosary, or at the end of the Psalms in the Divine Office.

---

[20] Constitution 25 of the Second Council of Lyons, convened in 1274 by Pope Gregory X (r. 1271-1276).

While the bow of the head is required at the mention of "Jesus" or "Jesus Christ," it is not required only at the mention of "Christ," which is a title as opposed to being the Name of the Second Person of the Blessed Trinity made flesh.

In our modern world, where so many people use the name of the Savior in curses or in exclamations of surprise, pain, or anger, we must do our part to make reparation for these grave sins against the Second Commandment. When we hear such offenses, we should instruct the blasphemer to cease and desist, unless it is probable that by doing so he will only increase his blasphemous use of Our Lord's Name. Furthermore, we should make an Act of Reparation for Blasphemies Uttered against the Holy Name of Jesus, pray the Divine Praises, or pray the Golden Arrow prayer. This prayer was given to Sister Mary of St. Peter in an apparition by Our Lord Himself in France in August 1843. Sister Mary said of this prayer that it is "an Act of Praise that Our Lord Himself dictated to me, notwithstanding my unworthiness, for the reparation of Blasphemy against His Holy Name."[21]

May the Golden Arrow prayer be on our nightstands as we, the members of the Church Militant, are implored to ever increase our acts of reparation for the proliferation of sin in the world. The text of this prayer is as follows: "May the most holy, most sacred, most adorable, most incomprehensible and unutterable Name of God be always praised, blessed, loved, adored and glorified in Heaven, on earth, and under the earth, by all the creatures of God, and by the Sacred Heart of Our Lord Jesus Christ, in the Most Holy Sacrament of the Altar. Amen."

Conclusion

In its closing remarks on this Second Article of the Creed, the Roman Catechism calls upon parish priests to "remind the faithful that from Christ we take our name and are called Christians; that we cannot be ignorant of the extent of His favors, particularly since by His gift of faith we are enabled to understand all these things. We, above all others, are under the obligation of devoting and consecrating ourselves forever, like faithful servants, to our Redeemer and our Lord."

---

[21] *The Golden Arrow: The Revelations of Sr. Mary of St. Peter*, Dorothy Scallan, 2010.

III

Who Was Conceived by the Holy Ghost, Born of the Virgin Mary

Third Article of the Creed

God Became Man to Ransom Us from the Devil

"O wondrous exchange! The Creator of Man, having assumed a living body, deigned to be born of a Virgin, and having become Man without Man's aid, enriched us with His divinity."[22]

The Roman Catechism prefaces the third article of the Creed with a statement on its central importance to our Catholic Faith: "From what has been said in the preceding article, the faithful can understand that in bringing us from the relentless tyranny of Satan into liberty, God has conferred a singular and surpassing blessing on the human race. But if we place before our eyes also the plan and means by which He deigned chiefly to accomplish this, then, indeed, we shall see that there is nothing more glorious or magnificent than this divine goodness and beneficence towards us."

Although Holy Mother Church teaches the mystery of the Incarnation using precise language, even Catholics today fail to understand this core truth of the Faith. And if we should fail to know with theological precision this mystery, how can we defend the perpetual virginity of Mary, the divinity of Jesus Christ, or the supremacy of God Who is One in nature and Three in Persons? The answer is to carefully and prayerfully study the Catechism so that we may know true doctrine in order to pass it on to others.

---

[22] First Antiphon of Vespers for the Feast of the Circumcision (taken from the Baronius Press 1961 Roman Breviary in Latin and English).

He Was Conceived by the Holy Ghost

If we were to conduct a poll of one hundred Catholics and ask them when the life of Jesus Christ began, I highly suspect that most would say His life began in the Crib of Bethlehem. While that may be a common answer, it would also be a wrong answer.

The Baltimore Catechism explains, "The Son of God was conceived and made man by the power of the Holy Ghost, in the womb of the Blessed Virgin Mary."[23] But unlike us who did not exist before our human conception, Jesus Christ did exist. And we as Catholics should know, as the Baltimore Catechism further expounds, "Jesus Christ was always God, as He is the Second Person of the Blessed Trinity, equal to His Father from all eternity"; however, "Jesus Christ was not always man but became man at the time of His Incarnation."[24]

When we speak of the life of Christ, it is important to note that we are talking about His *earthly* life. St. John teaches us in the profound beginning of his Gospel account aforementioned (Jn. i. 1-3).

Jesus is God, and God did not have a beginning like we do. All things were created through the Word, and since nobody can create themselves, we know that the Word is uncreated. After all, if He created all things, and He could not have created Himself, and "without Him was made nothing that was made," then we know that the Word is uncreated. The only uncreated being is God, so, just like St. John tells us, "the Word was God." In light of this truth, the Church confesses that the Son (Jesus) is co-eternal with the Father and the Holy Ghost – in other words, He has always existed as the Second Person of the Blessed Trinity. When we talk about "the life of Our Lord," we should preface such remarks as referring to the beginning of His *earthly* life, and because His life here on earth happened at a specific time and place, we can say it began.

Immediately after Our Lady said to the Angel Gabriel: *Behold the handmaid of the Lord; be it done to me according to thy word* (Lk. i. 38), Jesus was conceived in her womb and the Incarnation occurred: *And the Word was made flesh, and dwelt among us* (Jn. i. 14).

That precise moment of the Incarnation is the center of human history. It is the most important point in time. Nothing like this had ever happened before, and nothing like this will ever happen again. We cannot adequately compare the Incarnation to any other historical event because it is not like

---

[23] *New Saint Joseph Baltimore Catechism* No. 3, Question 342.
[24] Ibid., Question 339 and 340.

anything else. We may feel a natural attraction to images of the Passion, of the Nativity, of the Resurrection, or other scenes which depict external happenings. Yet, in the Incarnation, which was the beginning of our salvation, we can too often overlook its singular importance because it is not something which can accurately be depicted by an artist. Nevertheless, we should not grow remiss in meditating often on this first mystery of the Holy Rosary.

In the Incarnation, the Second Person of the Trinity took on a full human nature while remaining fully God. That is the central mystery of the Incarnation. Other religions have had mythological half-god, half-man figures like Hercules, or talked about men becoming gods, but never had anyone claimed that the Almighty God would empty Himself and become human.

The Roman Catechism succinctly affirms this mystery when it states, "That such is the meaning of the [third article of the Creed] is clear from the Creed of the Holy Council of Constantinople, which says: *Who for us men, and for our salvation,, came down from heaven, and became incarnate by the Holy Ghost of the Virgin Mary, and was made man.* The same truth we also find unfolded by St. John the Evangelist, who imbibed from the bosom of the Lord and Savior Himself the knowledge of this most profound mystery. For when he had declared the nature of the Divine Word as follows: *In the beginning was the Word, and the Word was with God, and the Word was God,* he concluded: *And the Word was made flesh and dwelt among us.*"

The Mystery of the Holy Trinity: Three Persons in One God

By introducing to us the Name of the "Holy Ghost," the Roman Catechism expresses the reality that Almighty God – the one and only God – is in fact a Trinity of Persons. The Catechism explains the role of the three Divine Persons in the Incarnation:

> It is a principle of Christian faith that whatever God does outside Himself in creation is common to the Three Persons, and that one neither does more than, nor acts without another. But that one emanates from another, this only cannot be common to all; for the Son is begotten of the Father only, and the Holy Ghost proceeds from the Father and the Son. Anything, however, which proceeds from them extrinsically is the work of the Three Persons without difference of any sort, and of this latter description is the Incarnation of the Son of God.

> Of those things, nevertheless, that are common to all, the Sacred Scriptures often attribute some to one Person, some to another. Thus, to the Father they attribute power over all things; to the Son, wisdom; to the Holy Ghost, love. Hence, as the mystery of the Incarnation manifests the singular and boundless love of God towards us, it is therefore in some sort peculiarly attributed to the Holy Ghost.

The Baltimore Catechism succinctly states, "In God there are three Divine Persons, really distinct, and equal in all things – the Father, the Son, and the Holy Ghost."[25]

We are not polytheists. We do not believe in three gods but in one God. The Athanasian Creed, one of the earliest confessions of faith written in the fifth century, declares: "Therefore, the Father is God, the Son is God, and the Holy Spirit is God; and yet there are not three Gods but one God. In the same way, the Father is Lord, the Son is Lord, and the Holy Spirit is Lord; yet there are not three Lords, but there is one Lord; for just as we are compelled by Christian truth to confess each Person individually as God and Lord, just so the Catholic religion forbids us to say that there are three Gods or three Lords."[26]

How is it, then, that there is a God the Father, a God the Son, and a God the Holy Spirit, but only one God? There is one divine substance, and three Divine Persons. You and I only have one substance and one person, but God has one substance and three Persons. Each of the Persons shares fully in the divine substance. This is not a construct invented by the early Church, as Jesus Himself said in the passage quoted above, *I and the Father are one* (Jn. x. 30).

Because God is perfect in and of Himself, He cannot become any more perfect. The Greek Church Fathers taught that God's substance is all perfection; the substance of God is being and existence itself. God is He Who is (cf. Ex. 3:14).

We know that there must be a Supreme Being from which everything else derives its existence, and we also know that there cannot be more than one Supreme Being. The Baltimore Catechism again states for our edification, "There can be but one God because God, being supreme and infinite,

---

[25] *New Saint Joseph Baltimore Catechism* No. 3, Question 186.
[26] Denzinger-Hünermann (D.H.), *Enchiridion Symbolorum* 43rd Latin-English Edition (San Francisco: Ignatius Press, 2012), n. 75 (p. 40).

cannot have an equal."[27] Thus, we can say with absolute certainty that God is One, and because of that, God is one in substance or nature.

Hence, the Trinity is One. The three Divine Persons do not each possess a part of the one divine nature; rather, each of them possesses it whole and entire. In the words of the Fourth Lateran Council (1215): "...each of the Persons is that supreme reality, that is, that divine substance, essence, or nature which alone is the beginning of all things, apart from which nothing else can be found."[28] Those who deny the ability of God to become man or to exist as a Trinity of Persons, whether they be Arians or Muslims, deny the ability of Almighty God to do what He pleases. God Himself can do all things, and this is what makes Him supreme. To claim as heretics and pagans do that God *could not* become a man, blaspheme the omnipotence of God Who can do all things whatsoever except commit sin, which is contrary to His perfect goodness.

The Second Person of the Trinity was Born to a Perpetual Virgin

The Roman Catechism continues in its explanation of the Third Article of the Creed by stating, "The faithful are bound to believe that Jesus the Lord was not only conceived by the power of the Holy Ghost but was also born of the Virgin Mary." Elsewhere, referring to the birth of the Second Person of the Blessed Trinity, the Catechism explains this sublime mystery on the Virgin Birth:

> As the rays of the sun penetrate, without breaking or injuring, in the least, the substance of glass; after a like, but more incomprehensible manner, did Jesus Christ come forth from his mother's womb without injury to her maternal virginity. This immaculate and perpetual virginity forms, therefore, the just theme of our eulogy.

In 2006, *The Nativity Story* film premiered and it was rightfully boycotted by some Traditional Catholics, despite having its premier in Vatican City, since it depicted Mary, the New Eve, in child birthing pains, which is heretical. The reality is that the birth of Christ was miraculous, but did not include birth pains. Likewise, some Protestants and non-believers alike attempt to claim that the Virgin Mary had other children with either St. Joseph or with other husbands by twisting the words of the Gospel of Mark 6:3 and the Gospel of Matthew 13:55–56, failing to understand, as Rev. George Leo Haydock explains in his illustrious Bible commentary published in 1859, "These were the children of Mary, the wife of Cleophas,

---

[27] New Saint Joseph Baltimore Catechism No. 3, Question 183.
[28] D.H. 804.

sister of our blessed Lady and therefore, according to the usual style of the Scripture, they were called brethren, that is, near relations to our Savior."

The central mystery of the Catholic Faith – namely, the Incarnation of Jesus Christ in the womb of the Blessed Virgin Mary – is beyond our full comprehension. Yet, rather than twisting the Scriptures and Church history to fit heretical views, we pray that we can slowly come to better understand this marvelous mystery on how God Himself took human flesh and was born of only one biological parent. This mystery harkens back to the beginning of Creation with Adam and Eve, and in Christ and Our Lady the Catechism rightfully calls them the Second Adam and the Second Eve:

> The Apostle sometimes calls Jesus Christ the second Adam, and compares Him to the first Adam; for as in the first all men die, so in the second all are made alive: and as in the natural order Adam was the father of the human race, so in the supernatural order Christ is the author of grace and of glory.

> The Virgin Mother we may also compare to Eve, making the second Eve, that is, Mary, correspond to the first, as we have already shown that the second Adam, that is, Christ, corresponds to the first Adam.

Sister Lucia, one of the three children to whom Our Lady appeared at Fatima in 1917, was subsequently visited by Our Lady on Dec. 10, 1925, who came to request the practice of the Five First Saturdays devotion. Several months later in the summer of 1930, Sister Lucia related in a letter to her confessor what Our Lord communicated to her on May 30, 1930, namely, that the request for reparation on five consecutive Saturdays corresponds to the five kinds of blasphemies uttered against His Mother. One of those five blasphemies is the denial of Our Lady's perpetual virginity. Not only would we do well by learning and sharing this truth of Our Lady's perpetual virginity, we should also make reparation for those who blaspheme against her by attributing child birthing pains to the Blessed Mother.

Conclusion

In its closing remarks on this Third Article of the Creed, the Roman Catechism calls upon parish priests to "impress deeply on the minds and hearts of the faithful these mysteries, *which were written for our learning*; first, that by the commemoration of so great a benefit they may make some return of gratitude to God, its author, and next, in order to place before their eyes, as a model for imitation, this striking and singular example of humility." After having considered and meditated upon the humility of God Himself to become a man, how can we ever express pride or envy with our fellow man? And yet, Our Lord did not just give us the example of becoming man for our edification and a guide in humility, He chose to subject Himself to the torment and agony of His Passion to show us both His true love for us and the horror of sin.

IV

Suffered under Pontius Pilate; Was Crucified, Dead, and Buried

Fourth Article of the Creed

Christ Became Obedient for Our Sake unto Death

The Roman Catechism opens its chapter on the Passion of our Redeemer by reminding parish priests of the supreme importance of teaching this article of the Creed to the souls entrusted to their care: "The pastor, therefore, should exercise the greatest care and pains in giving a thorough explanation of this subject in order that the faithful being moved by the remembrance of so great a benefit may give themselves entirely to the contemplation of the goodness and love of God towards us."

The Passion, Death, and Burial of Our Lord Jesus Christ, the Second Person of the Blessed Trinity, are a source of immense spiritual wisdom. In fact, the Cross itself is a school in every virtue, as St. Thomas Aquinas remarks: "Whoever wishes to live perfectly should do nothing but disdain what Christ disdained on the cross and desire what He desired, for the cross exemplifies every virtue." And in a similar way, we can often learn more by meditating upon the Crucified Lord than through many other pious means or a life of study. Therefore, not for the hope of intellectual gain or worldly knowledge do we consider this article of the Creed. We do so for the sole benefit of enriching our minds and hearts with the sentiments of the Redeemer's cruel suffering, death, and burial so that we may take these reflections before the Crucifix and there more perfectly contemplate the dying Son of God, Who became obedient for our sake *unto death, even the death of the cross* (Philip. ii. 8).

He Really Suffered the Torment of His Executioners

Every facet of our Redeemer's Passion was filled with anguish and torture. Our Lord really suffered from the abandonment of His disciples in the Garden, the betrayal by His own friend, the whippings and beatings, the mocking, the false accusations, and the rejection by His own people to the ripping of His flesh in the Scourging, the crushing weight of the Cross, and the three hours of suffocating agony on the Cross. While He was always in control by virtue of His Divinity, He nevertheless experienced both physical and mental agony unlike anything we will ever experience. The Roman Catechism succinctly explains why when it states:

> ...for as He really assumed human nature, it is a necessary consequence that He really, and in His soul, experienced a most acute sense of pain. Hence these words of the Savior: *My soul is sorrowful even unto death.* Although human nature was united to the Divine Person, He felt the bitterness of His Passion as acutely as if no such union had existed, because in the one Person of Jesus Christ were preserved the properties of both natures, human and divine; and therefore what was passible and mortal remained passible and mortal; while what was impassible and immortal, that is, His Divine Nature, continued impassible and immortal.

Christ Chose the Cross

In the infinite wisdom of God, the Cross, the most barbaric and cruel of all punishments, was chosen to be the means of our salvation. The Roman Catechism explains, "The fact that He suffered death precisely on the wood of the cross must also be attributed to a particular counsel of God, which decreed that life should return by the way whence death had arisen. The serpent who had triumphed over our first parents by the wood (of a tree) was vanquished by Christ on the wood of the cross." In fact, this same mystery is recounted in the Preface of the Holy Cross, prayed by the priest at Holy Mass during Passiontide as well as on the Feast of the Most Precious Blood and the Exaltation of the Holy Cross:

> It is truly meet and just, right and for our salvation, that we should at all times, and in all places, give thanks unto Thee, O holy Lord, Father almighty, everlasting God: Who didst establish the salvation of mankind on the tree of the Cross: that whence death came thence also life might arise again, and that he who overcame by the tree, by a tree also might be overcome...

By the wood of the Cross, Our Lord undid the crime of Adam. Stripped naked and adorned only with His laurel of thorns, both of His hands were nailed on the Cross's transept so that He was only able to slump His shoulders forward and downward. Likewise, His feet were securely fastened in a manner which allowed Him to push upward supported only by the spikes hammered therethrough. He could not do both concurrently. Pinned thusly to the Cross, His chest muscles and diaphragm were unable to function properly together. As a result, in order to inhale, Jesus was forced to push upward supporting His entire body weight against the spikes securing His feet, or to slacken the weight of His Body from His feet to transfer the pressure of His weight to His hands in His effort to exhale.

His muscles slowly failed, and suspended in this manner, He began to slowly suffocate. He also suffered deep dehydration. After three hours of this excruciating torment, the King of the Universe ignobly died. Crucifixion itself was so horrific and humiliating that the words of King David could apply to someone dying on a cross as he struggled to breathe: *But I am a worm, and no man* (Ps. xxi. 7). And yet it was the Cross that at last undid the ancient crime. According to ancient tradition, the site of the Crucifixion occurred above the very burial place of Adam himself. Thus, not only mystically but even literally the Blood of Jesus Christ blotted out the iniquity of Adam.

The Second Person of the Blessed Trinity suffered intensely. However, keep in mind that neither God the Father nor God the Holy Ghost died on the Cross. To claim that God the Father suffered on the Cross in any way is the heresy of Patripassianism. The only Divine Person to have suffered on the Cross was Jesus Christ, Who despite His complete divine nature also possessed a complete human nature, and through His human nature, our Redeemer suffered torments.

There was another group of heretics, the Docetists, who denied the reality of the Incarnation and argued that Jesus only appeared to be human. The problem with such a claim is that if Jesus was not truly man, then He did not actually save our fallen human race. On the contrary, the perennial teaching of the Church is explicated in the Roman Catechism:

> Moreover, as Christ was true and perfect man, He of course was capable of dying. Now man dies when the soul is separated from the body. When, therefore, we say that Jesus died, we mean that His soul was disunited from His body. We do not admit, however, that the Divinity was separated from His body. On the contrary, we firmly believe and profess that when His soul was

dissociated from His body, His Divinity continued always united both to His body in the sepulcher and to His soul in limbo. It became the Son of God to die, *that, through death, he might destroy him who had the empire of death that is the devil, and might deliver them, who through the fear of death were all their lifetime subject to servitude.*

Why Did Christ Suffer So Much?

There are four principal fruits of the Lord's Passion and Death:

> In the first place, then, the Passion of our Lord was our deliverance from sin; for, as St. John says, *He hath loved us, and washed us from our sins in his own blood...* In the next place He has rescued us from the tyranny of the devil, for our Lord Himself says: *Now is the judgment of the world; now shall the prince of this world be cast out. And I if I be lifted up from the earth, will draw all things to myself...* Again He discharged the punishment due to our sins. And as no sacrifice more pleasing and acceptable could have been offered to God, He reconciled us to the Father, appeased His wrath, and made Him favorable to us... Finally, by taking away our sins He opened to us heaven, which was closed by the common sin of mankind.

God could have chosen another means than the Cross to bring about the salvation of the human race. Nevertheless, He chose the Cross as the means to bring about these fruits for humanity. St. Thomas addressed this question in his *Summa Theologiae* as follows: "Speaking simply and absolutely, it was possible for God to deliver mankind otherwise than by the Passion of Christ, because *no word shall be impossible with God* (Lk. i. 37). Yet it was impossible if some supposition be made. For since it is impossible for God's foreknowledge to be deceived and His will or ordinance to be frustrated, then, supposing God's foreknowledge and ordinance regarding Christ's Passion, it was not possible at the same time for Christ not to suffer, and for mankind to be delivered otherwise than by Christ's Passion" (III q46 a2). Thus, *by the determinate counsel and foreknowledge of God* (Acts ii. 23), God became man in order to save His wayward creatures.

The death of Jesus on the Cross was reprehensible in its barbarity. It was excruciating, slow, and it is horrifying, even today, to contemplate. But contemplate it we must, because we were and continue to be the cause of His agony. He died for every sin we have committed or will commit in our lifetimes and for all sins that everyone else committed or will commit since Adam and Eve were expelled from the Garden of Eden. In the words of Holy Scripture, *He is the propitiation for our sins: and not for ours only, but also for those of the whole world* (I Jn. ii. 2).

But was it necessary for Him to suffer so much? According to the Baltimore Catechism, "It was not necessary for Christ to suffer so much in order to redeem us, for the least of His sufferings was more than sufficient to atone for all the sins of mankind. By suffering so much He showed His great love for us."[29] Likewise, the Roman Catechism expounds on this mystery:

> The reasons why the Savior suffered are also to be explained, that thus the greatness and intensity of the divine love towards us may the more fully appear. Should anyone inquire why the Son of God underwent His most bitter Passion, he will find that besides the guilt inherited from our first parents the principal causes were the vices and crimes which have been perpetrated from the beginning of the world to the present day and those which will be committed to the end of time. In His Passion and death, the Son of God, our Savior, intended to atone for and blot out the sins of all ages, to offer for them to His Father a full and abundant satisfaction.

The very least of Christ's sufferings and Blood shed during His Circumcision eight days after His birth could have redeemed the whole world. Yet, the Lord chose to endure all manner of sufferings to show us His infinite love and to be for all people a source of grace. There is no category of suffering we can endure that Our Lord did not endure already. As St. Thomas Aquinas affirms, "But, speaking generically, He did endure every human suffering. ... For Christ suffered from friends abandoning Him; in His reputation, from the blasphemies hurled at Him; in His honor and glory, from the mockeries and the insults heaped upon Him; in things, for He was despoiled of His garments; in His soul, from sadness, weariness, and fear; in His body, from wounds and scourging" (III q46 a5).

Why Did Jesus Die?

As we covered in the last chapter, the Roman Catechism begins its discussion of the "Reasons Why Christ Suffered" by stating "that thus the greatness and intensity of the divine love towards us may the more fully appear." Going on, the text explains:

---

[29] Baltimore Catechism No. 3, q. 379.

> Should anyone inquire why the Son of God underwent His most bitter Passion, he will find that besides the guilt inherited from our first parents [i.e. Original Sin] the principal causes were the vices and crimes which have been perpetrated from the beginning of the world to the present day and those which will be committed to the end of time. In His Passion and death the Son of God, our Savior, intended to atone for and blot out the sins of all ages, to offer for them to His Father a full and abundant satisfaction.

It is highly controversial nowadays to state that the Jews were at all responsible for the death of our Divine Lord. But what does the Church really teach? The first overarching issue is to determine what we mean by "responsible." How can some say that the Jews are responsible for Christ's death while others maintain that they are not responsible? The difference is precisely a lack of continuity in terminology.

What we must first consider is the philosophical notion that has been part of Catholic theology for over 1,000 years: the four causes. Aristotle was the first philosopher to identify all four types of causes which Aquinas would later incorporate into his *Summa Theologiae*. Each cause is a different kind of answer to the question: *why?*

Imagine being inside an art museum and admiring a statue, for example, Michelangelo's *David*. A bystander asks, "Why is this a statue?" In reply, Aristotle would give four different answers: This is a statue (1) because it is made of marble; (2) because it is in the shape of David; (3) because Michelangelo sculpted it; and (4) because Michelangelo wanted to depict the figure of David in marble (because he needed the money, perhaps). These answers correspond to the four causes of being, namely: (1) material, (2) formal, (3) efficient, and (4) final.

Now, let us turn to the question, "Are the Jews responsible for the death of Christ?" Or, slightly rephrased, "Are the Jews a cause of the death of Christ?" Let us first consider the material cause of Christ's death. The *material* cause of a thing is the matter or physical stuff causing it to be. Thus, the material cause of Our Lord's death—the physical stuff that brought about His death—was the nails and the wood of the Cross. The *formal* cause was the use of the nails and wood in a manner designed to kill.

But what about the *final* cause of Christ's death? The final cause is the end (*telos* in Greek) for which something is done. We know from Sacred

Scripture that our Divine Redeemer willingly gave up His life on the Cross for the salvation of mankind (cf. John 10:18). In this sense, many people will rightfully say that all sinners—thus, all mankind, aside from the Redeemer Himself and Immaculate Mary—are the final cause of Our Lord's death. After all, since Our Lord died in order to save sinners, we are the cause of Christ's death.

Who Caused His Death?

Nevertheless, we must also acknowledge the *efficient* cause of Christ's death. The efficient cause of a thing is "the source of the primary principle of change or stability."[30] In other words, it is the agent that brings about an effect. Thus, the efficient cause of Our Lord's death was primarily the Jewish leaders, who demanded of Pilate *out of envy* (Mk. xv. 10) that Jesus be crucified. They are the ones who *"moved the people"* (Mark 15:11) to cry out, "Crucify Him, crucify Him" (John 19:6), and moved Pilate to "deliver Him unto them to be crucified" (Matt. 27:26). This is why St. Peter in his first proclamation of the Gospel to the Jews says *you [Jews] by the hands of wicked men have crucified and slain* (Acts ii. 23) and St. Paul as well says *the Jews killed the Lord Jesus* (I Th. ii. 15). St. Thomas Aquinas concurs by affirming, "The Jews therefore sinned, as crucifiers not only of the Man-Christ, but also as of God" (III q47 a5 ad3).

Thus, it is correct to say that the Jews were responsible for the death of Christ as the primary efficient cause, the secondary efficient cause being the Roman soldiers who carried out Pilate's orders and actually nailed Our Lord to the Cross.

Let us not shy away from this truth that the Jews in one sense are to be held responsible, while also recognizing with St. Thomas that "those of lesser degree—namely, the common folk—who had not grasped the mysteries of the Scriptures, did not fully comprehend that He was the Christ or the Son of God" and "were seduced by the rulers" (III q47 a5). Likewise St. Peter says to the Jews *the author of life you killed* yet, just as Christ did on the Cross, he seeks their forgiveness: *brethren, I know that you did it through ignorance, as did also your rulers* (Acts iii. 17).

Let us, therefore, pray and work as we should for the conversion of the Jews, and all peoples, to the one true Catholic Faith. *For this is good and acceptable in the sight of God our Savior, Who will have all men to be saved, and to come to the knowledge of the truth* (I Tim. ii. 3-4). And let us also keep in mind and heart these sobering words found in the Roman

---

[30] Aristotle, *Physics* Book II, 3.

Catechism concerning the role that our own sins played in the Passion and death of Our Lord:

> In this guilt are involved all those who fall frequently into sin; for, as our sins consigned Christ the Lord to the death of the cross, most certainly those who wallow in sin and iniquity crucify to themselves again the Son of God, as far as in them lies, and make a mockery of Him [cf. Heb. vi. 6]. This guilt seems more enormous in us than in the Jews, since according to the testimony of the same Apostle [St. Paul]: *If they had known it, they would never have crucified the Lord of glory* [I Cor. ii. 8]; while we, on the contrary, professing to know Him, yet denying Him by our actions, seem in some sort to lay violent hands on Him.

Laid to Rest in a Clean Linen Cloth

Through the boldness and generosity of St. Joseph of Arimathea and St. Nicodemus, who sought the Body of Our Lord from Pilate (cf. Jn. xix. 38) despite the consequences they would suffer from the Jewish leaders, Our Lord's Body was given a proper burial as the Scriptures affirm: *And Joseph taking the body, wrapped it up in a clean linen cloth. And laid it in his own new monument, which he had hewed out in a rock. And he rolled a great stone to the door of the monument and went his way* (Mt. xxvii. 59-60). In imitation of the humility of the Lord, Who was buried in a simple linen cloth, the altar at Mass is likewise clothed in a simple linen cloth, as St. Bede the Venerable relates: "The Church's custom has prevailed for the sacrifice of the altar to be offered not upon silk, nor upon dyed cloth, but on linen of the earth; as the Lord's Body was buried in a clean winding-sheet."[31]

Yet more than merely having a reference to it in the altar cloth, we are privileged to still have on this earth the actual burial cloth of Our Lord, which is known as the Shroud of Turin, since the holy relic has remained in the city of Turin, Italy for centuries. The Shroud of Turin has been subjected to a variety of rigorous examinations to confirm its authenticity using scientific methods, despite the rather obvious conclusion that the intricacy and detail on the Shroud could not have been created by Medieval or even modern technology. In fact, the Turin Shroud Center of Colorado has demonstrated that the fold marks found on the Shroud indicate it once resided in Constantinople in the 10th-11th centuries, in contrast to those

---

[31] Bede Commentary on Mark 15:46 quoted in ST III q51 a2 ad 3.

who claim that the shroud was a 14th century forgery.[32] This corroborates the claim of historians who maintain that the Lord's burial cloth was in the possession of eastern Roman emperors before the Sack of Constantinople in A.D. 1204.[33]

The Holy See remained silent on the Shroud until the middle of the 20th century when, in 1940, Sister Maria Pierina De Micheli obtained authorization from the Archdiocese of Milan to produce the Holy Face Medal with the image of the Holy Shroud. Pope Pius XII subsequently approved the image in 1958 in connection with devotion to the Holy Face and the Feast of the Holy Face, which he instituted to be said on Shrove Tuesday of each year in reparation for the offenses of Mardi Gras.[34] Further corroborating the approval of devotion to the Shroud is the celebration of the special feast in honor of the Most Holy Shroud of Our Lord Jesus Christ in Turin, which was observed on the Friday after the Second Sunday of Lent in Turin in the pre-1955 Roman Missal.[35]

Closer to our times, Joseph Cardinal Ratzinger further expressed his own belief in the authenticity of the Shroud of Turin as the Lord's own burial cloth by calling it "a truly mysterious image, which no human artistry was capable of producing. In some inexplicable way, it appeared imprinted upon cloth and claimed to show the true face of Christ, the crucified and risen Lord."[36] Yet while the Church has officially not decreed that the Shroud of Turin is the actual burial cloth of the Lord, the scientific evidence of the Turin Center of Colorado points to this reality. As Holy Mother Church affirms in her actions, whether or not the cloth is authentic has no bearing on the validity of what Our Lord taught or on the saving power of His death and Resurrection.

God-Made-Man was Buried in the Earth

After having reflected on the Passion and death of the Redeemer, the Roman Catechism now turns to Our Lord's burial:

---

[32] For more information, www.shroudofturin.com.

[33] Emmanuel Poulle, "Les sources de l'histoire du linceul de Turin. Revue critique," *Revue d'histoire ecclésiastique* (Dec. 2009), 104 (3–4): 747–782.

[34] Matthew Plese, "Reparation to the Holy Face for the Offenses of Mardi Gras," *A Catholic Life* (Feb 19, 2018) <https://acatholiclife.blogspot.com/2018/02/reparation-to-holy-face-for-offenses-of.html>, accessed August 12, 2022.

[35] Matthew Plese, "Feast of The Holy Shroud (Friday after the Second Sunday in Lent)," *A Catholic Life* (March 6, 2015) <https://acatholiclife.blogspot.com/2015/03/feast-of-the-holy-shroud-friday-after.html>, accessed August 12, 2022.

[36] Joseph Ratzinger, *The Spirit of the Liturgy*, new ed. (Ignatius Press, 2014), 119.

There are, however, two things which demand particular attention; the one, that the body of Christ was in no degree corrupted in the sepulcher, according to the prediction of the Prophet: *Thou wilt not give thy holy one to see corruption* [Ps. xv. 10]; the other, and it regards the several parts of this Article, that burial, Passion, and also death, apply to Christ Jesus not as God but as man.

Our Lord experienced an actual death since His sacred Body and Soul were separated. The Lord was truly buried as a dead man—not one who merely appeared to be dead, as the Muslims claim. But the Lord's work was not yet done. The Holy Fathers in Limbo who had preceded Our Lord awaited Him, and the Redeemer did not leave them but came to preach to them (cf. I Pet. iii. 18-20) and show them His Sacrifice for them. But through it all, the Body of the Son of God remained guarded by angels in anticipation for the greatest miracle ever performed in the history of the world, the Resurrection, which we will cover in detail next chapter.

Conclusion

In its closing remarks on this Fourth Article of the Creed, the Roman Catechism piously exclaims:

> Would to God that these mysteries were always present to our minds, and that we learned to suffer, die, and be buried together with Our Lord; so that from henceforth, having cast aside all stain of sin, and rising with Him to newness of life, we may at length, through His grace and mercy, be found worthy to be made partakers of the celestial kingdom and glory.

St. Paul himself remarked, *For I judged not myself to know anything among you, but Jesus Christ, and Him crucified* (I Cor. ii. 2). How often do we truly contemplate the mystery of Our Lord's Passion and death?

In the words of Archbishop Fulton J. Sheen:

> Our Lord finished His work, but we have not finished ours. He pointed the way we must follow. He laid down the Cross at the finish, but we must take it up. He finished Redemption in His physical Body, but we have not finished it in His Mystical Body.

He has finished salvation; we have not yet applied it to our souls. He has finished the Temple, but we must live in it. He has finished the model Cross; we must fashion ours to its pattern. He has finished sowing the seed, we must reap the harvest. He has finished filling the chalice, but we have not finished drinking its refreshing draughts. He has planted the wheat field; we must gather it into our barns. He has finished the sacrifice of Calvary; we must finish the Mass.

The Crucifixion was not meant to be an inspirational drama, but a pattern act on which to model our lives. We are not meant to sit and watch the Cross as something done and ended like the life of Socrates. What was done on Calvary avails for us only in the degree that we repeat it in our own lives.[37]

---

[37] Fulton J. Sheen, *Calvary and the Mass*, Chapter 6 – The *Ite, Missa Est*.

V

He Descended into Hell;
The Third Day He Rose Again from the Dead

Fifth Article of the Creed

Christ Descended into Hell

After having carefully considered the sacred Passion and Death of the Son of God, which we addressed over the past two chapters, the Roman Catechism opens its chapter on the Resurrection of the Lord with the sublime words: "To know the glory of the burial of our Lord Jesus Christ, of which we last treated, is highly important; but of still higher importance is it to the faithful to know the splendid triumphs which He obtained by having subdued the devil and despoiled the abodes of hell. Of these triumphs, and also of His Resurrection, we are now about to speak."

Furthermore, the wisdom of the Church continues in the opening of the Fifth Article of the Creed by clearly stating, "[W]e profess that immediately after the death of Christ His soul descended into hell, and dwelt there as long as His body remained in the tomb; and also that the one Person of Christ was at the same time in hell and in the sepulchre."

Seeking to clarify the meaning of Christ's descent to hell, the Catechism of St. Pius X explains: "Hell here means the Limbo of the holy Fathers, that is, the place where the souls of the just were detained, in expectation of redemption through Jesus Christ."[38] The Roman Catechism corroborates this understanding by explaining for the faithful: "Hell, then, here signifies those secret abodes in which are detained the souls that have not obtained the happiness of heaven. In this sense the word is frequently used in Scripture" (cf. Philip. ii. 10).

---

[38] Catechism of St. Pius X, Fifth Article of the Creed, answer to second question.

Our Lord's descent into the abode of Limbo is likewise recounted in the private revelations of Ven. Anne Catherine Emmerich as recorded in *The Dolorous Passion of Our Lord Jesus Christ*. According to her visions of the Lord, immediately following His death on the Cross He descended to the Limbo of the Fathers.[39] In the Limbo of the Fathers, He preached to the patriarchs, prophets, and holy people that had died before Heaven was opened by His death (cf. I Pet. iv. 6). In her visions, Emmerich also saw that our Divine Lord commanded nearly one hundred of the holy people in Limbo to re-enter their bodies temporarily. He then commanded them to visit their relatives and preach the truth of His salvific death, a miraculous event to which the Scriptures testify (cf. Matt. xxvii. 52-53). Yet, the souls of those who rose from the graves in their bodies did not look like Jesus does in His glorified body. They merely re-entered their bodies temporarily to fulfill the divine command. Afterwards, their souls again left their bodies and returned to Limbo. Upon Our Lord's Ascension into Heaven, the souls of the Just at last entered into Heaven and on that day, the Limbo of the Fathers was closed forever.

The Two-Folded Purpose of Christ's Descent to the Souls in Limbo

Our Divine Redeemer descended to Limbo, as the Roman Catechism explains, for two chief reasons. Firstly, He descended to the souls of the just who awaited the Messiah to liberate them; and secondly, to proclaim His power. As the Catechism expounds:

> ...Christ the Lord descended into hell in order that, having despoiled the demons, He might liberate from prison those holy Fathers and the other just souls, and might bring them into heaven with Himself. This He accomplished in an admirable and most glorious manner; for His august presence at once shed a celestial luster upon the captives and filled them with inconceivable joy and delight. He also imparted to them that supreme happiness which consists in the vision of God, thus verifying His promise to the thief on the cross: *This day thou shalt be with Me in paradise* [Lk. xxiii. 43]. ...

> Another reason why Christ the Lord descended into hell is that there, as well as in heaven and on earth, He might proclaim His power and authority, and that *every knee should bow, of those that are in heaven, on earth, and under the earth* [Philip. ii. 10].

---

[39] Ven. Anne Catherine Emmerich, *The Dolorous Passion of Our Lord Jesus Christ* (Cosimo Classics, 1923), 320.

And here, who is not filled with admiration and astonishment when he contemplates the infinite love of God for man! Not satisfied with having undergone for our sake a most cruel death, He penetrates the inmost recesses of the earth to transport into bliss the souls whom He so dearly loved and whose liberation from thence He had achieved.

Limbus Patrum vs. Limbus Infantium

The Limbo of the Fathers (*limbus patrum*) – the place of waiting for the souls of the just who died prior to Our Lord's coming – is not to be confused with the Limbo of the infants (*limbus infantium*). Often called simply "Limbo" instead of "Limbo of the infants," it refers to the place of natural happiness to which the souls of unbaptized children go who die before attaining the age of reason. Indeed, one of the greatest crimes of abortion is the deprivation of baptismal grace from the unborn child's soul. Since Baptism, "or a desire for it" (Council of Trent), is necessary for salvation, these souls cannot enter Heaven.[40] Yet, due to the love of God, they do not suffer the pains of hell with the souls of the damned. Pope St. Pius X and other theologians have asserted that the Limbo of the infants is a place of eternal rest, yet without the joy of seeing God face-to-face. And whereas some in the Church have tried in recent years to discredit the existence of this Limbo, such efforts directly contradict the teaching of Pope Pius VI in *Auctorem Fidei* (Aug. 28, 1794):

> The doctrine which rejects as a Pelagian fable, that place of the lower regions (which the faithful generally designate by the name of the limbo of children) in which the souls of those departing with the sole guilt of original sin are punished with the punishment of the condemned, exclusive of the punishment of fire [... is] false, rash, injurious to Catholic schools. (Denz. 1526)

Consequently, whereas some modern translations refer to Christ's descent "unto the dead" as a means of clarifying that Christ did not descend into the hell of the damned (called *gehenna* by Our Lord), it is still appropriate to pray the Creed with the words "He descended into hell," as long as we maintain the proper meaning of the words, as discussed above. Furthermore, Our Lord's descent to hell in no way obscures His unblemished sanctity, as the Roman Catechism teaches: "But although Christ descended into hell, His supreme power was in no degree lessened,

---

[40] Session VI, Decree on Justification (Jan. 13, 1547), Ch. 4 (Denz. 796).

nor was the splendor of His sanctity obscured by any blemish. His descent served rather to prove that whatever had been foretold of His sanctity was true; and that, as He had previously demonstrated by so many miracles, He was truly the Son of God."

He Rose Again by His Own Power on the Third Day

Throughout the New Testament, we see the phrase "the third day" used in reference to Our Lord's Resurrection. Christ told His Apostles on three different occasions that He would *be put to death, and the third day rise again* (Matt. xvi. 21; cf. xvii. 22, xx. 19). Likewise, after His Resurrection, St. Peter preached that *God raised up [Jesus] the third day* (Acts x. 40), and St. Paul, *that He rose again the third day, according to the Scriptures* (I Cor. xv. 4). Regarding how Christ our Lord could have been in the tomb three days if He died on Friday afternoon and rose on Sunday morning, the answer lies in the ancient Jewish custom of counting where each part of one day was considered to be a day. In turning to the Roman Catechism, we read: "But as He lay in the sepulchre one full day, a part of the preceding and a part of the following day, He is said, with strictest truth, to have lain in the grave for three days, and on the third day to have risen again from the dead."

The Resurrection of Jesus Christ is the foundation of our Faith, as the Scriptures affirm: *And if Christ be not risen again, your faith is vain, for you are yet in your sins* (I Cor. xv. 17). Similarly, the Catechism affirms this reality in its succinct assertion on the uniqueness of the Lord's Resurrection: "By the word *Resurrection*, however, we are not merely to understand that Christ was raised from the dead, which happened to many others, but that He rose by His own power and virtue, a singular prerogative peculiar to Him alone. For it is incompatible with nature and was never given to man to raise himself by his own power, from death to life. ...Thus, He was able by His own power to return to life and rise from the dead."

Some question why Our Lord rose from the dead on the third day. To them, the Roman Catechism addresses these words: "To prove that He was God He did not delay His Resurrection to the end of the world; while, on the other hand, to convince us that He was truly man and really died, He rose not immediately, but on the third day after His death, a space of time sufficient to prove the reality of His death." Similarly, the Catechism of St. Pius X plainly states, "Jesus Christ deferred His own resurrection until the third day to show clearly that He was really dead."

The Resurrection of Jesus Christ is a Historical Reality

There are several common theories people put forth to deny the Resurrection and, by extension, the divinity of Christ (see below). It is important to remember these unquestionable facts when engaging in apologetics with such individuals:

1) Three days after His Crucifixion, eyewitnesses claimed to see the Resurrected Christ;

2) Many of these eyewitnesses suffered torture and death for their belief;

3) Paul, who was violently opposed to Christianity, converted suddenly and suffered martyrdom for his belief in the Resurrection;

4) The tomb was empty; and

5) Billons of people have accepted the Resurrection as true, and many Christians have suffered and died for their belief.

With these facts in mind, let us briefly consider the theories that question the Resurrection and the reasons why these theories are false.

The Stolen Body Theory

People who believe this will say that the Apostles stole Jesus' body and fabricated the story about the Resurrection. Of all the theories that deny Our Lord's Resurrection, this is the only one mentioned in the Gospels—a desperate attempt on the part of the Jewish leaders to explain the empty tomb (cf. Matt. xxviii. 11-15). Regarding the merits of this theory, it fails completely because it does not explain why the Apostles or other disciples would spend their entire lives spreading a lie which ultimately brought them persecution, suffering, and death. It is patently absurd to think they would have subjected themselves to such misery (humanly speaking) unless they believed, as the Gospels proclaim, *The Lord is risen indeed* (Lk. xxiv. 34) and, consequently, *that the sufferings of this time are not worthy to be compared with the glory to come, that shall be revealed in us* (Rom. viii. 18).

The Resuscitation Theory

This theory says that Jesus didn't really die on the Cross, but that He just lost consciousness and that His eventual recovery served as the basis for the story of His Resurrection. The problem here is that it assumes the Roman soldiers (who were professional executioners) did not make certain that Jesus was dead (despite stabbing Him in the heart with a lance). The theory also fails to explain how anyone who survived flagellation (many people died while being scourged, before they were crucified), nails through their hands and feet, hours of crucifixion, and a lance to the heart could survive at all.[41]

The Evolution Theory

This theory claims that over the decades and centuries following Jesus' death, the Apostles and early Christians gradually told more and more dramatic stories until they finally came up with a myth about His Resurrection. This theory is especially prominent today, appearing in books like *Constantine's Sword* by James Carroll. At first glance, this theory might sound more reasonable than the first two, but it fails for several reasons. The theory assumes that there was no bad faith on the part of the people who believed these stories (because then they could not explain why the people would die for their faith), and so it must argue that this process of making the myth up went on over several generations. However, within 20 to 30 years of Jesus' death the Synoptic Gospels (Matthew, Mark, and Luke) were already written proclaiming the Resurrection, and many Christians had already suffered martyrdom for their faith in the Risen Christ. It is a historically verifiable fact. A non-Christian historian could attempt to argue that the Resurrection is false, but he certainly cannot argue against the faith of the early Christians, thousands of whom chose to die a martyr's death rather than deny the Resurrection.

The Psychological Theory

This theory claims that the Apostles were so grief stricken that they convinced one another of His Resurrection as a psychological defense to counter their grief. These visions were subsequently copied by others who were grief stricken, and the story spread. St. Paul is the first problem with this theory, because he would have had absolutely no reason to "see" Jesus. Saul, as he was known before his conversion, hated Christians and did not believe in Jesus, and yet when Jesus appeared to him (cf. Acts ix. 1-19), he converted and eventually died for his belief in Jesus. The second and more crucial problem with this theory is that the tomb was actually empty. If the Apostles had fake visions and started claiming that Jesus was resurrected and the tomb was not empty, the Jewish leaders and Romans would simply

---

[41] For a detailed medical account of what Our Lord endured, from His agony in the garden to His last breath on the Cross, see Lee Strobel, *The Case for Christ: A Journalist's Personal Investigation of the Evidence for Jesus* (Grand Rapids: Zondervand Publishing House, 1998), 191-204.

have produced His body and ended the whole issue. However, the tomb was truly empty, and this theory totally fails to explain how that occurred.

Fr. John Laux in *Catholic Apologetics Book IV* poignantly affirms this conclusion when he writes:

> If their testimony is not true, what testimony is true? If we doubt the simple, definite, unanimous story of the Evangelists, the blood-sealed testimony of the Apostles, can we believe anything? Must we not despair of ever attaining truth on testimony? If these were deceived, then all the impressions registered by our senses, by sight, touch, and hearing, are illusions. It is an illusion when a thousand sane men and women see the sunshine at midday, when ten thousand hear the roar of the storm wind that uproots the giants of the forest. If these men deceived, then we are not sure of our lives in the company of our dearest friends. If the Resurrection of Jesus is not a fact, a reality, then all is a delusion and an idle dream.

Our Lord Possesses a Glorified Body

Although our Redeemer's Body was torn apart in the brutality of His Passion, His Body after the Resurrection was not only restored but also glorified. It was the same body, not a newly created one, but it was different in its properties. In its discussion of Article XI of the Creed, the Roman Catechism expounds upon the qualities of a resurrected body as possessing 1) impassibility, 2) brightness, 3) agility, and 4) subtility.

The eyewitnesses of the Resurrection not only saw Our Lord consume food (cf. Lk. xxiv. 41-43), evidence that He possessed a true body, they also saw Him pass through the walls of the Upper Room (cf. Jn. xx. 19) as if the walls were not there. And to those who will one day enter Heaven, the Catechism states clearly that such a glorified state will be given to our mortal bodies as well: "And as His body, rising to immortal glory, was changed, so shall our bodies also, before frail and mortal, be restored and clothed with glory and immortality."

The Resurrection is a Call to the Life of Grace

Those who believe in the Resurrection do not believe only in a historical reality. Belief in the Resurrection implies a conversion of life, one that requires putting away *the old man* and putting on *the new man, who according to God is created in justice and holiness of truth* (Eph. iv. 22,

24). The Apostle Paul plainly admonished the Colossians as such when he wrote, *If you have risen with Christ, seek the things that are above, where Christ is seated at the right hand of God... Mortify therefore your members which are upon the earth; fornication, uncleanness, lust, evil concupiscence, and covetousness, which is the service of idols. For which things the wrath of God cometh upon the children of unbelief, in which you also walked some time, when you lived in them* (Col. iii. 1, 5-6).

In her wisdom, Holy Mother Church reiterates these sentiments in the Catechism with these words:

> From the Resurrection of Christ, therefore, we should draw two lessons: the one, that after we have washed away the stains of sin, we should begin to lead a new life, distinguished by integrity, innocence, holiness, modesty, justice, beneficence and humility; the other, that we should so persevere in that newness of life as never more, with the divine assistance, to stray from the paths of virtue on which we have once entered.

And the wisdom of the Catechism continues:

> The principal signs of this resurrection from sin which should be noted are taught us by the Apostle. For when he says: *If you be risen with Christ, seek the things that are above, where Christ is sitting at the right hand of God*, he distinctly tells us that they who desire to possess life, honor, repose and riches, there chiefly where Christ dwells, have truly risen with Christ.

How often do we examine our own conscience against these references? Do we truly live a life through which others will recognize a follower of the Risen Lord?

Conclusion

It is important to note that although historical analysis helps to confirm our faith, we do not have faith because the history backs it up. We have faith because it is revealed to us by God as a gift. Faith is aided by reason and history, but it is not based solely on reason and history. Even if every scientist and historian in the world denied the existence of the Resurrection, we should still believe the Resurrection because it was revealed to us by God through the Church. (Thankfully, as the First Vatican Council assures us, "although faith is above reason, nevertheless, between faith and reason no true dissension can ever exist, since the same God Who reveals mysteries and infuses faith has bestowed on the human soul the light of reason; moreover, God cannot deny Himself, nor ever contradict truth with truth."[42])

As Catholics, we must be uncompromising in doctrine as well as unblemished in our conduct, always striving for the perfection of charity towards God and neighbor. Souls will only be converted by the grace of God operating through our persistent efforts of *doing the truth in charity* (Eph. iv. 15). But souls will be lost in only a few moments if they see us living in a manner that contradicts the Faith we profess in the Risen Lord. May this thought, and the holy fear of causing scandal, motivate us to *be blameless, and sincere children of God* (Philip. ii. 15) in order to help as many souls as possible embrace faith in the Risen Lord and enter His one true Church

---

[42] Dogmatic Constitution *Dei Filius* on the Catholic Faith (Apr. 24, 1870), Ch. 4 (Denz. 1797).

VI

He Ascended into Heaven, Sitteth at the Right Hand of God the Father Almighty

Sixth Article of the Creed

Christ Ascended Body and Soul into Heaven

After having carefully examined the mystery of Our Lord Jesus Christ's death and glorious Resurrection into Heaven, the Roman Catechism turns to His triumphant Ascension into Heaven:

> Filled with the Spirit of God and contemplating the blessed and glorious Ascension of our Lord, the Prophet David exhorts all to celebrate that splendid triumph with the greatest joy and gladness: *Clap your hands, all ye nations: shout unto God with the voice of joy.... God is ascended with jubilee.* The pastor will hence learn that this mystery should be explained with the greatest diligence; and that he should take care that the people not only perceive it with faith and understanding, but that they also strive as far as possible, with the Lord's help to reflect it in their lives and actions.

Ascension Thursday in the liturgical year marks the 40th day after Easter Sunday and the day we celebrate Our Lord's Ascension into Heaven from earth. The Ascension has three principal parts: (1) the departure of Jesus from earth, (2) His going up into Heaven, and (3) taking His place at the right hand of the Father. To the faithful who understand the reason for Our Lord's ascent, it is not only a historical reality but also an occasion for us to reflect on our lives. Are we in the state of grace and worthy to follow Our Lord into Heaven?

Rogation Days in Preparation for the Ascension

While many Catholics today will often unfortunately overlook the Ascension, the traditional liturgy of the Church saw the Ascension as a crowning achievement of Our Lord's victory over sin and death. As such, not only was the Ascension celebrated as an Octave for eight days but also it was preceded by fasting and vigils. These days of preparation were known as the Minor Rogation. These days have their ancient origin in 470 by Bishop Mamertus of Vienna. In time, they were eventually adopted as part of the Church's universal calendar. The word "Rogation" comes from the Latin verb *rogare*, which simply means "to ask", and was applied to these days because the Gospel reading for the previous Sunday before the Ascension included the verse, *Ask and you shall receive* (Jn. xvi. 24).

For hundreds of years, the faithful would observe these Minor Rogations – the third of which occurs on the day before Ascension Thursday, the Vigil of the Ascension – by prayer and fasting. At this time of year, it is customary to have the crops in one's fields blessed by a priest in violet colored vestments. Rogation Days were characterized by the Rogation procession in which parishioners, led by the priest, would proceed around the boundary of their parish and pray for its protection in the forthcoming year.

According to St. Augustine, the Feast of the Ascension is of Apostolic origin. As early as the fifth century, documentation of this feast is preserved. Since the ninth century during the Pontificate of Pope Leo III (r. 795-816) and up until the Second Vatican Council, the Ascension had an associated Octave attached to it. Predating this Octave is the long-established practice of having a Vigil for the Ascension.

While the Feast of the Ascension – despite its high rank as one of the most important holy days in the year – has fallen into obscurity and lack of observance in many areas (often transferred to the following Sunday), it is still a public holiday in many countries (e.g. Austria, Belgium, Colombia, Denmark, Finland, France, Germany, Haiti, Iceland, Indonesia, Liechtenstein, Luxembourg, Madagascar, Namibia, The Netherlands, Norway, Sweden, Switzerland and Vanuatu). As such, Catholic culture underscores the importance of the Ascension through its customs that precede and follow Ascension Thursday.

How Did Jesus Ascend?

After establishing the importance of reflecting on the Ascension, the Roman Catechism immediately follows with an explanation as to how our

Blessed Lord, Who was *physically* resurrected and likewise *physically* ascended into Heaven:

> The pastor is also to teach that He ascended by His own power, not being taken up by the power of another, as was Elias, who was carried to heaven in a fiery chariot; or, as the Prophet Habacuc, or Philip, the deacon, who were borne through the air by the divine power, and traversed great distances.

> Neither did He ascend into heaven solely by the exercise of His supreme power as God, but also by virtue of the power which He possessed as man. Although human power alone was insufficient to accomplish this, yet the virtue with which the blessed soul of Christ was endowed was capable of moving the body as it pleased, and His body, now glorified, readily obeyed the behest of the soul that moved it. Hence, we believe that Christ ascended into heaven as God and man by His own power.

Fr. Leonard Goffine in *The Church's Year* succinctly affirms that the Ascension was performed by Christ's own power when he writes, "Christ ascended into heaven by His own power, because He is God, and now in His glorified humanity He sits at the right hand of His Father, as our continual Mediator."

Unlike Elias, who was taken up into Heaven, or the Blessed Virgin Mary, who was assumed by the power of God body and soul into Heaven at the end of her earthly life, the Lord Jesus ascended by His own power. No mere man has the power to fly, much less to ascend out of the earth's atmosphere and into the furthest reaches of space to Heaven. But Jesus, Who is fully God and fully man, possessed the power to do so, thus performing another miracle to the approximately 125 people who saw Him ascend.[43]

---

[43] Baltimore Catechism No. 3, Q. 416: "From various parts of Scripture we may conclude there were about 125 persons – though traditions tell us there was a greater number – present at the Ascension. They were the Apostles, the Disciples, the pious women and others who had followed Our Blessed Lord. The souls of the just who were waiting in Limbo for the redemption ascended with Christ."

Where Did Jesus Ascend?

Our Blessed Lord ascended from the Mount of Olives into Heaven. As Fr. Goffine concisely teaches, "*Where and how did Christ ascend into heaven?* From Mount Olivet where His sufferings began, by which we learn that where our crosses and afflictions begin, which we endure with patience and resignation, there begins our reward." The Baltimore Catechism concurs when it states, "Christ ascended into heaven from Mount Olivet, the place made sacred by His agony on the night before His death."[44] Thus, by meditating on the place of the Ascension we have before us a source of great spiritual consolation, yet so few Catholics seem to have meditated on the connection between the Agony and the Ascension.

Likewise, the "Golden Legend" by Blessed Jacobus de Varagine, published in the late Middle Ages, further aids our meditation on the Mount of Olives in its account of the Ascension:

> The first point, note that He rose to heaven from the Mount of Olives, out toward Bethany. This mountain, following another translation, was also called the Mount of Three Lights, because from the west the light from the Temple fell upon it by night, for a fire burned continually on the altar; in the morning it caught the sun's rays from the east before they reached the city; and the hill's olive trees produced a plentiful supply of oil, which feeds light.

Today, a chapel sits on the Mount of Olives at the exact place of Our Lord's Ascension. According to Sulpicius Severus, bishop of Jerusalem, when a church was built on the Mount of Olives the spot where Christ had stood could never be covered with pavement; and more than that, the marble slabs placed there burst upwards into the faces of those who were laying them. He also says that the footmarks in the dust there prove that the Lord had stood on that spot. Those footprints are still discernible, and the ground still retains the depressions His sacred feet left as a remarkable display of Our Lord's last footstep on this earth.

Why Did Jesus Ascend into Heaven?

The answer to this fundamental question is found in the Preface for the Ascension (a Preface found in the Traditional Roman Rite, but unfortunately lost in the Novus Ordo) in which it states that the Lord ascended "so that He might make us partakers of His Godhead." As the

---

[44] Baltimore Catechism No. 3, Q. 415.

Roman Catechism likewise expounds on the reasons for the Lord's Ascension:

> *Ascending on high, he led captivity captive: He gave gifts to men. ...*
>
> He also ascended into heaven, according to the Apostle, *that he may appear in the presence of God for us*, and discharge for us the office of advocate with the Father. ...
>
> Finally, by His Ascension He has prepared for us a place, as He had promised, and has entered, as our head, in the name of us all, into the possession of the glory of heaven.

Our Lord ascended for us. He ascended so that we might have a share in His divinity in Heaven. Up until our Lord's Ascension, the doors of Heaven were closed as a result of Adam's sin. While the debt for this sin was paid through the death and Resurrection of Christ, the doors remained closed until He, the Victor over death, should open them and be the first to walk through them. Ascension Thursday recalls this sublime mystery: the opening of Heaven to the souls who had waited in the Limbo of the Fathers. It was on the day of the Lord's Ascension that humanity, in the Person of Christ, first entered Heaven.

The renowned Dom Prosper Guéranger, O.S.B. describes this sublime reason for Our Lord's Ascension thusly:

> Jesus ascended into heaven. His Divinity had never been absent; but, by Ascension, His Humanity was also enthroned there, and crowned with the brightest diadem of glory. This is another phase of the mystery we are now solemnizing. Besides a triumph, the Ascension gave to the sacred Humanity a place on the very throne of the eternal Word, to whom it was united in unity of Person. From this throne, it is to receive the adoration of men and of angels.[45]

Likewise, the Roman Catechism succinctly affirms the reality that Jesus Christ, true man and true God, physically entered into Heaven on Ascension Day: "This, then, the faithful must believe without hesitation, that Jesus Christ, having fully accomplished the work of Redemption,

---

[45] Dom Prosper Guéranger, *The Liturgical Year: Paschal time, Volume 3* (Duffy, 1871), 206.

ascended as man, body and soul, into heaven; for as God He never forsook heaven, filling as He does all places with His Divinity."

Archbishop Fulton J. Sheen likewise develops this reality by commenting on Our Lord's Ascension in His human nature:

> In the Ascension the Savior did not lay aside the garment of flesh with which He had been clothed; for His human nature would be the pattern of the future glory of other human natures, which would become incorporated to Him through a sharing of His life. Intrinsic and deep was the relation between His Incarnation and His Ascension. The Incarnation or the assuming of a human nature made it possible for Him to suffer and redeem. The Ascension exalted into glory that same human nature that was humbled to the death.[46]

He Sits at the Father's Right Hand

After *making purgation of sins*, as St. Paul says in his Epistle to the Hebrews, Our Lord ascended gloriously into Heaven and *sitteth on the right hand of the majesty on high* (Heb. i. 3). In his *Summa Theologiae*, St. Thomas Aquinas describes the immense honor signified in this mystery of the Faith:

> Christ is said to sit at the Father's right hand inasmuch as He is on equality with the Father in respect of His Divine Nature, while in respect of His humanity, He excels all creatures in the possession of Divine gifts. But each of these belongs exclusively to Christ. Consequently, it belongs to no one else, angel or man, but to Christ alone, to sit at the right hand of the Father (III q58 a4).

The Roman Catechism clarifies the meaning of this reality by stating in clear terms:

> As among men he who sits at the right hand is considered to occupy the most honorable place, so, transferring the same idea to celestial things, to express the glory which Christ as man has obtained above all others, we confess that He sits at the right hand of the Father.

---

[46] Fulton J. Sheen, *The Life of Christ* (Crown Publishing Group, 2008), 647.

To sit does not imply here position and posture of body, but expresses the firm and permanent possession of royal and supreme power and glory which He received from the Father, and of which the Apostle says: *Raising him up from the dead, and setting him on his right hand in the heavenly places, above all principality, and power, and virtue, and domination, and every name that is named, not only in this world, but also in that which is to come; and he hath subjected all things under his feet.*

While many of us are familiar with the image of Christ sitting at the right hand of the Father, the Scriptures do in one instance mention Christ standing – not sitting – at the right hand of the Father. This instance is during the stoning of St. Stephen. Reflecting upon this truly unique passage, St. Gregory says in a homily on the Ascension (Hom. xxix in Evang.), "It is the judge's place to sit, while to stand is the place of the combatant or helper. Consequently, Stephen in his toil of combat saw Him standing whom He had as his helper. But Mark describes Him as seated after the Ascension, because after the glory of His Ascension He will at the end be seen as judge."

The mystery of our Redeemer's Ascension further confirms us in hope, despite the reality of the judgment that awaits us at death. In another example of the great wisdom contained in the Roman Catechism, we are reassured:

[T]he Ascension of Christ into heaven contributes much to confirm our hope. Believing that Christ, as man, ascended into heaven, and placed our nature at the right hand of God the Father, we are animated with a strong hope that we, as members, shall also ascend thither, to be there united to our Head, according to these words of our Lord Himself: *Father, I will that where I am, they also whom thou hast given me may be with me.*

Conclusion

The Roman Catechism emphasizes the importance of the Ascension by affirming that "all other mysteries refer to the Ascension as to their end and find in it their perfection and completion; for as all the mysteries of religion commence with the Incarnation of our Lord, so His sojourn on earth terminates with His Ascension."

And likewise, the final words of the Catechism on the sixth article of the Creed comfort us by affirming: "For although we owe our Redemption and salvation to the Passion of Christ, whose merits opened heaven to the just, yet His Ascension is not only proposed to us as a model, which teaches us to look on high and ascend in spirit into heaven, but it also imparts to us a divine virtue which enables us to accomplish what it teaches."

In the Ascension, the sacred humanity of Christ entered heavenly glory for the first time. This was the first time that Heaven had opened. This is the first time that our human flesh had entered Heaven. But Our Lord brought something with Him into Heaven. He brought in His five glorious wounds. Those wounds will remain on His sacred Body for eternity. And thus Christ, the High Priest, offers to His Father His Sacrifice and daily pleads for us to His heavenly Father. And His heavenly Father sees in Christ our mortal flesh and the five glorious wounds that brought about our redemption. The Ascension is not just a time to feel sadness because Our Lord leaves us and goes to Heaven. Rather, this is a time of great joy. The Paschal Mystery, which began with Holy Thursday, is complete. Heaven is open to mortal men for the first time. And we too are called to follow Our Lord into Heaven, but we may do so only if we die as Catholics in the state of sanctifying grace.

Archbishop Fulton J. Sheen in *The Life of Christ* remarked in the prologue: "Christianity, unlike any other religion in the world, begins with catastrophe and defeat. Sunshine religions and psychological inspirations collapse in calamity and wither in adversity. But the Life of the Founder of Christianity, having begun with the Cross, ends with the empty tomb and victory."[47] And whereas those who are uncatechized may point to the Resurrection as the end of the Lord's work, the actual completion of the work of our Redemption further included not only His glorious Ascension into Heaven at the Father's right hand but also the sending of the Holy Ghost. But before we reach Pentecost, let us turn to the final article about Our Lord.

---

[47] Fulton J. Sheen, *The Life of Christ* (Crown Publishing Group, 2008), xxiii.

VII

From Thence He Shall Come to Judge the Living and the Dead

Seventh Article of the Creed

Christ Himself Will Come as Judge

In its opening for the Seventh Article of the Apostle's Creed, the Roman Catechism eloquently summarizes the three offices of our Divine Redeemer as follows:

> For the glory and adornment of His Church Jesus Christ is invested with three eminent offices and functions: those of Redeemer, Mediator, and Judge. Since in the preceding Articles it was shown that the human race was redeemed by His Passion and death, and since by His Ascension into heaven it is manifest that He has undertaken the perpetual advocacy and patronage of our cause, it remains that in this Article we set forth His character as Judge. The scope and intent of the Article is to declare that on the last day Christ the Lord will judge the whole human race.

Concerning this role of Judge, St. Peter the Apostle wrote in his First Epistle that we shall all *render account to Him*, that is, to Christ, *Who is ready to judge the living and the dead* (I Pet. iv. 5). The Catechism, in turn, expounds upon this point, stressing that this belief is of apostolic origin:

> Hence when the Prince of the Apostles had expounded in the house of Cornelius the chief dogmas of Christianity, and had taught that Christ was suspended from a cross and put to death by the Jews and rose the third day to life, he added: *And he commanded us to preach to the people, and to testify that this is He, who*

was appointed of God, to be the Judge of the living and the dead [Acts x. 42].

The Particular Judgment at the Moment of Death

It is a dogmatic teaching of the Faith that at the moment of our death we will appear *before the judgment seat of Christ* (II Cor. v. 10), Who will pronounce our eternal sentence: ultimate life in Heaven, though likely after cleansing in Purgatory, or an eternity of uninterrupted and unspeakable torment in hell.

Writing of the Particular Judgement, the Catechism of the Council of Trent explains:

> The first [judgment] takes place when each one of us departs this life; for then he is instantly placed before the judgment seat of God, where all that he has ever done or spoken or thought during life shall be subjected to the most rigid scrutiny. This is called the particular judgment.

Likewise, in the same spirit but with the docility of a pastor who yearned for the salvation of all men, St. John Vianney wrote on the Particular Judgment:

> Our catechism tells us, my children, that all men will undergo a particular judgment on the day of their death. No sooner shall we have breathed our last sigh than our soul, without leaving the place where it has expired, will be presented before the tribunal of God. Wherever we may die, God is there to exercise His justice. The good God, my children, has measured out our years, and of those years that He has resolved to leave us on this earth, He has marked out one which shall be our last; one day which we shall not see succeeded by other days; one hour after which there will be for us no more time.[48]

While the certainty of the particular judgment has been known since apostolic times, the particulars of the immediate consequences of our sentence was the subject of theological debate throughout the high periods of western Christendom (1100-1348). Seeking to end a period of debate on whether the blessed will have the vision of God immediately after their

---

[48] St. Jean-Marie Vianney, *The Little Catechism of the Curé of Ars* (TAN Books, 1994).

sentence or if they must wait until the General Judgment at the end of time, Pope Benedict XII issued *Benedictus Deus* (On the Beatific Vision of God) in the year of Our Lord 1336, thus ending the debate vis-à-vis a dogmatic definition:

> By this Constitution which is to *remain in force forever*, We, with apostolic authority, define the following: According to the general disposition of God, the souls of all the saints who departed from this world before the passion of Our Lord Jesus Christ and also of the holy apostles, martyrs, confessors, virgins and other faithful who died after receiving the holy baptism of Christ – provided they were not in need of any purification when they died, or will not be in need of any when they die in the future, or else, if they then needed or will need some purification, after they have been purified after death – and again the souls of children who have been reborn by the same baptism of Christ or will be when baptism is conferred on them, if they die before attaining the use of free will: all these souls, immediately after death and, in the case of those in need of purification, after the purification mentioned above, since the Ascension of our Lord and Savior Jesus Christ into heaven, already before they take up their bodies again and before the general judgment, have been, are and will be with Christ in heaven, in the heavenly kingdom and paradise, joined to the company of the holy angels.

> …we define that according to the general disposition of God, the souls of those who die in actual mortal sin go down into hell immediately after death and there suffer the pain of hell. Nevertheless, on the day of judgment, all men will appear with their bodies *before the judgment seat of Christ* to give an account of their personal deeds, *so that each one may receive good or evil, according to what he has done in the body* (II Cor. 5.10) (*Emphasis added*).

The Last Judgment at the End of the World

In addition to the Particular Judgment of each individual soul immediately after death, the Church solemnly teaches that there shall also be a second and final judgment, which will occur at the End of Time. This final judgment is also known as the General Judgment and will occur at the very end of the world, when our Blessed Lord comes again to judge the living and dead as we profess in the Creed. At that time, as our Savior Himself has told us, He shall *sit upon the seat of his majesty. And all nations shall be gathered together before Him, and He shall separate them one from another, as the shepherd separateth the sheep from the goats* (Mt. xxv. 31-32). Elsewhere in the Gospel, Our Lord described the Last Judgment with these words: *Wonder not at this; for the hour cometh, wherein all that are in the graves shall hear the voice of the Son of God. And they that have done good things, shall come forth unto the resurrection of life; but they that have done evil, unto the resurrection of judgment* (Jn. v. 28-29).

Similarly, St. John the Apostle wrote the following in his Book of the Apocalypse, the last book of the Holy Bible:

> And I saw the dead, great and small, standing in the presence of the throne, and the books were opened; and another book was opened, which is the book of life; and the dead were judged by those things which were written in the books, according to their works. And the sea gave up the dead that were in it, and death and hell gave up their dead that were in them; and they were judged everyone according to their works. And hell and death were cast into the pool of fire. This is the second death. And whosoever was not found written in the book of life, was cast into the pool of fire (Apoc. xx. 12-15).

The Catholic Church teaches that at the time of the Last Judgment, Christ will come in His glory, *and all the angels with Him* (Mt. xxv. 31), and in His presence the truth of each man's relationship with God will be laid bare. Each person who has ever lived will be judged with the perfect justice of an omnipotent and omniscient God. Those already in Heaven will remain in Heaven, those already in hell will remain in hell, and those in Purgatory will be released into Heaven. After the Last Judgment, the universe itself will be renewed there will be *a new heaven and a new earth* (Apoc. xxi. 1).

If the Last Judgment will in no way alter the verdict of our own particular judgment, some may ask why the Last Judgment is even necessary. In her wisdom, Holy Mother Church in the Seventh Article of the Creed in the Roman Catechism expounds on the reason:

> Those who depart this life sometimes leave behind them children who imitate their conduct, dependents, followers and others who admire and advocate their example, language and actions. Now by all these circumstances the rewards or punishments of the dead

must needs be increased, since the good or bad influence of example, affecting as it does the conduct of many, is to terminate only with the end of the world. Justice demands that in order to form a proper estimate of all these good or bad actions and words a thorough investigation should be made. This, however, could not be without a general judgment of all men.

In a similar though more succinct manner, the Baltimore Catechism explains the rationale for the Last Judgment by stating: "There is need of a general judgment, though everyone is judged immediately after death, that the providence of God, which, on earth, often permits the good to suffer and the wicked to prosper, may in the end appear just before all men."[49] And further, "There are other reasons for the general judgment, and especially that Christ Our Lord may receive from the whole world the honor denied Him at His first coming, and that all may be forced to acknowledge Him as their God and Redeemer."

The Last Judgment will make our sins and the sins of every person in history known to everyone else. Nothing will remain secret any longer, according to Our Lord's own words: *For there is not any thing secret that shall not be made manifest, nor hidden, that shall not be known and come abroad* (Lk. viii. 17). All will be revealed, and all bad will be punished and all good, even the hidden good for which we never received recognition on earth, will be rewarded openly before all.

Likewise, the Roman Catechism affirms the reality of the Last Judgment when it states:

> The second [judgment] occurs when on the same day and in the same place all men shall stand together before the tribunal of their Judge, that in the presence and hearing of all human beings of all times each may know his final doom and sentence. The announcement of this judgment will constitute no small part of the pain and punishment of the wicked; whereas the good and just will derive great reward and consolation from the fact that it will then appear what each one was in life. This is called the general judgment.

The time when Jesus will return is given many names: The Day of the Lord, the Parousia (Greek for "arrival" or "coming"), the end times, and the Second Coming of Christ. The Parousia will be unmistakable because it

---

[49] Baltimore Catechism No. 3, Q. 416 & Q. 1389.

will be accompanied by unprecedented signs: *For just as lightning comes from the east and is seen as far as the west, so will the coming* [parousia] *of the Son of Man be* (Mt. xxiv. 27). Some signs are general events concerning the evangelization of the world: *And this gospel of the kingdom will be preached throughout the world as a witness to all nations, and then the end will come* (Mt. xxiv. 14). Other signs are more proximate. Matthew (Ch. XXIV), Mark (Ch. XIII), and Luke (Ch. XXI) all describe the unmistakable signs with apocalyptic images. St. Paul likewise comments on the signs of the End of Times in his Second Epistle to St. Timothy:

> But understand this: there will be terrifying times in the last days. People will be self-centered and lovers of money, proud, haughty, abusive, disobedient to their parents, ungrateful, irreligious, callous, implacable, slanderous, licentious, brutal, hating what is good, traitors, reckless, conceited, lovers of pleasure rather than lovers of God, as they make a pretense of religion but deny its power. Reject them (II Tim. iii. 1-5).

The Catholic Church teaches that we should avoid pointless speculations about the time, the details of the signs, or the nature of the difficulties. The Church focuses instead on the need for living the commands of the Gospel as the only fitting preparation for the Parousia, whenever it happens. Once again, in the words of St. Peter, Prince of the Apostles and first Pope:

> Wherefore having the loins of your mind girt up, being sober, trust perfectly in the grace which is offered you in the revelation of Jesus Christ, as children of obedience, not fashioned according to the former desires of your ignorance: But according to Him that hath called you, Who is holy, be you also in all manner of conversation holy: Because it is written: You shall be holy, for I am holy (I Pet. i. 13-16).

Similarly, the Church entirely rejects the false Protestant notion of the Rapture (assumption of the faithful prior to Our Lord's Second Coming) and the related error of Millennialism, which claims there will be a 1,000-year temporal reign of Christ on earth after His return.

While the Church admonishes the faithful to avoid pointless speculations on the time or characteristics of when the Last Judgment will occur, she is nevertheless adamant that a true bodily resurrection will occur. The Fourth Lateran Council in 1215 A.D. clearly taught: "He [Christ] will come at the end of the world; He will judge the living and the dead; and He will reward all, both the lost and elect, according to their works. And all these will rise with their own bodies which they now have so that they may receive according to their works, whether good or bad; the wicked, a perpetual punishment with the devil; the good, eternal glory with Christ."

Conclusion

In its great wisdom and prudence, the Roman Catechism admonishes us to have before our eyes the reality that one day we will be judged in both the Particular Judgment and then openly before all peoples at the End of Time. This is inevitable:

> And if, from the beginning of the world that day of the Lord, on which He was clothed with our flesh, was sighed for by all as the foundation of their hope of deliverance; so also, after the death and Ascension of the Son of God, we should make that other day of the Lord the object of our most earnest desires, *looking for the blessed hope and coming of the glory of the great God* [Tit. ii. 13].

In light of this reality, we must ask ourselves how often we are going to Confession. How often do we sin? How many days left will the Lord give us to make spiritual progress before our eternal sentence is pronounced? Those who go to the Judgment Seat of God with mortal sin on their souls are lost for all eternity. Aware of this sobering reality but equally aware of God's immense generosity in the confessional, this Seventh Article of the Creed should inspire us to regularly receive the Sacrament of Penance and diligently put into practice the following admonition found in Scripture: *In all thy works remember thy last end, and thou shalt never sin* (Ecclus. vii. 40).

Venerable Mary of Agreda remarked, "The majority of souls appear before the Judgment empty-handed. They did nothing good for eternity." What merit are you winning for your soul? Are you engaging in corporal and spiritual works of mercy? Take some time to write down ways that you will help spread the Faith, teach the Faith, instruct those ignorant of the Faith, console those who are doubting in matters of Faith, help those in need of material goods, or care for those who are poor or in prison. Yet, as the Church teaches, our works are worthless if they are not performed in the state of grace. As St. Teresa of Jesus wrote, "Our works are of no value if they be not united to the merits of Jesus Christ."

VIII

I Believe in the Holy Ghost

Eighth Article of the Creed

Revisiting the Purpose of Religious Instruction

Before examining the Eighth Article of the Creed, it is worthwhile to step back and remember our purpose in studying the Roman Catechism. Rather than being a merely intellectual exercise, the purpose of religious instruction is ultimately for our salvation and that of others. We do not study these articles for mere curiosity, which St. Thomas Aquinas identifies as a sin (II-II q167), or out of a pride based on the notion that only Traditional Catholics should know these truths. Those who believe that these truths were meant only for a select group of chosen individuals would fall into the heresy of Gnosticism.

Rather, our purpose in studying the Creed and the teachings of the Catholic Faith as expounded upon in the Catechism of the Council of Trent, under the direction of St. Charles Borromeo, is entirely for our own salvation and that of those whom we encounter. The entire human race is called to life in the Catholic Church and adherence to the Church's teachings since her dogmatic teachings are ultimately God's teachings.

The principles and teachings of the Faith should lead to real, concrete actions in our lives, all centered around living the teachings of the Faith in the state of grace. These truths are necessary for salvation. However, to merely know the teachings of the Faith without praying, without frequenting the Sacraments, without striving to live in the state of grace at all times, or without sharing it for the salvation of the souls of others, would be foolish. As the saintly Curè of Ars once remarked, "My children, I often think that most of the Christians who are lost are lost for want of instruction; they do not know their religion."[50] Let us not be among the many who are lost and do not reach Heaven.

A Distinct Divine Person

The Holy Ghost, known also as the Holy Spirit, the Paraclete, or the Spirit of Truth,[51] is the Third Person of the Blessed Trinity. The Holy Ghost is not a feeling or a pious thought but a real and true Person. As the Roman Catechism explains, "the Holy Ghost is equally God with the Father and the Son, equally omnipotent and eternal, infinitely perfect, the supreme good, infinitely wise, and of the same nature as the Father and the Son."

While the Holy Ghost did not die on the Cross or take flesh of the Virgin Mary, the Holy Ghost is still nonetheless a real, divine Person. Each year, the Church celebrates one of her highest-ranking feasts on Pentecost Sunday, which commemorates the Descent of the Holy Ghost on the Apostles and the Blessed Virgin Mary ten days after Our Lord's Ascension. This event is described in the Book of Acts (ii. 1-13) and fulfilled Our Lord's promise to send us *another Paraclete* (Jn. xiv. 16), One Who would guide the Church into *all truth* (Jn. xvi. 13). That Advocate, Whom we call the Holy Ghost, is truly a divine Person distinct from the Father and the Son, yet there are not three gods but only one God in three divine Persons.

That the Holy Ghost is a distinct Person is confirmed by both Scripture and Tradition. There can be no debate on the existence of the Holy Ghost and His role as a distinct Person, as the Catechism further explains:

> To say nothing of other testimonies of Scripture, the form of Baptism, taught by our Redeemer, shows most clearly that the Holy Ghost is the Third Person, self-existent in the Divine Nature and distinct from the other Persons. It is a doctrine taught also by the Apostle when he says: *The grace of our Lord Jesus Christ, and the charity of God, and the communication of the Holy Ghost, be with you all. Amen.*
>
> This same truth is still more explicitly declared in these words added to this Article of the Creed by the Fathers of the First Council of Constantinople to refute the impious folly of Macedonius: *And in the Holy Ghost, the Lord and Giver of life, Who proceedeth from the Father*

---

[50] St. Jean-Marie Vianney, *The Little Catechism of the Curé of Ars* (TAN Books, 1994).
[51] Cf. Baltimore Catechism No. 3, Q. 422.

and the Son; Who together with the Father and the Son,
is adored and glorified; Who spoke by the prophets.

In referencing Macedonius, the Catechism addresses the heresy known as Macedonianism – also called the Pneumatomachian heresy – which Macedonius developed in the 4th century. This heresy taught that the Holy Ghost was created by the Son and was inferior to the Father and the Son. St. Athanasius of Alexandria in *Letters to Serapion* and St. Basil the Great of Caesarea in *On the Holy Ghost* countered these errors as against both Scripture and Tradition. Shortly thereafter at the First Council of Constantinople (381 AD), the Macedonians were officially condemned when the Creed of Nicaea, originally promulgated in 325 AD, was expanded to counter this grave error.

The Catechism explains that the Scriptures attest to the divinity of the Third Person of the Trinity:

> Again, the Sacred Scriptures join the Person of the Holy Ghost to those of the Father and the Son, as, for example, when Baptism is commanded to be administered *in the Name of the Father, and of the Son, and of the Holy Ghost.* There is thus no room left us of doubting the truth of this mystery. For if the Father is God, and the Son God, we must admit that the Holy Ghost, Who is united with Them in the same degree of honor, is also God.

> Besides, baptism administered in the name of any creature can be of no effect. *Were you baptized in the name of Paul?* says the Apostle, to show that such baptism could have availed nothing to salvation. Since, therefore, we are baptized in the name of the Holy Ghost, we must acknowledge the Holy Ghost to be God.

Furthermore, the Catechism expounds upon this reality with a clear presentation of Scripture which assigns to the Holy Ghost the attributes of God Himself:

> Wherefore to Him is ascribed the honour of temples, as when the Apostle says: *Know you not that your members are the temple of the Holy Ghost?* Scripture also attributes to Him the power to sanctify, to vivify, to search the depths of God, to speak by the Prophets, and to be present in all places, all of which can be attributed to God alone.

In its article on the Holy Ghost, the Roman Catechism does not present any novelties but only the enduring and apostolic teachings of the Faith, drawing upon such orthodox sources as the writings of St. Augustine and the Athanasian Creed, which originated in the late fifth or early sixth centuries and explicitly attests to the distinction of the three divine Persons. This Creed was for centuries prayed on Trinity Sunday during the Canonical Hour of Prime until the changes brought about the Second Vatican Council. Those who continue to pray the pre-conciliar Divine Office still recite this Creed, which declares in part:

> For there is one Person of the Father, another of the Son, and another of the Holy Ghost. But the Godhead of the Father, of the Son, and of the Holy Ghost, is all one; the Glory equal, the Majesty coeternal. Such as the Father is, such is the Son, and such is the Holy Ghost. The Father uncreated, the Son uncreated, and the Holy Ghost uncreated. The Father unlimited, the Son unlimited, and the Holy Ghost unlimited. The Father eternal, the Son eternal, and the Holy Ghost eternal. And yet they are not three eternals, but one eternal. As also there are not three uncreated nor three infinites, but one uncreated, and one infinite. So likewise, the Father is Almighty, the Son Almighty, and the Holy Ghost Almighty. And yet they are not three Almighties, but one Almighty. So, the Father is God, the Son is God, and the Holy Ghost is God. And yet they are not three Gods, but one God.

Lord and Giver of Life

After naming the Holy Ghost, the Nicene Creed then calls Him "Lord." The Catechism explains: "By confessing the Holy Ghost to be Lord [the Fathers of the First Council of Constantinople] declare how far He excels the Angels, who are the noblest spirits created by God...." By next professing the Holy Ghost as the Giver of Life, the Council Fathers address the role of the Holy Ghost in our own souls as the Catechism explains: "They also designate the Holy Ghost the giver of life because the soul lives more by its union with God than the body is nourished and sustained by its union with the soul."

It was by the will of God that we came into existence. Our entire existence, our life, and our family are all the will of the Holy Ghost, Almighty God, Who governs the world and orders all of Creation. But of all His gifts which He showers upon us, the greatest gift of all is that of justification, as the Catechism teaches:

> ...the grace of justification, *which signs us with the Holy Spirit of promise, who is the pledge of our inheritance,* transcends all His other most ample gifts. It unites us to God in the closest bonds of love, lights up within us the sacred flame of piety, forms us to newness of life, *renders us partakers of the divine nature,* and enables us *to be called and really to be the sons of God.*

Our purpose in life is to get to Heaven and we can do so only if we die in the state of sanctifying grace with charity in our soul. Stated another way, we can be saved only if we die with the Holy Ghost dwelling in our souls. The illustrious Father Reginald Garrigou-Lagrange, O.P. in his monumental work on the spiritual life, *The Three Ages of the Interior Life,* explains the connection of the Holy Ghost with charity:

> Charity is the bond of perfection because it is the highest of the virtues which unites our soul to God. Charity in fact vivifies all other virtues by rendering their acts meritorious. Without charity, the most excellent extraordinary gifts are of no avail for eternal life because without charity we do not fulfill the first commandment of God. By charity, we become temples of the Holy Ghost, and the more we love God, the more we know Him by the supernatural knowledge that is divine wisdom. According to this doctrine, perfection does not consist chiefly in humility, nor in poverty, nor in the virtue of religion, but it lies primarily in the love of God and of neighbor. The others are just means to the end.[52]

The Gifts of the Holy Ghost

The Catholic Church has always taught that through the Sacrament of Baptism Original Sin, inherited from our first parents (Adam and Eve), is forgiven and completely washed away along with all personal sins committed up to that moment. In addition, all punishment due to those sins is removed, meaning there is no need for penance or time in purgatory to expunge the effects of those sins forgiven through Baptism. At the moment of our Baptism, *the charity of God is poured forth in our hearts, by the Holy Ghost, Who is given to us* (Rom. v. 5). The Holy Ghost fills us with sanctifying grace – a participation in the divine life of the Blessed Trinity – and infuses in our souls the three theological virtues (faith, hope, and charity) as well as His seven gifts of wisdom, knowledge, understanding,

---

[52] Rev. Fr. Reginald Garrigou-Lagrange, O.P., *The Three Ages of the Interior Life* (Catholic Way Publishing, 2014), 199.

counsel, fortitude, piety, and fear of the Lord. As we grow and mature in the spiritual life, the Holy Ghost produces within us *the fruit of the Spirit*, namely, *charity, joy, peace, patience, benignity, goodness, longanimity, mildness, faith, modesty, continency, chastity* (Gal. v. 22-23). St. Thomas Aquinas teaches that the seven gifts of the Holy Ghost are in all souls in the state of grace since they are connected with charity. Regarding the plentiful gifts which the Holy Ghost showers on us, the Catechism states:

> These gifts of the Holy Ghost are numerous. Not to mention the creation of the world, the propagation and government of all created beings, discussed in the first Article, we have just shown that the giving of life is particularly attributed to the Holy Ghost, and this is further confirmed by the testimony of Ezechiel: *I will give you spirit and you shall live.*

> The Prophet (Isaias), however, enumerates the chief effects which are most properly ascribed to the Holy Ghost: The spirit of wisdom and understanding, the spirit of counsel and fortitude, the spirit of knowledge and piety, and the spirit of the fear of the Lord. These effects are called the gifts of the Holy Ghost.

The Gift of Wisdom: The principal and greatest of the gifts of the Holy Ghost. The gift of wisdom is much different than that which secular man considers to be wisdom. God's gift of wisdom instills within us the desire to contemplate the things of God. It allows us to "sort out" what is godly and what is of the world. Wisdom gives us godly insight into the secular world in which we live. Therefore, wisdom allows us to properly set our priorities in accordance with God's will. God's gift of wisdom is the ultimate perfection of the theological virtue of Faith.

The Gift of Understanding: While wisdom leads us to contemplate godly concepts, understanding helps us grasp the truths of these concepts. While man can never fully understand the ways of God, understanding strengthens our insight into these truths. Understanding takes our faith to a higher level.

The Gift of Counsel (right judgment): This gift closely correlates with and is the perfection of the moral virtue of prudence. Counsel bestows proper judgment. When we walk with the Spirit of Counsel, we can, almost instinctively, do the proper thing in any situation.

The Gift of Fortitude: Fortitude and courage are synonyms, although godly fortitude allows us to stay faithful to our beliefs even when such faithfulness could lead us into danger or martyrdom. Fortitude allows us to boldly but not overbearingly share the True Faith with others.

The Gift of Knowledge: This gift is often confused with both the gifts of wisdom and understanding. While wisdom allows us to sort out godly matters, and understanding allows us to grasp Godly Truths, the gift of knowledge allows us constant awareness of living in God's plan for our lives. We can also depend on the gift of knowledge to properly prepare us for the Sacrament of Confession by bringing us mindfully to know our sins. Like the gift of wisdom, this gift helps to perfect the theological virtue of faith.

The Gift of Piety: This gift helps us to love and worship God, not only as a matter of justice, but more so out of filial reverence and affection. Piety increases our awareness that we truly are *the sons of God* (I Jn. iii. 1) and helps us relate to our heavenly Father with great confidence and simplicity as His little children.

The Gift of Fear of the Lord: This holy fear is more an awe and wonder at the magnificence of God and a loathing of any sin that remains in our lives which might offend Him. Again, as with the gift of knowledge, the gift of the fear of the Lord can help us to properly prepare for Confession.

These gifts, available to us in their fullness at our Confirmation, are to be used to bear fruit in the form of our own salvation and those of others around us. The Sacrament of Confirmation equips us with these means to live a virtuous life *in* the world but not *of* the world. And if we are truly cultivating these gifts and living a life of grace to make progress in the spiritual life, we will see in our own lives the fruits of the Spirit. If we do not see these fruits in our own lives this is a sign of an issue in our own interior life.

Conclusion

If we are serious about desiring to grow and advance in the spiritual life, we should invoke the Holy Ghost daily, asking Him to inspire us, to preserve us in grace, and to show us God's will for us in every circumstance of life. Ask the Holy Ghost to bless and protect the Church, to help restore order to our fallen world, and to inspire the Pope and all the bishops of the world to consecrate Russia to the Immaculate Heart of Mary, as God Himself instructed them through Our Lady of Fatima. Lastly, do not neglect to invoke the all-too-often forgotten Third Person of the Blessed Trinity by asking Him to send you an increase of His gifts.

Come, Holy Spirit, Sanctifier, all-powerful God of love, Thou Who didst fill the Virgin Mary with grace, Thou Who didst wonderfully transform the hearts of the Apostles, Thou Who didst endow all Thy martyrs with a miraculous heroism, come and sanctify us, illumine our minds, strengthen our wills, purify our consciences, rectify our judgments, set our hearts on fire and preserve us from the misfortune of resisting Thine inspirations. Amen.[53]

---

[53] *The Raccolta* (Loreto Publications, 2010), p. 205.

IX

I Believe in the Holy Catholic Church, the Communion of Saints

Ninth Article of the Creed

The Catholic Church is the means that Jesus Christ established to preserve and pass on the doctrine He taught while on earth. The Church is a divine institution led by finite, fallen men. As a result, there is often confusion on what Catholics truly believe about the Church.

In its opening on this article of the Creed, the Roman Catechism explains that "the Prophets spoke more plainly and openly of the Church than of Christ, foreseeing that on this a much greater number may err and be deceived than on the mystery of the Incarnation." Indeed, there is no institution in the world like the Catholic Church as the Church is the only institution in our world that was established by Jesus Christ: "Other bodies rest on human reason and prudence, but the Church reposes on the wisdom and counsels of God who has called us inwardly by the inspiration of the Holy Ghost, who opens the hearts of men; and outwardly, through the labor and ministry of pastors and preachers."

The Meaning of "Church"

Before considering who is part of the Church or the marks of the true Church established by Christ, the Catechism of the Council of Trent begins by explaining the various meanings of the word "church." The Church is referred to as the flock of Christ, the House of God, and the Spouse of Christ. In Scripture, the word "church" is often used to describe the assemblies of the faithful. Far more than describing a mere building or even the communities in which we gather on Sundays to assist at the Holy Sacrifice of the Mass, the Church collectively refers to the totality of all those who are baptized Catholics in communion with the Lord's established religion. The Catechism: "In a word, *The Church*, says St. Augustine, *consists of the faithful dispersed throughout the world.*"

Such a statement is echoed by the Baltimore Catechism: "The means instituted by Our Lord to enable men at all times to share in the fruits of His Redemption are the Church and the Sacraments. The Church is the congregation of all those who profess the faith of Christ, partake of the same Sacraments, and are governed by their lawful pastors under one visible head."[54]

The Role of the Church in the Plan of Salvation

> And Jesus answering, said to him: Blessed art thou, Simon Bar-Jona: because flesh and blood hath not revealed it to thee, but My Father Who is in heaven. And I say to thee: That thou art Peter; and upon this rock I will build My Church, and the gates of hell shall not prevail against it. And I will give to thee the keys of the kingdom of heaven. And whatsoever thou shalt bind upon earth, it shall be bound also in heaven: and whatsoever thou shalt loose upon earth, it shall be loosed also in heaven (Matt. 16:17-19).

This solemn declaration by Our Lord is the first instance in which He promised to build His Church. In fact, this is the first time the Lord used the word "church" and He did so by telling St. Peter, who would become the first Pope, that He would establish the Church on Peter. And Our Lord gave Simon a new name, *Petros* (Peter), meaning "rock." The Roman Catechism expresses this divine origin of the Church by stating:

> This Church was founded not by man, but by the immortal God Himself, who built her upon a most solid rock. ...

> Since this power, therefore, cannot be of human origin, divine faith can alone enable us to understand that the keys of the kingdom of heaven are deposited with the Church, that to her has been confided the power of remitting sins, of denouncing excommunication, and of consecrating the real body of Christ...

While Jesus Christ is the invisible head of the Church, He chose to build His Church on St. Peter. The Pope is the visible head of the Church who

---

[54] Baltimore Catechism No. 3, Q. 114-115.

occupies the Chair of Peter and acts as Christ's representative, His Vicar, on earth. Yet, Christ remains the ultimate head of the Church. The Church preserves the Faith as taught by the Lord and handed down over the centuries in her teachings. She also passes down the ability to confer the Sacraments through Apostolic Succession. Catholic priests today are ordained in an unbroken line that can be traced back, bishop by bishop, to the Apostles, who were ordained by Christ Himself at the Last Supper.

Church Triumphant and Church Militant

The Church is not only composed of those who are on earth but also those who have gone before us in the Faith and died in the state of grace. The blessed in Heaven, who constitute the Church Triumphant, see the face of God (the Beatific Vision) and possess perfect happiness forever. The Church Suffering consists of those souls who have died in the state of grace but who are currently undergoing purification in Purgatory before they enter the joys of Heaven.

Concerning this truth, the Roman Catechism expounds: "The Church consists principally of two parts, the one called the Church triumphant; the other, the Church militant. The Church triumphant is that most glorious and happy assemblage of blessed spirits, and of those who have triumphed over the world, the flesh, and the iniquity of Satan, and are now exempt and safe from the troubles of this life and enjoy everlasting bliss. The Church militant is the society of all the faithful still dwelling on earth. It is called militant, because it wages eternal war with those implacable enemies, the world, the flesh and the devil."

The Latin word *militans* has a primary meaning of "serving as a soldier, military," but it acquired a secondary meaning of "to struggle, to make an effort." Christians on earth (the Church Militant) are still struggling against sin in order that, when they die, they might ultimately reach Heaven and be members of the Church Triumphant, those who have triumphed over sin. While we have not yet merited Heaven and could lose it if we die in the state of mortal sin, we are still nonetheless part of the Church despite our imperfections.

As Our Lord alluded to in parables, the Church is composed of those at all levels from those baptized souls highest in perfection to those unfortunate souls who live a life in mortal sin. Regarding this reality, the wisdom of the Catechism of the Council of Trent affirms: "The Church militant is composed of two classes of persons, the good and the bad, both professing the same faith and partaking of the same Sacraments, yet differing in their manner of life and morality. ... [T]he Church militant, is compared to a net cast into the sea, to a field in which tares were sown with the good grain, to a threshing floor on which the grain is mixed up with the chaff, and also to ten virgins, some of whom were wise, and some foolish."

Despite our sins and imperfections, we nonetheless are members of the same Church to which the Saints in Heaven belong. Only three categories of persons are not members of the Church and they are enumerated by the Roman Catechism:

> Hence there are but three classes of persons excluded from the Church's pale: infidels, heretics and schismatics, and excommunicated persons. Infidels are outside the Church because they never belonged to, and never knew the Church, and were never made partakers of any of her Sacraments. Heretics and schismatics are excluded from the Church, because they have separated from her and belong to her only as deserters belong to the army from which they have deserted. ... Finally, excommunicated persons are not members of the Church, because they have been cut off by her sentence from the number of her children and belong not to her communion until they repent.

The Four Marks of the Church

In order to determine which institution on earth is the true Church, there are four marks which distinguish it from all false religions and institutions. They are *unity, holiness, catholicity,* and *apostolicity.*

One: It was the first and is the one Church founded by Christ (cf. Rom. xii. 5; I Cor. x. 17, xii. 13). St. Paul in his Epistle to the Ephesians asserted that there is *one Lord, one faith, one baptism* (Eph. iv. 5). The Church is one because she was founded by Jesus, the one and only Son of God, Who taught one unified body of doctrine. Granted, there is great diversity in the Church regarding cultures, gifts, ways of life, and offices, yet there is unity in government (under the visible head, the Pope), faith, and sacraments. The Roman Catechism explains, "The first mark of the true Church is described in the Nicene Creed, and consists in unity...." Likewise, the Baltimore Catechism teaches, "The Church is one because all its members agree in one faith, are all in one communion, and are all under one Head."[55]

Holy: The Church is holy because she teaches holy doctrine and her Founder is the Source of all holiness (cf. Eph. v. 25-27; Apoc. xix. 7-8). Christ joined the Church to Himself as His Mystical Body and gave her the

---

[55] Baltimore Catechism No. 3, Q. 129.

gift of the Holy Ghost. Through Him and in Him, she becomes the means of sanctification for others. On this second mark, the Roman Catechism states: "The Church is called holy because she is consecrated and dedicated to God.... The Church is also to be called holy because she is united to her holy Head, as His Body; that is, to Christ the Lord, the fountain of all holiness.... Moreover, the Church alone has the legitimate worship of sacrifice, and the salutary use of the Sacraments, which are the efficacious instruments of divine grace, used by God to produce true holiness. Hence, to possess true holiness, we must belong to this Church."

There is a genuine paradox between the holiness of the divine dimension and human dimension of the Church. The divine dimension of the Church is holy, but the human dimension contains sinful members. Concerning this paradox, the wisdom of the Roman Catechism again helps clarify the matter: "It should not be deemed a matter of surprise that the Church, although numbering among her children many sinners, is called holy. For as those who profess any art, even though they depart from its rules, are still called artists, so in like manner the faithful, although offending in many things and violating the engagements to which they had pledged themselves, are still called holy, because they have been made the people of God and have consecrated themselves to Christ by faith and Baptism."

Catholic: The term literally means "universal." The Church is the *universal* body of believers established by Christ and meant for all people of all corners of the world for all times (cf. Matt. xxviii. 18-20; Apoc. v. 9-10). The etymology of the word "catholic" is the Greek adjective *katholikos*, which is related to the adverb *katholou*, meaning "in general" or "according to the whole." This definition helps communicate the fact that the Catholic Faith is for people of every place, culture, and class. There is no one who is not called to be a member of the true Faith. As St. John relates in the Book of the Apocalypse: *Thou art worthy, O Lord, to take the book, and to open the seals thereof; because Thou wast slain, and hast redeemed us to God, in Thy blood, out of every tribe, and tongue, and people, and nation* (Apoc. v. 9).

Apostolic: The title of "apostle" comes from the Greek word *apostolos*, which means "to be sent." Through the unbroken line of bishops going back to the Twelve Apostles themselves, the *foundation* upon which the Church was built, we can trace our Faith back to Christ Himself, Who is *the chief cornerstone* (Eph. ii. 20). As the Baltimore Catechism succinctly states: "The Church is apostolic because it was founded by Christ on His Apostles, and is governed by their lawful successors, and because it has never ceased, and never will cease, to teach their doctrine."[56]

---

[56] Baltimore Catechism No. 3, Q. 132.

The Church is founded on the Apostles in three ways. First, the Apostles were the actual witnesses of what Christ taught and then were sent to evangelize by Christ. This is the origin of the Church.

Second, the Church has the "Deposit of Faith" (Scripture and Tradition) through the Apostles. The Deposit of Faith is the body of saving truth entrusted by Christ to the Apostles and handed on by them to be preserved and proclaimed. Jesus ordered them to teach the nations *all things whatsoever I have commanded you* and assured them, *I am with you always, even until the consummation of the world* (Mt. xxviii. 18-20). Sacred Scripture and Sacred Tradition are the two unique sources of public Revelation, which together form the one Deposit of Faith.

The third way that the Church is apostolic is through Apostolic Succession. The whole Church continues to be guided by the Apostles through their successors, the bishops, as well as priests. The whole Church is apostolic because she is sent into the whole world and all members of the Church share in her mission to pray and work for the conversion of all non-Catholics, as well as the return of all Catholics who have fallen away from the Faith.

The Necessity of Organized Religion

The purpose of the Catholic Church is to be the means of salvation for the entire world. Fr. John Laux in "Catholic Apologetics, Book IV" explains:

> From this commission of Christ (i.e. Matthew 28:18-20), it is evident that His followers form an organized society under the leadership and guidance of the Apostles and their successors, with the right to teach and to command on one side, and the duty to be taught and to obey on the other. Everything is visible about His great institution: Baptism, which is necessary for membership, the other Sacraments which He commanded His followers to receive, the rulers and lawgivers whom the faithful must obey, the tribunal before which the faithful are judged and to which they have a right to appeal.

It is not possible to be spiritual and not religious. Jesus Christ, God-made-man, instituted a visible, organized religion. It is not possible to follow Him without religion. And it is not possible to be pleasing to God in any other religion than the divinely established Catholic Religion.

Outside of the Church There is No Salvation

While institutional religion is necessary for salvation, not all so-called "churches" are equal. Only the Catholic Church can properly be called an *ecclesia* (assembly of the faithful) as other self-described "churches" are break-away sects which splintered away in the past from the Catholic Church or from each other. The Catholic Church alone possess the four marks of the divinely established Church instituted by Jesus Christ. There is only "one, holy, Catholic, and apostolic Church" on earth, as we profess in the Nicene Creed, and outside of this one true Church there is no salvation. St. Augustine famously remarked, "No one can find salvation except in the Catholic Church. Outside the Church, you can find everything except salvation. You can have dignities, you can have Sacraments, you can sing 'Alleluia,' answer 'Amen,' have the Gospels, have faith in the name of the Father, the Son, and the Holy Ghost, and preach it, too. But never can you find salvation except in the Catholic Church."

The Church has always taught that there is no salvation outside of the Catholic Church – in Latin, *extra Ecclesiam nulla salus* – for the simple fact that we must be united to Christ through His Body, the Church, in order to have the fruits of Redemption applied to our souls. As the Council of Trent taught, "After the promulgation of the Gospel, this transition [i.e. from the state of Original Sin to the state of grace] cannot take place without the bath of regeneration [Baptism] or the desire for it, as it is written: 'Unless one is reborn of water and the Spirit, he cannot enter the kingdom of God [John 3:5].'"[57] Some may be saved at the moment of death, where to our eyes they may appear to have died as a non-Catholic, but through an extraordinary grace granted by God, they became Catholic in their last earthly moments. However, the Church also teaches that this is rare, and no one should ever presume to rely upon receiving such an exceptional grace.

Ultimately, as Pope Innocent III asserted, "There is but one universal Church of the faithful, outside which no one at all is saved" (Fourth Lateran Council, 1215). Likewise, Pope Boniface VIII declared: "We declare, say, define, and pronounce that it is absolutely necessary for the salvation of every human creature to be subject to the Roman Pontiff" (Bull *Unam Sanctam*, 1302).

In 1441, Pope Eugene IV stated the same doctrine with even greater clarity: "The most Holy Roman Church firmly believes, professes and preaches

---

[57] Council of Trent, Session VI (Jan. 13, 1547), Decree on Justification (Denz. 796; D.S. 1524). For more on this subject, see the Letter of the Holy Office to the Archbishop of Boston (Aug. 8, 1949) (D.S. 3866-3873).

that none of those existing outside the Catholic Church, not only pagans, but also Jews and heretics and schismatics, can have a share in life eternal; but that they will go into the eternal fire which was prepared for the devil and his angels, unless before death they are joined with Her; and that so important is the unity of this ecclesiastical body that only those remaining within this unity can profit by the sacraments of the Church unto salvation, and they alone can receive an eternal recompense for their fasts, their almsgivings, their other works of Christian piety and the duties of a Christian soldier. No one, let his almsgiving be as great as it may, no one, even if he pours out his blood for the Name of Christ, can be saved, unless he remain within the bosom and the unity of the Catholic Church" (Bull *Cantate Domino*).

And closer to our own times, Pope Pius IX confirmed: "It is to be held of faith that none can be saved outside the Apostolic Roman Church ... but nevertheless it is equally certain that those who are ignorant of the true religion, if that ignorance is invincible, will not be held guilty in the matter in the eyes of the Lord" (Solemn Allocution *Singulari Quadam*, Dec. 9, 1854).

The Church is the one means of salvation. Those who reject the Catholic Church necessarily reject Jesus Christ and thus reject salvation. No one can change these teachings – not the Pope's own personal opinions, not interpretations of Vatican II documents, and not any Catholic priest's sermons. Nothing can change what the Church has authoritatively and infallibly taught since its founding, including the truth that the Catholic Faith alone is the one true religion.

The Communion of the Faithful

The members of the Church, both those who have died in the state of grace and those still alive on earth, form a true communion of the faithful. This communion is established first and foremost by our shared Sacraments. Regarding this connection, the Roman Catechism expounds: "That this communion of Saints implies a communion of Sacraments, the Fathers declare in these words of the Creed: *I confess one Baptism.* After Baptism, the Eucharist holds the first place in reference to this communion, and after that the other Sacraments."

Furthermore, the communion of saints implies a communion of good works amongst the Church's members. On this point, the wisdom of the Roman Catechism uniquely shines:

> In the human body there are many members, but though
> many, they yet constitute but one body, in which each

performs its own, not all the same, functions. All do not enjoy equal dignity, or discharge functions alike useful or honorable; nor does one propose to itself its own exclusive advantage, but that of the entire body. Besides, they are so well organized and knit together that if one suffers, the rest likewise suffer on account of their affinity and sympathy of nature; and if, on the contrary, one enjoys health, the feeling of pleasure is common to all.

The same may be observed in the Church. She is composed of various members; that is, of different nations, of Jews, Gentiles, freemen and slaves, of rich and poor; when they have been baptized, they constitute one body with Christ, of which He is the Head. To each member of the Church is also assigned his own peculiar office. As some are appointed apostles, some teachers, but all for the common good; so to some it belongs to govern and teach, to others to be subject and to obey.

Conclusion

As Catholics, we hold fast to the Deposit of Faith entrusted to the Church, which transcends individual priests, bishops, cardinals, and even the Pope. If any Catholic, regardless of his rank, were to preach heresy or teach falsehood, we would be compelled to resist him and hold fast to what the Church has always taught. For example, if a priest were to encourage or support abortion, homosexual "marriage," the ordination of women, or changing any defined Church doctrine, we would be required to resist such efforts.

Our duty as lay Catholics is to hold fast to the enduring and timeless teachings of the Church and to pray for the Church. We are to receive the Sacraments and thus remain in communion with the Mystical Body of Christ. We know that there will be sinful members in God's Church, but that is because the devil only seeks to attack and discredit that which he knows is the true Church: one, holy, Catholic, and apostolic.

X

The Forgiveness of Sin

Tenth Article of the Creed

In its introduction to the tenth article of the Apostle's Creed, the Roman Catechism reminds priests: "…it is the duty of the pastor to teach that, not only is forgiveness of sins to be found in the Catholic Church, as Isaias had foretold in these words: *The people that dwell therein shall have their iniquity taken away from them*; but also that in her resides the power of forgiving sins…." Such an important teaching cannot be overstated since man is prone to sin, even after Baptism, and should have frequent recourse throughout his entire life to the Sacrament of Penance in order to receive the forgiveness of sins. In the grand design of the universe, God has permitted sin and yet has also instituted a means for us to receive forgiveness for offending Him through the Sacraments of the Church. Addressing this subject in his *Summa Theologiae*, St. Thomas Aquinas remarks:

> It is written (Ps. cxliv. 9): *His tender mercies are over all His works*, and in a collect [Tenth Sunday after Pentecost] we say: 'O God, Who dost show forth Thine all-mightiness most by pardoning and having mercy,' and Augustine, expounding the words, *greater than these shall he do* (Jn. xiv. 12) says that 'for a just man to be made from a sinner, is greater than to create heaven and earth' (I-II q113 a9).

Baptism Remits Original and Personal Sin

After introducing the tenth article of the Creed, the Roman Catechism begins to explain the extent of this power entrusted to the Church by wisely separating the discussion on forgiveness into two categories: forgiveness for those sins that precede Baptism and those that follow it:

When we first make a profession of faith and are cleansed in holy Baptism, we receive this pardon entire and unqualified; so that no sin, original or actual, of commission or omission, remains to be expiated, no punishment to be endured. The grace of Baptism, however, does not give exemption from all the infirmities of nature. On the contrary, contending, as each of us has to contend, against the motions of concupiscence, which ever tempts us to the commission of sin, there is scarcely one to be found among us, who opposes so vigorous a resistance to its assaults, or who guards his salvation so vigilantly, as to escape all wounds.

It being necessary, therefore, that a power of forgiving sins, distinct from that of Baptism, should exist in the Church, to her were entrusted the keys of the kingdom of heaven, by which each one, if penitent, may obtain the remission of his sins, even though he were a sinner to the last day of his life. This truth is vouched for by the most unquestionable authority of the Sacred Scriptures. In St. Matthew the Lord says to Peter: *I will give to thee the keys of the kingdom of heaven; and whatsoever thou shalt bind upon earth, shall be bound also in heaven; and whatsoever thou shalt loose on earth, shall be loosed also in heaven*; and again: *Whatsoever you shall bind upon earth, shall be bound also in heaven; and whatsoever you shall loose on earth, shall be loosed also in heaven*. Further, the testimony of St. John assures us that the Lord, breathing on the Apostles, said: *Receive ye the Holy Ghost, whose sins you shall forgive they are forgiven them; and whose sins you shall retain, they are retained.*

Baptism, *the laver of regeneration and renovation of the Holy Ghost* (Tit. iii. 5), remits both Original Sin (inherited from Adam and Eve) and all the actual (personal) sins one has committed up to the moment of Baptism (for those baptized after attaining the age of reason). In addition to forgiving these sins and saving one from eternal punishment, Baptism also removes all temporal punishment due to sin, meaning that no penance is necessary for a person just baptized, nor time in Purgatory (if they were to die after having just been baptized).

Finally, Baptism also makes us friends of God, placing us in the state of sanctifying grace for the first time. However, as the Catechism mentions,

Baptism does not remove concupiscence, which is the "insubordination of man's desires to the dictates of reason and the propensity of human nature to sin as a result of Original Sin."[58] Consequently, our life will continue to be, even after our Baptism, a struggle against the evil inclinations of our fallen nature (including our own bad habits) and a struggle against the temptations of the devil (cf. I Pet. v. 8).

Sacrament of Penance for Sins After Baptism

In describing the effects of the Sacrament of Penance, the Catechism of St. Pius X states: "[It] confers sanctifying grace by which are remitted the mortal sins and also the venial sins which we confess and for which we are sorry; it changes eternal punishment into temporal punishment, of which it even remits more or less according to our dispositions; it revives the merits of the good works done before committing mortal sin; it gives the soul aid in due time against falling into sin again, and it restores peace of conscience."[59]

The Jesuit Father Horacio de la Costa wrote, "Life is a Warfare: a warfare between two standards: the Standard of Christ and the Standard of Satan. It is a warfare older than the world, for it began with the revolt of the angels. It is a warfare wide as the world; it rages in every nation, every city, in the heart of every man... Two armies, two Standards, two generals... and to every man there comes the imperious cry of command: Choose! Christ or Satan? Choose! Sanctity or Sin? Choose! Heaven or Hell? And in the choice he makes is summed up the life of every man."

It is through the Sacrament of Penance, instituted by Our Lord Jesus Christ Himself, that man can fight the battle against Satan and cleanse his soul of sin after having already received the Sacrament of Baptism. Even if a man were to live under the standard of Satan and sin for decades, he is never too evil to receive forgiveness and reconciliation with God. Should a sinner begin to despair of God's mercy for his repeated failures, the Roman Catechism consoles such a one with the assurance that no sin is beyond the power of God's mercy to forgive:

> Nor is the exercise of this power [of forgiving sins] restricted to particular sins. No crime, however heinous, can be committed or even conceived which the Church has not power to forgive, just as there is no sinner, however abandoned, however depraved, who should not

---

[58] Fr. John Hardon, *Modern Catholic Dictionary*, accessed via <http://www.therealpresence.org/cgi-bin/getdefinition.pl>.
[59] *Catechism of St. Pius X* (St. Michael's Press, 2010), 106.

confidently hope for pardon, provided he sincerely repent of his past transgressions.

Furthermore, the exercise of this power is not restricted to particular times. Whenever the sinner turns from his evil ways he is not to be rejected, as we learn from the reply of our Savior to the Prince of the Apostles. When St. Peter asked how often we should pardon an offending brother, whether seven times, *Not only seven times*, said the Redeemer, *but till seventy times seven*.

Consequence of Mortal Sin

There is no greater evil in the world than sin, which is nothing other than an offense against an all-loving and all-holy God Who created us out of nothing and yet gained no greater honor, glory, or benefit by doing so. He has given us all that we possess – our intellect, our memory, our imagination, our free will, our senses, everything – and yet we are prone to rebel against Him even after knowing that He has redeemed us through the bloody torture of the Cross. In its words on the horror of sin, the Roman Catechism expounds:

> For whoever offends God, even by one mortal sin, instantly forfeits whatever merits he may have previously acquired through the sufferings and death of Christ, and is entirely shut out from the gate of heaven which, when already closed, was thrown open to all by the Redeemer's Passion. When we reflect on this, the thought of our misery must fill us with deep anxiety. But if we turn our attention to this admirable power with which God has invested His Church; and, in the firm belief of this Article, feel convinced that to every sinner is offered the means of recovering, with the assistance of divine grace, his former dignity, we must exult with exceeding joy and gladness, and must offer immortal thanks to God.

> If, when we are seriously ill, the medicines prepared for us by the art and industry of the physician are wont to be welcome and agreeable to us, how much more welcome and agreeable should those remedies prove which the wisdom of God has established to heal our souls and restore us to the life of grace, especially since they bring with them, not, indeed, uncertain hope of recovery, like

the medicines that are applied to the body, but assured health to such as desire to be cured!

The medicine that God has given to us is present in the confessional. As Archbishop Fulton J. Sheen eloquently remarked, "Hospitals are built because people have sick bodies, and the Church builds confessional boxes because they also have sick souls." And the Lord has entrusted the administration of these "hospitals of the soul" to the Apostles and their successors in the New Covenant priesthood (bishops and priests).

Christ Has Given Such Power to Priests

Continuing on, the Catechism explains that the power of forgiving sins has been entrusted only to certain members of the Church and not to everyone: "Our Lord gave not the power of so sacred a ministry to all, but to Bishops and priests only." The bishops and priests who exercise this ministry do so through the power of God, Who acts through them by virtue of the Sacrament of Holy Orders. While absolution may only be received from a validly ordained priest or bishop, it is ultimately God Who forgives sins through His sacred ministers. No mere man has the power to forgive sins by his own authority: "The remission of sins seems to bear an exact analogy to the cancelling of a pecuniary debt. None but the creditor can forgive a pecuniary debt. Hence, since by sin we contract a debt to God alone – wherefore we daily pray: *forgive us our debts* – sin, it is clear, can be forgiven by Him alone, and by none else."

Through her life-giving Sacraments, the Church continues to bring the forgiveness and healing of Jesus Christ to all mankind. The priests of the Holy Catholic Church have the unique ability to forgive sins because Our Lord gave them the ability to do so in His Name. In the three years that the disciples journeyed with the Lord in His public life, He taught them the Faith. Our Lord gave His Apostles *power and authority* (Lk. ix. 1), and later, after His Resurrection, He gave them the unique power to forgive sins:

> [Jesus] said therefore to them again: Peace be to you. As the Father hath sent Me, I also send you. When He had said this, He breathed on them; and He said to them: Receive ye the Holy Ghost. Whose sins you shall forgive, they are forgiven them; and whose sins you shall retain, they are retained (Jn. xx. 21-23).

With these words, Our Lord Jesus Christ instituted the Sacrament of Confession. Such has the Church also believed and taught, according to the testimony of the Holy Scriptures and the unanimous consent of the Fathers.

In response to the heresies of the Protestant revolt, the Council of Trent solemnly declared:

> If anyone says that these words of the Lord Savior [Jn. xx. 21-23] ... are not to be understood as referring to the power of forgiving and retaining sins in the Sacrament of penance, as the Catholic Church has always understood them from the beginning; but if he distorts them, in contradiction with the institution of this Sacrament, to make them refer to the authority of preaching the Gospel, let him be anathema.

And further:

> If anyone denies that sacramental confession was instituted and is necessary for salvation by divine law; or says that the manner of confessing secretly to a priest alone, which the Catholic Church has always observed from the beginning and still observes, is at variance with the institution and command of Christ and is a human invention, let him be anathema.

Centuries later, in order to combat the errors of the Modernists, Pope St. Pius X proscribed (condemned) the following proposition in *Lamentabili Sane*: "The words of the Lord, 'Receive the Holy Spirit; whose sins you shall forgive, they are forgiven them; and whose sins you shall retain, they are retained,' in no way refer to the Sacrament of Penance, in spite of what it pleased the Fathers of Trent to say."

Regarding the awesome power given by God, *Who is rich in mercy* (Eph. ii. 4), to His Church so that men might be forgiven and restored to His friendship, the Roman Catechism beautifully expounds:

> This wonderful and divine power was never communicated to creatures, until God became man. Christ our Savior, although true God, was the first one who, as man, received this high prerogative from His heavenly Father. *That you may know that the son of man hath power on earth to forgive sins (then said he to the man sick of the palsy), rise. take up thy bed, and go into thy house.* As, therefore, He became man, in order to bestow on man this forgiveness of sins, He communicated this power to Bishops and priests in the Church, previous to His Ascension into heaven, where He sits forever at the right hand of God. Christ, however,

as we have already said, remits sin by virtue of His own
authority; all others, by virtue of His authority delegated
to them as His ministers.

In the Holy Scriptures, the only other reference to God breathing upon
someone is recorded in Genesis 2:7, when God breathed upon Adam and
gave him life. In John 20:21-23, we understand that God Incarnate is truly
giving the eleven Apostles this profound ability to forgive sins and restore
supernatural life, just as He truly gave Adam the gift of natural life.

While on this earth, Jesus would go through the streets of Jerusalem and
heal and forgive those that desired forgiveness. But today, Jesus is not
walking in the streets. After His Resurrection, He gave the Apostles the
duty to go forth and forgive sins. He never told anyone to pray to Him for
forgiveness in the privacy of their home. Rather, He told the Apostles to
forgive the sins of penitents. Today, the Church's bishops and priests,
ordained in apostolic succession, continue to forgive our sins by the power
of God.

Conclusion

Do not neglect going to the Sacrament of Confession and receiving the
pardon and peace of God. Truly, the change in a soul that occurs when a
penitent receives absolution is a greater work than the moment when out
of nothingness God created the visible world.

Our ability to obtain forgiveness of sins would not be possible had it not
been for Almighty God's will to die for our sins, as the Roman Catechism
reminds us: "It was His will that our offences should be expiated by the
Blood of His Only Begotten Son; that His Son should voluntarily assume
the imputability of our sins, and suffer a most cruel death, the just for the
unjust, the innocent for the guilty." Yet, how often do we thank God for
this awesome privilege? And how often do we make reparation for the
millions of souls who do not know Christ or who know Him and openly
reject His invitation to the Sacrament of Penance?

Let us, then, make frequent use of this holy Sacrament, remembering the
following words of St. John the Apostle: *If we confess our sins, He is
faithful and just, to forgive us our sins, and to cleanse us from all iniquity*
(I Jn. i. 9).

XI

The Resurrection of the Body

Eleventh Article of the Creed

Supported by Sacred Scripture

But if there be no resurrection of the dead, then Christ is not risen again. And if Christ be not risen again, then is our preaching vain, and your faith is also vain (I Cor. xv. 13-14).

Having completed a study of the first ten articles of the Apostles Creed over the past year, in this chapter we reflect on the second to last article of the Creed as taught in the Roman Catechism. In its introduction to the eleventh article of the Creed, the Catechism, after quoting the words of St. Paul to the Corinthians, insightfully explains why the Apostles chose the specific words "the resurrection of the body" in formulating the Creed:

> That in this Article the resurrection of mankind is called the resurrection of the body, is a circumstance which deserves special attention. ...

> Although in Sacred Scripture the word *flesh* often signifies the whole man, as in Isaias, *All flesh is grass* [Is. xl. 6], and in St. John, *The Word was made flesh* [Jn. i. 14]; yet in this place it is used to express the body only, thus giving us to understand that of the two constituent parts of man, soul and body, one only, that is, the body, is corrupted and returns to its original dust, while the soul remains incorrupt and immortal. As then, a man cannot be said to return to life unless he has previously died, so the soul could not with propriety be said to rise again.

The words of the Creed teach us of the immortality of the soul, which upon death appears before the judgment seat of God (cf. Rom. xiv. 10; II Cor. v. 10) and is then taken to Heaven, Hell, Purgatory, or the Limbo of the Infants. From the moment of our death until the End of Time, our body remains here on earth and is over time reduced to ashes while our soul continues in the afterlife.

After presenting various objections that some people raise against the resurrection of the body, St. Thomas Aquinas in his *Summa Theologica* sets out the following explanation based on Sacred Scripture and Our Lord's own testimony before responding to the objections:

> It is written (Job xix. 25-26): 'I know that my Redeemer liveth, and in the last day I shall rise out of the earth, and I shall be clothed again with my skin,' etc. Therefore, there will be a resurrection of the body. Further, the gift of Christ is greater than the sin of Adam, as appears from Romans 5:15. Now death was brought in by sin, for if sin had not been, there had been no death. Therefore, by the gift of Christ man will be restored from death to life.
>
> Further, the members should be conformed to the head. Now our Head lives and will live eternally in body and soul, since 'Christ rising again from the dead dieth now no more' (Rom. vi. 8). Therefore, men who are His members will live in body and soul; and consequently, there must needs be a resurrection of the body (Suppl q75, a1)

Supported by Logic and Reason

In its exposition on the dogma that our bodies will be resurrected at the End of Times, the Church does not only rely on the Sacred Scriptures but also on reason itself:

> In the first place, as the soul is immortal, and has, as part of man, a natural propensity to be united to the body, its perpetual separation from it must be considered as unnatural. But as that which is contrary to nature and in a state of violence, cannot be permanent, it appears fitting that the soul should be reunited to the body, and consequently that the body should rise again. This argument our Savior Himself employed, when in His disputation with the Sadducees He deduced the resurrection of the body from the immortality of the soul.

The Catechism presents several arguments centered on logic and concludes with a compelling argument by which we can understand how the body would need to be restored so those in Heaven are lacking in nothing:

> Again, while the soul is separated from the body, man cannot enjoy that full happiness which is replete with every good. For as a part separated from the whole is imperfect, the soul separated from the body must be imperfect. Therefore, that nothing may be wanting to fill up the measure of its happiness, the resurrection of the body is necessary.

Our Actual Body Will Be Resurrected

When we speak of the resurrection of the body in the Creed, we are not speaking of the soul's resurrection but of our current, mortal body's eventual resurrection. The Creed continues to express this reality with absolute clarity by affirming:

> The word *body* is also mentioned, in order to confute the heresy of Hymeneus and Philetus, who, during the lifetime of the Apostle, asserted that whenever the Scriptures speak of the resurrection, they are to be understood to mean not the resurrection of the body, but that of the soul, by which it rises from the death of sin to the life of grace. The words of this Article, therefore, as is clear, exclude that error, and establish a real resurrection of the body.

The Church unequivocally preaches the resurrection of the very body each person possesses. Regardless of a person's body after death, whether it be reduced to ash or decomposed and strewn across whole oceans or land masses, the very selfsame body will be restored and resurrected by the power of God, Who alone has the ability to work such a marvel. The Council of Toledo XI in A.D. 675 plainly taught:

> Thus, according to the example of our Head, we confess that there is a true resurrection of the flesh for all the dead. And we do not believe that we shall rise in ethereal or any other flesh, as some foolishly imagine, but in this very flesh in which we live and are and move.

And while the same body we currently use will be resurrected, it will not be restored to its present state and remain susceptible to injury, exhaustion, or death. Like Our Lord and Our Lady before us, we too will possess a glorified body, as the Roman Catechism plainly teaches:

> But as it is of vital importance to be fully convinced that the identical body, which belongs to each one of us during life, shall, though corrupt and dissolved into its original dust, be raised up again to life, this too is a subject which demands accurate explanation on the part of the pastor. ...

> We have said that the body is to rise again, that *every one may receive the proper things of the body, according as he hath done, whether it be good or evil* [II Cor. v. 10]. Man is, therefore, to rise again in the same body with which he served God, or was a slave to the devil; that in the same body he may experience rewards and a crown of victory, or endure the severest punishments and torments.

The Four Characteristics of a Glorified Body

After our bodies are resurrected and reunited with our souls, some may be curious as to what age we will appear. Will the body look the age of its death? Will it appear fat or frail, depending on how we looked in life? Again, with great clarity that is not found in modern catechisms, the wisdom of the Roman Catechism shines (quoting from *The City of God* by St. Augustine):

> There shall then be no deformity of body; if some have been overburdened with flesh, they shall not resume its entire weight. All that exceeds the proper proportion shall be deemed superfluous. On the other hand, should the body be wasted by disease or old age, or be emaciated from any other cause, it shall be repaired by the divine power of Christ, who will not only restore the body unto us, but will repair whatever it shall have lost through the wretchedness of this life.

In fact, the Church affirms that the bodies of those who are *faithful unto death* and thus obtain *the crown of life* (Apoc. ii. 10) will not only be restored and free from deformity but also will possess the four characteristics of a glorified body: (1) impassability, (2) subtlety, (3) agility, and (4) clarity.

Impassibility refers to freedom from physical ills of all kinds, including sickness and death. The glorified body is incapable of suffering hunger, thirst, cold, heat, or any displeasures. On the other hand, as the Roman Catechism teaches, "The bodies of the damned, though incorruptible, will not be impassible; they will be capable of experiencing heat and cold and of suffering various afflictions."

Subtlety relates to the ability of the glorified body to penetrate matter. Imagine being able to walk through walls, closed doors, or even entire mountains. Just as Our Lord was able to appear in His glorified body to His Apostles after His Resurrection, even though the doors of the Cenacle were closed (cf. Jn. xx. 19), so too will those who attain to *the resurrection of life* (Jn. v. 29) be able to do likewise. Hence, we should all continue to *work out [our] salvation with fear and trembling* (Philip. ii. 12) in order to attain this great gift.

Agility refers to the soul's ability to move the body with ease and speed. The glorified body will be able to traverse the greatest distances at the speed of thought. Within the blink of an eye, the blessed citizens of Heaven will be able to traverse the *new heavens, and a new earth* (Isa. lxv. 17; II Pet. iii. 13) which God will establish after the Second Coming of Christ, the general resurrection, and the final judgment (cf. Apoc. xxi-xxii).

Clarity, also known as beauty, is the final characteristic which refers to the body's freedom from all defects and possession of utter beauty and radiance. In her revelations to St. Bridget, the Most Blessed Virgin Mary once said: "The Saints stand around my Son like countless stars, whose glory is not to be compared with any temporal light. Believe me, if the Saints could be seen shining with the glory they now possess, no human eye could endure their light; all would turn away, dazzled and blinded."[60] Do we live our lives in conformity with the Church so that we can one day be among their number?

Both the Saved and the Damned Will Rise

Amen, amen, I say unto you, that the hour cometh, and now is, when the dead shall hear the voice of the Son of God: and they that hear shall live. ... Wonder not at this; for the hour cometh, wherein all that are in the graves shall hear the voice of the Son of God. And they that have done good things, shall come forth unto the resurrection of life; but they that have done evil, unto the resurrection of judgment (Jn. v. 25, 28-29).

---

[60] Rev. Fr. Martin von Cochem, *The Four Last Things: Death, Judgment, Hell, Heaven* (Benziger Brothers, 1899).

While the souls in Heaven will at last receive their bodies and experience the never-ending blessedness of Heaven with their glorified bodies, those unhappy souls who have merited eternal damnation as a result of dying in the state of mortal sin will also receive their bodies, though it will be for their further agony and suffering. As the Fourth Lateran Council (A.D. 1215) solemnly declared:

> He [Christ] shall come at the end of time to judge the living and the dead and to render to each one according to his works, to the reprobate as well as to the elect. All of them will rise again with their own bodies which they now bear to receive according to their works, whether these have been good or evil, the ones perpetual punishment with the devil and the others everlasting glory with Christ.

Such a truth is expounded upon in the Roman Catechism, which sets out for the faithful an understanding of why the souls of the damned must also receive their bodies:

> The wicked, too, shall rise with all their members, even with those lost through their own fault. The greater the number of members which they shall have, the greater will be their torments; and therefore this restoration of members will serve to increase not their happiness but their sorrow and misery…. To those, therefore, who shall have done penance, they shall be restored as sources of reward; and to those who shall have contemned it, as instruments of punishment.

Appealing to the very essence of justice, St. Thomas Aquinas similarly affirms the reason for the resurrection of the body for all when he succinctly writes:

> Further, the resurrection is necessary in order that those who rise again may receive punishment or reward according to their merits. Now either punishment or reward is due to all, either for their own merits, as to adults, or for others' merits, as to children. Therefore, all will rise again (Suppl q75 a2).

Conclusion

God has in store for us, our family, and our friends such a blessed and happy resurrection of our bodies. All He asks is that we live and die in the state of sanctifying grace. Truly, if we love Him and wish to find ourselves in the joys of Heaven with our body, we must keep His Commandments (cf. Jn. xiv. 15).

"Another important advantage to be derived from reflection on this Article," says the Roman Catechism, "is that in it we shall find consolation both for ourselves and others when we mourn the death of those who were endeared to us by relationship or friendship. Such was the consolation which the Apostle himself gave the Thessalonians when writing to them concerning those who are asleep."

As the Roman Catechism concludes its exposition on the eleventh article of the Creed, it offers a poignant admonishment to praise God for such wonders He has in store for us in the future, should we find ourselves worthy of Heaven, when the section concludes with the words:

> The same thought must also prove a powerful incentive
> to the faithful to use every exertion to lead lives of
> rectitude and integrity, unsullied by the defilement of sin.
> For if they reflect that those boundless riches which will
> follow after the resurrection are now offered to them as
> rewards, they will be easily attracted to the pursuit of
> virtue and piety.

Offer up prayers for the souls in Purgatory, that the Lord may hasten their purification and admittance into heavenly glory.

XII

I Believe in Life Everlasting. Amen.

Twelfth Article of the Creed

A Future, Deathless Life

But, as it is written: That eye hath not seen, nor ear heard, neither hath it entered into the heart of man, what things God hath prepared for them that love him. But to us God hath revealed them, by this Spirit. For the Spirit searcheth all things, yea, the deep things of God (I Cor. ii. 9-10).

Having arrived at the final article of the Creed, the Roman Catechism begins by asserting the importance of this article for all Christians and its worthwhile position as the final article of the Apostles' Creed:

> The holy Apostles, our guides, thought fit to conclude the Creed, which is the summary of our faith, with the Article on eternal life: first, because after the resurrection of the body the only object of the Christian's hope is the reward of everlasting life; and secondly, in order that perfect happiness, embracing as it does the fullness of all good, may be ever present to our minds and absorb all our thoughts and affections.

As the Catechism makes plainly clear, "life everlasting" refers to a perpetuity of happiness in a future, deathless life to which the happy souls of the blessed in Heaven will possess for all eternity without fear of losing God's grace ever again.

> The faithful, therefore, are to be informed that the words, *life everlasting*, signify not only continuance of existence, which even the demons and the wicked possess, but also that perpetuity of happiness which is to satisfy the desires of the blessed. In this sense they were understood by the lawyer mentioned in the Gospel when

he asked the Lord our Savior: *What shall I do to possess everlasting life?* [Mt. xix. 16; Mk. x. 17; Lk. xviii. 18] as if he had said, *What shall I do in order to arrive at the enjoyment of perfect happiness?* In this sense these words are understood in the Sacred Scriptures, as is clear from many passages.

As a consoling Mother, the Church puts forth these same sentiments during the Preface of the Canon of the Mass for funeral and Requiem Masses by assuring us:

> It is truly meet and just, right and for our salvation, that we should at all times and in all places give thanks to Thee, holy Lord, Father almighty, eternal God, through Christ our Lord: in Whom the hope of a blessed resurrection hath beamed upon us: so that those who are saddened by the certainty of dying may be consoled by the promise of a future deathless life. For to Thy faithful people, Lord, life is changed, not taken away; and when the home of this earthly sojourn is dissolved, an eternal dwelling is made ready in Heaven.

Everlasting Happiness in Heaven

In its exposition on the words "life everlasting," the Creed makes clear that the happiness of a soul in Heaven is eternal. This happiness cannot by lost by sin any longer:

> These words, *life everlasting*, also teach us that, contrary to the false notions of some, happiness once attained can never be lost. Happiness is an accumulation of all good without admixture of evil, which, as it fills up the measure of man's desires, must be eternal. He who is blessed with happiness must earnestly desire the continued enjoyment of those goods which he has obtained. Hence, unless its possession be permanent and certain, he is necessarily a prey to the most tormenting apprehension.

However, such an absolute assurance of happiness is not possible in this life. It is possible only to souls who die in the state of grace. Contrary to the false Protestant view of merely accepting Jesus as one's personal Savior and thus assuring oneself of salvation, those still on earth can lose their salvation if they choose mortal sin over the love of God and neighbor. Only after crossing the threshold from life to death does judgment occur, and the verdict rendered at that time is the one that will continue without end for all eternity.

Death Shall Be No More

Rather than believing in a never-ending cycle of births and deaths, as some pagan religions do which believe in reincarnation, the Roman Catechism makes clear that we are to die only once and after this one death enter a future, endless life:

> For it is written in the Apocalypse: *They shall no more hunger nor thirst, neither shall the sun fall on them, nor any heat* [Apoc. vii. 16]; and again, *God shall wipe away all tears from their eyes: and death shall be no more, nor mourning nor crying, nor sorrow shall be any more, for the former things are passed away* [Apoc. xxi. 4].

Death shall be no more. According to reincarnation, however, all people receive a new body after death; thus, the body that a person has now is not the body that he will have in the future. Some religions even teach that a person could be re-born after death as a creature other than a human. A human being is a union of body and soul. The substance of a human person is not merely his soul, which some falsely believe can travel from body to body and occupy them at whim. Rather, a human person's substance is a union of body and soul and it is impossible for a human being to become any other creature.

Believers in reincarnation directly contradict the Creed which professes a resurrection of the same body that a person currently possesses and a future, never-ending life. Our Lord's triumph over death on Easter Sunday shows us a model since we are to follow Him in His Passion, Death, and Resurrection of the same body since He Himself has foretold it (Jn. xiii. 36).

Christ did not inherit a new body. Christ's body in Heaven still bears the same wounds from the Cross. It is for that reason that St. Thomas was told by Christ to put his hand into the Sacred Side of Our Lord so that Thomas would believe in the Resurrection (Jn. xx. 24-29). Just as Christ *died* once *for our sins* (I Pet. iii. 18) and *dieth now no more* (Rom. vi. 9), so also *it is appointed unto men* once *to die, and after this the judgment* (Heb. ix. 27).

This teaching was expressed with great clarity in the Catechism of the Council of Trent in the Eleventh Article of the Creed, which complements the teachings of the Twelfth Article: "Man is, therefore, to rise again in the same body with which he served God, or was a slave to the devil; that in the same body he may experience rewards and a crown of victory, or endure the severest punishments and torments."

To See God is Eternal Happiness

In addition to the negative elements of eternal life ("negative" in the sense of exemption from all physical and moral evils forever), the Roman Catechism also expounds upon the positive elements, the highest of which is the Beatific Vision – seeing God *as He is* (I Jn. iii. 2):

> For the blessed always see God present and by this greatest and most exalted of gifts, being made partakers of the divine nature, they enjoy true and solid happiness. Our belief in this happiness should be joined with an assured hope that we too shall one day, through the divine goodness, attain it. This the Fathers [of Constantinople I, A.D. 381] declared in their Creed, which says: *I expect the resurrection of the dead and the life of the world to come.*

Far beyond the inability to suffer and die ever again, the chief happiness of the blessed in Heaven is the enjoyment of God Himself. To those faithful souls who persevere in His grace and finish the race victorious (I Cor. ix. 24-25; II Tim. iv. 7), they shall see the face of God and live. To gaze upon the Holy and Undivided Trinity, and for Him to gaze upon us, *is* the essential and eternal happiness of Heaven:

> Solid happiness, which we may designate by the common appellation, *essential*, consists in the vision of God, and the enjoyment of His beauty Who is the source and principle of all goodness and perfection. *This*, says Christ our Lord, *is eternal life: that they may know Thee, the only true God, and Jesus Christ, Whom Thou hast sent.* [Jn. xvii. 3] These words St. John seems to interpret when he says: *Dearly beloved, we are now the sons of God; and it hath not yet appeared what we shall be. We know that when he shall appear, we shall be like to him: because we shall see him as he is* [I Jn. 3:2]. He shows, then, that beatitude consists of two things: that we shall behold God such as He is in His own nature and substance; and that we ourselves shall become, as it were, gods.

This happiness is possible only for those who die in the state of God's grace. It is not made possible to those who merely preach Christ or who

117

believe in Him but who do not strive to keep His commandments and thus end up departing this life in mortal sin. Neither Our Lord nor His Apostles taught that mere belief in God, or even profession of the true (Catholic) Faith, guaranteed salvation. St. Paul himself wrote: *Know you not that the unjust shall not possess the kingdom of God? Do not err: neither fornicators, nor idolaters, nor adulterers, nor the effeminate, nor liars with mankind, nor thieves, nor covetous, nor drunkards, nor railers, nor extortioners shall possess the kingdom of God* (I Cor. vi. 9-10). Likewise, St. James exhorts us: *Do you see that by works a man is justified; and not by faith only? And in like manner also Rahab the harlot, was not she justified by works, receiving the messengers, and sending them out another way? For even as the body without the spirit is dead, so also faith without works is dead* (Ja. ii. 24-26).

In succinct words, the Baltimore Catechism attests that the joys of eternal happiness are available only to those who die in the state of grace and merit Heaven:

> Those are rewarded in heaven who have died in the state of grace and have been purified in purgatory, if necessary, from all venial sin and all debt of temporal punishment; they see God face to face and share forever in His glory and happiness.[61]

Accessory Happiness

Aside from the vision of God, which is perfect happiness, the blessed souls in Heaven will possess several additional gifts which the Catechism calls accessory happiness:

> To this happiness, however, are added certain gifts which are common to all the blessed, and which, because more within the reach of human comprehension, are generally found more effectual in moving and inflaming the heart. These the Apostle seems to have in view when, in his Epistle to the Romans, he says: *Glory and honor, and peace to everyone that worketh good* [Rom. ii. 10].

Glory consists in the "clear and distinct knowledge which each (of the blessed) shall have of the singular and exalted dignity of his companions (in glory)." Honor will consist in being the friends, brethren, and sons of God. The Catechism beautifully states:

---

[61] Baltimore Catechism, No. 3, Q. 186.

> The Redeemer will address His elect in these most loving and honorable words: *Come, ye blessed of my Father, possess you the kingdom prepared for you* [Mt. xxv. 34]. Justly, then, may we exclaim: *Thy friends, O God, are made exceedingly honorable* [Ps. cxxxviii. 17]. They shall also receive the highest praise from Christ the Lord, in presence of His heavenly Father and His Angels.

Indeed, the Catechism admits: "To enumerate all the delights with which the souls of the blessed shall be filled would be an endless task. We cannot even conceive them in thought. With this truth, however, the minds of the faithful should be deeply impressed – that the happiness of the Saints is full to overflowing of all those pleasures which can be enjoyed or even desired in this life, whether they regard the powers of the mind or of the perfection of the body; albeit this must be in a manner more exalted than, to use the Apostle's words, eye hath seen, ear heard, or the heart of man conceived.

Amen

The final word of the Creed as set forth by the Apostles themselves is the word, "Amen." After becoming so accustomed to ending our prayers with this word, we are prone to forget the power and meaning in such an ancient and venerable term. The Baltimore Catechism explains:

> By the word 'Amen,' with which we end the Apostles' Creed, is meant, 'So it is,' or, 'So be it'; the word expresses our firm belief in all the doctrines that the Creed contains.[62]

Fiat. So be it. We affirm with this word all that we have taught in the previous installments on the Articles of the Creed. We believe them all without hesitation because they come from God, "Who can neither deceive nor be deceived" (Act of Faith).

Conclusion

As the Roman Catechism concludes this final article of the Holy Creed, we should read the following with the purpose of reflecting on our own lives and asking ourselves how we can better prepare our own soul for the Judgment Seat of Christ:

> The pastor, therefore, should not only encourage the faithful to seek this happiness, but should frequently remind them that the sure way of obtaining it is to

---

[62] Baltimore Catechism, No. 3, Q. 187.

possess the virtues of faith and charity, to persevere in prayer and the use of the Sacraments, and to discharge all the duties of kindness towards their neighbor.

Thus, through the mercy of God, Who has prepared that blessed glory for those who love Him, shall be one day fulfilled the words of the Prophet: *My people shall sit in the beauty of peace, and in the tabernacle of confidence, and in wealthy rest* [Is. xxxii. 18].

XIII

On the Sacraments in General

The Unique Importance of the Sacraments

Having concluded its series of lessons on the Apostle's Creed, Part II of the Roman Catechism provides the Church's authoritative teaching on each of the seven Sacraments: Baptism, Confirmation, Holy Eucharist, Penance, Extreme Unction, Holy Orders, and Matrimony. Before beginning its thorough explanation of Baptism, the first of the Sacraments, the wisdom of the Catechism presents an important introduction on the theology of the Sacraments in general. Its opening words emphasize for priests the importance of preaching frequently on the Sacraments, while underscoring for the laity the importance of understanding the Sacraments and frequenting them:

> The exposition of every part of Christian doctrine demands knowledge and industry on the part of the pastor. But instruction on the Sacraments, which, by the ordinance of God, are a necessary means of salvation and a plenteous source of spiritual advantage, demands in a special manner his talents and industry. By accurate and frequent instruction on the Sacraments, the faithful will be enabled to approach worthily and with salutary effect these inestimable and most holy institutions.

Efficacious Signs and Channels of Grace

To truly understand Our Lord's plan of salvation for us, it is imperative that we as Catholics know with clarity the definition of a Sacrament. The Roman Catechism quotes from St. Augustine of Hippo (A.D. 354-430) and St. Bernard of Clairvaux (1090-1153) in order to provide the best definition of the term:

> [T]here is [no definition] more comprehensive, none more perspicuous, than the definition given by St. Augustine and adopted by all scholastic writers. *A*

> *Sacrament*, he says, *is a sign of a sacred thing*; or, as it has been expressed in other words of the same import: *A Sacrament is a visible sign of an invisible grace, instituted for our justification.*

In similar language, the Baltimore Catechism states, "A sacrament is an outward sign instituted by Christ to give grace."[63] And the Catechism of St. Pius X defines grace as "an inward and supernatural gift given to us without any merit of our own, but through the merits of Jesus Christ in order to gain eternal life."[64] Expounding on how a Sacrament is a visible sign of an invisible reality, the Roman Catechism continues with Baptism as an example:

> [A Sacrament] makes known to us by a certain appearance and resemblance that which God, by His invisible power, accomplishes in our souls. Let us illustrate what we have said by an example. Baptism, for instance, which is administered by external ablution, accompanied with certain solemn words, signifies that by the power of the Holy Ghost all stain and defilement of sin is inwardly washed away, and that the soul is enriched and adorned with the admirable gift of heavenly justification; while, at the same time, the bodily washing, as we shall hereafter explain in its proper place, accomplishes in the soul that which it signifies.

The Author of All the Sacraments

All seven Sacraments were instituted by Our Lord Jesus Christ. While some may incorrectly think that St. John the Baptist instituted the Sacrament of Baptism or that the Apostles instituted the Sacrament of Extreme Unction, the Church's clear teaching is that Christ alone instituted all seven Sacraments:

> For since human justification comes from God, and since the Sacraments are the wonderful instruments of justification, it is evident that one and the same God in Christ, must be acknowledged to be the author of justification and of the Sacraments.

---

[63] Baltimore Catechism No. 3, Q. 304.
[64] Fr. Marshall Roberts, Catechism of St. Pius X (St. Michael's Press, 2010), p. 106.

The Sacraments ultimately exist because Our Lord instituted them as the means of conferring grace – and more specifically, *sanctifying* grace, by which we are *made partakers of the divine nature* (II Pet. i. 4). And since all justification has its foundation in the salvific death and resurrection of our Redeemer, the Roman Catechism points out that all the Sacraments are connected to the Sacrifice of Our Lord on Calvary:

> [F]or all of them declare not only our sanctity and justification, but also two other things most intimately connected with sanctification, namely, the Passion of Christ our Redeemer, which is the source of our sanctification, and also eternal life and heavenly bliss, which are the end of sanctification.

St. Paul himself makes this connection manifest when he writes, *Know you not that all we, who are baptized in Christ Jesus, are baptized in His death?* (Rom. vi. 3).

Ex Opere Operato

In Sacramental Theology, the Church teaches that the Sacraments work *ex opere operato* (Latin, "from the work performed"), an expressed used by the Council of Trent.[65] As Fr. John Hardon (1914-2000) explains in his *Modern Catholic Dictionary*, the Fathers of Trent dogmatically defined that grace is always conferred by a Sacrament "in virtue of the rite performed and not as a mere sign that grace has already been given, or that the sacrament stimulates the faith of the recipient and thus occasions the obtaining of grace, or that what determines the grace is the virtue of either the minister or recipient of a sacrament."[66]

Thus, provided there is no obstacle placed in the way (e.g., invalid matter or form, absence of right intention on the part of the minister), every Sacrament properly administered confers the grace intended by the Sacrament. The reception of a Sacrament does not depend on the sanctity of the individual priest conferring it since it is ultimately Christ Himself Who confers grace through each Sacrament. As St. Thomas Aquinas (1225-1274) teaches in his *Summa Theologiae*, "the sacrament is not perfected by the righteousness of the minister ... but by the power of God" (III q68 a8).

---

[65] Council of Trent, Canons on the Sacraments in General, Can. 8 (Denzinger-Hünermann, 1608).
[66] Fr. John A. Hardon, S.J., *Modern Catholic Dictionary*, "Ex Opere Operato" (available online at http://www.therealpresence.org/dictionary/adict.htm).

Distinguishing Sacraments from Other Sacred Things

Our Lord instituted seven Sacraments. Their number, as determined by Him, can never be increased or decreased by anyone on earth. But what is it, precisely, that makes each Sacrament a channel of grace? What distinguishes the seven Sacraments from other sacred ceremonies such as the blessing of religious articles, consecrations of chalices or altars, or coronations of popes and kings? The Roman Catechism explains the important distinction:

> In order, therefore, to explain more fully the nature of a Sacrament, it should be taught that it is a sensible object which possesses, by divine institution, the power not only of signifying, but also of accomplishing holiness and righteousness. Hence it follows, as everyone can easily see, that the images of the Saints, crosses and the like, although signs of sacred things, cannot be called Sacraments.

Clarifying the nature and purpose of Sacramentals, which includes blessings, consecrations, and exorcisms, the Baltimore Catechism states: "Sacramentals are holy things or actions of which the Church makes use to obtain for us from God, through her intercession, spiritual and temporal favors. The sacramentals obtain favors from God through the prayers of the Church offered for those who make use of them, and through the devotion they inspire."[67] Succinctly stated, Sacramentals do not work *ex opere operato*, nor were they instituted directly by Christ; thus, they are not Sacraments. The blessing of a consecrated virgin, the coronation of a king, the "christening" of church bells, or the blessing of scapulars are still a part of the Catholic Faith, but Our Lord did not institute these ceremonies as Sacraments of His Church. While the number of Sacraments may never be increased or decreased, Sacramentals may be increased or decreased according to the judgment of the Church.

Why Christ Instituted the Sacraments

In answer to the basic question of why the Sacraments were instituted, the Roman Catechism enumerates several reasons:

> The first of these reasons is the feebleness of the human mind. We are so constituted by nature that no one can aspire to mental and intellectual knowledge unless through the medium of sensible objects. In order,

---

[67] Baltimore Catechism No. 3, Q. 469-470.

therefore, that we might more easily understand what is accomplished by the hidden power of God, the same sovereign Creator of the universe has most wisely, and out of His tender kindness towards us, ordained that His power should be manifested to us through the intervention of certain sensible signs.

As human beings who perceive using our senses, we are unable to grasp merely spiritual reality. Even St. Nicodemus, when conversing with the Lord Himself as His teacher, was unable to grasp only spiritual realities without sensible objects (Jn. iii. 1–21).

Another reason is because the mind yields a reluctant assent to promises. Hence, from the beginning of the world, God was accustomed to indicate, and usually in words, that which He had resolved to do; but sometimes, when designing to execute something, the magnitude of which might weaken a belief in its accomplishment, He added to words other signs, which sometimes appeared miraculous. ... As, then, in the Old Law, God ordained that every important promise should be confirmed by certain signs, so in the New Law, Christ our Savior, when He promised pardon of sin, divine grace, the communication of the Holy Spirit, instituted certain visible and sensible signs by which He might oblige Himself, as it were, by pledges, and make it impossible to doubt that He would be true to His promises.

The Old Testament is replete with examples of the Lord's gratuitous expression of signs to the people, including the miracles He performed in Egypt to the amazement of both the Egyptians and the Israelites.

A third reason is that the Sacraments, to use the words of St. Ambrose, may be at hand, as the remedies and medicines of the Samaritan in the Gospel, to preserve or recover the health of the soul. For, through the Sacraments, as through a channel, must flow into the soul the efficacy of the Passion of Christ, that is, the grace which He merited for us on the altar of the cross, and without which we cannot hope for salvation.

As previously expounded upon in the study of the Apostle's Creed, the word "Catholic" refers to the universality and unity of the faithful, despite the differences in gender, race, nationality, language, and time separating them. Despite these external differences, the Sacraments provide a unifying mark which unites all the faithful. Baptism, which produces an indelible mark on the soul, will be present among the souls in Heaven and those in hell who received the Sacrament. That mark can never be erased.

> A fourth reason why the institution of the Sacraments seems necessary is that there may be certain marks and symbols to distinguish the faithful; particularly since, as St. Augustine observes, no society of men, professing a true or a false religion, can be, so to speak, consolidated into one body, unless united and held together by some bond of sensible signs.

Matter and Form

For a Sacrament to be validly conferred and for the recipient to receive the inward grace it signifies, it is necessity for the Sacrament to be conferred using valid matter and form, together with the intention to do what the Church does. The Roman Catechism explains:

> Every Sacrament consists of two things: *matter*, which is called the *element*, and *form*, which is commonly called *the word*. ...

> In order to make the meaning of the rite that is being performed easier and clearer, words had to be added to the matter. Water for example, has the quality of cooling as well as of making clean, and may be symbolic of either. In Baptism, therefore, unless the words were added, it would not be certain which meaning of the sign was intended. When the words are added, we immediately understand that the Sacrament possesses and signifies the power of cleansing. ...

> But although God is the author and dispenser of the Sacraments, He nevertheless willed that they should be administered by men in His Church, not by Angels. ...

> Since the ministers of the Sacraments represent in the discharge of their sacred functions, not their own, but the person of Christ, be they good or bad, they validly perform and confer the Sacraments, provided they make use of the matter and form always observed in the Catholic Church according to the institution of Christ, and provided they intend to do what the Church does in their administration.

Baptism, for instance, is only valid when it has the proper matter (i.e., water poured thrice over the head of the baptized) and proper form (i.e., the words, "I baptize you in the Name of the Father, of the Son, and of the Holy Ghost"). Without proper matter and form, there is no valid Sacrament and thus no reception of a Sacrament at all.

While matter and form are both essential for the validity of each Sacrament, the form of the Sacraments may vary slightly according to the different rites of the Catholic Church. For example, the Latin (or Roman) Rite observed the following form of words for Confirmation for many centuries (prior to Vatican II): "*N., signo te signo crucis + et confirmo te chrismate salutis, in nomine Patris + et Filii + et Spiritus + Sancti*" [*Name*, I sign thee with the sign of the cross and confirm thee with the Chrism of Salvation]. In the Byzantine Rite, however, Chrismation (as Confirmation is called throughout the Christian East) is administered with these words: "The sign of the seal of the Holy Spirit…" Despite the difference in form (words), both are valid, provided that valid matter and right intention are also employed. We will discuss this further in the next chapter.

While anyone may baptize validly in cases of necessity (assuming they use the proper matter and form), only a priest is able to confect the Holy Eucharist, confirm souls in Confirmation (although a bishop is the ordinary minister in the Latin Rite), absolve sins in Confession, and administer Extreme Unction to those in danger of death. A validly ordained priest is necessary for these Sacraments. The Sacrament of Holy Orders, in turn, requires a bishop to administer it.

Matrimony is unique in that the spouses administer the Sacrament to one another by means of their mutual free consent to enter into a permanent union, with the primary end of their union being the procreation and education of children. However, as the Roman Catechism teaches (in accord with the Council of Trent), "there can be no true and valid marriage unless it be contracted in the presence of the parish priest, or of some other priest commissioned by him, or by the Ordinary [local bishop], and that of a certain number of witnesses."

Regarding Baptism, the Church accepts most Protestant baptisms as valid since a Catholic minister is not required for validity, provided that valid matter, form, and intention are employed. The so-called "baptisms" of certain pseudo-Christian sects such as Mormons or Jehovah's Witnesses, however, are not valid due to the lack of correct form (words) and/or intention. Questions of validity may also arise in relation to certain Protestant baptisms due to their erroneous conceptions of Original Sin and the role of Baptism. Anyone seeking to convert to the Catholic Faith who was baptized in a Protestant denomination should consult with a priest on whether they might need to be conditionally baptized, in the event that the validity of their Protestant baptism is doubtful.[68]

The Significance of Having Seven Sacraments

Before concluding its introduction on the Sacraments, the authors of the Roman Catechism sought to set forth an insightful explanation of why God, in His wisdom, chose to establish *seven* Sacraments, as opposed to a different number:

> The Sacraments of the Catholic Church are seven in number, as is proved from Scripture, from the tradition handed down to us from the Fathers, and from the authority of Councils. Why they are neither more nor less in number may be shown, at least with some probability, from the analogy that exists between the natural and the spiritual life. In order to exist, to preserve existence, and to contribute to his own and to the public good, seven things seem necessary to man: to be born, to grow, to be nurtured, to be cured when sick, when weak to be strengthened; as far as regards the public welfare, to have magistrates invested with authority to govern, and to perpetuate himself and his species by legitimate offspring. Now, since it is quite clear that all these things are sufficiently analogous to that life by which the soul lives to God, we discover in them a reason to account for the number of the Sacraments.

Conclusion

In concluding its teachings on the Sacraments in general, the Roman Catechism summarizes in two primary points the key takeaways:

> The first is that the faithful understand the high honour, respect and veneration due to these divine and celestial gifts. The second is that, since the Sacraments have been established by the God of infinite mercy for the common salvation of all, the people should make pious and religious use of them, and be so inflamed with the desire of Christian perfection as to deem it a very great loss to

---

[68] Baltimore Catechism No. 3, Q. 612-615 provides information on the conditional conferring of Sacraments.

be for any time deprived of the salutary use, particularly
of Penance and the Holy Eucharist. ...

For as we are ushered into spiritual life by means of the
Sacraments, so by the same means are we nourished and
preserved, and grow to spiritual increase.

The importance of the Sacraments cannot be overstated. As the venerable
king of France, St. Louis IX (r. 1226-1270), famously remarked: "I think
more of the place where I was baptized than of Rheims Cathedral where I
was crowned. It is a greater thing to be a child of God than to be the ruler
of a Kingdom. This last I shall lose at death, but the other will be my
passport to an everlasting glory."

We should fervently pray that, before we receive any Sacrament, we are
prepared to do so with the proper dispositions. To summarize, the
Sacraments are seven in number and were instituted by Our Lord Jesus
Christ for the salvation and sanctification of all men. Beginning with
Baptism, each Sacrament confers sanctifying grace (divine life), together
with the particular (sacramental) graces proper to it. Some Sacraments are
necessary for salvation (e.g., Baptism), while others are not (e.g.,
Matrimony).

XIV

On the Sacrament of Baptism

What is Baptism?

After discussing the seven Sacraments in general, the Roman Catechism proceeds to offer a more focused look at each Sacrament beginning with Baptism, the gateway to the other Sacraments. As the Catechism states, "Baptism is, as it were, the gate through which we enter into the fellowship of the Christian life and begin thenceforward to obey the Commandments."

Baptism is the means by which we are made children of God and have the stain of Original Sin removed from our souls. While all seven Sacraments were instituted by Our Lord Jesus Christ, Baptism itself is explicitly mentioned several times in Sacred Scripture (Jn. iii. 3-5, Mt. xxviii. 19, and Acts ii. 38-39 are three such instances). The Roman Catechism, in referencing the Scriptures which bear explicit testimony to the Sacrament, defines Baptism as: "The Sacrament of regeneration by water in the word. By nature, we are born from Adam children of wrath, but by Baptism we are regenerated in Christ, children of mercy. For He gave power to men *to be made the sons of God, to them that believe in His Name, who are born, not of blood, nor of the will of the flesh, nor of the will of man, but of God* [Jn. i. 12-13]."

Proper Matter and Form of Baptism

As the Catechism previously set forth, the validity of all Sacraments depends on proper matter and proper form; both are essential. Baptism is no exception to this universal rule. The Sacrament of Baptism consists not only of water but also the necessary words that must be said, as the Roman Catechism explains:

> ...the faithful are to be informed that this Sacrament consists of ablution, accompanied necessarily, according to the institution of our Lord, by certain solemn words. This is the uniform doctrine of the holy Fathers, as is proved by the following most explicit testimony of St.

Augustine: *The word is joined to the element, and it becomes a Sacrament.*

It is all the more necessary to impress this on the minds of the faithful lest they fall into the common error of thinking that the baptismal water, preserved in the sacred font, constitutes the Sacrament. The Sacrament of Baptism can be said to exist only when we actually apply the water to someone by way of ablution, while using the words appointed by our Lord.

Shortly before His Ascension, Our Lord Jesus Christ told His disciples the exact formula that must be used for a valid Baptism when He said: *All power is given to Me in heaven and in earth. Going therefore, teach ye all nations, baptizing them in the Name of the Father, and of the Son, and of the Holy Ghost. Teaching them to observe all things whatsoever I have commanded you: and behold I am with you all days, even to the consummation of the world* (Mt. xxviii. 18-20).

Everyone who is baptized must be baptized in the Name of the Father, the Son, and the Holy Ghost. To be baptized only in the Name of Jesus does not constitute an authentic baptism because it does not follow the Trinitarian formula established by Our Lord. As previously stated, each Sacrament must be administered using the form and matter proper to it. "The matter, then, or element of [Baptism]," the Roman Catechism states, "is any sort of natural water, which is simply and without qualification commonly called water, be it sea water, river water, water from a pond, well, or fountain." As for the proper form, water must be poured over the individual's head three times, or immersed three times in water, while the words, "I baptize you in the Name of the Father, and of the Son, and of the Holy Ghost," are pronounced by the one baptizing (ordinarily a priest).

Immersion is Unnecessary

In addition to infusion (pouring water over the head), Baptism by aspersion (sprinkling) or by immersion is also valid. On this topic, the Roman Catechism states:

> [Pastors] should briefly explain that, according to the common custom and practice of the Church, Baptism may be administered in three ways, by immersion, infusion or aspersion.

> Whichever of these rites be observed, we must believe that Baptism is rightly administered. For in Baptism

water is used to signify the spiritual ablution which it accomplishes, and on this account, Baptism is called by the Apostle a *laver* [Eph. v. 26]. Now this ablution is not more really accomplished by immersion, which was for a considerable time the practice in the early ages of the Church, than by infusion, which we now see in general use, or by aspersion, which there is reason to believe was the manner in which Peter baptized, when on one day he converted and gave Baptism to about three thousand souls.

For around twelve centuries, immersion was the common form practiced in the Catholic Church. However, St. Thomas Aquinas, who lived in the 13th century, plainly states, "Baptism can be conferred by sprinkling and also by pouring." Tertullian, who was born c. 160 A.D., said that Baptism is a "sprinkling with any kind of water" (*De Bapt.*, Ch. 6).

The Didache (The Teaching of the Apostles) holds that baptismal water may be poured when there is not enough water for immersion. St. Thomas Aquinas explains what the Catechism said above: that the three thousand converts baptized by St. Peter on the first Pentecost (cf. Acts ii. 41) were most likely not baptized by immersion because there was not enough water in Jerusalem at the time to have done so. Similarly, St. Thomas also argued that it is highly unlikely that the jailer baptized in the prison at Philippi (cf. Acts xvi. 25-40) or the Gentiles in the home of Cornelius (cf. Acts 10) were immersed in water.

The Baptism of St. John Was Not the Sacrament of Baptism

As the Catechism taught in its opening on the seven Sacraments in general, Our Lord Jesus Christ is the author of all the Sacraments. Some may incorrectly think that St. John the Baptist instituted the Sacrament of Baptism. This, however, is false.

> When these things have been explained, it will also be expedient to teach and remind the faithful that, in common with the other Sacraments, Baptism was instituted by Christ the Lord. On this subject the pastor should frequently teach and point out that there are two different periods of time which relate to Baptism—one the period of its institution by the Redeemer; the other, the establishment of the law regarding its reception.

St. John the Baptist preached a *baptism of penance* (Mk. i. 4; Lk. iii. 3; Acts xiii. 24, xix. 4) which called for those who received it to repent. It was not the Sacrament of Baptism which Our Lord instituted. It was more of what we would consider a sacramental. For that reason, St. Paul baptized those believers he encountered in Ephesus who had only received *John's baptism* with the actual Sacrament of Baptism after Our Lord's Ascension (cf. Acts xix. 1-5). Concerning this incident, St. Jerome writes, "Those who were baptized with John's baptism needed to be baptized with the baptism of our Lord." Likewise, St. Augustine says, "Our sacraments are signs of present grace, whereas the sacraments of the Old Law were signs of future grace."

Why, then, did our Blessed Lord consent to be baptized with the "baptism of penance" by St. John? The wisdom of the Roman Catechism explains:

> With regard to the former, it is clear that this Sacrament was instituted by our Lord when, having been baptized by John, He gave to water the power of sanctifying. St. Gregory Nazianzen and St. Augustine testify that to water was then imparted the power of regenerating to spiritual life. In another place St. Augustine says: *From the moment that Christ is immersed in water, water washes away all sins.* And again: *The Lord is baptized, not because He had need to be cleansed, but in order that, by the contact of His pure flesh, He might purify the waters and impart to them the power of cleansing.*
>
> A very strong argument to prove that Baptism was then instituted by our Lord might be afforded by the fact the most Holy Trinity, in whose Name Baptism is conferred, manifested Its divine presence on that occasion. The voice of the Father was heard, the Person of the Son was present, the Holy Ghost descended in the form of a dove; and the heavens, into which we are enabled to enter by Baptism, were thrown open.

Is Baptism Necessary for Salvation?

While Baptism was instituted by Christ at His own Baptism by St. John, it was not yet made necessary for salvation until after Our Redeemer's triumphant Resurrection. At that time, it became necessary for salvation:

> Holy writers are unanimous in saying that after the Resurrection of our Lord, when He gave to His Apostles the command to go and *teach all nations: baptizing them in the name of the Father, and of the Son, and of the Holy*

Ghost [Mt. xxviii. 19], the law of Baptism became
obligatory on all who were to be saved.

The Council of Trent affirmed what the Church has taught from the
beginning, namely, that Baptism is necessary for salvation: "If anyone says
that baptism is optional, that is, not necessary for salvation, let him be
anathema." The necessity of Baptism for the salvation of every single
human person is also plainly attested to in the Roman Catechism:

> ...the law of Baptism, as established by our Lord,
> extends to all, so that unless they are regenerated to God
> through the grace of Baptism, be their parents Christians
> or infidels, they are born to eternal misery and
> destruction. Pastors, therefore, should often explain
> these words of the Gospel: *Unless a man be born again
> of water and the Holy Ghost, he cannot enter into the
> kingdom of God* [Jn. iii. 5].

Who May Baptize?

The Roman Catechism explains that there are three categories of persons
who may serve as ministers of the Sacrament of Baptism. "Bishops and
priests hold the first place. To them belongs the administration of this
Sacrament, not by any extraordinary concession of power, but by right of
office; for to them, in the persons of the Apostles, was addressed the
command of our Lord: *Go, baptize.*" In short, bishops and priests are the
ordinary ministers of Baptism.

The second category belongs to deacons, who are the extraordinary
ministers of Baptism: "Next among the ministers are deacons, for whom,
as numerous decrees of the holy Fathers attest, it is not lawful without the
permission of the Bishop or priest to administer this Sacrament."

And lastly, the minister in case of necessity: "Those who may administer
Baptism in case of necessity, but without its solemn ceremonies, hold the
last place; and in this class are included all, even the laity, men and women,
to whatever sect they may belong. This office extends in case of necessity,
even to Jews, infidels and heretics, provided, however, they intend to do
what the Catholic Church does in that act of her ministry. These things
were established by many decrees of the ancient Fathers and Councils; and
the holy Council of Trent denounces anathema against those who dare to
say, that Baptism, even when administered by heretics, in the name of the
Father, and of the Son, and of the Holy Ghost, with the intention of doing
what the Church does, is not true Baptism."

Why are even non-Christians allowed to baptize? Because of the grave necessity of Baptism for salvation: "And here indeed let us admire the supreme goodness and wisdom of our Lord. Seeing the necessity of this Sacrament for all, He not only instituted water, than which nothing can be more common, as its matter, but also placed its administration within the power of all."

Consequently, anyone, even an unbaptized person, may baptize someone so long as they use the proper matter and form and have the intention to do what the Church does.

What are the Effects of Baptism?

After clearly defining the Sacrament of Baptism, its institution by Our Lord, and the necessity of receiving it for salvation, the Roman Catechism proceeds to discuss the six principal effects of Holy Baptism.

First and foremost, the Sacrament is administered for the remission of sin, both *original* (inherited from Adam and Eve) and *actual* (personal): "[The faithful] are to be taught, in the first place, that such is the admirable efficacy of this Sacrament that it remits original sin and actual guilt, however unthinkable its enormity may seem." Most Protestants view baptism as the covering up of our sins. That is not correct. Baptism completely washes the soul clean. Every human person aside from the Blessed Virgin Mary was conceived with Original Sin and thus stands in need of Baptism.[69]

The second effect of Baptism is the removal of all temporal punishment due to sin that has been incurred up until the moment of Baptism. As Catholics, we should understand that the sins which we commit are forgiven in the Sacrament of Confession, but the punishment due to those sins must be expiated through penance. For this reason, we are enjoined by the Church to obtain indulgences and perform pious works for the purpose of paying this debt. However, the sins forgiven in Baptism also have the temporal punishment paid in full:

---

[69] Our Blessed Lord was also conceived without original sin, but He is a Divine Person, not a human person. And St. John the Baptist, a human person, was born without Original Sin, but he was conceived with Original Sin. He was cleansed from Original Sin when he leapt in his mother's womb, a miracle we remember as part of the Visitation of Mary to Elizabeth. As stated by the Catholic Encyclopedia: "Then was accomplished the prophetic utterance of the angel that the child should 'be filled with the Holy Ghost even from his mother's womb.' Now as the presence of any sin whatever is incompatible with the indwelling of the Holy Ghost in the soul, it follows that at this moment John was cleansed from the stain of original sin."

In Baptism not only is sin forgiven, but with it all the punishment due to sin is mercifully remitted by God. To communicate the efficacy of the Passion of Christ our Lord is an effect common to all the Sacraments; but of Baptism alone does the Apostle say, that by it we die and are buried together with Christ.

Hence holy Church has always understood that to impose those works of piety, usually called by the holy Fathers works of satisfaction, on one who is to be cleansed in Baptism, would be injurious to this Sacrament in the highest degree.

The third effect of Baptism is the infusion of sanctifying grace – the divine life of God – into our souls. Through Baptism, we become *partakers of the divine nature* (II Pt. i. 4) of the Blessed Trinity. We become sons of God and temples of the Holy Ghost. In Baptism, we are *born again*, as St. Peter writes, *not of corruptible seed, but incorruptible, by the word of God who liveth and remaineth forever* (I Pt. i. 23). We are also buried with Christ so that we might rise with Him (cf. Rom. vi. 3-4). In the words of the Roman Catechism, "by virtue of this Sacrament we are not only delivered from what are justly deemed the greatest of all evils, but [we] are also enriched with invaluable goods and blessings. Our souls are replenished with divine grace, by which we are rendered just and children of God and are made heirs to eternal salvation."

The fourth effect is the infusion into our souls of the virtues and incorporation into Christ our Lord: "By Baptism we are also united to Christ, as members to their Head. As therefore from the head proceeds the power by which the different members of the body are moved to the proper performance of their respective functions, so from the fullness of Christ the Lord are diffused divine grace and virtue through all those who are justified, qualifying them for the performance of all the duties of Christian piety."

The fifth effect of Baptism is the indelible spiritual seal or character imprinted upon the soul, forever marking it as Christian. Even if a baptized person goes to hell, this seal will remain for all eternity on the soul. Baptism is a Sacrament that lasts forever, which is why it cannot be repeated after it has been validly received: *One Lord, one faith, one baptism* (Eph. iv. 5).

And finally, the sixth effect, "to which all the others seem to be referred, is that it opens to us the portals of heaven which sin had closed against us."

Are Non-Catholic Baptisms Valid?

Since the Church requires the baptizer to do what the Church intends, the one who baptizes must intend to wash away sin (original and actual), infuse grace, and incorporate the baptized person into the Mystical Body of Christ, the Church. As such, the Church *may* accept the validity of most Protestant baptisms since a validly ordained minister is not required for this particular Sacrament, so long as those baptisms used the proper matter, form, and intention. For this reason, the alleged baptisms of certain groups like the Mormons or Jehovah's Witnesses are not valid due to lack of proper matter, form, and intention.

The primary issue for those who were baptized in a Protestant sect is determining whether the baptizer had the right intention. Due to many Protestants having erroneous conceptions of Original Sin and the nature of Baptism, doubt may exist regarding the validity of such baptisms. Anyone seeking to convert to the Catholic Faith who was baptized in a Protestant denomination should consult with a priest to determine if they need to be conditionally baptized. The Roman Catechism provides the formula used by the Church in such cases: "*If thou art baptized, I baptize thee not again; but if thou art not yet baptized, I baptize thee in the name of the Father, and of the Son, and of the Holy Ghost.* In such cases Baptism is not to be considered as impiously repeated, but as holily, yet conditionally, administered."

Infant Baptism

The one to be baptized must possess three necessary dispositions: intent to be baptized, faith, and "repentance for past sins, and a fixed determination to avoid all sin in the future," in the words of the Roman Catechism. As a result, some have erroneously claimed that only adults should receive the Sacrament of Baptism.

The Church has always taught that Baptism can and should be conferred on children. As previously mentioned, in Baptism we are "born again" to the supernatural life of grace that continues into eternity. Since Baptism is the beginning of supernatural life, a child should be baptized as soon as possible that they might have a share in divine sonship.

Likewise, the wisdom of the Catechism of the Council of Trent explains this unambiguously: "That this law [regarding the necessity of Baptism, according to Jn. iii. 5] extends not only to adults but also to infants and children, and that the Church has received this from Apostolic tradition, is confirmed by the unanimous teaching and authority of the Fathers. Besides, it is not to be supposed that Christ the Lord would have withheld the

Sacrament and grace of Baptism from children, of whom He said: *Suffer the little children, and forbid them not to come to Me; for the kingdom of heaven is for such* [Mt. xix. 14]; whom also He embraced, upon whom He imposed hands, to whom He gave His blessing. Moreover, when we read that an entire family was baptized by Paul, it is sufficiently obvious that the children of the family must also have been cleansed in the saving font."

Furthermore, the Third Council of Carthage (A.D. 253), together with St. Cyprian, taught that infants should be baptized as soon as possible after birth. The Council of Milevis (A.D. 416) also affirmed the necessity of Baptism for infants. This same position has been reaffirmed at the Fourth Lateran Council (1215) as well as the Councils of Vienne (1311-1312), Florence (1431-1447), and Trent (1545-1563).

However, since Baptism requires a proper intention by the recipient, how can infants consent? The Roman Catechism answers: "This disposition [i.e., the desire and intent to receive Baptism] even infants are presumed to have, since the will of the Church, which promises for them, cannot be mistaken."

Concerning the important role of godparents, through whom infants profess the Faith, they are enjoined by the Church with the solemn responsibility to see to the religious instruction of their godchildren (in cooperation with the parents, of course), to be good examples of the Christian life, and to pray for them. Quoting St. Augustine, the Roman Catechism reminds godparents of their duty: "They ought to admonish [their godchildren] to observe chastity, love justice, cling to charity; and above all they should teach them the Creed, the Lord's Prayer, the Ten Commandments, and the rudiments of the Christian religion."

Conclusion

After its lengthy instruction on this most essential of Sacraments, the Catechism concludes:

> We have explained the meaning of the word *Baptism*, the nature and substance of the Sacrament, and also the parts of which it is composed. We have said by whom it was instituted; who are the ministers necessary to its administration; who should be, as it were, the tutors whose instructions should sustain the weakness of the person baptized; to whom Baptism should be administered; and how they should be disposed; what are the virtue and efficacy of the Sacrament; finally, we have developed, at sufficient length for our purpose, the rites

and   ceremonies   that   should   accompany   its
administration.

We should reflect on our own baptism, whether we received the Sacrament as an infant or an adult, and thank God our Father for the ransom of our souls and incorporation into His Son's Mystical Body through this august Sacrament. Pray also for all of the souls who are in this world now who are not yet baptized. Ask yourself if there is anything you can do to help encourage them to receive the Sacrament of Baptism, which is necessary for salvation

XV

On the Sacrament of Confirmation

What is Confirmation?

After explaining the Sacrament of Baptism, the Roman Catechism turns to the Sacrament of Confirmation, which completes the holy anointing begun at Baptism. For this reason, the Sacrament is called Confirmation since it *confirms* and *completes* the graces of holy Baptism. As the Catechism teaches, "a baptized person, when anointed with the sacred chrism by the Bishop, with the accompanying solemn words…becomes stronger with the strength of a new power, and thus begins to be a perfect soldier of Christ."

Confirmation is not a mere "graduation" from religious education, as it is sadly often treated in our era. Rather, Confirmation makes a Catholic a soldier for Christ who is called upon to live, defend, and spread the Faith to others. As a testimony to this fact, the traditional Confirmation rite calls for the minister of the sacrament (ordinarily, a bishop) to gently slap the cheek of the confirmandi (person being confirmed) as a physical reminder that "he should be prepared to endure with unconquered spirit all adversities for the name of Christ."

While the word "confirmation" is not mentioned explicitly in Holy Scripture, the Roman Catechism explains that various Scriptural texts nevertheless bear witness to Confirmation as an anointing whereby a soul is sealed with the gifts of the Holy Ghost:

> [The Early Church Fathers] were so persuaded that no doubt could exist as to the reality of this Sacrament that they even taught and confirmed the doctrine by passages of Scripture, the one testifying that to the Sacrament of Confirmation apply these words of the Apostle: *Grieve not the Holy Spirit of God, whereby you are sealed* [Eph. iv. 30]; the other, these words of the Psalmist: *Like the precious ointment on the head, that ran down upon the beard, the beard of Aaron* [Ps. cxxxii. 2], and also these words of the same Apostle: *The charity of God is poured*

forth in our hearts by the Holy Ghost, Who is given to us
[Rom. v. 5].

Confirmation is a Distinct Sacrament

While acknowledging the intimate connection between Confirmation and Baptism, the Roman Catechism does emphasize that they are, in fact, two distinct Sacraments rather than two phases of the same Sacrament:

> Although said by [Pope] Melchiades [r. ca. 310/311-314 A.D.] to have a most intimate connection with Baptism, Confirmation is still not to be regarded as the same, but as a very different Sacrament; for the variety of the grace which each of the Sacraments confers, and of the sensible sign employed to signify that grace, evidently render them distinct and different Sacraments.

> Since, then, by the grace of Baptism we are begotten unto newness of life, whereas by that of Confirmation we grow to full maturity, having put away the things of a child, we can sufficiently understand that the same difference that exists in the natural life between birth and growth exists also between Baptism, which regenerates, and Confirmation, by virtue of which growth and perfect spiritual strength are imparted to the faithful.

Furthermore, the Sacrament of Confirmation is not an invention of the Church but was instituted by Our Lord Jesus Christ, as were all of the Sacraments, and administered by the Apostles. Pope St. Clement I, who reigned as the fourth pope (A.D. 92-99), is explicitly referenced as bearing witness to Confirmation as a distinct Sacrament of apostolic origin:

> That in Confirmation is contained the true and proper nature of a Sacrament has always been acknowledged by the Catholic Church, as Pope Melchiades and many other very holy and very ancient Pontiffs expressly declare. The truth of this doctrine St. Clement could not confirm in stronger terms than when he says: *All should hasten without delay to be born again unto God, and afterwards to be signed by the Bishop, that is, to receive the sevenfold grace of the Holy Ghost; for, as has been handed down to us from St. Peter, and as the other Apostles taught in obedience to the command and of our Lord, he who culpably and voluntarily, and not from necessity, neglects to receive this Sacrament, cannot*

141

possibly be a perfect Christian. This same faith has been confirmed, as may be seen in their decrees, by Popes Urban, Fabian and Eusebius, who, filled with the same spirit, shed their blood for the name of Christ.

All Should Be Confirmed

Concerning the importance of Confirmation, the words of the Roman Catechism, written nearly 500 years ago, express even to the modern pastor the importance of preaching on this Sacrament: "If ever there was a time demanding the diligence of pastors in explaining the Sacrament of Confirmation, in these days certainly it requires special attention, when there are found in the holy Church of God many by whom this Sacrament is altogether omitted; while very few seek to obtain from it the fruit of divine grace which they should derive from its participation."

Strictly speaking, Confirmation is not required for salvation. However, it certainly should not be neglected or treated as unnecessary for a Christian. The wisdom of the Roman Catechism explains: "Although not essential, however, it ought to be omitted by no one, but rather, on the contrary, in a matter so full of holiness through which the divine gifts are so liberally bestowed, the greater care should be taken to avoid all neglect. What God has proposed in common unto all for their sanctification, all should likewise most earnestly desire."

The Baltimore Catechism likewise expresses the importance of receiving Confirmation when it reminds the faithful that, while Confirmation is not required for salvation, deliberating neglecting Confirmation is actually a sin: "It is a sin to neglect Confirmation, especially in these evil days when faith and morals are exposed to so many and such violent temptations.... Confirmation is not so necessary for salvation that we could not be saved without it, for it is not given to infants even in danger of death; nevertheless, there is a divine command obliging all to receive it, if possible. Persons who have not been confirmed in youth should make every effort to be confirmed later in life."[70]

Valid Matter and Form of Confirmation

As discussed in previous chapters, the validity of all Sacraments depends upon the use of valid matter and form; both are essential and admit no exceptions. The Sacrament of Confirmation consists of an anointing with sacred chrism while the proper words are said, as the Roman Catechism explains:

---

[70] Baltimore Catechism, No. 3, Q. 694, 696.

We now come to treat of the component parts of the Sacrament, and first of its matter. This is called *chrism*, a word borrowed from the Greek language... which is composed of oil and balsam with the solemn consecration of the Bishop. A mixture of two material things, therefore, furnishes the matter of Confirmation; and this mixture of different things not only declares the manifold grace of the Holy Ghost given to those who are confirmed but also sufficiently shows the excellence of the Sacrament itself. ...

The form of Confirmation, then, is comprised in these words: *I sign thee with the sign of the cross, and I confirm thee with the chrism of salvation, in the name of the Father, and of the Son, and of the Holy Ghost.*

Although the matter of Confirmation has always been sacred chrism, the form (words) of the Sacrament has varied somewhat throughout Church history according to local custom – unlike Baptism, for example, whose form was specified by Our Lord and is explicit in Scripture (cf. Matt. xxviii. 19).

Following the Second Vatican Council (1962-1965) and the introduction of the *Novus Ordo Missae* (1969), Pope Paul VI published an Apostolic Constitution (Aug. 15, 1971) by which he changed the words used to confer the Sacrament of Confirmation in the Latin Church (effective Jan. 1, 1973). The revised words, *Accipe signaculum doni Spiritus Sancti* ("Be sealed with the Gift of the Holy Spirit"), mirror the valid form used in the Byzantine Rite: *Signaculum doni Spiritus Sancti* ("The Seal of the Gift of the Holy Spirit"). The traditional Rite of Confirmation, still used for those assisting at the Traditional Latin Mass, maintains the old Roman form: "I sign thee with the sign of the cross, and I confirm thee with the chrism of salvation, in the Name of the Father, and of the Son, and of the Holy Ghost."

Who May Administer Confirmation?

The Sacrament of Confirmation requires a validly ordained minister, unlike Baptism, which may be administered by anyone in cases of necessity. While the ordinary minister of Confirmation is a bishop, priests likewise possess the ability to confirm souls. Canon 882 of the 1983 Code of Canon Law states: "The ordinary minister of confirmation is a bishop; a presbyter provided with this faculty in virtue of universal law or the special grant of the competent authority also confers this sacrament validly." The 1917 in

Canon 782 similarly affirmed that the ordinary minister of Confirmation is a bishop and that priests are extraordinary ministers of Confirmation by virtue of an apostolic indult granted to that effect.

Consequently, a bishop or priest may administer Confirmation, but a deacon may not. On this point, the Roman Catechism explains this distinction by referring to the administration of Confirmation by the Apostles:

> Now the Holy Scriptures show that the Bishop alone is the ordinary minister of this Sacrament, because we read in the Acts of the Apostles that when Samaria had received the Word of God, Peter and John were sent to them, who prayed for them *that they might receive the Holy Ghost*: for He was *not as yet come upon any of them, but they were only baptized* [Acts viii. 14]. Here we may see that he who had baptized, having been only a deacon, had no power to confirm; but that its administration was reserved to a more perfect order of ministers, that is, to the Apostles. The same may be observed whenever the Sacred Scriptures make mention of this Sacrament.

When May Confirmation Be Received?

Confirmation in the Roman Catholic Church is ordinarily received in adolescence, often around the beginning of high school. Adult converts ordinarily receive Confirmation along with the other Sacraments of Initiation, Baptism and Holy Communion, at the same time. Starting in 1995, the Diocese of Saginaw, Michigan became the first American diocese to implement the "restored order of the Sacraments," moving Confirmation to around second grade so that it is received before First Holy Communion. Since then, eleven other dioceses throughout the United States have followed suit: Great Falls-Billings (1996), Portland, Maine (1997), Spokane (1998), Fargo (2002), Gaylord (2003), Tyler (2005), Phoenix (2005), Honolulu (2015), Denver (2015), Manchester (2017), and Gallup (2019).

While the Roman Catechism states that Confirmation may be received at various ages, it clarifies that the administration of the Sacrament is properly deferred until a child has at least reached the age of reason: "Here it is to be observed, that, after Baptism, the Sacrament of Confirmation may indeed be administered to all; but that, until children shall have attained the use of reason, its administration is inexpedient. If it does not seem well to defer (Confirmation) to the age of twelve, it is most proper to postpone this Sacrament at least to that of seven years."

Concerning the time of year for the administration of the Sacrament, while acknowledging that Confirmation may be administered throughout the year, the time around Pentecost Sunday is the most appropriate. Again, turning to the clear teachings as contained in the Roman Catechism: "It has also been a matter of solemn religious observance in the Church of God that this Sacrament should be administered principally at Pentecost, because on that day especially were the Apostles strengthened and confirmed by the power of the Holy Ghost. By the recollection of this supernatural event the faithful should be admonished of the nature and magnitude of the mysteries contained in the sacred unction."

What are the Effects of Confirmation?

Confirmation is not a diploma signifying the completion of religious education. It is an actual Sacrament which confers actual graces on the soul that receives it. On this essential point, the Roman Catechism explains the primary effects of Confirmation by admonishing pastors to "teach that, in common with the other Sacraments, Confirmation, unless some obstacle be present on the part of the receiver, imparts new grace."

As implied by the name of the Sacrament, the first effect of the Sacrament, as stated by the Catechism, is to "perfect the grace of Baptism." "But not only does it confirm," the Catechism goes on, "it also increases (divine grace), as says [Pope] Melchiades : *The Holy Ghost, whose salutary descent upon the waters of Baptism, imparts in the font fullness to the accomplishment of innocence, in Confirmation gives an increase of grace*; and not only an increase, but an increase after a wonderful manner."

The power of Confirmation in the soul is further manifest in the lives of the Apostles, who received the fullness of the gifts of the Holy Ghost on Pentecost. This same marvelous power from on high is available for all those who have been confirmed, if only they open their souls to the effect of God's grace:

> So weak and timid were [the Apostles] before, and even
> at the very time of the Passion, that no sooner was our
> Lord apprehended, than they instantly fled; and Peter,
> who had been designated the rock and foundation of the
> Church, and who had displayed unshaken constancy and
> exalted magnanimity, terrified at the voice of one weak
> woman, denied, not once nor twice only, but a third time,
> that he was a disciple of Jesus Christ; and after the

Resurrection they all remained shut up at home for fear of the Jews. But, on the day of Pentecost, so great was the power of the Holy Ghost with which they were all filled that, while they boldly and freely disseminated the Gospel confided to them, not only through Judea, but throughout the world, they thought no greater happiness could await them than that of *being accounted worthy to suffer* contumely, chains, torments and crucifixion, *for the name of Christ* [Acts v. 41].

Likewise, the Catechism of St. Pius X succinctly explains: "The sacrament of Confirmation makes us perfect Christians by confirming us in the faith and perfecting the other virtues and gifts received in Baptism; hence, it is called Confirmation.... The gifts of the Holy Ghost received in Confirmation are these seven: Wisdom, Understanding, Counsel, Fortitude, Knowledge, Piety, and the Fear of the Lord."

In his teaching on the Gifts of the Holy Ghost, St. Thomas Aquinas says that four of these gifts (wisdom, understanding, knowledge, and counsel) direct the intellect, since the intellect seeks to know the truth of God, while the other three gifts (fortitude, piety, and fear of the Lord) direct the will toward God, since the will seeks to do the will of God.

Why Are Sponsors Needed?

As in Baptism, a sponsor is chosen to present the confirmandi. The sponsor should be a baptized and confirmed Catholic who is at least fourteen years of age, is of the same sex as the confirmandi, and is well instructed in the Faith. Those unable to serve as a sponsor include members of religious orders, spouses in respect to each other, parents in respect to their own children, infidels, heretics, members of condemned secret societies, and public sinners. The 1917 Code of Canon Law excludes godparents from being sponsors except in cases of emergency, while the 1983 Code of Canon Law recommends the opposite, namely, that the godparent should act as sponsor at Confirmation if possible in order to better tie Baptism and Confirmation together.

Sponsors, like godparents, are charged with a solemn responsibility by Holy Mother Church. Do not take this responsibility likely if you are asked to be a sponsor. As the Baltimore Catechism cautions, "Sponsors are necessary in Confirmation, and they must be of the same good character as those required at Baptism, for they take upon themselves the same duties and responsibilities. They also contract a spiritual relationship, which, however, unlike that in Baptism, is not an impediment to marriage."[71] On this point, the Roman Catechism explains by way of metaphor:

> A sponsor is also required, as we have already shown to be the case in Baptism. For if they who enter the fencing lists have need for someone whose skill and counsel may teach them the thrusts and passes by which to overcome their adversaries, while remaining safe themselves; how much more will the faithful require a leader and monitor, when, sheathed, as it were, in the stoutest armor by this Sacrament of Confirmation, they engage in the spiritual conflict, in which eternal salvation is the proposed reward. With good reason, therefore, are sponsors employed in the administration of this Sacrament also; and the same spiritual affinity is contracted in Confirmation, which, as we have already shown, is contracted by sponsors in Baptism, so as to impede the lawful marriage of the parties.

Are Non-Catholic Confirmations Valid?

Unlike the Sacrament of Baptism, which does not require a validly ordained minister, the Sacrament of Confirmation requires a bishop to consecrate the sacred chrism as well as a bishop or at least a priest to administer the chrism with the proper words. Non-Catholic denominations like Lutherans and Anglicans which claim to administer the Sacrament of Confirmation, however, do not actually confer the Sacrament since Protestants do not possess a valid priesthood. As a result, only Catholic or Eastern Orthodox Confirmations are valid. Protestants who convert to the Catholic Faith after having received "Confirmation" in a Protestant denomination, even if their Baptism is determined to have been valid, still need to receive the actual Sacrament of Confirmation.

Those who do receive the Sacrament of Confirmation validly receive an indelible mark, called a character, on their souls. Turning again to the Roman Catechism, we read: "Confirmation has also the effect of impressing a character. Hence, as we before said of Baptism, and as will be more fully explained in its proper place with regard to the Sacrament of Orders also, it can on no account ever be repeated."

Like Baptism and Holy Orders, Confirmation may never be repeated once validly conferred, nor can it ever be "undone" due to the permanence of the sacramental character. Even a soul in hell would retain the mark of

---

[71] Baltimore Catechism No. 3, Q. 697

Confirmation on his soul, all to his greater suffering for having squandered the grace of God and losing forever the crown of eternal life (cf. I Cor. ix. 24-27).

When legitimate doubt exists regarding whether one has received a valid Confirmation, a person may receive the Sacrament of Confirmation conditionally (the same as with Baptism). Conditional Confirmations, when done, are administered out of an abundance of caution, often if there is uncertainty regarding the validity of the bishop who confirmed the person in question or if all sacramental records are lost and the recipient is uncertain if they received Confirmation. Converts from some Old Roman Catholic or Orthodox Churches often seek conditional Confirmation for such reasons.

Conclusion

The Roman Catechism concludes its explanation of the Sacrament of Confirmation with an admonition which is worth meditating upon:

> Let this, then, serve as a summary of those things which pastors are to expound touching the Sacrament of chrism. The exposition, however, should not be given so much in empty words and cold language, as in the burning accents of pious and glowing zeal, so as to seem to imprint them on the souls and inmost thoughts of the faithful.

We should reflect on our own Confirmation, if we have received this admirable Sacrament, and ask ourselves if we are doing enough to serve as a soldier for Christ. Are we a model example of a traditional Catholic or are we a cause of scandal that the enemies of Holy Mother Church could set forth as an example of Catholic hypocrisy? Likewise, are we doing enough to encourage our family members who have neglected Confirmation to start studying for this Sacrament and receive it

XVI

On the Most Holy Sacrament of the Altar

After explaining the Church's infallible teachings on the Sacraments of Baptism and Confirmation, the Roman Catechism turns to the greatest of all the Sacraments, the Most Holy Eucharist. Known as the Sacrament of the Altar, the Holy Eucharist, or Holy Communion, this Sacrament is none other than God Himself – the most precious Body, Blood, Soul, and Divinity of the Incarnate Word, Our Lord Jesus Christ. In its opening paragraph on the Most Holy Eucharist, the Catechism affirms:

> As of all the sacred mysteries bequeathed to us by our Lord and Savior as most infallible instruments of divine grace, there is none comparable to the most holy Sacrament of the Eucharist; so, for no crime is there a heavier punishment to be feared from God than for the unholy or irreligious use by the faithful of that which is full of holiness, or rather which contains the very Author and Source of holiness.

Likewise, the Catechism of St. Pius X expresses this sublime reality: "The Eucharist is a sacrament in which, by the marvelous conversion of the whole substance of bread into the Body of Jesus Christ, and that of wine into His precious Blood, is contained truly, really, and substantially, the Body, the Blood, the Soul and Divinity of the same Lord Jesus Christ, under the appearance of bread and wine as our spiritual food."[72] Plainly stated, the Most Holy Eucharist is the Body, Blood, Soul, and Divinity of Jesus Christ under the mere appearance of bread and wine.

The Eucharist is worthy, says the Roman Catechism, of "divine honors" because this Sacrament when confected at Mass is God Himself. Hence, the Council of Trent condemns anyone who asserts that "Christ, the only-begotten Son of God, is not to be adored in the holy sacrament of the Eucharist with the worship of *latria*, including external worship...."

---

[72] Fr. Marshall Roberts, Catechism of St. Pius X (St. Michael's Press, 2010), p. 88.

The Institution of the Eucharist

Our Redeemer instituted the Sacrament of His Body and Blood on the night before His Passion and death. That the Eucharist was instituted by Jesus Christ Himself at the Last Supper is affirmed by the Roman Catechism:

> That its institution was as follows, is clearly inferred from the Evangelist. Our Lord, *having loved His own, loved them to the end* [Jn. xiii. 1]. As a divine and admirable pledge of this love, knowing that the hour had now come that He should pass from the world to the Father, that He might not ever at any period be absent from His own, He accomplished with inexplicable wisdom that which surpasses all the order and condition of nature. For having kept the supper of the Paschal lamb with His disciples, that the figure might yield to the reality, the shadow to the substance, *He took bread, and giving thanks unto God, He blessed, and brake, and gave to the disciples, and said: 'Take ye and eat, this is My Body which shall be delivered for you; this do for a commemoration of Me.' In like manner also, He took the chalice after He had supped, saying: 'This chalice is the new testament in My blood; this do, as often as you shall drink it, in commemoration of Me.'* [Mt. xxvi. 26; Mk. xiv. 22; Lk. xxii. 19; I Cor. xi. 24].

Two-Fold Sacramental Matter

Before describing the matter and form for this most august Sacrament, the Roman Catechism insightfully explains the uniqueness of this Sacrament as contrasted with the Sacraments studied thus far:

> How much this Sacrament differs from all the others is easily inferred. For all the other Sacraments are completed by the use of the material, that is, while they are being administered to someone. Thus, Baptism attains the nature of a Sacrament when the individual is actually being washed in the water. For the perfecting of the Eucharist on the other hand, the consecration of the material itself suffices, since neither species ceases to be a Sacrament, though kept in the pyx.
>
> Again, in perfecting the other Sacraments there is no change of the matter and element into another nature. The water of Baptism, or the oil of Confirmation, when

> those Sacraments are being administered, do not lose
> their former nature of water and oil; but in the Eucharist,
> that which was bread and wine before consecration, after
> consecration is truly the substance of the Body and
> Blood of the Lord.

Thus, the Holy Eucharist is affirmed as a unique Sacrament instituted by
Our Lord both by the writings of the early Church as well as by the very
definition of a Sacrament. On this latter point (definition of a Sacrament),
the Catechism expounds: "For there are in It signs that are external and
subject to the senses. In the next place, It signifies and produces grace.
Moreover, neither the Evangelists nor the Apostle leave room for doubt
regarding Its institution by Christ. Since all these things concur to establish
the fact of the Sacrament, there is obviously no need of any other
argument."

The sacramental matter for the Holy Eucharist is two-fold: wheat bread and
wine. While many other catechisms fail to explain why the Holy Eucharist
must be confected from wheat bread only, the Roman Catechism addresses
this by the testimony of Sacred Scripture:

> There are, however, various sorts of bread, either
> because they consist of different materials, such as
> wheat, barley, pulse and other products of the earth; or
> because they possess different qualities, some being
> leavened, others altogether without leaven. It is to be
> observed that, with regard to the former kinds, the words
> of the Savior show that the bread should be wheaten; for,
> according to common usage, when we simply say bread,
> we are sufficiently understood to mean wheaten bread.
> This is also declared by a figure in the Old Testament,
> because the Lord commanded that the loaves of
> proposition, which signified this Sacrament, should be
> made of fine flour.

An interesting question arises on whether the Sacrament must be confected
from unleavened or if leavened wheat bread is equally valid. On this point,
the Roman Catechism makes clear that the Eucharist "was consecrated and
instituted by Him on the first day of unleavened bread, on which it was not
lawful for the Jews to have anything leavened in their house," but the text
continues, "This quality of the bread, however, is not to be deemed so
essential that, if it be wanting, the Sacrament cannot exist." Thus, we see a
difference between the Church of Rome and the Eastern Churches, since
the Latin Rite uses unleavened bread while the Eastern Rites use leavened
bread. Despite such a difference, all else being equal, the matter is valid in

both instances, although it would be illicit (but not invalid) for a Roman Catholic priest to consecrate leavened bread at Mass.

Along with wheaten bread, wine constitutes the other required component for the matter of the Sacrament. The wine is not optional and may not be replaced by any other liquid, for any reason, in virtue of Our Lord's own command:

> That in the institution of this Sacrament our Lord and Savior made use of wine has been at all times the doctrine of the Catholic Church, for He Himself said: *I will not drink from henceforth of this fruit of the vine until that day* [Mt. xxvi. 29; Mk. xiv. 25]. On this passage Chrysostom observes: *He says, 'Of the fruit of the vine,' which certainly produced wine not water*; as if he had it in view, even at so early a period, to uproot the heresy which asserted that in these mysteries water alone is to be used.

During Mass, the priest will add a drop of water into the chalice along with the wine. Why? The Catechism explains: "First, because Christ the Lord did so, as is proved by the authority of Councils and the testimony of St. Cyprian; next, because by this mixture is renewed the recollection of the blood and water that issued from His side." But the Catechism appropriately clarifies: "But although there are reasons so grave for mingling water with the wine that it cannot be omitted without incurring the guilt of mortal sin, yet its omission does not render the Sacrament null."

Therefore, wine along with wheaten bread constitutes the matter for the Sacrament, as summarized by the Roman Catechism: "These, then, are the only two elements of this Sacrament; and with reason has it been enacted by many decrees that, although there have been those who were not afraid to do so, it is unlawful to offer anything but bread and wine." The gifts of bread and wine are presented to Almighty God during the offertory of the Mass and from that moment forward may only be offered in divine worship. They may not be used for any other purpose aside from the Holy Sacrifice of the Mass.

Words of Consecration

Concerning the form of this Sacrament – that is, the words by which the matter (bread and wine) is changed into the Body and Blood of Christ – *Hoc est enim Corpus Meum* ("For this is My Body") are the exact words required for the consecration of the bread into our Blessed Lord. The words

"Take and eat" immediately before "This is My Body" should "by all means…be pronounced by the priest…. But they are not necessary to the validity of the Sacrament." The Roman Catechism further explains:

> We are then taught by the holy Evangelists, Matthew and Luke, and also by the Apostle, that the form consists of these words: *This is My Body*; for it is written: Whilst they were at supper, Jesus took bread, and blessed it, and brake, and gave to His disciples, and said: *Take and eat, This is My Body*.

On the consecration of the wine, the Catechism similarly explains:

> We are then firmly to believe that [the form for the wine] consists in the following words: *This is the chalice of My Blood, of the new and eternal testament, the mystery of faith, which shall be shed for you and for many, to the remission of sins*. Of these words the greater part are taken from Scripture; but some have been preserved in the Church from Apostolic tradition.

The double consecration of both the bread and wine must occur at Mass. Should a priest die after the Consecration of the bread but before the Consecration of the wine, a different priest must, as soon as possible, resume the Holy Sacrifice. Canon 927 in the Code of Canon Law promulgated in 1983 affirms that it is absolutely forbidden, even in cases of necessity, for a priest to consecrate only one of the two necessary species. The Sacrifice, once it has begun, must be accomplished.

Transubstantiation

The changing of the bread and wine into the Body, Blood, Soul, and Divinity of Our Lord Jesus Christ is known as *transubstantiation*. The substance of bread and the substance of wine give way to the substance of Our Lord Himself when the words of consecration are said.

At the moment of this divine act, accomplished through the words of a validly ordained bishop or priest, each particle of bread and each particle of wine become the entire Christ. The former wine is not only the Blood of Christ, and likewise, the former bread is not only the Body of the Lord. Each particle of the Eucharist is the fullness of the God-Man. On this point, the Baltimore Catechism teaches:

> Jesus Christ is whole and entire both under the form of bread and under the form of wine. After the substance of

the bread and wine had been changed into the substance of the Body and Blood of our Lord there remained only the appearances of bread and wine. By the appearances of bread and wine I mean the figure, the color, the taste, and whatever appears to the senses. This change of the bread and wine into the Body and Blood of our Lord is called Transubstantiation.[73]

For this reason, the Fathers of the Council of Trent solemnly decreed: "If anyone denies that in the venerable sacrament of the Eucharist the whole Christ is contained under each species and under each part of either species when separated, let him be anathema."

Likewise, in this Sacrament the fullness of Christ, including His Divinity, is present. Jesus Christ, the God-Man, can never be separated from His Divinity. Wherever His humanity is present, as it is under the appearances of bread and wine in the Holy Eucharist, there also is His Divinity. Consequently, the Roman Catechism warns that "it would be impious to suppose that the Body of Christ, which is contained in the Sacrament, is separated from His Divinity." As a result, in Holy Communion, when we receive the Sacred Host that was consecrated on the altar, we receive not only the sacred humanity of our Redeemer but also His Soul and His Divinity. *We receive God.*

The Lord plainly said to His disciples: *Take ye and eat. This is My Body* (Mt. xxvi. 26). St. Cyril of Jerusalem succinctly remarks on these words: "Since Christ Himself has said, 'This is My Body,' who shall dare to doubt that It is His Body?" St. Augustine likewise declares: "Christ held Himself in His hands when He gave His Body to His disciples, saying: 'This is My Body.' No one partakes of this Flesh before he has adored It."

The Accidents

After the consecration, the only elements of bread and wine remaining are the accidents. While the substance of what used to be bread and wine cease to exist, we refer to the species of bread or the species of wine remaining. On the term "species", Fr. John Hardon's *Modern Catholic Dictionary* defines "species" as, "Appearances, especially those of bread and wine, after the Eucharistic consecration." Fr. Hardon continues, "The term 'species' is used by the Council of Trent to identify the accidents, i.e., the size, weight, color, resistance, taste, and odor of bread, which remain exactly the same after transubstantiation. They are not mere appearances as though these physical properties were unreal. But they are appearances

---

[73] Baltimore Catechism No. 3, Q. 243 – 246

because after the consecration they lack any substance that underlies them or in which they inhere."

To summarize, when a validly ordained bishop or priest speaks the proper words of consecration and uses proper matter, transubstantiation occurs. Bread and wine become our Blessed Lord and remain as such as long as the species (appearances) of bread and wine remain. The only properties of bread and wine remaining are the accidental properties perceivable by our senses. Thus, when we affirm our belief in the Real Presence of Christ in the Eucharist, we truly affirm in the words of the Roman Catechism: "that the true Body of Christ the Lord, the same that was born of the Virgin, and is now seated at the right hand of the Father in heaven, is contained in this Sacrament."

Consubstantiation Condemned

Transubstantiation is not to be confused with the Lutheran teaching of consubstantiation, a belief that the bread and wine continue to exist alongside the Lord's Body and Blood. The Roman Catechism states, "none of the substance of the bread and wine remains in the Sacrament."

Lutherans and Anglicans, unlike most other Protestant denominations, generally believe in the presence of Christ in the Sacrament of the Altar. Other sects tend to view the Eucharist as only a symbol and neither a Sacrament nor Christ's Body and Blood, directly contrary to two millennia of doctrine. However, neither Lutherans nor Anglicans have valid Holy Orders and thus do not have valid priests. As a result, they cannot confect the Holy Eucharist, so the "sacrament" they propose to their followers does not actually contain Christ's presence. It remains only bread and wine. However, as to their theology, they believe it to be both Christ's Presence in addition to remaining bread and wine. Such a view is called consubstantiation, which is in direct contradiction to transubstantiation. The Council of Trent addressed and condemned the error of consubstantiation as follows:

> If anyone says that in the most holy sacrament of the Eucharist the substance of bread and wine remains together with the Body and Blood of our Lord Jesus Christ and denies that wonderful and unique change of the whole substance of the bread into His Body and of the whole substance of the wine into His Blood while only the species of bread and wine remain, a change which the Catholic Church very fittingly calls transubstantiation, let him be anathema.

The Eucharist is a Sacrifice

After the Consecration, the priest, who acts in *persona Christi*, offers to the Eternal Father the Sacrifice of Jesus Christ. During the Canon of the Mass, Jesus Christ, acting through His priest, offers Himself present on the altar to His Father in Heaven. The Mass is therefore the very same Sacrifice of Christ on the Cross which is made present again on the altar. Our Lord is not sacrificed again before us; rather, we are mystically present before the one and selfsame Sacrifice. This marvelous reality is beautifully expressed in the words of the Roman Catechism:

> We therefore confess that the Sacrifice of the Mass is and ought to be considered one and the same Sacrifice as that of the cross, for the victim is one and the same, namely, Christ our Lord, who offered Himself, once only, a bloody Sacrifice on the altar of the cross. The bloody and unbloody Victim are not two, but one victim only, whose Sacrifice is daily renewed in the Eucharist...

> The priest is also one and the same, Christ the Lord; for the ministers who offer Sacrifice, consecrate the holy mysteries, not in their own person, but in that of Christ, as the words of consecration itself show, for the priest does not say: *This is the Body of Christ*, but, *This is My Body*; and thus, acting in the Person of Christ the Lord [*in persona Christi*], he changes the substance of the bread and wine into the true substance of His Body and Blood.

Apostolic Origin of the Eucharistic Fast

Transitioning to the application of these truths in our own lives, the Roman Catechism reminds us of the necessity of observing the Eucharistic Fast before approaching the Most Holy Sacrament.

On the requirement to fast before receiving Holy Communion, the Roman Catechism is unambiguous: "It is not, however, lawful to consecrate or partake of the Eucharist after eating or drinking, because, according to a custom wisely introduced by the Apostles, as ancient writers have recorded, and which has ever been retained and preserved, Communion is received only by persons who are fasting."

St. Paul admonished those who approach Holy Communion with the purpose of merely eating food with condemnation: *For everyone taketh before his own supper to eat. And one indeed is hungry, and another is drunk. What, have you not houses to eat and to drink in? Or despise ye the Church of God; and put them to shame that have not? What shall I say to you? Do I praise you? In this I praise you not* (I Cor. xi. 21-22). Likewise, in the Acts of the Apostles, St. Luke mentions a connection between those present at the liturgy, *ministering to the Lord*, and fasting (cf. Acts xiii. 2).

Although the specifics have changed over time, fasting before receiving Our Lord in Holy Communion is certainly of apostolic origin. St. Hippolytus (c. 170–235 A.D.) in his *Apostolic Tradition* writes, "The faithful shall be careful to partake of the Eucharist before eating anything else." At the Synod of Hippo in 393, the Eucharistic fast was codified in Canon 29, and again a few years later it was likewise codified at the Synod of Carthage in Canon 28.

St. Augustine bears witness to the universality of the fast before Holy Communion in his writings: "Must we therefore censure the universal Church because the sacrament is everywhere partaken of by persons fasting? Nay, verily, for from that time it pleased the Holy Spirit to appoint, for the honour of so great a sacrament, that the Body of the Lord should take the precedence of all other food entering the mouth of a Christian; and it is for this reason that the custom referred to is universally observed."[74]

While the discipline of the Eucharistic fast was changed by Pope Pius XII in 1953 and 1957, and by Pope Paul VI in 1964 and 1973, the requirement of fasting for some time before receiving the Lord's Body and Blood remains.[75] The words which Padre Pio once uttered could apply equal to us: "My children, we can never prepare ourselves too much for Holy Communion." No amount of preparation is too onerous when we consider that God the Son Incarnate allows us to eat His very Flesh and consume His Most Precious Blood.

Conclusion

Concluding its lengthy explanation of the holiest of the Sacraments, the Roman Catechism encourages us to reflect on the Mass and the dispositions we should bring before the altar:

---

[74] William John Sparrow-Simpson, *The Works of Saint Augustine* (The MacMillan Company, 1919), 286.

[75] The current discipline requires communicants "to abstain for at least one hour before holy communion from any food and drink, except for only water and medicine" (1983 Code of Canon Law, Can. 919 §1). For many centuries, however, the Church required communicants to abstain from all food and drink "at least from the preceding midnight until the moment of Communion" (Roman Catechism).

...the sacred and holy Sacrifice of the Mass is not a Sacrifice of praise and thanksgiving only, or a mere commemoration of the Sacrifice performed on the cross, but also truly a propitiatory Sacrifice, by which God is appeased and rendered propitious to us. If, therefore, with a pure heart, a lively faith, and affected with an inward sorrow for our transgressions, we immolate and offer this most holy victim, we shall, without doubt, obtain mercy from the Lord, and grace in time of need; for so delighted is the Lord with the odor of this victim that, bestowing on us the gift of grace and repentance, He pardons our sins.

St. Ignatius of Antioch (died ca. 110 A.D.) wrote in his Epistle to the Smyrnaeans that "the Eucharist is the Flesh of our Savior Jesus Christ, Flesh which suffered for our sins and which the Father, in His goodness, raised up again." Let us recall, then, that we should visit Our Lord in the tabernacle and pray before His living Flesh with the words, "O Sacrament most holy, O Sacrament divine, all praise and all thanksgiving be every moment thine."

XVII

On the Sacrament of Penance

After having carefully considering each of the three Sacraments of Initiation (Baptism, Confirmation, and the Holy Eucharist), the Roman Catechism next turns its attention to the Sacrament of Penance. In contrast to Baptism and Confirmation, whose valid reception may occur only once in a lifetime, the Sacrament of Confession may be frequented often. Like the Most Blessed Sacrament of the Altar, the Sacrament of Penance is one which Catholics will most often experience. Yet, familiarity often breeds forgetfulness. Even lifelong Catholics can benefit from carefully reflecting upon the wisdom of St. Charles Borromeo and the writers of the Roman Catechism in its chapter on this remarkable sacrament.

Importance of the Sacrament

In its introductory remarks on the subject, the Roman Catechism asserts the paramount importance of proper instruction on the Sacrament of Penance (also known as Confession), emphasizing the necessity of this sacrament for those who sin after Baptism:

> If, therefore, the diligence of pastors should be proportioned to the weight and importance of the subject, we must admit that in expounding this Sacrament they can never be sufficiently diligent. Nay, it should be explained with more care than Baptism. Baptism is administered but once and cannot be repeated; Penance may be administered and becomes necessary, as often as we may have sinned after Baptism. Hence the Council of Trent declares: *For those who fall into sin after Baptism the Sacrament of Penance is as necessary to salvation as is Baptism for those who have not been already baptized.* The saying of St. Jerome that Penance is a second plank, is universally known and highly commended by all subsequent writers on sacred things. As he who suffers shipwreck has no hope of safety, unless, perchance, he seize on some plank from the wreck, so he that suffers the shipwreck of baptismal innocence, unless he cling to

the saving plank of Penance, has doubtless lost all hope
of salvation.

This admonition is aimed not only at priests (to encourage them to preach
often on the subject) but also at the laity, that they may rediscover the
importance of Confession for their own spiritual lives:

> These instructions are intended not only for the benefit of pastors,
> but also for that of the faithful at large, to awaken attention, lest
> they be found culpably negligent in a matter so very important.
> Impressed with a just sense of the frailty of human nature, their
> first and most earnest desire should be to advance with the divine
> assistance in the ways of God, without sin or failing. But should
> they at any time prove so unfortunate as to fall, then, looking at
> the infinite goodness of God, who like the good shepherd binds
> up and heals the wounds of His sheep, they should not postpone
> recourse to the most saving remedy of Penance.

What is the Sacrament of Penance?

Penance is truly and properly a sacrament instituted by Our Lord for the
forgiveness of sins after Baptism:

> As Baptism is a Sacrament because it blots out all sins,
> and especially original sin, so for the same reason
> Penance, which takes away all the sins of thought and
> deed committed after Baptism, must be regarded as a true
> Sacrament in the proper sense of the word.

> Moreover – and this is the principal reason – since what
> is exteriorly done, both by priest and penitent, signifies
> the inward effects that take place in the soul, who will
> venture to deny that Penance is invested with the nature
> of a proper and true Sacrament? For a Sacrament is a sign
> of a sacred thing. Now the sinner who repents plainly
> expresses by his words and actions that he has turned his
> heart from sin; while from the words and actions of the
> priest we easily recognize the mercy of God exercised in
> the remission of sins.

How May Mortal Sins Be Forgiven?

The Sacrament of Penance is the means our Divine Lord has established so
that we may receive forgiveness for our sins. Ordinarily, this means that

only in Confession can a soul in the state of mortal sin be restored to the life of grace and friendship with God.

However, the Church also teaches that there is one additional means to receive forgiveness of mortal sins in cases of necessity (when sacramental confession is not possible): making a perfect act of contrition. How does an act of perfect contrition work in the soul? The Catechism of St. Pius X explains: "Perfect sorrow or contrition produces this effect, because it proceeds from charity which cannot exist in the soul together with sin."[76]

Perfect vs. Imperfect Contrition

On the subject of contrition, the Catholic Encyclopedia states: "Catholic teaching distinguishes a twofold hatred of sin; one, perfect contrition, rises from the love of God Who has been grievously offended; the other, imperfect contrition, arises principally from some other motives, such as loss of heaven, fear of hell, the heinousness of sin, etc. (Council of Trent, Sess. XIV, ch. Iv, *de Contritione*)."[77]

While those who are dying without Confession and with mortal sin on their souls will need to make such a perfect act of contrition in order to avoid hell, we too can seek to make perfect acts of contrition whenever we sin.

However, as an important clarification, even those who make a perfect act of contrition must confess their sins in the Confessional at the next available opportunity as the Catechism of St. Pius X clarifies: "Perfect sorrow does not obtain us pardon of our sins independently of confession, because it always includes the intention to confess them."[78]

Why did Jesus Institute the Sacrament of Penance?

If it is possible to receive forgiveness outside of the Sacrament of Confession, why did Our Lord institute a special sacrament for the purpose of forgiving post-baptismal sins? He did so (shortly before His Ascension into Heaven) for two primary reasons. The Roman Catechism explains:

> One of His reasons certainly was to leave us no room for
> doubt regarding the remission of sin which was promised
> by God when He said: *If the wicked do penance, etc.* For
> each one has good reason to distrust the accuracy of his

---

[76] Catechism of St. Pius X, n. 41.
[77] Edward Hanna, "Contrition," The Catholic Encyclopedia. Vol. 4. (New York: Robert Appleton Company, 1908).
[78] Catechism of St. Pius X, n. 40.

own judgment on his own actions, and hence we could not but be very much in doubt regarding the truth of our internal penance. It was to destroy this, our uneasiness, that our Lord instituted the Sacrament of Penance, by means of which we are assured that our sins are pardoned by the absolution of the priest; and also to tranquilize our conscience by means of the trust we rightly repose in the virtue of the Sacraments. The words of the priest sacramentally and lawfully absolving us from our sins are to be accepted in the same sense as the words of Christ our Lord when He said to the paralytic: *Son, be of good heart: thy sins are forgiven thee.*

While we may receive forgiveness through a perfect act of contrition, we do not know the exact state of our souls and thus cannot determine if our act of contrition was perfect or imperfect. As a result, only in the Sacrament of Confession can we receive assurance of our pardon, assuming valid form and matter. Thus, there is another reason why Our Lord chose to institute this sacrament:

In the second place, no one can obtain salvation unless through Christ and the merits of His Passion. Hence it was becoming in itself, and highly advantageous to us, that a Sacrament should be instituted through the force and efficacy of which the Blood of Christ flows into our souls, washes away all the sins committed after Baptism, and thus leads us to recognize that it is to our Savior alone we owe the blessing of reconciliation.

When Did Our Lord Institute the Sacrament?

In the three years that the disciples journeyed with Jesus in His public life, He taught them the Faith. He gave His Apostles *power and authority* (Lk. ix. 1), and later, after His Resurrection, the unique power to forgive sins:

He said therefore to them again: Peace be to you. As the Father hath sent me, I also send you. When He had said this, He breathed on them; and He said to them: Receive ye the Holy Ghost. Whose sins you shall forgive, they are forgiven them; and whose sins you shall retain, they are retained (Jn. xx. 21-23).

With these words, Our Lord Jesus Christ instituted the Sacrament of Penance. Pope St. Pius X in *Lamentabili Sane* condemned those who deny that our Lord instituted the Sacrament of Penance with these words:

Therefore, after a very diligent investigation and consultation with the Reverend Consultors, the Most Eminent and Reverend Lord Cardinals, the General Inquisitors in matters of faith and morals have judged the following propositions to be condemned and proscribed... The words of the Lord, 'Receive the Holy Spirit...etc. (Jn. xx. 22-23), in no way refer to the Sacrament of Penance, in spite of what it pleased the Fathers of Trent to say."[79]

In the Holy Scriptures, the only other reference to God breathing upon someone is recorded in Genesis II. 7, when God breathed upon Adam and gave him life. In John XX. 21-23 we understand that God is truly giving the eleven Apostles this profound ability to forgive sins, just as He truly gave Adam the unique gift of life.

Some people may object to the Sacrament of Confession by citing I John I. 9, which states, *If we confess our sins, He is faithful and just, to forgive us our sins, and to cleanse us from all iniquity.* This passage is referring to the confession of sins and not the way it is achieved. It can only be inferred that St. John would refer to the confession of sins to the Apostles, of which he wrote in the 20th chapter of his Gospel (see above).

Sacramental Matter

As with all the sacraments, proper matter and form are required for the validity of Confession. The "matter" for Confession is unique, however, in that it is supplied by the penitent, while the matter for each of the Sacraments of Initiation consists of physical material supplied by the priest (e.g. water, chrism, bread and wine). The Roman Catechism explains:

> There is nothing that should be better known to the faithful than the matter of this Sacrament; hence they should be taught that Penance differs from the other Sacraments in this that while the matter of the other Sacraments is something, whether natural or artificial, the matter, as it were, of the Sacrament of Penance is the acts of the penitent – namely, contrition, confession and satisfaction – as has been declared by the Council of Trent.

---

[79] Pope St. Pius X, Lamentabili Sane #47
(https://www.papalencyclicals.net/pius10/p10lamen.htm).

Mortal sins must be confessed in kind, number, and any circumstances that change the gravity or nature of the sin. As the Code of Canon Law promulgated in 1983 states:

> A member of the Christian faithful is obliged to confess in kind and number all grave sins committed after baptism and not yet remitted directly through the keys of the Church nor acknowledged in individual confession, of which the person has knowledge after diligent examination of conscience.

Deliberating concealing a known mortal sin in Confession is a sacrilege, as is downplaying the number of times a particular mortal sin was committed when the penitent knows he committed the sin more often. Such a confession, explains the Baltimore Catechism, is invalid:

> It is a grievous offense willfully to conceal a mortal sin in Confession, because we thereby tell a lie to the Holy Ghost and make our Confession worthless. He who has willfully concealed a mortal sin in Confession must not only confess it but must also repeat all the sins he has committed since his last worthy Confession.[80]

Returning to the proper matter of the sacrament, the Roman Catechism explains the importance of contrition:

> By the Fathers of the Council of Trent, contrition is defined: A sorrow and detestation for sin committed, with a purpose of sinning no more and a little further on the Council, speaking of the motion of the will to contrition, adds: *If joined with a confidence in the mercy of God and an earnest desire of performing whatever is necessary to the proper reception of the Sacrament, it thus prepares us for the remission of sin.*

Contrition is the most difficult of the conditions required since the verbal confession of all sins without contrition would be invalid. The Roman Catechism explains that contrition must be supreme, universal, and intense. Above all, contrition is a detestation of sin as an offense against the almighty and all-loving God Who made us, redeemed us, and never ceases watching us.

---

[80] Baltimore Catechism No. 2, Q. 216-217.

To be clear, though, the Sacrament of Confession does not require the actual shedding of tears or perfect contrition; imperfect contrition (fear of punishment) is valid matter for the sacrament: "But although contrition is defined as sorrow, the faithful are not thence to conclude that this sorrow consists in sensible feeling; for contrition is an act of the will...."

Lastly, the Roman Catechism addresses the importance of the firm purpose of amendment, which is also required for validity of the sacrament:

> That a sorrow for sin and a firm purpose of avoiding sin for the future are two conditions indispensable to contrition nature and reason clearly show. He who would be reconciled to a friend whom he has wronged must regret to have injured and offended him, and his future conduct must be such as to avoid offending in anything against friendship.

> ... Likewise if, by word or deed he has injured his neighbor's honor or reputation, he is under an obligation of repairing the injury by procuring him some advantage or rendering him some service. Well known to all is the maxim of St. Augustine: *The sin is not forgiven unless what has been taken away is restored.*

Furthermore, the amendment of life must entail forgiving others who trespass against us: "Again, not less necessary for contrition than the other chief conditions is a care that it be accompanied by entire forgiveness of the injuries which we may have received from others. This our Lord and Savior admonishes when He declares: *If you will forgive men their offences, your heavenly Father will forgive you also your offences, but if you will not forgive men, neither will your Father forgive you your offences.*"

In sum, true sorrow for sin along with a desire to amend one's life, confession in number and kind (for all mortal sins – not necessary for venial), and the intention to perform the penance imposed by the priest are all required for valid matter.

Sacramental Form

In addition to its lengthy consideration of the matter, the Roman Catechism also addresses the proper form of the Sacrament of Penance:

> Pastors should not neglect to explain the form of the Sacrament of Penance. A knowledge of it will excite the

faithful to receive the grace of this Sacrament with the greatest possible devotion. Now the form is: *I absolve thee*, as may be inferred not only from the words, *whatsoever you shall bind upon earth shall be bound also in heaven*, but also from the teaching of Christ our Lord, handed down to us by the Apostles.

The form of the sacrament is expressed in the words of absolution. The traditional Roman absolution formula (in use prior to Vatican II) states: "May Our Lord Jesus Christ absolve you, and I, by His authority, absolve you from every bond of excommunication and interdict as far as I can and you may need. I absolve you from your sins in the name of the Father, and of the Son, and of the Holy Ghost. Amen."

As with the other sacraments, the words for Confession were changed following the Second Vatican Council (1962-1965). Thus, the current absolution formula (1970) states: "God, the Father of mercies, through the death and resurrection of His Son has reconciled the world to Himself and sent the Holy Spirit among us for the forgiveness of sins; through the ministry of the Church may God give you pardon and peace, and I absolve you from your sins in the Name of the Father, and of the Son, and of the Holy Spirit."

Note, however, that both forms contain the essential words, "I absolve you" (*ego te absolvo* in Latin).

It is also important to recall that the Sacrament of Confession, like all the sacraments, must be received in person from a priest and is not validly conferred over the telephone or video. The Pontifical Council on Social Communications on the Church and the Internet published a document in 2002 reiterating that the sacraments may not be validly received through electronic communication:

> Virtual reality is no substitute for the Real Presence of Christ in the Eucharist, the sacramental reality of the other sacraments, and shared worship in a flesh-and-blood human community. There are no sacraments on the Internet; and even the religious experiences possible there by the grace of God are insufficient apart from real-world interaction with other persons of faith.[81]

---

[81] Pontifical Council on Social Communications on the Church, "The Church and the Internet," 2002.

The Minister of Confession

Beyond valid form and matter, the Sacrament of Confession requires a validly ordained priest who possesses the faculties to forgive sins in the Name of Christ Himself:

> That the minister of the Sacrament of Penance must be a priest possessing ordinary or delegated jurisdiction the laws of the Church sufficiently declare. Whoever discharges this sacred function must be invested not only with the power of orders, but also with that of jurisdiction. Of this ministry we have an illustrious proof in these words of our Lord, recorded by St. John: *Whose sins you shall forgive, they are forgiven them; and whose sins you shall retain, they are retained*, words addressed not to all, but to the Apostles only, to whom, in this function of the ministry, priests succeed.

How do priests obtain these faculties? The 1983 Code of Canon Law explains: "A priest can be given this faculty either by the law itself or by a grant made by the competent authority... In addition to the Roman Pontiff, cardinals have the faculty of hearing the confessions of the Christian faithful everywhere in the world by the law itself. Bishops likewise have this faculty and use it licitly everywhere unless the diocesan bishop has denied it in a particular case."

Where may an ordinary priest hear confessions? The Code further states: "Those who possess the faculty of hearing confessions habitually whether by virtue of office or by virtue of the grant of an ordinary of the place of incardination or of the place in which they have a domicile can exercise that faculty everywhere unless the local ordinary has denied it in a particular case."

How Often Should We Go to Confession?

The third precept of the Church requires all Catholics who have made their First Confession to confess their sins in the Sacrament of Penance at least once a year. While we are only required under the penalty of mortal sin to confess our sins sacramentally once a year, we are encouraged to receive the sacrament more often. Frequent Confession restores sanctifying grace in our souls if we were in a state of mortal sin before our Confession, absolves all venial and mortal sins, strengthens our resolve, and helps us grow in virtue. The Roman Catechism reminds the faithful that the Sacrament of Confession is never exhausted:

The faithful should be careful above all to cleanse their consciences from sin by frequent confession. When a person is in mortal sin nothing can be more salutary, so precarious is human life, than to have immediate recourse to confession. But even if we could promise ourselves a long life, yet it would be truly disgraceful that we who are so particular in whatever relates to cleanliness of dress or person, were not at least equally careful in preserving the luster of the soul unsullied from the foul stains of sin.

Typically, Catholics should strive to go to Confession every two to four weeks, though some may need to go more or less often. Those who struggle with mortal sins may need to go more often, whereas those who are prone to scrupulosity (the feeling that everything is a sin) should go less often. Every Catholic should have an honest discussion with their confessor to determine how often they should receive the sacrament.

Conclusion

Without Our Lord's institution of this sacrament, we would be without a sure means of receiving forgiveness after falling into sin after Baptism. The Sacrament of Confession is not only the means for obtaining forgiveness, it is a gift of inexpressible compassion to us. On this point, St. John Chrysostom tells us, "Let no one mourn that he has fallen again and again; for forgiveness has risen from the grave." And all Catholics should encourage others to return to this wellspring of forgiveness if they have fallen away.

XVIII

On the Sacrament of Extreme Unction

In the Traditional Rite of Extreme Unction, before the priest anoints a person's eyes, ears, nose, mouth, hands, and feet, he prays: "In the Name of the Father, and of the Son, and of the Holy Ghost; may any power the devil has over you be destroyed by the laying on of of our hands and by calling on the glorious and blessed Virgin Mary, Mother of God, her illustrious spouse, St. Joseph, and all holy angels, archangels, patriarchs, prophets, apostles, martyrs, confessors, virgins, and all the saints."

This Sacrament, most often the last Sacrament a person receives before death, is intended to bring spiritual and sometimes physical help to a dying person. Yet, it is very often misunderstood. Extreme Unction, "also called by our predecessors in the faith the Sacrament of the anointing of the sick, and also the Sacrament of the dying" (*Roman Catechism*), is a Sacrament which was instituted by Christ Himself and which confers actual graces. It is not a mere blessing, as some have come to erroneously believe; it is a true Sacrament, the same as Baptism, Confirmation, Confession, the Holy Eucharist, etc.

The Importance of the Sacrament

In its introductory remarks on the Sacrament of Extreme Unction, the Roman Catechism highlights its connection with death and its importance for our journey into eternity:

> The Sacrament of Extreme Unction, because inseparably associated with recollection of the day of death, should, it is obvious, form a subject of frequent instruction, not only because it is right to explain the mysteries of salvation, but also because death, the inevitable doom of all men, when recalled to the minds of the faithful, represses depraved passion. Thus shall they be less disturbed by the approach of death, and will pour forth their gratitude in endless praises to God, who has not only opened to us the way to true life in the Sacrament of Baptism, but has also instituted that of Extreme

Unction, to afford us, when departing this mortal life, an easier way to heaven.

Extreme Unction is A Real Sacrament Instituted by Christ

Scripture and Tradition clearly demonstrate that there are seven Sacraments, which are outward signs instituted by Christ to give grace. The Council of Trent unequivocally affirmed that Extreme Unction is one of the seven Sacraments instituted by our Redeemer:

> If anyone says that the sacraments of the New Law were not all instituted by Jesus Christ our Lord; or that they are more or fewer than seven, that is: Baptism, Confirmation, the Eucharist, Penance, Extreme Unction, Order, and Matrimony; or that any one of these seven is not truly and properly a sacrament, let him be anathema.

The Roman Catechism likewise asserts that the Sacrament of Extreme Unction is a true Sacrament instituted by Our Lord with a firm basis in both Sacred Tradition and Sacred Scripture:

> That Extreme Unction is strictly speaking a Sacrament, is first to be explained; and this the words of St. James the Apostle, promulgating the law of this Sacrament, clearly establish. *Is any man*, he says, *sick amongst you? Let him bring in the priests of the church, and let them pray over him, anointing him with oil in the name of the Lord: and the prayer of faith shall save the sick man; and the Lord shall raise him up; and if he be in sins, they shall be forgiven him.* [Jam. v. 14] When the Apostle says that sins are forgiven, he ascribes to Extreme Unction the nature and efficacy of a Sacrament.
>
> That such has been at all times the doctrine of the Catholic Church on Extreme Unction, many Councils testify, and the Council of Trent denounces anathema against all who presume to teach or think otherwise. Innocent I also recommends this Sacrament with great earnestness to the attention of the faithful.

Similarly, the Baltimore Catechism affirms that Our Lord Jesus Christ instituted the Sacrament of which St. James bears witness, although the account of its institution is not mentioned in the Sacred Scriptures:

Extreme Unction was instituted at the time of the Apostles, for James the Apostle exhorts the sick to receive it. It was instituted by Our Lord Himself – though we do not know at what particular time – for He alone can make a visible act a means of grace, and the Apostles and their successors could never have believed Extreme Unction a Sacrament and used it as such unless they had Our Lord's authority for so doing.[82]

While the institution of Extreme Unction is not explicitly mentioned in Sacred Writ (as are Baptism and Confession, for example), the Roman Catechism mentions that Scripture nevertheless alludes to it:

Our Savior Himself, however, seems to have given some indication of it, when He sent His disciples two and two before Him; for the Evangelist informs us that *going forth, they preached that all should do penance; and they cast out many devils, and anointed with oil many who were sick, and healed them* [Mk. vi. 12-13].

Sacramental Matter

As a Sacrament, Extreme Unction is composed of both matter and form, which are required for its valid administration. Concerning its sacramental matter, the oil of the sick, consecrated by the Bishop at the Chrism Mass (traditionally held on Holy Thursday), constitutes the necessary matter:

Its element, then, or matter, as defined by Councils, particularly by the Council of Trent, consists of oil consecrated by the Bishop. Not any kind of oil extracted from fatty or greasy substances, but olive oil alone (can be the matter of this Sacrament).

Thus, its matter is most significant of what is inwardly effected in the soul by the Sacrament. Oil is very efficacious in soothing bodily pain, and the power of this Sacrament lessens the pain and anguish of the soul. Oil also restores health, brings joy, feeds light, and is very efficacious in refreshing bodily fatigue. All these effects signify what the divine power accomplishes in the sick man through the administration of this Sacrament. So much will suffice in explanation of the matter.

---

[82] Baltimore Catechism No. 3, Q. 961.

Sacramental Form

The form of the Sacrament consists of the words that the priest uses in the anointing. While the priest anoints the eyes, ears, nostrils, tongue, hands and feet of the sick person, he says the prayers prescribed in the Roman Ritual. These words are the form of Extreme Unction:

> The form of the Sacrament is the word and solemn prayer which the priest uses at each anointing: *By this Holy Unction may God pardon thee whatever sins thou hast committed by the evil use of sight, smell or touch.*

> That this is the true form of this Sacrament we learn from these words of St. James: *Let them pray over him ... and the prayer of faith shall save the sick man.* Hence, we can see that the form is to be applied by way of prayer. The Apostle does not say of what particular words that prayer is to consist; but this form has been handed down to us by the faithful tradition of the Fathers, so that all the Churches retain the form observed by the Church of Rome, the mother and mistress of all Churches.

The Roman Catechism likewise explains that even slight wording changes between Catholic rites all constitute valid sacramental form:

> Some, it is true, alter a few words, as when for *God pardon thee*, they say (God) *remit*, or (God) *spare*, and sometimes, *May* (God) *remedy all the evil thou hast committed.* But as there is no change of meaning, it is clear that all religiously observe the same form.

Further, though the Rite of Extreme Unction consists of several prayers said at the various anointings of a sick person's body, the prayers together form but one Sacrament. Each anointing is not a separate administration of the Sacrament, as the Catechism explains:

> Pastors, therefore, should teach that Extreme Unction is a true Sacrament, and that, although administered with many anointings, each given with a peculiar prayer, and under a peculiar form, it constitutes not many, but one Sacrament. It is one, however, not in the sense that it is composed of inseparable parts, but because each of the parts contributes to its perfection, as is the case with every object composed of many parts. As a house which consists of a great variety of parts derives its perfection

> from unity of plan, so is this Sacrament, although composed of many and different things and words, but one sign, and it effects only that one thing of which it is the sign.

And as we observed when treating the Sacraments of Confession and the Most Holy Eucharist, the Sacrament's form must be administered by a validly ordained priest:

> Who the minister of Extreme Unction is we learn from the same Apostle that promulgated the law of the Lord; for he says: *Let him bring in the priests* (presbyters) [Ja. v. 14]. By which name, as the Council of Trent has well explained, he does not mean persons advanced in years, or of chief authority among the people, but priests who have been duly ordained by Bishops with the imposition of hands.

Who May Receive Extreme Unction?

After explaining the matter and form for this Sacrament, the Roman Catechism clarifies: "But although instituted for the use of all, Extreme Unction is not to be administered indiscriminately to all."

For reception of the Sacrament, a person must be a baptized Catholic who has reached the age of reason and is in danger of death from infirmity or old age. Care should be given to ensure that everyone who receives the Sacrament of Extreme Unction has the proper dispositions. Close relatives and the priest should also do their best to help the infirm receive the Sacrament as worthily as possible. The Catechism of the Council of Trent explains that factors which affect a worthy reception of this Sacrament include sorrow for past sins, piety, faith, trust in God, and loving resignation to His holy will.

As stated in the Baltimore Catechism, "Extreme Unction may be given to all Christians dangerously ill, who have ever been capable of committing sin after baptism and who have the right dispositions for the Sacrament. Hence, it is never given to children who have not reached the use of reason, nor to persons who have always been insane."[83]

The Baltimore Catechism enumerates three specific dispositions which must be present by those who receive this Sacrament: a resignation to the will of God in regards to recovery, being in the state of grace or at least

---

[83] Baltimore Catechism No. 3, Q. 959.

contrition for sins committed, and a general desire to receive the Sacrament. As a result of these dispositions, the Sacrament of Extreme Unction is never given to heretics "because they cannot be supposed to have the intention necessary for receiving it, nor the desire to make use of the Sacrament of Penance in putting themselves in a state of grace."[84] Consequently, Protestants may not receive this Sacrament. The rubrics also imply that the Sacrament may only be given to the living, not to those who have already passed on to their particular judgment.

When May We Receive the Sacrament?

Extreme Unction is often as associated with the phrase "Last Rites" because it is given to those who are sick to such a degree that there is a legitimate concern of death:

> In the first place, it is not to be administered to persons in sound health, according to these words of St. James: *Is anyone sick amongst you?* This is also proved by the fact that Extreme Unction was instituted as a remedy not only for the diseases of the soul, but also for those of the body. Now only the sick need a remedy, and therefore this Sacrament is to be administered to those only whose malady is such as to excite apprehensions of approaching death.

The Catechism further clarifies that the danger of death must arise from some cause already present within the body, such as disease. Anticipated external dangers – as in the case of a soldier going into battle, for instance, or a criminal about to be executed, or someone who is scheduled to undergo an elective surgery – are not appropriate occasions for this Sacrament. Only those in danger from sickness and accident may receive the Sacrament:

> Extreme Unction, then, can be administered to no one who is not dangerously sick; not even to those who are in danger of death, as when they undertake a perilous voyage, or enter into battle with the sure prospect of death, or have been condemned to death and are on the way to execution.

Unfortunately, since the close of the Second Vatican Council (1962-1965), the practice has emerged for the elderly who are in good health to regularly receive the Sacrament. Often administered in a communal setting, this practice is a sharp departure from Catholic Tradition. Not only have the prayers radically changed since the Rite was altered in 1972, but also its

---

[84] Ibid., Q. 960.

administration to those not suffering from life-threatening illness stands in contrast to the clear teaching in the Roman Catechism. If the recipient is not in danger of death, no Sacrament is conferred even though the outward rite may be perfectly performed.

While the Sacrament is given to those in danger of death, the family of a sick person should never wait to the last hour to call for a priest. The Baltimore Catechism advises: "We should not wait until we are in extreme danger before we receive Extreme Unction, but if possible, we should receive it whilst we have the use of our senses."[85] And the Roman Catechism echoes these sentiments:

> It is, however, a very grievous sin to defer the Holy Unction until, all hope of recovery being lost, life begins to ebb, and the sick person is fast verging into a state of insensibility. It is obvious that if the Sacrament is administered while consciousness and reason are yet unimpaired, and the mind is capable of eliciting acts of faith and of directing the will to sentiments of piety, a more abundant participation of its graces must be received. Though this heavenly medicine is in itself always salutary, pastors should be careful to apply it when its efficacy can be aided by the piety and devotion of the sick person.

Like the Sacrament of Penance, the Sacrament of Extreme Unction may be repeated throughout a person's life as necessary:

> Here it is to be observed that, during the same illness, and while the danger of dying continues the same, the sick person is to be anointed but once. Should he, however, recover after he has been anointed, he may receive the aid of this Sacrament as often as he shall have relapsed into the same danger of death. This Sacrament, therefore, is evidently to be numbered among those which may be repeated.

What are the Effects of Extreme Unction?

For those who are properly disposed and able to receive Extreme Unction, its effects are three-fold:

---

[85] Baltimore Catechism No. 3, Q. 967.

> "To comfort us in the pains of sickness and to strengthen us against temptations; To remit venial sins and to cleanse our soul from the remains of sin; To restore us to health, when God sees fit."[86]

Clarifying the meaning of the remains of sin, the Baltimore Catechism explains: "By the remains of sin I mean the inclination to evil and the weakness of the will which are the result of our sins, and which remain after our sins have been forgiven."[87]

Extreme Unction, therefore, is chiefly aimed at a sick person's salvation, not their bodily recovery, unless it be God's will that they recover. On this point, the Catechism clarifies that while Extreme Unction may remit venial sins, the purpose of this Sacrament is not to remit mortal sins. Mortal sins are removed by the Sacraments of Baptism and Confession:

> As all care should be taken that nothing impede the grace of the Sacrament, and as nothing is more opposed to it than the consciousness of mortal guilt, the constant practice of the Catholic Church must be observed of administering the Sacrament of Penance and the Eucharist before Extreme Unction. ...

> Pastors, therefore, should teach that by this Sacrament is imparted grace that remits sins, and especially lighter, or as they are commonly called, venial sins; for mortal sins are removed by the Sacrament of Penance. Extreme Unction was not instituted primarily for the remission of grave offences; only Baptism and Penance accomplish this directly.

Conclusion

For those of us who continue to *fight the good fight of faith* (I Tim. vi. 12) as members of the Church Militant on earth, let us make it clear to our family that we wish to receive the traditional form of Extreme Unction should we fall into sudden illness or injury. In a similar vein, every Catholic should clearly stipulate in their wills their desires and ensure that a truly Catholic executor is appointed to administer our estate. And our families should also know that when we draw close to death, they should call the priest and request the Sacrament of Extreme Unction and the Apostolic Pardon to be administered to us sufficiently before we take our leave of

---

[86] Baltimore Catechism No. 3, Q. 969.
[87] Ibid., Q. 973.

this world. Let us invoke St. Joseph, Patron of the dying, to intercede for us with the Lord, that we may be protected from a sudden and unprovided-for death.

XIX

On the Sacrament of Holy Orders

The Importance of the Sacrament

In its opening remarks on the Sacrament of Holy Orders, the Roman Catechism immediately explains its foundational importance in the sacramental economy:

> If one attentively considers the nature and essence of the other Sacraments, it will readily be seen that they all depend on the Sacrament of Orders to such an extent that without it some of them could not be constituted or administered at all; while others would be deprived of all their solemn ceremonies, as well as of a certain part of the religious respect and exterior honor accorded to them.

The study of Holy Orders should not be relegated only to priests or those who are clerics. Even lay Catholics should study the Sacrament of Holy Orders for two primary reasons, as the Catechism explains: "first, because it enables them to understand the respect due to the Church's ministers, and secondly, because as it often happens that many may be present who have destined their children, while yet young, for the Church's service, or who desire to embrace that life themselves, it is far from right that such persons should be unacquainted with the principal truths regarding this particular state."

As seen through our examination of the other Sacraments, the study of Holy Orders should likewise increase greater devotion in our own hearts for God and His plan of salvation. As in centuries past, so also today do our priests possess a unique dignity and an unbroken line of succession going back to Our Lord Jesus Christ Himself. On this point, the Catechism poignantly elaborates:

> In all ages, priests have been held in the highest honor; yet the priests of the New Testament far exceed all

others. For the power of consecrating and offering the Body and Blood of our Lord and of forgiving sins, which has been conferred on them, not only has nothing equal or like to it on earth, but even surpasses human reason and understanding.

And as our Savior was sent by His Father [cf. Jn. viii. 42], and as the Apostles and disciples were sent into the whole world by Christ our Lord [cf. Mt. xxviii. 19], so priests are daily sent with the same powers, for the perfecting of the saints, *for the work of the ministry, and the edifying of the body of Christ* [Eph. iv. 12].

On this point, the Catechism of St. Pius X further explains: "The Catholic Priesthood is necessary in the Church, because without it the faithful would be deprived of the Holy Sacrifice of the Mass and of the greater part of the sacraments; they would have no one to instruct them in the faith; and they would be as sheep without a shepherd, a prey to wolves; in short, the Church, such as Christ instituted it, would no longer exist."[88]

If no bishops remained on earth – those who possess the fulness of the priesthood and the only ones able to transmit it – the Sacrament of Holy Orders would end. The priesthood would end. Without the priesthood, we would have no ability to have our sins absolved after Baptism. If the priesthood were to die out, there would be no Holy Sacrifice of the Mass and no Holy Eucharist. The perfect oblation that is offered on the altar every single day throughout the world in satisfaction for sins (cf. Mal. i. 11) would die out. Confirmation would no longer occur (recall that bishops are the ordinary ministers of this sacrament). There would be no teaching authority to guide the Church. Last Rites would never be imparted again to the dying.

We truly would be a flock without a shepherd and the wolves would devour us. Only the Sacraments of Baptism and Holy Matrimony would be able to continue. All of the others, which require a validly ordained priest, would cease.

Holy Orders is a Sacrament

---

[88] Fr. Marshall Roberts, Catechism of St. Pius X (St. Michael's Press, 2010), p. 130.

Holy Orders is therefore a necessary sacrament in the Church. The Catechism of St. Pius X explains: "Holy Orders is a sacrament which gives power to exercise the sacred duties connected with the worship of God and the salvation of souls, and which imprints the character of Minister of God on the soul of him who receives it."[89] The 1983 Code of Canon Law, in describing the Sacrament of Holy Orders, states in greater detail:

> By divine institution, the sacrament of orders establishes some among the Christian faithful as sacred ministers through an indelible character which marks them. They are consecrated and designated, each according to his grade, to nourish the people of God, fulfilling in the person of Christ the Head the functions of teaching, sanctifying, and governing. They are conferred by the imposition of hands and the consecratory prayer which the liturgical books prescribe for the individual grades.

The Roman Catechism beautifully explains in its own language what Holy Orders is when it states:

> That Sacred Ordination is to be numbered among the Sacraments of the Church, the Council of Trent has established by the same line of reasoning as we have already used several times. Since a Sacrament is a sign of a sacred thing, and since the outward action in this consecration denotes the grace and power bestowed on him who is consecrated, it becomes clearly evident that Order must be truly and properly regarded as a Sacrament. Thus the Bishop, handing to him who is being ordained a chalice with wine and water, and a paten with bread, says: *Receive the power of offering sacrifice,* etc. In these words, pronounced along with the application of the matter, the Church has always taught that the power of consecrating the Eucharist is conferred, and that a character is impressed on the soul which brings with it grace necessary for the due and proper discharge of that office, as the Apostle declares thus: *I admonish thee that thou stir up the grace of God which is in thee, by the imposition of my hands; for God hath not given us the spirit of fear, but of power, and of love, and of sobriety* [II Tim. i. 6].

---

[89] Fr. Marshall Roberts, *op. cit.*, p. 130.

Since Holy Orders is a Sacrament, it follows that it must have been instituted by Our Lord. Since all the Sacraments were instituted by our Divine Savior, Holy Orders is no exception. This Sacrament was instituted at the Last Supper, as the Catechism of St. Pius X further explains:

> Jesus Christ instituted the Sacerdotal Order at the Last Supper when He conferred on the Apostles and their successors the power of consecrating the Blessed Eucharist. Then on the day of His resurrection He conferred on them the power of remitting and retaining sin, thus constituting them the first Priests of the New Law in all the fullness of their power.

The Degrees of Orders

While Holy Orders is often synonymous with the priesthood in the minds of the faithful, the Sacrament encompasses more than the priesthood alone. It concerns all of the orders to which a man is ordained leading up to his ultimate ordination as a priest of the New Testament. On this point, the Roman Catechism explains, quoting the Council of Trent's teaching on the subject:

> The ministry of so sublime a priesthood being a thing all divine, it is but befitting its worthier and more reverent exercise that in the Church's well-ordered disposition there should be several different orders of ministers destined to assist the priesthood by virtue of their office, orders arranged in such a way that those who have already received clerical tonsure should be raised, step by step, from the lower to the higher orders.

Regarding these "lower" and higher" degrees of Holy Orders – distinguished as *minor* and *major*, respectively – the Roman Catechism further states:

> It should be taught, therefore, that these orders are seven in number, and that this has been the constant teaching of the Catholic Church. These orders are those of porter, lector, exorcist, acolyte, subdeacon, deacon and priest.
>
> That the number of ministers was wisely established thus may be proved by considering the various offices that are necessary for the celebration of the Holy Sacrifice of the Mass and the consecration and administration of the

Blessed Eucharist, this being the principal scope of their institution.

They are divided into major or sacred, and minor orders. The major or sacred orders are priesthood, deaconship and subdeaconship; while the minor orders are those of acolyte, exorcist, lector and porter, concerning each of which we shall now say a few words so that the pastor may be able to explain them to those especially whom he knows to be about to receive any of the orders in question.

In 1972, following the novel spirit of the Second Vatican Council Pope Paul VI abolished the minor orders of porter and exorcist, as well as the major order of subdeacon, and decreed that the orders of lector and acolyte would henceforth be called "ministries" open to laymen and would no longer be considered necessary as preparation for priestly ordination.[90] However, priestly societies and religious orders which have retained the liturgical books in force in 1962 or before continue to confer the first five orders, whose origin dates back to at least Pope St. Caius. St. Caius served as Supreme Pontiff from A.D. 283- 296. Concerning his pontificate, the 1960 Roman Breviary recounts: "Caius was a Dalmatian, of the kindred of the emperor Diocletian. He decreed that these several orders and grades of honor in the Church should lead up to the episcopate, namely: doorkeeper, lector, exorcist, acolyte, subdeacon, deacon, and priest. Fleeing from the cruelty of Diocletian towards the Christians, he hid himself for some time in a cave; then… received the crown of martyrdom together with this brother Gabinus and was buried in the cemetery of Callistus."

The Minor Orders

Whereas Paul VI wanted "entrance into the clerical state [to be] joined to the diaconate,"[91] traditionally a man would enter the clerical state by his tonsure, a ceremony in which he would receive a small piece of his hair cut off, says the Catechism, "for by the cutting off of hair is signified the character and disposition of him who desires to devote himself to the sacred ministry." After tonsure, the cleric would receive four minor orders over the initial years of his formation: porter, lector, exorcist, and acolyte.

Porter (Doorkeeper): In the early Church, the porter was charged with ringing the bells for Mass and for the offices, opening the church and the sacristy, holding the book in front of the preacher and keeping troublesome

---

[90] Pope Paul VI, Apostolic Letter *Ministeria Quaedam* (Aug. 15, 1972).
[91] Ibid.

persons out of the church. Spiritually, this symbolizes closing oneself to the devil and opening oneself to God by one's words and examples, our souls being temples of the Holy Ghost. In conferring this order, the bishop has the candidate touch the keys, saying: "Comport yourself as if you were to render account unto God, of all that you close with these keys."

Lector: Those ordained lectors have the privilege to read Lessons and Prophesies during the liturgy. The bishop thus exhorts them, "Apply yourselves to reading the word of God... to instruct and edify the faithful."

Exorcist: The bishop has the candidates touch the ritual book containing the rite of exorcism. He instructs them, saying, "As you drive forth the devil from the bodies of your brothers, be sure to reject from your spirit and body all impurity and iniquity, so as not to be slaves of him from whom you deliver others." Today, however, recipients of this minor order do not actually receive faculties (permission) to exorcise (i.e., drive out demons), this is left to priests who receive the necessary permission from their bishop.

Acolyte: The acolyte carries candles during ecclesiastical functions and presents wine and water at Mass. When conferring this minor order, the bishop quotes the Gospel according to St. Matthew, saying, *Let your light shine before men that they may see your good works and glorify your Father that is in heaven* (Mt. v. 16).

Again, the ordination of men as lectors and acolytes according to the Church's traditional rites differs from the modern practice of "instituting" (Paul VI's term) men to perform these functions, including those who have no intention of preparing for the priesthood.

The Subdiaconate

After briefly explaining the four minor orders, the Roman Catechism immediately turns to the first of the major orders: the subdiaconate. The role of the subdeacon, as the name implies, is to assist the deacon:

> Its function, as the name itself indicates, is to serve the deacon at the altar. It is the subdeacon who should prepare the altar linen, the vessels and the bread and wine necessary for the celebration of the Holy Sacrifice. He also it is who presents water to the Bishop or priest when he washes his hands during the Sacrifice of the Mass. It is also the subdeacon who now reads the Epistle which in former times was read at Mass by the deacon. He assists as witness at the Holy Sacrifice, and guards the

celebrant from being disturbed by anyone during the sacred ceremonies.

Traditionally in the Latin Rite, the vow to perpetually observe celibacy is made at the reception of the subdiaconate, the first of the major orders, which is consequently the "point of no return" (so to speak) in preparation for the priesthood. The practice of celibacy, a tell-tale mark of the priest in secular culture, is often misunderstood. Writing in 1935, Pope Pius XI explains the connection of celibacy to Our Lord's earthly life:

> But the Christian priesthood, being much superior to that of the Old Law, demanded a still greater purity. The law of ecclesiastical celibacy, whose first written traces presuppose a still earlier unwritten practice, dates back to a canon of the Council of Elvira, at the beginning of the fourth century, when persecution still raged. This law only makes obligatory what might in any case almost be termed a moral exigency that springs from the Gospel and the Apostolic preaching. For the Divine Master showed such high esteem for chastity, and exalted it as something behind the common power; He Himself was the Son of a Virgin Mother, and was brought up in the virgin family of Joseph and Mary....[92]

Continuing on, Pope Pius XI explains the rationale for maintaining celibacy among those in major orders:

> Priests have a duty which, in a certain way, is higher than that of the most pure spirits 'who stand before the Lord.' Is it not right, then, that he live an all but angelic life? A priest is one who should be totally dedicated to the things of the Lord. Is it not right, then, that he be entirely detached from the things of the world, and have his conversation in Heaven? A priest's charge is to be solicitous for the eternal salvation of souls, continuing in their regard the work of the Redeemer. Is it not, then, fitting that he keep himself free from the cares of a family, which would absorb a great part of his energies?[93]

---

[92] Pope Pius XI, Encyclical *Ad Catholici Sacerdottii* on the Catholic Priesthood (Dec. 20, 1935), n. 43.
[93] Ibid., n. 45.

The reception of the subdiaconate also binds a man to the recitation of the Divine Office (cf. *Baltimore Catechism* #3, Q.981). Subdeacons, deacons, priests, bishops, choir monks, and nuns in temporary or solemn vows who are part of a choir in a cloistered convent or monastery are all bound to pray the Divine Office, notwithstanding exceptions.

The Diaconate

The diaconate traditionally refers to the order that a man receives before his ordination to the priesthood. The purpose of the deacon is well summarized in the Roman Catechism:

> The second degree of Sacred Orders is that of the deacons, whose functions are much more extensive and have always been regarded as more holy. His duty it is to be always at the side of the Bishop, guard him while he preaches, serve him and the priest during the celebration of the divine mysteries, as well as during the administration of the Sacraments, and to read the Gospel in the Sacrifice of the Mass. In former times he frequently warned the faithful to be attentive to the holy mysteries; he administered our Lord's Blood in those churches in which the custom existed that the faithful should receive the Eucharist under both species; and to him was entrusted the distribution of the Church's goods, as well as the duty of providing for all that was necessary to each one's sustenance. To the deacon also, as the eye of the Bishop, it belongs to see who they are in the city that lead a good and holy life, and who not; who are present at the Holy Sacrifice and sermons at appointed times, and who not; so that he may be able to give an account of all to the Bishop, and enable him to admonish and advise each one privately, or to rebuke and correct publicly, according as he may deem more profitable.

The introduction of the "permanent diaconate" by Pope Paul VI, in accord with Vatican II's *Lumen Gentium* (Dogmatic Constitution on the Church, art. 29), as well as his tampering with all of the orders below the diaconate, represents an obvious rupture with the immemorial tradition of the Church. As a result of these changes, including the elimination of the tonsure, a man is not considered a cleric until he has been ordained a deacon (excepting traditional communities, of course), a dramatic departure from the Church's perennial understanding and practice.

The Priesthood

Only a bishop, who has the fullness of the Catholic priesthood, can ordain a priest. The Roman Catechism explains:

> Beyond all doubt, it is to the Bishop that the administration of orders belongs, as is easily proved by the authority of Holy Scripture, by most certain tradition, by the testimony of all the Fathers, by the decrees of the Councils, and by the usage and practice of Holy Church.
>
> It is true that permission has been granted to some abbots occasionally to administer those orders that are minor and not sacred; yet there is no doubt whatever that it is the proper office of the Bishop, and of the Bishop alone to confer the orders called holy or major.
>
> To ordain subdeacons, deacons and priests, one Bishop suffices; but in accordance with an Apostolic tradition that has been always observed in the Church, Bishops are consecrated by three Bishops.

The ordination rite is the means whereby the man is given the priestly character. The sacrament of Holy Orders is administered, after many prayers, by the imposition of the hands of the bishop. Then all the priests present impose their hands also on the man.

Ordination to the priesthood involves the conferral of a two-fold power, as the Roman Catechism wisely explains:

> This power is twofold: the powers of orders and the power of jurisdiction. The power of orders has for its object the real body of Christ our Lord in the Blessed Eucharist. The power of jurisdiction refers altogether to the mystical body of Christ. The scope of this power is to govern and rule the Christian people and lead them to the unending bliss of heaven.

After the imposition of hands, which constitutes the essential matter of the sacrament,[94] the priest's hands are consecrated with the oil of the catechumens that he might be able to handle holy things, bless, and consecrate. Then comes the reception of the chalice and paten, when the

---

[94] Pope Pius XII, Apostolic Constitution *Sacramentum Ordinis* (Nov. 30, 1947), art. 4.

bishop tells the newly ordained priest, "Receive the power to offer sacrifice to God, and to celebrate Masses, both for the living and the dead." Next, he is vested with the chasuble, a symbol of the charity with which his soul must be filled. And finally, kneeling down in the sanctuary, he concelebrates the Mass together with the ordaining bishop, reciting in a low voice all of the prayers.

The newly ordained priest receives Holy Communion from the hands of the bishop. Afterwards, he is reminded that he must now be a friend of Our Lord Jesus Christ. His chasuble, which to this moment was folded in half in the back, is dropped down. The priest receives the power to forgive sins, he solemnly promises obedience to his bishop and his successors, and he receives the kiss of peace from the bishop. The man is now a priest forever (cf. Heb. 7:17). All of these sacred ceremonies visibly convey the function of the priest as expressed in the Catechism: "The office of a priest, then, is to offer Sacrifice to God and to administer the Sacraments of the Church."

The Importance of Holy Priests

In 1908, Pope St. Pius X wrote the following on the paramount importance of holiness among priests in *Haerent Animo* (Apostolic Exhortation on Priestly Sanctity), words which apply all the more in our own times:

> ... we will begin this exhortation by stimulating you to that sanctity of life which the dignity of your office demands. ... The priest then is the light of the world and the salt of the earth. Everyone knows that he fulfills this function chiefly by the teaching of Christian truth; and who can be unaware that this ministry of teaching is practically useless if the priest fails to confirm by the example of his life the truths which he teaches? ... [A] priest who neglects his own sanctification can never be the salt of the earth.

By practicing the heroic virtues and developing one's interior life, a man can truly be a friend of Our Lord and thus grow in holiness. It is of this holiness that St. Pius X speaks when he further affirms:

> Sanctity alone makes us what our divine vocation demands, men crucified to the world and to whom the world has been crucified, men walking in newness of life who, in the words of St. Paul, show themselves as ministers of God in labors, in vigils, in fasting, in chastity, in knowledge, in long-suffering, in kindness, in the Holy Spirit, in sincere charity, in the word of truth [II

Cor. vi. 5-7]; men who seek only heavenly things and strive by every means to lead others to them.

As a result, there are three primary qualifications for the priesthood: holiness of life, competent knowledge, and canonical fitness. As the Roman Catechism teaches:

> The chief and most necessary quality requisite in him who is to be ordained a priest is that he be recommended by integrity of life and morals....

> In the second place there is required of the priest not only that knowledge which concerns the use and administration of the Sacraments; but he should also be versed in the science of Sacred Scripture, so as to be able to instruct the people in the mysteries of the Christian faith and the precepts of the divine law, lead them to piety and virtue, and reclaim them from sin. ...

> This Sacrament should not be conferred on children, nor on the insane or mad, because they are devoid of the use of reason. ... As for the precise age requisite for the reception of the various orders, this will easily be found in the decrees of the Council of Trent.

Conclusion

At the Last Supper, Our Savior's words, *This is My Body*, and, *this is My Blood* (Mt. xxvi. 26, 28) truly changed the bread and wine into His Body and Blood. To the Apostles and their successors alone were given this power, passed down through the Sacrament of Holy Orders. Our priests today have this same power to stand at the altar because of their ordination. Our same priests have the power to baptize (cf. Mt. xxviii. 19) and forgive sins (cf. John xx. 19-23), as well as to bless and preach. Their hands are anointed to make them worthy to touch the Most Holy Eucharist.

In the words of St. John Vianney (1786-1859), the Holy Cure of Ars, "Without the Sacrament of Holy Orders, we would not have the Lord. Who put Him there in that tabernacle? The priest. Who welcomed your soul at the beginning of your life? The priest. Who feeds your soul and gives it strength for its journey? The priest. Who will prepare it to appear before God, bathing it one last time in the Blood of Jesus Christ? The priest, always the priest. And if this soul should happen to die [as a result of sin], who will raise it up, who will restore its calm and peace? Again, the priest… After God, the priest is everything! … Only in heaven will he fully realize what he is".[95]

In light of the vital importance of the priesthood, we have divine assurance that it will persist on earth until Our Lord's glorious return. "In spite of the war that hell wages against it," the Catechism of St. Pius X explains, "the Catholic Priesthood will last until the end of time, because Jesus Christ has promised that the powers of hell shall never prevail against His Church."[96]

Today, offer your prayers and sacrifices for the good of our priests and for many more holy religious vocations. And we should likewise offer prayers of reparation for the priests who have violated their sacred vows and who have used their authority to abuse others, causing immense scandal and the loss of souls. These wolves in sheep's clothing (cf. Mt. vii. 15) are in no way representative of the true priests of Our Lord Jesus Christ.

---

[95] Quoted by Pope Benedict XVI, "Letter Proclaiming a Year for Priests" (June 16, 2009).
[96] Fr. Marshall Roberts, *op. cit.*, p. 130.

XX

On the Sacrament of Holy Matrimony

What is Holy Matrimony?

St. Robert Bellarmine (1542-1621), a contemporary of St. Charles Borromeo (1538-1584), once remarked, "Love is a marvelous and heavenly thing. It never tires and never thinks it has done enough." While love may be manifested in all vocations and should be present in the life of all Catholics (cf. Col. 3:14), those in the married state manifest their love through bearing and raising children in the Catholic Faith. As affirmed in the 1917 Code of Canon Law, "The primary end of matrimony is the procreation and the education of children."[97]

Holy Matrimony is the seventh and final Sacrament explained by the Roman Catechism. In its introductory remarks, the Catechism presents a clear definition of this Sacrament: "Matrimony, according to the general opinion of theologians, is defined: *The conjugal union of man and woman, contracted between two qualified persons, which obliges them to live together throughout life.*" The text further clarifies this definition by stating:

> The special character of this union is marked by the word *conjugal*. This word is added because other contracts, by which men and women bind themselves to help each other in consideration of money received or other reason, differ essentially from matrimony.

> Next follow the words *between qualified persons*; for persons excluded by law cannot contract marriage, and if they do their marriage is invalid. Persons, for instance, within the fourth degree of kindred, a boy before his fourteenth year, and a female before her twelfth, the ages established by law, cannot contract marriage.

---

[97] 1917 Code of Canon Law, Canon 1013 §1

The words, *which obliges them to live together throughout life*, express the indissolubility of the tie which binds husband and wife.

The Baltimore Catechism succinctly expresses the same reality when it states: "The Sacrament of Matrimony is the Sacrament which unites a Christian man and woman in lawful marriage."[98]

The Three Motives and Blessings of Marriage

Why should man and woman be joined in Holy Matrimony? While some are called to celibacy for the sake of the Kingdom of God on earth and serve the Lord as consecrated religious (cf. Mt. xix. 10-12), the vast majority of the faithful are called to marriage and to continue Our Lord's original command to *increase and multiply* (Gen. i. 28).

The Baltimore Catechism, mirroring the teachings in the Roman Catechism, lists three proper ends for the Sacrament of Matrimony: "To enable the husband and wife to aid each other in securing the salvation of their souls; to propagate or keep up the existence of the human race by bringing children into the world to serve God; to prevent sins against the holy virtue of purity by faithfully obeying the laws of the marriage state." Those who feel called to the married life must discern the vocation in order to know the will of God, as the Roman Catechism counsels:

> They should consider that they are about to enter upon a work that is not human but divine. The example of the Fathers of the Old Law, who esteemed marriage as a most holy and religious rite, although it had not then been raised to the dignity of a Sacrament, shows the singular purity of soul and piety (with which Christians should approach marriage).

And to those who are called to marriage and who receive Holy Matrimony, there are three primary blessings: children, fidelity, and the Sacrament:

> The first blessing, then, is a family, that is to say, children born of a true and lawful wife. So highly did the Apostle esteem this blessing that he says: *The woman shall be saved by bearing children* [I Tim. ii. 15]. These words are to be understood not only of bearing children, but also of bringing them up and training them to the practice of piety....

---

[98] Baltimore Catechism No. 3, Q. 1005.

The second advantage of marriage is faith, not indeed that virtue which we receive in Baptism; but the fidelity which binds wife to husband and husband to wife in such a way that they mutually deliver to each other power over their bodies, promising at the same time never to violate the holy bond of Matrimony. ...

The third advantage is called the Sacrament, that is to say, the indissoluble bond of marriage.

The Necessity of Consent

Consent is the core of marriage. As stated in the Catechism of St. Pius X, the couple themselves are the ministers of the Sacrament, who contract it themselves by their consent:

> The Ministers of this sacrament are the couple themselves, who together confer and receive the sacrament. This sacrament, preserving, as it does, the nature of a contract, is administered by the contracting parties themselves, who declare, in the presence of the parish priest, or another priest delegated by him, and of two witnesses, that they take each other in marriage.[99]

Consent, the cornerstone of marriage, must possess three qualities as enumerated in the Roman Catechism. It must be *mutual*, *external*, and *present*. The mutuality refers to the consent of both parties, which must be expressed externally (i.e., in words). And finally, such a consent must be expressed in the present, as future promises to marry do not contract a valid marriage. The consent must be in the present tense: "I do."

Consequently, it is the consent of each party and not the consummation of the marriage which confers the Sacrament, as the Roman Catechism clarifies:

> Hence pastors should teach the faithful that the nature and force of marriage consists in the tie and obligation; and that, without consummation, the consent of the parties, expressed in the manner already explained, is sufficient to constitute a true marriage. It is certain that our first parents before their fall, when, according to the

---

[99] Fr. Marshall Roberts, Catechism of St. Pius X (St. Michael's Press, 2010), p. 134.

holy Fathers, no consummation took place, were really united in marriage. Hence the Fathers say that marriage consists not in its use but in the consent. This doctrine is repeated by St. Ambrose in his book *On Virgins*.[100]

The Traditional Rite of Holy Matrimony retained in the 1962 liturgical books includes the prayer of the priest who ratifies and blesses the bond of marriage for the couple, noting however that the couple have themselves contracted marriage: "By the authority of the Church, I ratify and bless the bond of marriage you have contracted. In the Name of the Father, and of the Son, and of the Holy Ghost."

Marriage Was Instituted in the Garden of Eden

Marriage is the only Sacrament whose origin stretches back to the Garden of Eden, where God first instituted it. For this reason, it is called the primordial Sacrament.

> The faithful, therefore, are to be taught in the first place that marriage was instituted by God. We read in Genesis that *God created them male and female, and blessed them, saying: 'Increase and multiply'* [Gen. i. 27-28]; and also: *'It is not good for man to be alone: let us make him a help like unto himself'* [Gen. ii. 18]. And a little further on: *But for Adam there was not found a helper like himself. Then the Lord God cast a deep sleep upon Adam; and when he was fast asleep, he took one of his ribs, and filled up flesh for it. And the Lord God built a rib which he took from Adam into a woman, and brought her to Adam; and Adam said: 'This is now bone of my bones, and flesh of my flesh: she shall be called woman, because she was taken out of man: wherefore a man shall leave father and mother, and shall cleave to his wife; and they shall be two in one flesh'* [Gen. ii. 20-24]. These words, according to the authority of our Lord Himself, as we read in St. Matthew, prove the divine institution of Matrimony [cf. Mt. xix. 6]."[101]

In the 1962 Rite of Matrimony, the priest prays the following prayer to Almighty God shortly after the couple have voiced their consent and effected the Sacrament. The prayer references this institution by God at the

---

[100] Roman Catechism, *op. cit.*, pp. 341-342.
[101] Ibid.

beginning whose purpose is none other than the "continuation of the human race":

> We beg You, Lord, to look on these Your servants, and graciously to uphold the institution of marriage established by You for the continuation of the human race, so that they who have been joined together by Your authority may remain faithful together by Your help.

Marriage Raised to a Sacrament

While marriage was first established in the Garden, it was not yet a Sacrament of the New Law. Marriage was raised to the dignity of a Sacrament by our Lord Jesus Christ, Who alone instituted all of the Sacraments as the Church authoritatively teaches: "Matrimony was instituted by God Himself in the Garden of Paradise, and was raised to the dignity of a sacrament by Jesus Christ in the New Law."[102]

However, since marriage existed since Adam and Eve, why did Our Lord choose to elevate a pre-existing institution to a Sacrament? On this essential question, the wisdom of the Roman Catechism again teaches with clarity:

> For as marriage, as a natural union, was instituted from the beginning to propagate the human race; so was the sacramental dignity subsequently conferred upon it in order that a people might be begotten and brought up for the service and worship of the true God and of Christ our Savior.

> Thus, when Christ our Lord wished to give a sign of the intimate union that exists between Him and His Church and of His immense love for us, He chose especially the sacred union of man and wife. That this sign was a most appropriate one will readily appear from the fact that of all human relations there is none that binds so closely as the marriage, and from the fact that husband and wife are bound to one another by the bonds of the greatest affection and love. Hence it is that Holy Writ so frequently represents to us the divine union of Christ and the Church under the figure of marriage.

---

[102] Fr. Marshall Roberts, *op. cit.*

Since marriage was instituted before it became a Sacrament, some have questioned whether the Sacrament of Marriage could be separated from the contract of marriage. Put another way, is it possible for a Catholic to be validly married in any way that is not a Sacrament? The Catechism of St. Pius X wisely clearly answers: "No, in marriage among Christians the contract cannot be separated from the sacrament, because, for Christians, marriage is nothing else than the natural contract itself, raised by Jesus Christ to the dignity of a sacrament...Among Christians there can be no true marriage that is not a sacrament."[103]

As a Sacrament, Holy Matrimony confers grace on the recipients since all Sacraments by their definition confer grace. On this point, the teaching of the Church is further explained by the Roman Catechism:

> That grace is also signified and conferred by this Sacrament, which are two properties that constitute the principal characteristics of each Sacrament, is declared by the Council as follows: *By His passion Christ, the Author and Perfecter of the venerable Sacraments, merited for us the grace that perfects the natural love* (of husband and wife), *confirms their indissoluble union, and sanctifies them.* It should, therefore, be shown that by the grace of this Sacrament husband and wife are joined in the bonds of mutual love, cherish affection one towards the other, avoid illicit attachments and passions, and so keep their *marriage honorable in all things, ... and their bed undefiled* [Heb. xiii. 4].

The Laws of the Church on Marriage

While the couples contract marriage, Holy Mother Church requires Catholics to follow her laws in regard to the Sacrament. To observe the Church's laws on marriage is the sixth precept of the Church. And these laws include that marriage should take place before a priest, preferably with a nuptial Mass:

> To receive the Sacrament of Matrimony worthily it is necessary to be in the state of grace, and it is necessary also to comply with the laws of the Church.... Christians should prepare for a holy and happy marriage by receiving the Sacraments of Penance and Holy Eucharist; by begging God to grant them a pure intention

---

[103] Fr. Marshall Roberts, *op. cit.* p. 133.

> and to direct their choice; and by seeking the advice of
> their parents and the blessing of their pastors....
> Catholics should be married before the altar in the
> Church. They should be married in the morning, and
> with a Nuptial Mass if possible.

The Church further forbids marriages to those within three degrees of blood
relationships (e.g., second cousins and those nearer in blood relation)
without special dispensation.[104] And those who receive Matrimony are
likewise forbidden to marry privately without the blessing of the priest or
without witnesses.[105] Marriage in front of a non-Catholic minister is also
condemned, and in previous times, incurred excommunication; and further,
marriages should not be solemnized at forbidden times, that is, "during
Lent and Advent the marriage ceremony should not be performed with
pomp or a nuptial Mass."[106]

It is a grave responsibility of the priest to instruct the couple on these and
other matters concerning the contracting of marriage as the Roman
Catechism states: "The impediments of marriage are also to be explained,
a subject so minutely and accurately treated by many grave and learned
writers on the virtues and vices as to render it an easy task to draw upon
their labors, particularly as the pastor has occasion to have such works
continually in his hands."

Special instruction should be given by the priest to emphasize the consent
of one's parents before entering a martial union, as the Catechism also
wisely states:

> Among other things, children should be exhorted
> earnestly that they owe as a tribute of respect to their
> parents, or to those under whose guardianship and
> authority they are placed, not to contract marriage
> without their knowledge, still less in defiance of their
> express wishes. It should be observed that in the Old Law
> children were always given in marriage by their fathers;
> and that the will of the parent is always to have very great
> influence on the choice of the child, is clear from these
> words of the Apostle: *He that giveth his virgin in*
> *marriage doth well; and he that giveth her not, doth*
> *better* [I Cor. vii. 38].

---

[104] Baltimore Catechism No. 3, Q. 1360 & 1361.
[105] Ibid., Q. 1364.
[106] Ibid., Q. 1366.

Marriage is Indissoluble

Marriage has been a permanent union of a man and a woman since its creation. Only natural death can end a valid marriage. Divorce, simply put, does not exist for a Catholic, as stated in by the Council of Trent:

> Not only did God institute marriage; He also, as the Council of Trent declares, rendered it perpetual and indissoluble. *What God hath joined together*, says our Lord, *let not man separate.*

Whereas before Christ, divorce and polygamy were concessions permitted by God on account of the people's hardness of heart, these were suppressed when marriage was restored by our Redeemer to its original dignity:

> It should be added that if we consider the law of nature after the fall and the Law of Moses, we shall easily see that marriage had fallen from its original honor and purity. Thus under the law of nature we read of many of the ancient Patriarchs that they had several wives at the same time; while under the Law of Moses it was permissible, should cause exist, to repudiate one's wife by giving her a bill of divorce. Both these (concessions) have been suppressed by the law of the Gospel, and marriage has been restored to its original state.

The Gospel records Christ's teaching:

> For this cause a man shall leave his father and mother; and shall cleave to his wife. And the two shall be in one flesh. Therefore now they are not two, but one flesh. What therefore God hath joined together, let not man put asunder. (…) And he saith to them: Whosoever shall put away his wife and marry another, committeth adultery against her. And if the wife shall put away her husband, and be married to another, she committeth adultery" (Mk. x. 6–9; 11–12).

In his Epistle to the Ephesians, St. Paul further compares the union of spouses in marriage with the union of Christ and His Church:

> For this cause shall a man leave his father and mother, and shall cleave to his wife, and they shall be two in one flesh. This is a great sacrament; but I speak in Christ and in the church. Nevertheless, let every one of you in

particular love his wife as himself: and let the wife fear her husband (Eph. v. 31–32).

Just there is only one Savior, namely Our Jesus Christ, and only one Church, the Catholic Church which He founded, and their union is indissoluble, so it is with marriage. Holy Matrimony, the union of one man and one woman lasts for as long as both spouses are alive. It may not be broken by any human authority. Consequently, those who are civilly remarried are living in a state of sin contrary to that willed by Christ. This permanent and public state of grave sin makes them unworthy to receive Holy Communion and incapable of receiving its fruit. If this state is known by the priest, the priest is bound to refuse them Holy Communion publicly. If either of them however does receive our Lord in Holy Communion, it would be a sacrilegious Communion and one of the most serious of mortal sins. The Baltimore Catechism echoes these teachings:

> The bond of Christian marriage cannot be dissolved by any human... Divorce granted by courts of justice or by any human power does not break the bond of marriage, and one who makes use of such a divorce to marry again while the former husband or wife lives commits a sacrilege and lives in the sin of adultery. A civil divorce may give a sufficient reason for the persons to live apart and it may determine their rights with regard to support, the control of the children and other temporal things, but it has no effect whatever upon the bond and spiritual nature of the Sacrament.[107]

While the Church does at times permit a husband and wife to live apart, divorce is never an option. The indissolubility of marriage, for which St. Thomas More and others died defending, has several clear advantages as enumerated by the Roman Catechism:

> The first (beneficial consequence) is that men are given to understand that in entering Matrimony virtue and congeniality of disposition are to be preferred to wealth or beauty....
>
> In the second place, if marriage could be dissolved by divorce, married persons would hardly ever be without causes of disunion, which would be daily supplied by the old enemy of peace and purity; while, on the contrary, now that the faithful must remember that even though

---

[107] Baltimore Catechism No. 3, Q. 1023 & 1024.

separated as to bed and board, they remain none the less bound by the bond of marriage with no hope of marrying another, they are by this very fact rendered less prone to strife and discord.

Unfortunately, in the past several decades following Vatican II, more Catholics are treating annulments as a Catholic equivalent to divorce. From 1952 to 1955 there were a total of 392 annulments issued for the entire world. This is seemingly in line with what an annulment is: a statement that a marriage was never validly contracted in the beginning. One would logically expect that few of the people who claim to live a married life are in actuality not really married. But in 1997 there were 73,000 annulments issued worldwide.[108] It is simply ludicrous to believe that so many invalid marriages take place. If they do take place, shouldn't one of the greatest concerns in the Church and society be limiting the number of invalid unions?

Modern Crisis of Marriage

From divorce to annulments and the social acceptance of gay "marriage," the Sacrament of Holy Matrimony is under constant assault. Underpinning this war on marriage is a fundamental error – subjecting God's natural law, which is immutable and eternal, to human law.

Should someone who claims to be Catholic assert that human law supersedes natural law, that person would profess heresy. As St. Thomas Aquinas taught, "Human law is law only by virtue of its accordance with right reason; and thus, it is manifest that it flows from the eternal law. And in so far as it deviates from right reason it is called an unjust law; in such case it is no law at all, but rather a species of violence" (I-II q93 a3).

Pope Leo XIII affirmed the inability of human law to nullify God's law concerning marriage in his 1891 encyclical, *Rerun Novarum* (n. 12): "No human law can abolish the natural and original right of marriage, nor in any way limit the chief and principal purpose of marriage ordained by God's authority from the beginning: 'Increase and multiply.'"

From 1594 to 1634, our Blessed Mother appeared in Ecuador in a series of Church-approved apparitions to Mother Mariana de Jesus Torres, a Conceptionist nun. Under the title of "Our Lady of Good Success," our Blessed Mother warned that "the spirit of impurity" would "saturate the

---

[108] What We Have Lost and the Road to Restoration
(https://www.youtube.com/watch?v=hJxM7Lo2URw)

atmosphere" beginning "at the end of the 19th century and into the 20th century," stating further: "Like a filthy ocean, it will run through the streets, squares and public places with an astonishing liberty."[109]

In her apparition on Jan. 21, 1610, Our Lady also said that "the Sacrament of Matrimony, which symbolizes the union of Christ with His Church, will be attacked and profaned in the fullest sense of the word. Freemasonry, which will then be in power, will enact iniquitous laws with the objective of doing away with this Sacrament, making it easy for everyone to live in sin, encouraging the procreation of illegitimate children born without the blessing of the Church. The Catholic spirit will rapidly decay and the precious light of Faith will gradually be extinguished until it reaches the point that there will be an almost total and general corruption of customs. Added to this will be the effects of secular education, which will be one reason for the dearth of priestly and religious vocations."[110]

These prophecies have been fulfilled. We are now reaping the rotten fruits. Man is so blinded by sin that he can no longer understand the Natural Law. Let us remain faithful to God's unchanging Laws, and we will understand and embrace Holy Matrimony as God has created it.

Conclusion

Marriage is a sacrament at the service of community, which symbolizes and makes present God's love through the love, friendship, and self-giving love of husband and wife. Marriage was given by God to man and woman as a gift to be a public covenant of their love. It is life-long, monogamous, and unconditional. It requires a total gift of self by each spouse to the other. Accordingly, God protects this Sacrament with His grace, allowing the couple to grow in their union with each other for the purpose of raising children.

---

[109] Marian Therese Horvat, *Our Lady of Good Success: Prophecies for Our Times* (Tradition in Action, 1999), 54, 56.
[110] Ibid., 46.

XXI

The Ten Commandments

The First Commandment

After carefully explaining the twelve articles of the Creed and the seven Sacraments, the Roman Catechism next turns to the Ten Commandments.

Why Study the Ten Commandments?

Before addressing the First Commandment, the Roman Catechism opens its series of chapters on the Commandments with an important introduction as to why we should even study the Ten Commandments, also known as the Decalogue. The Catechism explains:

> St. Augustine in his writings remarks that the Decalogue is the summary and epitome of all laws: *Although the Lord had spoken many things, He gave to Moses only two stone tablets, called 'tables of testimony,' to be placed in the Ark. For if carefully examined and well understood, whatever else is commanded by God will be found to depend on the Ten Commandments which were engraved on those two tables, just as these Ten Commandments, in turn, are reducible to two, the love of God and of our neighbor, on which 'depend the whole law and the prophets.'*

The Catechism goes on to summarize six primary motives for the keeping of the Commandments: (1) God is the Giver of the Commandments; (2) the Commandments were proclaimed with great solemnity; (3) the observance of the Commandments is not difficult; (4) the observance of the Commandments is necessary; (5) the observance of the Commandments is attended by many blessings; and (6) God's goodness invites us to keep His Commandments.

Beyond the blessings we are given by keeping the Commandments, their observance is also necessary for our salvation, as the Catechism clearly states: "...no one who has arrived at the use of reason can be justified, unless he is resolved to keep all of God's Commandments." As similarly stated by Canon Francis Ripley, "Since the Ten Commandments represent God's law for all men, they are possible for all men to observe successfully. God would not make laws that are impossible to observe. Moreover, God always gives those graces necessary to observe the Commandments. Not only is it possible for all men to observe them, it is necessary and obligatory for them to do so. Therefore, everyone has the obligation to know them."[111]

The Ten Commandments Remain Valid

While the Ten Commandments must be observed in order to be saved, the greatest of the motives for keeping them is that God Himself is their Author:

> Now among all the motives which induce men to obey this law the strongest is that God is its author. ...But, lest the people, aware of the abrogation of the Mosaic Law, may imagine that the precepts of the Decalogue are no longer obligatory, it should be taught that when God gave the Law to Moses, He did not so much establish a new code, as render more luminous that divine light which the depraved morals and long continued perversity of man had at that time almost obscured. It is most certain that we are not bound to obey the Commandments because they were delivered by Moses, but because they are implanted in the hearts of all, and have been explained and confirmed by Christ our Lord.

In the Old Testament, the Ten Commandments were only ten of the 613 laws that the Jews were required to observe. By virtue of Christ's Sacrifice on the Cross, the ceremonial and civil laws of the Old Testament are no longer in effect, such as the law of circumcision or the law prohibiting pork. And that is where some Protestant sects such as the Seventh Day Adventists and the Messianic Jews fall into error. The Old Testament ritualistic laws were abrogated by Christ:

> Before the coming of Our Lord the Jews had three kinds of laws: Civil laws, regulating the affairs of their nation; Ceremonial laws, governing their worship in the temple; Moral laws, guiding their religious belief and actions.

---

[111] Canon Francis Ripley, *This is the Faith* (Gracewing Publishing, 1973), 53.

> The Ten Commandments belong to the moral law, because they are a compendium or short account of what we must do in order to save our souls; just as the Apostles' Creed is a compendium of what we must believe. The civil laws of the Jews ceased to exist when the Jewish people, shortly before the coming of Christ, ceased to be an independent nation. The ceremonial laws ceased to exist when the Jewish religion ceased to be the true religion; that is, when Christ established the Christian religion, of which the Jewish religion was only a figure or promise.

While the Mosaic Law is no longer in force by reason of Christ's Sacrifice on the Cross, we do have to keep in mind the words of the Redeemer Himself: *Do not think that I am come to destroy the law, or the prophets. I am not come to destroy, but to fulfill* (Mt. v. 17). Consequently, while the civil and ceremonial laws were abolished, the moral law of the Ten Commandments remains eternally valid:

> The moral laws of the Jews could not be abolished by the establishment of the Christian religion because they regard truth and virtue and have been revealed by God, and whatever God has revealed as true must be always true, and whatever He has condemned as bad in itself must be always bad."[112]

As the Roman Catechism explains in its concluding remarks in this introduction, the Ten Commandments apply to all people of all times and places without exception: "The Law, although delivered to the Jews by the Lord from the mountain, was long before written and impressed by nature on the heart of man, and was therefore rendered obligatory by God for all men and all times."

The Laws that we follow as Christians, which include the Ten Commandments and all the Laws of the Church (e.g., Mass attendance on Sundays and holy days of obligation, abstinence on Fridays) are all meant to set us apart as a special people — "the people of God" (I Pet. ii. 10). Through the observance of these laws, we will grow in the grace of God, and we will grow in virtue by learning to say no to sin and yes to the inspirations given to us by the Holy Ghost. Aware of the perpetual validity of the Ten Commandments, we begin with the First Commandment: "No False Gods."

---

[112] Baltimore Catechism No. 3, Q. 1139.

The First Commandment

The first three of the Commandments concern the service we are to render Almighty God and the remaining seven concern our interactions with our fellow man.

> The pastor should teach that the first part of the Decalogue contains our duties towards God; the second part, our duties towards our neighbor. The reason (for this order) is that the services we render our neighbors are rendered for the sake of God; for then only do we love our neighbor as God commands when we love him for God's sake. The Commandments which regard God are those which were inscribed on the first table of the Law.

Almighty God declares in the First Commandment: *I am the Lord thy God, who brought thee out of the land of Egypt, out of the house of bondage. Thou shalt not have strange gods before Me. Thou shalt not make to thyself a graven thing, nor the likeness of anything that is in heaven above, or in the earth beneath, nor of those things that are in the waters under the earth. Thou shalt not adore them, nor serve them. I am the Lord thy God, mighty, jealous, visiting the iniquity of the fathers upon the children, to the third and fourth generation of them that hate Me, and showing mercy unto thousands of them that love Me, and keep My commandments* (Ex. xx. 2-6).

Rather than merely providing a set of prohibitions, as some non-Christians assert, the Ten Commandments express both positive and negative precepts: "...the words just quoted contain a twofold precept, the one mandatory, the other prohibitory. When it is said: *Thou shalt not have strange gods before Me*, it is equivalent to saying: Thou shalt worship Me the true God; thou shalt not worship strange gods."

The Worship of the One True God

The First Commandment enjoins us not only to believe in God and worship Him but also to trust Him and love Him, as well as to encourage others to do likewise. Again, turning to the wisdom of the Roman Catechism:

> The (mandatory part) contains a precept of faith, hope and charity. For, acknowledging God to be immovable, immutable, always the same, we rightly confess that He is faithful and entirely just. Hence in assenting to His oracles, we necessarily yield to Him all belief and

obedience. Again, who can contemplate His omnipotence, His clemency, His willing beneficence, and not repose in Him all his hopes? Finally, who can behold the riches of His goodness and love, which He lavishes on us, and not love Him? Hence the exordium and the conclusion used by God in Scripture when giving His commands: *I, the Lord.*

Next, the Roman Catechism explains what the First Commandment forbids:

The (negative) part of this Commandment is comprised in these words: *Thou shalt not have strange gods before Me.* This the Lawgiver subjoins, not because it is not sufficiently expressed in the affirmative part of the precept, which means: *Thou shalt worship Me, the only God,* for if He is God, He is the only God; but on account of the blindness of many who of old professed to worship the true God and yet adored a multitude of gods. Of these there were many even among the Hebrews, whom Elias reproached with having *halted between two sides* [III Kngs xviii. 21], and also among the Samaritans, who worshipped the God of Israel and the gods of the nations [cf. IV Kngs xvii. 33].

Consequently, sins against the First Commandment include (among other things) failing to pray, failing to study the Faith, neglecting spiritual duties, taking part in the worship of non-Catholic religions, despair, presumption, idolatry, consulting fortune tellers, and observing superstitious practices like horoscopes. The Baltimore Catechism clearly reiterates this prohibition against spells and charms: "Those who make use of spells and charms, or who believe in dreams, in mediums, spiritists, fortune-tellers, and the like, sin against the First Commandment, because they attribute to creatures perfections which belong to God alone."[113]

Contrary to accusations from certain enemies of the Church, sacramentals are not charms and do not violate the First Commandment, as the Baltimore Catechism further clarifies: "Agnus Deis,[114] medals, scapulars, etc., which we wear about our bodies, are not charms, for we do not expect any help

---

[113] Baltimore Catechism No. 3, Q. 1151.

[114] The name *Agnus Dei* has been given to certain discs of wax impressed with the figure of a lamb and blessed at stated seasons by the Pope. The last Pope to have consecrated them was Pope Pius XII (r. 1939-1958).

from these things themselves, but, through the blessing they have received from the Church, we expect help from God, the Blessed Mother, or the Saint in whose honor we wear them. On the contrary, they who wear charms expect help from the charms themselves, or from some evil spirit."[115]

Idolatry as the Worst of Sins

While all mortal sins are worse than venial sins, there is still a ranking of mortal sins since some, by their very nature, are worse than others. For instance, the four sins which cry out to Heaven for vengeance, the seven deadly sins, and the sins that blaspheme the Holy Ghost are especially heinous. However, the worst mortal sin is not on any of these lists. As stated by the Catholic Encyclopedia, the worst mortal sin is actually *idolatry*, the sin which violates the very heart of the First Commandment. The Catholic Encyclopedia explains:

> Considered in itself, idolatry is the greatest of mortal sins. For it is, by definition, an inroad on God's sovereignty over the world, an attempt on His Divine majesty, a rebellious setting up of a creature on the throne that belongs to Him alone. Even the simulation of idolatry, in order to escape death during persecution, is a mortal sin, because of the pernicious falsehood it involves and the scandal it causes.

Even the simulation of idolatry – that is, pretending to offer incense or worship to idols – is still a serious mortal sin. In the Second Book of Maccabees, Chapter 6, the elderly scribe Eleazar was beaten to death for refusing to eat pork. When he was given the option to pretend to eat the pork but in fact eat a hidden piece of permitted meat on the dish, he refused saying that to do so would cause grave scandal to the young who would see him apparently eat the pork. And for this, he was martyred. While pork is no longer prohibited, the story illustrates the seriousness of simulating sins, especially those against the First Commandment, while also underscoring the seriousness of allowing anyone to worship pagan statues (e.g., Pachamama).

Veneration of Saints Does Not Violate First Commandment

After enumerating the types of sins which violate the First Commandment, the Roman Catechism next counters the Protestant claim that honoring the

---

[115] Baltimore Catechism No. 3, Q. 1153.

Saints or Angels violates the First Commandment. On this point, the Roman Catechism is clear:

> In explanation of this Commandment it should be accurately taught that the veneration and invocation of holy Angels and of the blessed who now enjoy the glory of heaven, and likewise the honor which the Catholic Church has always paid even to the bodies and ashes of the Saints, are not forbidden by this Commandment.

A basic study of Church history reveals that honoring the Saints and asking for their intercession is of apostolic origin. The term "saint" comes from the Latin *sanctus*, meaning "hallowed" or "consecrated." The first person honored individually as a saint was Stephen, the first martyr, whose death is recorded in the Book of the Acts of the Apostles, Chapters 6 and 7. For nearly four centuries, praying to St. Stephen was incredibly popular. Towards the end of the second century (late 100s A.D.), there were already special celebrations on the anniversaries of martyrs' deaths. These martyrs were witnesses of Christ. By the fourth century, sainthood was not just considered for martyrs but for all who led a holy life and died in God's grace.

Despite the historical evidence, however, Protestants often believe that the invocation of the Saints is contrary to Our Lord's role as Mediator. While Christ our Lord is the *one Mediator between God and man* (I Tim. ii. 5), as He is both fully divine and fully human, His role of Mediator does not forbid other mediators (intercessors) between us and Himself. St. Paul directly asked others to pray for him (cf. Rom. xv. 30-32; Eph. vi. 18-20; Col. iv. 3; I Thess. v. 25, II Thess. iii. 1) and assured others that he was praying for them, as well (cf. II Thess. i. 11). On this crucial point, contrary to the errors of the Protestants, the Roman Catechism expounds:

> True, there is but one Mediator, Christ the Lord, who alone has reconciled us to the heavenly Father through His Blood.... But it by no means follows that it is therefore unlawful to have recourse to the intercession of the Saints. If, because we have one Mediator Jesus Christ, it were unlawful to ask the intercession of the Saints, the Apostle [St. Paul] would never have recommended himself with so much earnestness to the prayers of his brethren on earth. For the prayers of the living would lessen the glory and dignity of Christ's Mediatorship not less than the intercession of the Saints in heaven.

The Book of the Apocalypse, written by St. John the Apostle, specifically mentions how the prayers of the Saints are presented before God in Heaven. The Saints in Heaven are very much aware of what is happening on earth because God has in His order of the world permitted them to know of prayers addressed to them. In Matthew XVII. 3-5, the prophets Moses and Elias were very much aware of what was taking place on the earth. The Saints themselves are witnesses of what occurs on earth, as St. Paul affirms in his Epistle to the Hebrews: *Therefore, since we are surrounded by so great a cloud of witnesses, let us rid ourselves of every burden and sin that clings to us and persevere in running the race that lies before us* (Heb. xii. 1). And Our Lord Himself, in Luke XV. 7-10, describes those in Heaven rejoicing over repentance on earth. How could they do so unless God has somehow permitted them to know and see what was happening on the earth?

If Scripture supported the notion that we should only pray to Jesus and not ask others to pray for us to God, then the Scripture would say it with such clarity. But on the contrary, the Scriptures emphasize praying for others. And God Himself, as the Roman Catechism also explains, indicates His approval of this practice by the working of miracles through the intercession of the Saints and the veneration of their relics. He would not work miracles through the Saints if it were somehow in violation of the First Commandment.

> But who would not be convinced of the honor due the Saints and of the help they give us by the wonders wrought at their tombs? Diseased eyes, hands, and other members are restored to health; the dead are raised to life, and demons are expelled from the bodies of men! These are facts which St. Ambrose and St. Augustine, most unexceptionable witnesses, declare in their writings, not that they heard, as many did, nor that they read, as did many very reliable men, but that they saw.

> But why multiply proofs? If the clothes, the handkerchiefs [cf. Acts xix. 12, 15], and even the very shadows of the Saints, while yet on earth, banished disease and restored health, who will have the hardihood to deny that God can still work the same wonders by the holy ashes, the bones and other relics of the Saints? Of this we have a proof in the restoration to life of the dead body which was accidentally let down into the grave of Eliseus, and which, on touching the body (of the Prophet), was instantly restored to life [cf. IV Kngs xiii. 21].

Graven Images

After establishing the worship of God alone, which is not violated by the veneration of the Angels and Saints, the Roman Catechism turns to the second part of the First Commandment: "Thou shalt not make to thyself a graven thing, nor the likeness of anything that is in heaven above, or in the earth beneath, nor of those things that are in the waters under the earth. Thou shalt not adore them, nor serve them."

Are all images connected with religion forbidden? Referring to Sacred Scripture, in the Book of Numbers XXI. 8, God commanded Moses to make a bronze serpent which is a prefigurement of Jesus Christ (cf. Jn. iii. 14). The making of it was not a sin; it is only destroyed after it is worshiped as an idol (cf. IV Kngs xviii. 4). And there were images of the cherubim angels in the temple (cf. III Kngs vi. 23-28), and God blessed the temple (cf. III Kings ix. 3). Not one line of Scripture ever condemned the creation of all images. What images are forbidden by the First Commandment? Once again, turning to the wisdom of the Roman Catechism, we find the answer:

> As far as this Commandment is concerned, it is clear that there are two chief ways in which God's majesty can be seriously outraged. The first way is by worshipping idols and images as God, or believing that they possess any divinity or virtue entitling them to our worship, by praying to, or reposing confidence in them, as the Gentiles did, who placed their hopes in idols, and whose idolatry the Scriptures frequently condemn. The other way is by attempting to form a representation of the Deity, as if He were visible to mortal eyes, or could be reproduced by colors or figures. ...

> When, therefore, the Lord had forbidden the worship of strange gods, He also forbade the making of an image of the Deity from brass or other materials, in order thus utterly to do away with idolatry.

Bishop Richard Challoner (1691–1781), in his renowned Scripture commentary, mirrors the Roman Catechism and explains that *idols*, not all images, are what the First Commandment forbids:

> All such images, or likenesses, are forbidden by this commandment, as are made to be adored and served; according to that which immediately follows, *thou shalt not adore them, nor serve them*. That is, all such as are

designed for idols or image-gods or are worshipped with divine honor. But otherwise images, pictures, or representations, even in the house of God, and in the very sanctuary so far from being forbidden, are expressly authorized by the word of God."[116]

The Roman Catechism likewise explains that representations of the Divine Persons – even God the Father and the Holy Ghost, Who did not take on human nature – and the Angels are not forbidden:

To represent the Persons of the Holy Trinity by certain forms under which they appeared in the Old and New Testaments no one should deem contrary to religion or the law of God. ...

Angels, also, are represented under human form and with wings to give us to understand that they are actuated by benevolent feelings towards mankind, and are always prepared to execute the Lord's commands; for *they are all ministering spirits, sent to minister for them who shall receive the inheritance of salvation* [Heb. i. 14].

Similarly, the First Commandment does not forbid the creation of any images of our Blessed Lord or His Saints:

But to make and honor the images of Christ our Lord, of His holy and virginal Mother, and of the Saints, all of whom were clothed with human nature and appeared in human form, is not only not forbidden by this Commandment, but has always been deemed a holy practice and a most sure indication of gratitude. This position is confirmed by the monuments of the Apostolic age, the General Councils of the Church, and the writings of so many among the Fathers, eminent alike for sanctity and learning, all of whom are of one accord upon the subject.

As the Catechism explains in succinct terms, *idols* are forbidden, not images which aid us in the worship of the One True God:

Let no one think that this Commandment entirely forbids the arts of painting, engraving or sculpture. The Scriptures inform us that God Himself commanded to be

---

[116] Commentary on Exodus 20:4 (http://www.drbo.org/chapter/02020.htm).

made images of Cherubim, and also the brazen serpent. The interpretation, therefore, at which we must arrive, is that images are prohibited only inasmuch as they are used as deities to receive adoration, and so to injure the true worship of God.

Conclusion

The First Commandment forbids all false religions, and the Catholic Church alone is the religion founded by God and necessary for salvation. As St. Augustine famously remarked, "No one can find salvation except in the Catholic Church. Outside the Church, you can find everything except salvation. You can have dignities, you can have Sacraments, you can sing 'Alleluia,' answer 'Amen,' have the Gospels, have faith in the name of the Father, the Son, and the Holy Ghost, and preach it, too. But never can you find salvation except in the Catholic Church."

We must reject religious indifferentism and seek to win as many souls from the devil and error as possible. By keeping the First Commandment and encouraging others to become Catholic, we observe this first and foundational Commandment.

XXII

The Second Commandment

Thou shalt not take the name of the Lord, thy God, in vain: for the Lord will not hold him guiltless that shall take the name of the Lord his God in vain (Ex. xx. 7). This is the Second Commandment of God. Like the First Commandment, which concerns the worship of the one true God alone, the Second Commandment also belongs to the virtue of religion. While the Second Commandment naturally follows from the First, the Roman Catechism explains why God saw fit to institute this distinct but related Commandment:

> The second Commandment of the divine law is necessarily comprised in the first, which commands us to worship God in piety and holiness. For He who requires that honor be paid Him, also requires that He be spoken of with reverence, and must forbid the contrary, as is clearly shown by these words of the Lord in Malachy: *The son honored the father and the servant his master if then I be a father, where is my honor?* However, on account of the importance of the obligation, God wished to make the law, which commands His own divine and most holy name to be honored, a distinct Commandment, expressed in the clearest and simplest terms.

A Positive and Negative Precept

The Second Commandment has both a positive precept as well as a prohibition. While we often think of the prohibition – not taking the Name of the Lord in vain – the Commandment also requires us to honor the Lord's Name. On this point, the Roman Catechism explains:

> But in the exposition of this Commandment it should first be shown that besides a negative, it also contains a positive precept, commanding the performance of a duty. To each of these a separate explanation should be given;

and for the sake of easier exposition what the Commandment requires should be first set forth, and then what it forbids. It commands us to honor the name of God, and to swear by it with reverence. It prohibits us to condemn the divine name, to take it in vain, or swear by it falsely, unnecessarily, or rashly.

Likewise, the Baltimore Catechism notes both parts of the Commandment: "We are commanded by the second Commandment to speak with reverence of God and of the saints, and of all holy things, and to keep our lawful oaths and vows."[117]

The Honor of the Name of God

How does one honor the name of God? The Roman Catechism lists five principal ways: the public profession of Faith, respect for the Word of God, praising God and rendering Him unbounded thanksgiving, invoking Him in prayer, and by taking a lawful oath:

> In the first place, God's name is honored when we publicly and confidently confess Him to be our Lord and our God; and when we acknowledge and also proclaim Christ to be the author of our salvation.

> (It is also honored) when we pay a religious attention to the word of God, which announces to us His will; make it the subject of our constant meditation; and strive by reading or hearing it, according to our respective capacities and conditions of life, to become acquainted with it.

> Again, we honor and venerate the name of God when, from a sense of religious duty, we celebrate His praises, and under all circumstances, whether prosperous or adverse, return Him unbounded thanks. ...

> The name of God is not less honored when we confidently invoke His assistance, either to relieve us from our afflictions, or to give us constancy and strength to endure them with fortitude. ...

> Finally, we honor the name of God when we solemnly call upon Him to witness the truth of what we assert. ...

---

[117] Baltimore Catechism No. 3, Q. 1219.

The honor of God's name is not merely an intellectual exercise. It necessitates real actions in our lives. One of the manifestations of this is the proper capitalization of God's name as well as all pronouns (e.g. He, Him, His) that refer to God, or any of the three divine persons. Known as reverential capitalization, this practice used to be commonplace until continued liberalism in education began to erode at this practice. As Catholics, we do our part to honor God's holy name by always capitalizing it and all references to the Divine Name.

Similarly, the Church in her worship prescribes that the priest bow his head "when the three Divine Persons are named together and at the names of Jesus, of the Blessed Virgin Mary, and of the Saint in whose honor Mass is being celebrated."[118] By extension, the faithful are admonished to also bow their heads whenever the Holy Name of Jesus is mentioned, even in casual conversation.

Oaths

What is an oath and how is it usually taken? The Baltimore Catechism states, "An oath is the calling upon God to witness the truth of what we say. An oath is usually taken by laying the hand on the Bible or by lifting the hand towards heaven as a sign that we call God to witness that what we are saying is under oath and to the best of our knowledge really true."[119] The fifth way in which we honor God's name – the taking of lawful oaths – is worthy of special clarification:

> "This mode of honoring God's name differs much from those already enumerated. Those means are in their own nature so good, so desirable, that our days and nights could not be more happily or more holily spent than in such practices of piety. *I will bless the Lord at all times*, says David, *His praise shall be always in my mouth*. On the other hand, although oaths are in themselves good, their frequent use is by no means praiseworthy.
>
> The reason of this difference is that oaths have been instituted only as remedies to human frailty, and a necessary means of establishing the truth of what we assert. As it is inexpedient to have recourse to medicine unless, when it becomes necessary, and as its frequent use is harmful; so with regard to oaths, it is not profitable

---

[118] *General Instruction of the Roman Missal* (GIRM), n. 275.
[119] Baltimore Catechism No. 3, Q. 1221–1222.

to have recourse to them, unless there is a weighty and just cause; and frequent recurrence to them, far from being advantageous, is on the contrary highly prejudicial.

Likewise the Baltimore Catechism echoes the Catechism of the Council of Trent in cautioning that no oath should be taken lightly: "We may take an oath when it is ordered by lawful authority or required for God's honor or for our own or our neighbor's good."[120] A distinction is also necessary to clarify how a valid oath is taken. Contrary to what some may believe, a valid oath does not require any certain words and, while often taken with a hand on the Bible or at least on the Holy Gospels, it does not require them:

> ...it is first to be observed, that to swear, whatever the form of words may be, is nothing else than to call God to witness; thus to say, *God is my witness*, and *By God*, mean one and the same thing.

> To swear by creatures, such as the holy Gospels, the cross, the names or relics of the Saints, and so on, in order to prove our statements, is also to take an oath. Of themselves, it is true, such objects give no weight or authority to an oath; it is God Himself who does this, whose divine majesty shines forth in them. Hence to swear by the Gospel is to swear by God Himself, whose truth is contained and revealed in the Gospel. This holds equally true with regard to those who swear by the Saints, who are the temples of God, who believed the truth of His Gospel, were faithful in its observance, and spread it far and wide among the nations and peoples.

What makes an oath lawful? Simply put, "To make an oath lawful it is necessary that what we swear to, be true, and that there be a sufficient cause for taking an oath."[121] The Roman Catechism expands on this point by noting three conditions for a lawful oath: truth, judgment, and justice:

> Although to constitute an oath it is sufficient to call God to witness, yet to constitute a holy and just oath many other conditions are required, which should be carefully explained. These, as St Jerome observes, are briefly enumerated in the words of Jeremias: *Thou shalt swear: as the Lord liveth, in truth and in judgment and in justice,*

---

[120] Baltimore Catechism No. 3, Q. 1225.
[121] Baltimore Catechism No. 2, Q. 349.

words which briefly sum up all the conditions that constitute the perfection of an oath, namely, truth, judgment, justice.

Continuing on, the Roman Catechism explains what is meant by the necessary qualities of truth, judgment, and justice:

> Truth, then, holds the first place in an oath. What is asserted must be true and he who swears must believe what he swears to be true, being influenced not by rash judgment or mere conjecture, but by solid reasons. ...

> The second condition of an oath is judgment. An oath is not to be taken rashly and inconsiderately, but after deliberation and reflection. When about to take an oath, therefore, one should first consider whether he is obliged to take it, and should weigh well the whole case, reflecting whether it seems to call for an oath. ...

> The last condition (of an oath) is justice, which is especially requisite in promissory oaths. Hence, if a person swear to do what is unjust or unlawful, he sins by taking the oath, and adds sin to sin by executing his promise. Of this the Gospel supplies an example. King Herod, bound by a rash oath, gave to a dancing girl the head of John the Baptist as a reward for her dancing [cf. Mk. ix. 28]. Such was also the oath taken by the Jews, who, as we read in the Acts of the Apostles, bound themselves by oath not to eat, until they had killed Paul [cf. Acts xxiii. 12].

Did the Lord Prohibit Oaths?

An important objection against oaths concerns Our Lord's own words as recorded in St. Matthew's Gospel: *Again you have heard that it was said to them of old, Thou shalt not forswear thyself: but thou shalt perform thy oaths to the Lord. But I say to you not to swear at all: neither by heaven, for it is the throne of God: Nor by the earth, for it is His footstool: nor by Jerusalem, for it is the city of the great king* (Mt. v. 33-35).

In his Scripture commentary, Bishop Challoner (1691–1781) explains the meaning of Our Lord's words: "It is not forbidden to swear in truth, justice and judgment; to the honor of God, or our own or neighbor's just defense: but only to swear rashly, or profanely, in common discourse, and without necessity."

On such an important clarification, the Roman Catechism again elaborates wonderfully:

> It cannot be asserted that these words condemn oaths universally and under all circumstances, since we have already seen that the Apostles and our Lord Himself made frequent use of them. The object of our Lord was rather to reprove the perverse opinion of the Jews, who had persuaded themselves that the only thing to be avoided in an oath was a lie. Hence in matters the most trivial and unimportant they did not hesitate to make frequent use of oaths, and to exact them from others. This practice the Redeemer condemns and reprobates and teaches that an oath is never to be taken unless necessity require it. For oaths have been instituted on account of human frailty. They are really the outcome of evil, being a sign either of the inconstancy of him who takes them, or of the obstinacy of him who refuses to believe without them. However, an oath can be justified by necessity.

> When our Lord says: *Let your speech be 'yea, yea'; 'no, no,'* He evidently forbids the habit of swearing in familiar conversation and on trivial matters. He therefore admonishes us particularly against being too ready and willing to swear; and this should be carefully explained and impressed on the minds of the faithful.

Oaths in Secret Societies

Lastly, the Baltimore Catechism further clarifies that oaths are never to be taken in secret societies: "It is never allowed to promise under oath, in secret societies or elsewhere, to obey another in whatever good or evil he commands, for by such an oath we would declare ourselves ready and willing to commit sin, if ordered to do so, while God commands us to avoid even the danger of sinning. Hence the Church forbids us to join any society in which such oaths are taken by its members."[122]

For this reason, amongst others, the Catholic Church unequivocally condemns Freemasonry and prohibits Catholics without exception to join Masonic organizations. The first condemnation against Freemasonry, given by Pope Clement XII per *In Eminenti* (1738), was repeated and even extended by Benedict XIV (1751), Pius VII (1821), Leo XII in *Quo*

---

[122] Baltimore Catechism No. 3, Q. 1227.

Graviora (1826), Pius VIII (1829), Gregory XVI (1832), Pius IX (1846, 1849, 1864, 1865, 1869, 1873), and by Pope Leo XIII in both *Humanum Genus* (1884) and *Custodi di Quella Fede* (1890).

The 1917 Code of Canon law explicitly declared that Catholics who joined a Masonic organization incurred a penalty of *ipso facto* excommunication (Can. 2335). Several decades later, the Congregation for the Doctrine of the Faith (CDF) reaffirmed the prohibition (and the gravity of the offense) vis-à-vis a 1983 declaration approved by Pope John Paul II and signed by then-Cardinal Joseph Ratzinger:

> It has been asked whether there has been any change in the Church's decision in regard to Masonic associations since the new Code of Canon Law does not mention them expressly, unlike the previous Code. This Sacred Congregation is in a position to reply that this circumstance is due to an editorial criterion which was followed also in the case of other associations likewise unmentioned inasmuch as they are contained in wider categories.
>
> Therefore, the Church's negative judgment in regard to Masonic association remains unchanged since their principles have always been considered irreconcilable with the doctrine of the Church and therefore membership in them remains forbidden. The faithful who enroll in Masonic associations are in a state of grave sin and may not receive Holy Communion.[123]

No oath may be taken lightly, and no oath may ever be taken in a secret society.

Vows

Like oaths, vows are not forbidden and should not be taken lightly. The Baltimore Catechism again succinctly explains the importance of vows and how they differ from oaths, even though both fall under the domain of the Second Commandment:

> A vow is a deliberate promise made to God to do something that is pleasing to Him. The vows most

---

[123] CDF, "Declaration on Masonic Associations" (Nov. 26, 1983) (https://www.vatican.va/roman_curia/congregations/cfaith/documents/rc_con_cfai th_doc_19831126_declaration-masonic_en.html).

frequently made are the three vows of poverty, chastity, and obedience, taken by persons living in religious communities or consecrated to God. Persons living in the world are sometimes permitted to make such vows privately, but this should never be done without the advice and consent of their confessor.[124]

And while vows often concern those in religious life, they do have a place for lay Catholics as well:

It has always been a custom with pious Christians to make vows and promises to God; to beg His help for some special end, or to thank Him for some benefit received. They have promised pilgrimages, good works or alms and they have vowed to erect churches, convents, hospitals or schools.[125]

Sins Against the Second Commandment

After carefully considering our obligation to honor God's Name and how that is manifested in practice, we now consider sins against the Second Commandment. Turning again to the Baltimore Catechism, we read: "The second Commandment forbids all false, rash, unjust, and unnecessary oaths, blasphemy, cursing, and profane words."[126] Concerning sinful oaths – whether they be unjust, rash, or taken by false gods – the Roman Catechism wisely explains:

This Commandment is also violated, if justice, which is one of the three conditions of an oath, be wanting. Hence he who swears to commit a mortal sin, for example, to perpetrate murder, violates this Commandment, even though he speak seriously and from his heart, and his oath possess what we before pointed out as the first condition of every oath, that is, truth. …

This Commandment is also sinned against, and judgment is violated when one swears to what is true and what he believes to be true if his motives are light conjectures and far-fetched reasons. …

---

[124] Baltimore Catechism No. 3, Q. 1233.
[125] Ibid., Q. 1235.
[126] Ibid., Q. 1239.

> To swear by false gods is likewise to swear falsely. What is more opposed to truth than to appeal to lying and false deities as to the true God?

The final three sins against the Second Commandment, as explained by the Roman Catechism, are irreverent speech, neglect of prayer, and blasphemy.

Irreverent speech, which includes profanity, can indeed be a mortal sin if done with great anger against another person. Language is a gift from God. It should be used wisely and not laden with profanities that are impolite, vulgar, and negative, in according with St. Paul's admonition: *Let no evil speech proceed from your mouth: but that which is good, to the edification of faith: that it may administer grace to the hearers* (Eph. iv. 29). Likewise, speaking irreverently of holy things (such as Scripture, when it is used in satire) is blatantly condemned by the Law of God.

Even worse that irreverent speech is blasphemy, one of the most serious misuses of God's Name, as the Roman Catechism warns:

> Still more enormous is the guilt of those who, with impure and defiled lips, dare to curse or blaspheme the holy name of God—that name which is to be blessed and praised above measure by all creatures, or even the names of the Saints who reign with Him in glory.

As the Baltimore Catechism also explains, blasphemy is contempt for God, expressed in thought, word, or action: "Blasphemy is any word or action intended as an insult to God. To say He is cruel or find fault with His works is blasphemy. It is a much greater sin than cursing or taking God's name in vain. Profane words mean here bad, irreverent or irreligious words."[127] Those who, for instance, invoke the Name of God to support torture, abortion, slavery, or to cover up criminal offenses commit blasphemy by their actions. Cursing (asking God to damn a soul to hell) is also a mortal sin.

Conclusion

Death and life are in the power of the tongue (Prov. xviii. 21). The Roman Catechism concludes its explanation on the Second Commandment with a worthy reflection: "If *for every idle word that men shall speak, they shall render an account on the day of judgment* [Mt. xii. 26], what shall we say of those heinous crimes which involve great contempt of the divine name?"

---

[127] Ibid., Q. 1241.

These are truly words that we should reflect upon as part of our daily examination of conscience as Cardinal Giovanni Bona wisely counseled:

> Be prudent in every conversation, suppressing that immoderate inclination which rashly hurries most people on to pass sentence upon their neighbor without due examination and deference to the case in question. Flee far from duplicity and deception, and without any ambiguity or equivocation deliver the pure sentiments of your mind. God has given you the faculty of speech that you may truly and candidly announce things as they really are. Before you speak, consult your conscience — as to whether you be influenced by any evil passion — nor should you permit your tongue to say a word until that influence cease; otherwise, you shall say many things of which you shall afterwards have to repent. You may easily keep silence if you allow no passion to disturb your heart and if you preserve your soul tranquil and serene. Your discourse and your mind ought to be stamped with the same character. If your mind be sound, temperate and composed, your discourse also will be prudent and temperate. If the former be corrupted, the latter will breathe corruption. It is language that reveals to us the character of him who speaks.[128]

St. James himself also cautioned, *If anyone thinks he is religious and does not bridle his tongue but deceives his heart, his religion is vain* (Ja. i. 26). Anyone who seeks to live a holy life must guard his speech, understanding that he will need to render an account to God of every vain, empty, or false word uttered.

---

[128] Taken from *The Hand that Leads to Heaven* by Cardinal Giovanni Bona, 1881. Republished by TAN Books under the title *Guidance to Heaven.*

XXIII

The Third Commandment

Remember that thou keep holy the sabbath day. Six days shalt thou labor and do all thy works; but on the seventh day is the sabbath of the Lord thy God; thou shalt do no work on it, neither thee nor thy son, nor thy daughter, nor thy man-servant, nor thy maid-servant, nor thy beast, nor the stranger that is within thy gates. For in six days the Lord made heaven and earth, and the sea, and all things that are in them, and rested on the seventh day; wherefore the Lord blessed the seventh day and sanctified it (Ex. xx. 8-11).

The Third Commandment requires the sabbath to be observed as a holy day — a day unlike the other days in the week. Continuing our study of the Roman Catechism, we begin by considering the purpose of this Commandment as summarized therein:

> This Commandment of the Law rightly and in due order prescribes the external worship which we owe to God; for it is, as it were, a consequence of the preceding Commandment. For if we sincerely and devoutly worship God, guided by the faith and hope we have in Him, we cannot but honor Him with external worship and thanksgiving. Now since we cannot easily discharge these duties while occupied in worldly affairs, a certain fixed time has been set aside so that it may be conveniently performed.

When Is the Sabbath?

Sunday is the preeminent holy day of the week. It is the day on which we refrain from servile work, attend Mass, devote ourselves to prayer, and engage in recreation, family time, and true leisure. But even some Catholics are surprised to learn that the original day of rest for the Jews was Saturday, not Sunday.

If Saturday is the Sabbath day, then why do we keep Sunday holy? Did the Church change the Sabbath day? Is working on Saturday a sin too since it does not, strictly speaking, keep the Sabbath holy? Should we honor both days?

Unlike what Seventh-day Adventists or Seventh Day Baptists allege, the observance of Sunday instead of Saturday is not a medieval invention of the Catholic Church. The change reflects the ultimate authority of the Apostles to govern the Church on earth – a charge given to them directly by Our Lord. On this matter, the Roman Catechism notes the difference in the ceremonial law as opposed to the moral law of the Jews:

> The other Commandments of the Decalogue are precepts of the natural law, obligatory at all times and unalterable. Hence, after the abrogation of the Law of Moses, all the Commandments contained in the two tables are observed by Christians, not indeed because their observance is commanded by Moses, but because they are in conformity with nature which dictates obedience to them.

> This Commandment about the observance of the Sabbath, on the other hand, considered as to the time appointed for its fulfilment, is not fixed and unalterable, but susceptible of change, and belongs not to the moral, but the ceremonial law. Neither is it a principle of the natural law; we are not instructed by nature to give external worship to God on that day, rather than on any other. And in fact, the Sabbath was kept holy only from the time of the liberation of the people of Israel from the bondage of Pharaoh. The observance of the Sabbath was to be abrogated at the same time as the other Hebrew rites and ceremonies, that is, at the death of Christ. Having been, as it were, images which foreshadowed the light and the truth, these ceremonies were to disappear at the coming of that light and truth, which is Jesus Christ.

In Galatians V. 1-6, St. Paul stated that the observance of circumcision and the requirements of the Law of Moses from the Old Testament were abrogated and no longer binding. The only remaining elements of the Old Testament that are required are the moral law; the ceremonial laws are not. And that is why the requirement for wearing tassels on your clothes (cf. Dt. xxii. 12), abstaining from pork or shellfish, or not using two different species to plow a field at the same time, are abrogated. The Jews count 613 different laws, but the ceremonial laws no longer apply since the New Testament has completed and fulfilled the Old Testament.

The Roman Catechism clarifies the relationship between the moral and the ceremonial law in regard to the Third Commandment, illustrating why this Commandment ultimately remains valid in light of the New Testament:

> This Commandment is like the others, not in so far as it is a precept of the ceremonial law, but only as it is a natural and moral precept. The worship of God and the practice of religion, which it comprises, have the natural law for their basis. Nature prompts us to give some time to the worship of God. This is demonstrated by the fact that we find among all nations public festivals consecrated to the solemnities of religion and divine worship.
>
> As nature requires some time to be given to necessary functions of the body, to sleep, repose and the like, so she also requires that some time be devoted to the mind, to refresh itself by the contemplation of God. Hence, since some time should be devoted to the worship of the Deity and to the practice of religion, this (Commandment) doubtless forms part of the moral law.

Sunday Established as New Sabbath by the Apostles

The ceremonial law concerning Jewish Sabbath has ceased by virtue of Christ. God Himself fulfilled the Jewish Sabbath and replaced it with Sunday, the Lord's Day, as the Baltimore Catechism affirms:

> The Church commands us to keep the Sunday holy instead of the Sabbath because on Sunday Christ rose from the dead, and on Sunday He sent the Holy Ghost upon the Apostles. We keep Sunday instead of Saturday holy also to teach that the Old Law is not now binding upon us, but that we must keep the New Law, which takes its place.[129]

The issue of observing Sunday as the holy day is ultimately based on the authority of the Church, which Our Lord established and to which He entrusted the power of binding and loosing (cf. Mt. xvi. 18-19, 18:18). The Church, therefore, by the authority given to her by Christ, has established Sunday as the day on which we are to render worship to Almighty God as the Roman Catechism teaches:

---

[129] Baltimore Catechism No. 3, Q. 1250 – 1251.

But the Church of God has thought it well to transfer the celebration and observance of the Sabbath to Sunday.

For, as on that day light first shone on the world, so by the Resurrection of our Redeemer on the same day, by whom was thrown open to us the gate to eternal life, we were called out of darkness into light; and hence the Apostles would have it called *the Lord's day*.

We also learn from the Sacred Scriptures that the first day of the week was held sacred because on that day the work of creation commenced, and on that day the Holy Ghost was given to the Apostles.

The early Church Fathers bear witness to the legitimacy of this change, as well. St. Ignatius of Antioch (died c. A.D. 110), for example, tells us, "[T]hose who were brought up in the ancient order of things [i.e., Jews] have come to the possession of a new hope, no longer observing the Sabbath, but living in the observance of the Lord's day, on which also our life has sprung up again by him and by his death."[130] Indeed, the Roman Catechism states that the institution of Sunday as the principal day of worship in place of Saturday is of apostolic origin:

The Apostles therefore resolved to consecrate the first day of the week to the divine worship and called it *the Lord's day*. St. John in the Apocalypse makes mention of 'the Lord's day' [Apoc. i. 10]; and the Apostle [Paul] commands collections to be made 'on the first day of the week' [I Cor. xvi. 2], that is, according to the interpretation of St. Chrysostom, on the Lord's day. From all this we learn that even then the Lord's day was kept holy in the Church.

Remember the Sabbath

Before discussing how the Sabbath must be honored (lest it be profaned), the Roman Catechism wisely pauses to reflect on the word "remember", the first word in the text of the Third Commandment. Why did God choose to add this particular word? The Roman Catechism expounds on this inclusion in a truly unique manner not found in other catechisms when it states:

The word *remember* is appropriately made use of at the beginning of the Commandment to signify that the

---

[130] St. Ignatius of Antioch, Letter to the Magnesians, Ch. 9 (c. A.D. 110).

sanctification of that particular day belonged to the ceremonial law. Of this it would seem to have been necessary to remind the people; for, although the law of nature commands us to devote a certain portion of time to the external worship to God, it fixes no particular day for the performance of this duty.

They [the faithful] are also to be taught, that from these words we may learn how we should employ our time during the week; that we are to keep constantly in view the Lord's day, on which we are, as it were, to render an account to God for our occupations and conduct; and that therefore our works should be such as not to be unacceptable in the sight of God, or, as it is written, be to us 'an occasion of grief, and a scruple of heart' [I Kngs. xxv. 31].

Remembering the Lord's Day necessitates that we plan for it and ensure that all of our errands and labors are completed before it begins. And similarly, the remembrance of the Lord's Day requires us to appropriately plan ahead our attendance at Mass and the other prayers that we intend to observe (e.g., the Family Rosary, the Breviary, Benediction) in order to appropriately sanctify the day.

Keeping Holy the Lord's Day

The primary means by which we keep Sunday holy is by (1) refraining from servile labor and (2) offering to God "works of piety and religion" – most especially, our assistance at Holy Mass. Says the Roman Catechism:

In the Scriptures keeping holy the Sabbath means a cessation from bodily labor and from business, as is clear from the following words of the Commandment: *Thou shalt do no work on it.* But this is not all that it means; otherwise, it would have been sufficient to say in Deuteronomy, *Observe the day of the sabbath*; but it is added, *and sanctify it*; and these additional words prove that the Sabbath is a day sacred to religion, set apart for works of piety and devotion.

We sanctify the Sabbath fully and perfectly, therefore, when we offer to God works of piety and religion. This is evidently the Sabbath, which Isaias calls *delightful*; for festivals are, as it were, the delight of God and of pious men. And if to this religious and holy observance of the

Sabbath we add works of mercy, the rewards promised us in the same chapter are numerous and most important. The true and proper meaning, therefore, of this Commandment tends to this, that we take special care to set apart some fixed time, when, disengaged from bodily labor and worldly affairs, we may devote our whole being, soul and body, to the religious veneration of God.

On the meaning of "a cessation from bodily labor," the Catechism further explains:

> *Thou shalt do no work on it, says the Lord, thou, nor thy son, nor thy daughter, nor thy man-servant, nor thy maid-servant, nor thy beast, nor the stranger that is within thy gates.*

> These words teach us, in the first place, to avoid whatever may interfere with the worship of God. Hence it is not difficult to perceive that all servile works are forbidden, not because they are improper or evil in themselves, but because they withdraw the attention from the worship of God, which is the great end of the Commandment.

> The faithful should be still more careful to avoid sin, which not only withdraws the mind from the contemplation of divine things, but entirely alienates us from the love of God.

Abstaining from Servile Works

Understanding the difference between servile labor and intellectual work is of paramount importance. As summarized in the Baltimore Catechism: "Servile works derive their name from the fact that such works were formerly done by slaves. Therefore, reading, writing, studying and, in general, all works that slaves did not perform are not considered servile works."[131]

Are servile works ever permitted on the Lord's Day? Turning to the Catechism of St. Thomas Aquinas, there are only four exceptions to the prohibition against servile work on Sundays and Holy Days of Obligation:

---

[131] Baltimore Catechism No. 3, Q. 1254.

We ought to know, however, that servile work can be done on the Sabbath for four reasons. The first reason is necessity. Wherefore, the Lord excused the disciples plucking the ears of corn on the Sabbath, as we read in St. Matthew (xii. 3-5). The second reason is when the work is done for the service of the Church, as we see in the same Gospel how the priests did all things necessary in the Temple on the Sabbath day. The third reason is for the good of our neighbor; for on the Sabbath the Savior cured one having a withered hand, and He refuted the Jews who reprimanded Him, by citing the example of the sheep in a pit (Mt. xxii. 9-15). And the fourth reason is the authority of our superiors. Thus, God commanded the Jews to circumcise on the Sabbath.

As a result, the Church's clear teaching on the Sabbath indicates that we refrain from unnecessary work for the purpose of God's worship. Works that support that worship (e.g., providing meals to priests, driving to Mass) do not violate the spirit or the letter of the Law.

Holy Days of Obligation

While the Third Commandment is often thought of as only concerning Sunday, it is closely related to the Church's authority to declare certain days as being Holy Days of Obligation, a topic discussed in the Roman Catechism:

From the very infancy of the Church and in the following centuries other days were also appointed by the Apostles and the holy Fathers, in order to commemorate the benefits bestowed by God. Among these days to be kept sacred the most solemn are those which were instituted to honor the mysteries of our redemption. In the next place are the days which are dedicated to the most Blessed Virgin Mother, to the Apostles, Martyrs and other Saints who reign with Christ. In the celebration of their victories the divine power and goodness are praised, due honor is paid to their memories, and the faithful are encouraged to imitate them.

The first precept of the Church requires Catholics to attend Holy Mass on all Holy Days of Obligation. These days have changed over the course of the centuries. The first catalog of Holy Days comes from the Decretals of Pope Gregory IX in 1234, which listed 45 Holy Days. In 1642, Pope Urban VIII issued the papal bull *Universa Per Orbem* which altered the required

Holy Days of Obligation for the Universal Church to consist of 35 such days, as well as the principal patrons of one's locality.

Some of the Holy Days of Obligation removed between 1234 and 1642 included Holy Monday through Holy Saturday, in addition to Easter Wednesday through Easter Saturday. In 1708, Pope Clement XI added the Conception of the Blessed Virgin to the list in his papal bull *Commissi Nobis Divinitus.*

However, these days were not held as obligatory in all places. We see a lot of variety in the observance of these days from region to region. The Church has approved different days and reduced days of precept for a long time. Before the 1900s, there was also a distinction between days of single or double precept. Days of double precept required Mass attendance as well as observing a sabbath rest. Days of single precept were days of Mass attendance, but the faithful were permitted to work on them. Throughout the late 1700s and into the 1800s, the number of observed days of precept began to wane.

In 1911, Pope St. Pius X in *Supremi disciplinæ* drastically reduced the number of Holy Days of Obligation in the Universal Church to eight. Shortly thereafter in 1917, Corpus Christi and St. Joseph were added back, bringing the total to ten. The ten currently observed on the Universal Calendar are the same as from 1917.

Holy Days of Obligation, which had remained the same in the United States since 1917, were further modified in the latter part of the century. On Dec. 13, 1991, the United States Bishops issued a directive further abrogating New Year's Day (traditionally called the Feast of the Circumcision), the Assumption on August 15, or All Saints on November 1 in years when the feast falls on a Saturday or a Monday. And on Mar. 23, 1992, in another reduction, the Bishop of Honolulu obtained an indult from the Holy See and approval from the United States episcopal conference to reduce the Holy Days of Obligation to only Christmas and the Immaculate Conception for Catholics in Hawaii.

The Roman Catechism, alluding to the decline already underway at the time of the Council of Trent, wisely laments:

> Had [God] commanded us to offer Him every day the tribute of religious worship, would it not be our duty, in return for His inestimable and infinite benefits towards us, to endeavor to obey the command with promptitude and alacrity? But now that the days consecrated to His worship are but few, there is no excuse for neglecting or

reluctantly performing this duty, which moreover obliges under grave sin.

When so few days are kept as Holy Days of Obligation, there can be no worthy excuse for not observing the few that remain.

First Precept of the Church

Missing Mass on a Sunday or a Holy Day of Obligation without a grave reason or without dispensation (e.g., illness, inability to reasonably obtain transportation) is a mortal sin. If someone is unable to attend the Holy Sacrifice of the Mass for a good reason, that person should still read the Missal for that day and pray the prayers from the Liturgy (e.g., Collect, Gradual, Communion), in addition to sanctifying the day through prayers like the Rosary, spiritual reading, and works of mercy.

Bishops may dispense the faithful from the obligation of attending the Holy Sacrifice of the Mass for a legitimate reason (e.g., dangerous storms, epidemics of illness). When this occurs, the Church dispenses souls from the precept of assisting at Mass; however, the obligation to sanctify Sundays and Holy Days (a precept of divine law) cannot be abrogated. The Roman Catechism lists a number of ways in which the faithful may honor the Lord's Day in addition to Mass attendance and reception of the Sacraments of Confession and the Most Holy Eucharist:

> The faithful should also listen with attention and reverence to sermons. Nothing is more intolerable, nothing more unworthy than to despise the words of Christ or hear them with indifference.

> Likewise, the faithful should give themselves to frequent prayer and the praises of God; and an object of their special attention should be to learn those things which pertain to a Christian life, and to practice with care the duties of piety, such as giving alms to the poor and needy, visiting the sick, and administering consolation to the sorrowful and afflicted. 'Religion clean and undefiled before God and the Father is this,' says St. James, 'to visit the fatherless and widows in their tribulation' [Ja. i. 27].

Canon Francis Ripley wisely wrote, "At present, we must remember that God's command is to keep Sunday holy. Attendance at Mass and abstinence from servile work are only two ways of doing this. One who merely goes to Mass and forgets about God for the rest of the day can scarcely be said to keep Sunday holy, although he may, thereby, avoid mortal sin."[132]

The Importance of the Commandment

In addition to fulfilling their duty to render external worship to God, the faithful who keep this Commandment also receive many blessings, as the Roman Catechism illustrates:

> Those who are faithful in its observance are admitted, as it were, into the divine presence to speak freely with God; for in prayer, we contemplate the divine majesty and commune with Him; in hearing religious instruction, we hear the voice of God, which reaches us through the agency of those who devoutly preach on divine things; and at the Holy Sacrifice of the Mass, we adore Christ the Lord, present on our altars. Such are the blessings which they preeminently enjoy who faithfully observe this Commandment.

Conversely, those who shun this Commandment commit a great crime. Pope Pius XII exclaimed in *Mediator Dei*, his 1947 Encyclical on the Sacred Liturgy: "...how will these Christians not fear spiritual death whose rest on Sundays and feast days is not devoted to religion and piety but given over to the allurements of the world! Sundays and holidays must be made holy by divine worship which gives homage to God and heavenly food to the soul.... Our soul is filled with the greatest grief when we see how the Christian people profane the afternoon of feast days...."[133]

The Roman Catechism confirms these sentiments:

> But those who altogether neglect its fulfilment resist God and His Church; they heed not God's command, and are enemies of Him and His holy laws, of which the easiness of the command is itself a proof. We should, it is true, be prepared to undergo the severest labor for the sake of God; but in this Commandment He imposes on us no labor; He only commands us to rest and disengage ourselves from worldly cares on those days which are to be kept holy. To refuse obedience to this Commandment is, therefore, a proof of extreme boldness; and the punishments with which its infraction has been visited

---

[132] Canon Francis Ripley, *This Is the Faith* (Gracewing Publishing, 1973), 78.
[133] Pius XII, Encyclical Mediator Dei (Nov. 20, 1947), n. 150.

by God, as we learn from the Book of Numbers [Num. xv. 35], should be a warning to us.

Sadly, those who fail to rest on the Lord's Day rob God of that which is due to him as St. John Vianney also warned:

> Sunday is the property of our good God; it is His own day, the Lord's day. He made all the days of the week: He might have kept them all; He has given you six and has reserved only the seventh for Himself. What right have you to meddle with what does not belong to you? You know very well that stolen goods never bring any profit. Nor will the day that you steal from Our Lord profit you either. I know two very certain ways of becoming poor: they are working on Sunday and taking other people's property.[134]

Our Lady has also warned us of the disasters that will result from the profanation of the Lord's Day. In 1846, when Melanie Calvat and Maximin Giraud were watching cattle in a pasture, they saw a globe of light that opened to reveal a most beautiful woman, clad in long dress and apron, with a shawl that crossed in front and tied in back. Around her neck was a crucifix that depicted the instruments of the Passion and on her head was a cap and roses. She sat on a rock with her face in her hands weeping. The Lady said that unless the people repented of working on Sundays and of blasphemy, she would be forced to let go her Son's arm because it had grown too heavy. She said that crop blights and famine would follow if her wishes were not heeded. That Lady was the Blessed Mother under the title of Our Lady of La Salette.

We must ask ourselves, do we do enough to truly keep holy the Lord's Day and all Holy Days of Obligation? Besides observing these days and encouraging others to do so, we can make reparation for these sins, specifically through the Holy Face Confraternity.[135]

---

[134] St. John Vianney, "On the Sanctification of Sunday," <https://catholicsaints.info/on-the-sanctification-of-sunday-by-saint-john-vianney>.
[135] <http://www.holyfacedevotion.com/devotion.htm>.

XXIV

The Fourth Commandment

Honor thy father and thy mother, that thou mayest be long lived upon the land which the Lord thy God will give thee (Ex. xx. 12).

The Two Tables of the Law

In its opening remarks, the Roman Catechism explains the relationship between the first three Commandments with the subsequent ones:

> The preceding Commandments are supreme both in dignity and in importance; but those which follow rank next in order because of their necessity. For the first three tend directly to God; while the object of the others is the charity we owe to our neighbor, although even these are ultimately referred to God, since we love our neighbor on account of God, our last end. Hence Christ our Lord has declared that the two Commandments which inculcate the love of God and of our neighbor are like unto each other.

All the Commandments, regardless of their particulars, have charity as their foundation. In particular, the Fourth Commandment requires us to honor and obey not only our parents and grandparents but also our superiors. It is under the Fourth Commandment that the clergy understand obedience to their superiors; and likewise, men and women understand obedience to their nations, employers, and rulers. On the other hand, parents and rulers are expected to provide for the spiritual well-being of their children and subjects.

While seemingly distinct from the preceding three Commandments, which concern our service to God, the Fourth Commandment is rooted in the same virtue of charity. As the Roman Catechism aptly remarks:

The advantages arising from the present subject can scarcely be expressed in words; for not only does it bring with it its own fruit, and that in the richest abundance and of superior excellence, but it also affords a test of our obedience to and observance of the First Commandment. *He that loveth not his brother whom he seeth,* says St. John, *how can he love God whom he seeth not?* [I Jn. iv. 20] In like manner, if we do not honor and reverence our parents whom we ought to love next to God and whom we continually see, how can we honor or reverence God, the supreme and best of parents, whom we see not? Hence we can easily perceive the similarity between these two Commandments.

While all the Commandments are rooted in charity, they do not all have the same immediate object or end. As the Catechism explains, Moses received the Commandments on two stone tablets. On the first was written the first, second, and third. And the remaining seven, including the Fourth Commandment, were inscribed on the second tablet. The division of Commandments in this manner is from God Himself:

This order of the Commandments is especially appropriate, since the very collocation points out to us their difference in nature. For whatever is commanded or prohibited in Scripture by the divine law springs from one of two principles, the love of God or of our neighbor: one or the other of these is the basis of every duty required of us. The three preceding Commandments teach us the love which we owe to God; and the other seven, the duties which we owe to our neighbors and to public society. The arrangement, therefore, which assigns some of the Commandments to the first and others to the second table is not without good reason.

Honor

The Fourth Commandments enjoins on everyone the responsibility to "honor" a group of individuals. What does "honor" mean in this regard? The Baltimore Catechism explains: "The word *honor* in this commandment includes the doing of everything necessary for our parents' spiritual and temporal welfare, the showing of proper respect, and the fulfillment of all our duties to them."[136]

---

[136] Baltimore Catechism No. 3, Q. 1258.

The eloquence of the Roman Catechism goes further in explaining honor, and how it differs from both love and fear, by stating:

> To honor is to think respectfully of anyone, and to hold in the highest esteem all that relates to him. It includes love, respect, obedience, and reverence.
>
> Very properly then is the word *honor* used here in preference to the word *fear* or *love*, although parents are also to be much loved and feared. Respect and reverence are not always the accompaniments of love; neither is love the inseparable companion of fear; but *honor*, when proceeding from the heart, combines both fear and love."

Who Is "Thy Father" and "Thy Mother"?

While the Fourth Commandment obviously applies to our natural parents, the Catechism next makes an important clarification that "father", in this context, refers to more than just our biological father:

> Besides our natural fathers, then, there are others who in Scripture are called fathers, as was said above, and to each of these, proper honor is due.
>
> In the first place, the prelates of the Church, her pastors and priests are called fathers, as is evident from the Apostle, who, writing to the Corinthians, says: *I write not these things to confound you; but I admonish you as my dearest children. For if you have ten thousand instructors in Christ, yet not many fathers. For in Christ Jesus by the gospel I have begotten you* [I Cor. iv. 14-16]. It is also written in Ecclesiasticus: *Let us praise men of renown, and our fathers in their generation* [Ecclus. xliv. 1].
>
> Those who govern the State, to whom are entrusted power, magistracy, or command, are also called fathers; thus, Naaman was called father by his servants [cf. IV Kngs v. 13].
>
> The name father is also applied to those to whose care, fidelity, probity, and wisdom others are committed, such as teachers, instructors, masters, and guardians; and hence the sons of the Prophets called Elias and Eliseus

236

their father [cf. IV Kings ii. 12, xiii. 14]. Finally, aged men, advanced in years, we also call fathers.

In similarly clear language, the Roman Catechism expounds on the rationale for mothers being explicitly mentioned: "The pastor should teach that the name *mother* is mentioned in this Commandment, in order to remind us of her benefits and claims in our regard, of the care and solicitude with which she bore us, and of the pain and labor with which she gave us birth and brought us up."

How to Honor Our Parents

After explaining our responsibility to our fathers and mothers, the Roman Catechism next carefully lists various means by which we honor them. Offering spontaneous and sincere love, offering respect, honoring their wishes and inclinations, imitating their good example, and relieving their necessities all follow from the Fourth Commandment of the Decalogue.

Canon Francis Ripley remarks in a similar fashion: "If we are commanded to love all men, how much more should we love our parents, to whom we owe so much. Such love corresponds to the most natural feeling of the heart. In practice, parents should receive from their children affection, thanks, good wishes, consideration, prayer, kindness in thought… and exact obedience."[137]

Special attention is given by the Catechism to the responsibility of caring for ill and elderly parents. While written hundreds of years ago, the wisdom of the Roman Catechism, especially in this passage, transcends times and applies as equally in our day as in the time of St. Charles Borromeo:

> But if at all times it is our duty to honor our parents, this duty becomes still more imperative when they are visited by severe illness. We should then see to it that they do not neglect Confession and the other Sacraments which every Christian should receive at the approach of death. We should also see that pious and religious persons visit them frequently to strengthen their weakness, assist them by their counsel, and animate them to the hope of immortality, that having risen above the concerns of this world, they may fix their thoughts entirely on God. Thus, blessed with the sublime virtues of faith, hope, and charity, and fortified by the helps of religion, they will not only look at death without fear, since it is necessary,

---

[137] Canon Francis Ripley, *This Is the Faith* (Gracewing Publishing, 1973), p. 78.

but will even welcome it, as it hastens their entrance into eternity.

The importance of caring for our parents' spiritual health is clearly emphasized. Care should be taken to ensure that, to the best of our ability, they die in the state of grace and fortified by the sacraments of the Church. Their funerals should also be properly arranged so they receive the respect they deserve with a devout and proper Catholic Requiem Mass. And great care should also be given to the management of their estate, ensuring that sufficient money is set aside to cover stipends for Masses to be said for their souls, especially Gregorian Masses. On the history and the value of Gregorian Masses, the Servants of the Holy Family explain:

> The practice of offering Gregorian Masses for the repose of the soul of a deceased person was started by Pope Saint Gregory the Great, who ruled the Church from 590 to 604. The event that started this pious practice took place while he was abbot of St. Andrew's monastery in Rome, prior to his election to the papacy. In the fourth book of his *Dialogues*, St. Gregory relates how one of the monks of his monastery, named Justus, did not keep his vow of poverty very well. When Justus died, St. Gregory feared that the good monk might have to spend a long time in Purgatory because of his failures with regard to poverty. He therefore ordered that the Holy Sacrifice of the Mass be offered up for Justus for thirty consecutive days. On the thirtieth day, Justus appeared to Copiosus, a brother monk, telling him that he was now freed from his sufferings because of the thirty Masses that St. Gregory had ordered to be said for him.
>
> Following St. Gregory's example, Catholic people throughout the ages have continued the pious custom of having thirty Masses said for their departed relatives and friends. The custom of praying thirty days for the dead can be traced back to the Old Testament (Deut. 34:8). The Sacred Congregation on Indulgences has declared, 'The offering of Gregorian Masses has a special efficacy for obtaining from God the speedy deliverance of a suffering soul, and that this is a pious and reasonable belief of the faithful.'"[138]

---

[138] <https://servi.org/product/gregorian-masses>, accessed October 20th, 2022.

The Limits of Obedience

While we are enjoined to honor our parents and respect them, this command is not absolute. If a parent, or anyone in authority over us, commands us to commit a sin, we must disobey since obeying such an immoral command would be a sin. On this essential caveat, the Baltimore Catechism counsels: "We should refuse to obey parents or superiors who command us to sin because they are not then acting with God's authority, but contrary to it and in violation of His laws."[139]

Rather than being one-sided, the Fourth Commandment also charges parents with a series of responsibilities toward their children too:

> As the law of God commands children to honor, obey, and respect their parents so are their reciprocal duties which parents owe to their children. Parents are obliged to bring up their children in the knowledge and practice of religion, and to give them the best rules for the regulation of their lives; so that, instructed and trained in religion, they may serve God holily and constantly.

Respect for Lawful Authorities

After expounding upon the honor due to our parents, the Roman Catechism next turns to the respect we owe our lawful authorities and superiors by affirming: "We are bound to honor not only our natural parents, but also others who are called fathers, such as bishops and priests, kings, princes and magistrates, tutors, guardians and masters, teachers, aged persons and the like, all of whom are entitled, some in a greater, some in a less degree, to share our love, our obedience, and our assistance."

St. Paul commands likewise: *Obey your prelates and be subject to them. For they watch as being to render an account of your souls; that they may do this with joy, and not with grief. For this is not expedient for you* (Heb. xiii. 17). Our Lord likewise affirmed the importance of rendering our dues to civil rulers and governments when He answered the question on whether it was lawful to pay taxes to Caesar:

> [The spies of the chief priests and scribes asked Jesus:] Is it lawful for us to give tribute to Caesar, or no? But [Jesus], considering their guile, said to them: Why tempt you Me? Show Me a penny. Whose image and inscription hath it? They answering, said to Him,

---

[139] Baltimore Catechism No. 3, Q. 1260.

> Caesar's. And He said to them: Render therefore to
> Caesar the things that are Caesar's: and to God the things
> that are God's (Lk. xx. 22-25).

Our Lord's command was to give to the civil authorities their rightful dues
but to give true worship to God alone. The Jews at the time of Our Lord
often clashed with the pagan Roman authorities. But even with their errors,
Our Lord affirmed that dues must nevertheless be paid to them. Even
wicked authorities, if they be legitimate, must be respected even if their
unlawful commands are not to be obeyed. Says the Roman Catechism:

> St. Peter says: *Be ye subject, therefore, to every human
> creature for God's sake; whether it be to the king as
> excelling, or to governors as sent by him* [I Pet. ii. 13].

> For whatever honor we show them is given to God, since
> exalted human dignity deserves respect because it is an
> image of the divine power, and in it we revere the
> providence of God who has entrusted to men the care of
> public affairs and who uses them as the instruments of
> His power.

> If we sometimes have wicked and unworthy officials it
> is not their faults that we revere, but the authority from
> God which they possess. Indeed, while it may seem
> strange, we are not excused from highly honoring them
> even when they show themselves hostile and implacable
> towards us. Thus, David rendered great services to Saul
> even when the latter was his bitter foe, and to this he
> alludes when he says: *With them that hated peace I was
> peaceable* [Ps. cxix. 7].

> However, should their commands be wicked or unjust,
> they should not be obeyed, since in such a case they rule
> not according to their rightful authority, but according to
> injustice and perversity.

Likewise, the Roman Catechism affirms the need to honor our bishops and
priests, even though we are never to obey commands to sin. These wise
words are well suited to our current era, when far too many priests are prone
to teach false doctrine or encourage weak discipline:

> The Apostle also teaches that they [the clergy] are
> entitled to obedience: *Obey your prelates and be subject
> to them; for they watch as being to render an account of*

your souls [Heb. xiii. 17]. Nay, more. Christ the Lord commands obedience even to wicked pastors: *Upon the chair of Moses have sitten the scribes and Pharisees: all things, therefore, whatsoever they shall say to you, observe and do; but according to their works do ye not, for they say and do not* [Mt. xxiii. 2-3].

In short, we must respect all who are legitimately placed over us, whether they be our bosses, our teachers, our priests, or our civil leaders, but we cannot follow their wishes if they instruct us to do anything sinful. In this way, the Fourth Commandment is subordinated to the First Commandment.

That We May Be Long Lived

After commanding us to honor our father and our mother, the Scriptures add: *that thou mayest be long lived upon the land which the Lord thy God will give thee* (Ex. xx. 12). Why does the Lord include this phrase in the Fourth Commandment? Indeed, few people even consider the reward for obeying the divine precept. However, the Roman Catechism uniquely explains:

> Children, therefore, who honor their parents, and gratefully acknowledge the blessing of life received from them are deservedly rewarded with the protracted enjoyment of that life to an advanced age.

> The (nature of the) divine promise also demands distinct explanation. It includes not only the eternal life of the blessed, but also the life which we lead on earth, according to the interpretation of St. Paul: *Piety is profitable to all things, having promise of the life that now is, and of that which is to come* [I Tim. iv. 8]. ...

> The additional words, *which the Lord thy God will give thee*, promise not only length of days, but also repose, tranquility, and security to live well; for in Deuteronomy it is not only said, *that thou mayest live a long time*, but it is also added, and *that it may be well with thee* [Dt. v. 16], words afterwards quoted by the Apostle [cf. Eph. vi. 3].

Yet, the Catechism also reminds us that for some it is God's will – for the person's ultimate good – that his life on earth be shortened:

Now this happens sometimes because it is better for him to depart from this world before he has strayed from the path of virtue and of duty; for *he was taken away lest wickedness should alter his understanding, or deceit beguile his soul* [Wis. vi. 10-11]. Or because destruction and general upheaval are impending, he is called away that he may escape the calamities of the times. *The just man*, says the Prophet, *is taken away from before the face of evil* [Isa. lvii. 1], lest his virtue and salvation be endangered when God avenges the crimes of men. Or else, he is spared the bitter anguish of witnessing the calamities of his friends and relations in such evil days. The premature death of the good, therefore, gives special reason for fear.

Conclusion

While many at least implicitly assume the Fourth Commandment only concerns young children, the Fourth Commandment applies to everyone, regardless of age. As our parents inevitably age, we have a grave responsibility to help provide for both their spiritual and material needs with the utmost care and attention. Our Lord Jesus Christ, in the honoring of the Blessed Virgin Mary, shows us the example of perfect observance of the Fourth Commandment. To those who are currently experiencing trials in caring for aging parents, the words of St. John Chrysostom on Our Lord's entrusting of His Mother to St. John serve as a source of inspiration to us:

> And He, having committed His Mother to John, said, 'Behold thy son' (John 19:26). O the honor! With what honor did He honor the disciple! when He Himself was now departing, He committed her to the disciple to take care of. For since it was likely that, being His Mother, she would grieve, and require protection, He with reason entrusted her to the beloved. To him He says, 'Behold thy Mother' (John 19:27).' This He said, knitting them together in charity; which the disciple understanding, took her to his own home. But why made He no mention of any other woman, although another stood there? To teach us to pay more than ordinary respect to our mothers. For as when parents oppose us on spiritual matters, we must not even own them, so when they do not hinder us, we ought to pay them all becoming respect, and to prefer them before others, because they begot us, because they bred us up, because they bare for

242

us ten thousand terrible things. And by these words He silences the shamelessness of Marcion; for if He were not born according to the flesh, nor had a mother, wherefore takes He such forethought for her alone?[140]

---

[140] St. John Chrysostom, Homilies on the Gospel of John, Homily 85.

XXV

The Fifth Commandment

Thou shalt not kill (Ex. xx. 13). While most Catholics are not guilty of the sin of homicide, the Fifth Commandment is not one that any Catholic may ignore. This Commandment both prohibits a number of a sins, of which homicide is only one, and also enjoins on everyone a commandment of charity towards one another. On this point, the Roman Catechism is clear:

> In the explanation of this Commandment the Lord points out its twofold obligation. The one is prohibitory and forbids us to kill; the other is mandatory and commands us to cherish sentiments of charity, concord and friendship towards our enemies, to have peace with all men, and finally, to endure with patience every inconvenience.

While the Commandments were first given to Moses on Mount Sinai, the prohibition against killing extends back further to the beginning of creation with our first parents. It was original sin, which is an attack against God Himself, that drove Adam and Eve from paradise and brought about the consequences of original sin to humanity. And in only one more generation, murder would enter human history as Cain murdered his brother Abel out of jealousy (cf. Gen. iv. 3-8). Even before Moses received the Tablets of the Law, the Lord spoke clearly about the seriousness of killing, as the Roman Catechism insightfully demonstrates:

> Immediately after the earth was overwhelmed in universal deluge, this was the first prohibition made by God to man. *I will require the blood of your lives*, He said, *at the hand of every beast and at the hand of man* [Gen. ix. 5]. In the next place, among the precepts of the Old Law expounded by our Lord, this Commandment was mentioned first by Him; concerning which it is written in the Gospel of St. Matthew: *It has been said thou shalt not kill* [Mt. v. 9], etc.

Sins Against the Fifth Commandment

The Fifth Commandment forbids willful murder, abortion, suicide, fighting (outside of self-defense, of course), quarreling, scandal, bad example, anger, hatred, and revenge. As stated by Canon Francis Ripley, "Life is man's greatest good, so God wishes to safeguard it against attack. God alone is the author of life; He alone may take life — apart from the circumstances of a just war, the execution of a criminal, and legitimate self-defense."[141] The Baltimore Catechism concurs: "The fifth Commandment forbids all willful murder, fighting, anger, hatred, revenge, and bad example."[142]

The wisdom of the Roman Catechism expounds on these prohibitions and mentions that the Commandment similarly condemns those who encourage or assist with the death of another, not merely those who commit the act. And further, that the Commandment applies to everyone without exception:

> As to the person who kills, the Commandment recognizes no exception whatever, be he rich or powerful, master or parent. All, without exception or distinction, are forbidden to kill.

> With regard to the person killed, the law extends to all. There is no individual, however humble or lowly his condition, whose life is not shielded by this law.

Suicide is also forbidden without exception, as the Roman Catechism affirms:

> It also forbids suicide. No man possesses such power over his own life as to be at liberty to put himself to death. Hence, we find that the Commandment does not say: *Thou shalt not kill another*, but simply: *Thou shalt not kill.*

> Finally, if we consider the numerous means by which murder may be committed, the law admits of no exception. Not only does it forbid to take away the life of another by laying violent hands on him, by means of a sword, a stone, a stick, a halter, or by administering poison; but also strictly prohibits the accomplishment of

---

[141] Canon Francis Ripley, *This Is the Faith* (Gracewing Publishing, 1973), p. 82.
[142] Baltimore Catechism No. 3, Q. 1277.

the death of another by counsel, assistance, help or any other means whatever.

Fr. Joseph Deharbe's "Complete Catechism of the Catholic Religion" explains the Church's immemorial practice of forbidding funerals to those guilty of suicide because of the scandal it causes for the faithful since, from our perspective, the prospects of someone repenting and making a perfect act of contrition before death are miniscule: "How does the Church, therefore, punish suicide, or self-murder? She refuses Christian burial to the self-murderer, for his own punishment, as well as to deter others from doing the same."[143] The logical consequence of this immemorial Commandment is that those who consent to euthanasia and those who assist, encourage, advocate, or perform it are guilty of this heinous offense.

The Killing of Animals

As Canon Ripley notes (see above), there are several exceptions to the universal prohibition against killing: "the circumstances of a just war, the execution of a criminal, and legitimate self-defense." The Roman Catechism adds a fourth by clarifying that killing, in this Commandment, refers only to human beings and not to animals:

> With regard to the prohibitory part, it should first be taught what kinds of killing are not forbidden by this Commandment. It is not prohibited to kill animals; for if God permits man to eat them, it is also lawful to kill them. *When*, says St. Augustine, *we hear the words, 'Thou shalt not kill,' we do not understand this of the fruits of the earth, which are insensible, nor of irrational animals, which form no part of human society.*

While killing of animals does not break the Fifth Commandment, torturing animals is a sin. Since God has made humans the caretakers of animals (cf. Gen. ii. 15), we are to treat His creatures with respect and care. The examples of St. Francis of Assisi, St. Francis of Paola, St. Philip Neri, and others express the gentleness and kindness we are to show to God's creatures out of love for the Lord.

Capital Punishment Approved by God

---

[143] Fr. Joseph Deharbe, "A Complete Catechism of the Catholic Religion" (Schwartz, Kirwin & Fauss, 1847), 198.

The lawful execution of a criminal is the second exception to the divine prohibition against killing. By law, certain crimes are punishable by death and the Church has always accepted the validity of capital punishment, contrary to certain claims made in recent years (especially by Pope Francis vis-à-vis his "updating" of the post-conciliar *Catechism of the Catholic Church*).[144] When asked under what circumstances human life may lawfully be taken, the Baltimore Catechism explains: "By the lawful execution of a criminal, fairly tried and found guilty of a crime punishable by death when the preservation of law and order and the good of the community require such execution."[145] And the ability to administer capital punishment, as taught by the Roman Catechism, is none other than the lawful authorities and not any private citizen: "Another kind of lawful slaying belongs to the civil authorities, to whom is entrusted power of life and death, by the legal and judicious exercise of which they punish the guilty and protect the innocent."

Far from being supported only in the Middle Ages, the Church has sanctioned the use of capital punishment at least since the time of Pope Innocent I (r. 401-417), who wrote the following in A.D. 405:

> It must be remembered that power was granted by God [to the magistrates], and to avenge crime by the sword was permitted. He who carries out this vengeance is God's minister (Rm. xiii. 1-4). Why should we condemn a practice that all hold to be permitted by God? We uphold, therefore, what has been observed until now, in order not to alter the discipline and so that we may not appear to act contrary to God's authority.[146]

St. Thomas Aquinas asserted two primary reasons for governments to execute criminals, the first of which is the preservation of the common good:

> Now every individual person is related to the entire society as a part to the whole. Therefore, if a man be dangerous and infectious to the community, on account

---

[144] For a thorough treatment of this subject, see Matt Gaspers, "Despite Papal Fiat, Death Penalty Remains Licit," *Catholic Family News*, Sept. 2018 issue <https://catholicfamilynews.com/blog/2018/12/19/despite-papal-fiat-death-penalty-remains-licit>, accessed October 20, 2022.
[145] Baltimore Catechism No. 3, Q. 1276.
[146] Innocent 1, Epist. 6, C. 3. 8, *ad Exsuperium, Episcopum Tolosanum*, 20 Feb. 405, PL 20, 495.

of some sin, it is praiseworthy and healthful that he be killed in order to safeguard the common good, since 'a little leaven corrupteth the whole lump' (II-II q64 a2).

The Roman Catechism concurs and expands upon the responsibilities of governments to provide for the protection of their citizens, which may necessitate the use of capital punishment against those who are fairly tried and found guilty of a crime sufficiently heinous to warrant execution:

> The just use of this power, far from involving the crime of murder, is an act of paramount obedience to this Commandment which prohibits murder. The end of the Commandment is the preservation and security of human life. Now the punishments inflicted by the civil authority, which is the legitimate avenger of crime, naturally tend to this end, since they give security to life by repressing outrage and violence. Hence these words of David: *In the morning I put to death all the wicked of the land, that I might cut off all the workers of iniquity from the city of the Lord* [Ps. c. 8].

The second benefit of capital punishment is its ability to bring about expiation for the sinner's crime, as St. Thomas Aquinas affirmed:

> "They...have at that critical point of death the opportunity to be converted to God through repentance. And if they are so obstinate that even at the point of death their heart does not draw back from malice, it is possible to make a quite probable judgment that they would never come away from evil.[147]

On this purpose of capital punishment as a means of expiation, Pope Pius XII insisted: "Even in the case of the death penalty, the State does not dispose of the individual's right to life. Rather public authority limits itself to depriving the offender of the good of life in expiation for his guilt, after he, through his crime, deprived himself of his own right to life."[148] As a result, the Church affirms the legitimacy of capital punishment, however, the greatest care should be taken, though, to ensure that no innocent person is ever executed for a crime he did not commit.

Killing in A Just War

---

[147] *Summa Contra Gentiles*, Book III, Chapter 146.
[148] Pope Pius XII, Address to the First International Congress of Histopathology of the Nervous System, 14 Sept. 1952, XIV, 328.

A just war is the third exception to the general rule. A just war permits a soldier to take the life of another in armed combat, as the Roman Catechism demonstrates in light of the Old Testament:

> In like manner, the soldier is guiltless who, actuated not by motives of ambition or cruelty, but by a pure desire of serving the interests of his country, takes away the life of an enemy in a just war.
>
> Furthermore, there are on record instances of carnage executed by the special command of God. The sons of Levi, who put to death so many thousands in one day, were guilty of no sin; when the slaughter had ceased, they were addressed by Moses in these words: *You have consecrated your hands this day to the Lord* [Ex. xxxii. 29].

Writing in the early part of fifth century, St. Augustine wrote: "Peace should be the object of your desire; war should be waged only as a necessity…in order that peace may be obtained. Therefore, even in waging a war, cherish the spirit of a peacemaker, that, by conquering those whom you attack, you may lead them back to the advantages of peace…. As violence is used toward him who rebels and resists, so mercy is due to the vanquished or captive."[149] His wise words have helped to form the Catholic teaching on a just war, which obliges a soldier to protect both captives and civilians. For this reason, heinous attacks on innocent civilians, such as the dropping of the nuclear bombs in Japan, constitute a grave sin. Let us recall that we may never do or formally cooperate with evil on the pretext that good may come of it (cf. Rom. iii. 8).

Death by Accident or Self Defense

Death by accident is the fourth exception. Sin requires consent of the will; thus, accidentally causing the death of another is generally not a sin, as the Roman Catechism explains:

> Such accidental deaths, because inflicted without intent or design, involve no guilt whatever, and this is confirmed by the words of St. Augustine: *God forbid that what we do for a good and lawful end shall be imputed to us, if, contrary to our intention, evil thereby befall anyone.*

---

[149] St. Augustine, Letter 189.

There are, however, two cases in which guilt attaches (to accidental death). The first case is when death results from an unlawful act; when, for instance, a person kicks or strikes a woman in a state of pregnancy, and abortion follows. The consequence, it is true, may not have been intended, but this does not exculpate the offender, because the act of striking a pregnant woman is in itself unlawful. The other case is when death is caused by negligence, carelessness or want of due precaution.

And similarly, killing in self-defense is also without sin, assuming it is used as a last resort: "If a man kill another in self-defense, having used every means consistent with his own safety to avoid the infliction of death, he evidently does not violate this Commandment."

The Grave Sin of Abortion

One form of homicide deserves special attention due to its heinous consequences, which deprive its victim not only of life on earth but also eternal life in Heaven. That is none other than abortion, a mortal sin which carries with it the penalty of automatic excommunication: "Often disguised as 'termination of pregnancy,' it deprives a child of Heaven forever. It is punished by the Church with excommunication."[150]

Excommunication is defined as, "An ecclesiastical censure by which one is more or less excluded from communion with the faithful. It is also called *anathema*, especially if it is inflicted with formal solemnities on persons notoriously obstinate to reconciliation. Two basic forms of excommunication are legislated by the Code of Canon Law, namely inflicted penalties (*ferendae sententiae*) and automatic penalties (*latae sententiae*). In the first type, a penalty does not bind until after it has been imposed on the guilty party. In the second type, the excommunication is incurred by the very commission of the offense, if the law or precept expressly determines this (Canon 1314). Most excommunications are of the second type."[151]

Abortion is condemned without exception by the Church and has been condemned since the time of the Apostles: "You shall not murder a child by abortion nor kill that which is begotten."[152] There is no exception — no

---

[150] Ripley, *This Is the Faith, op. cit.*, p. 82.
[151] Fr. John Hardon, *Modern Catholic Dictionary*, "Excommunication" (accessed via http://www.therealpresence.org/dictionary/adict.htm).
[152] The Didache, Ch. 2.

one can claim to be a 'devout Catholic' and support abortion in any manner at the same time. It is a serious sin to support abortion, encourage it, undergo it, perform it, or even vote for politicians who advance a pro-abortion agenda. Those who encourage abortion in any way are guilty of this grave crime which cries to Heaven for vengeance.

Long before the sin of abortion became commonplace in society, Fr. Deharbe's Catechism (published in 1847) specifically singled out this abominable crime: "The deliberate destruction of infant life before birth, even in its earliest stages, as is sometimes done by surgeons, physicians, nurses, and others is nothing less than willful murder."[153]

Whoever is Angry is Guilty of Murder

But besides these various manifestations of actual killing, the Fifth Commandment prohibits the root cause of them all: hatred. The Baltimore Catechism plainly states: "Fighting, anger, hatred and revenge are forbidden by the Fifth Commandment because they are sinful in themselves and may lead to murder. The commandments forbid not only whatever violates them, but also whatever may lead to their violation."[154] Once again, the brilliant clarity of the Roman Catechism expounds on this crucial point:

> The Jews, with singular dullness of apprehension, thought that to abstain from taking life with their own hands was enough to satisfy the obligation imposed by this Commandment. But the Christian, instructed in the interpretation of Christ, has learned that the precept is spiritual, and that it commands us not only to keep our hands unstained, but our hearts pure and undefiled; hence what the Jews regarded as quite sufficient, is not sufficient at all. For the Gospel has taught that it is unlawful even to be angry with anyone: *But I say to you that whosoever is angry with his brother, shall be in danger of the judgment. And whosoever shall say to his brother, 'Raca,' shall be in danger of the council. And whosoever shall say, 'Thou fool,' shall be in danger of hell fire* [Mt. v. 22].

The Catechism explains the meaning of those words of Our Lord, which are taken from the Gospel of St. Matthew:

---

[153] Fr. Joseph Deharbe, "A Complete Catechism of the Catholic Religion" (Schwartz, Kirwin & Fauss, 1847), 197.
[154] Baltimore Catechism No. 3, Q. 1280.

From these words it clearly follows that he who is angry with his brother is not free from sin, even though he conceals his resentment; that he who gives indication of his wrath sins grievously; and that he who does not hesitate to treat another with harshness, and to utter contumelious reproaches against him, sins still more grievously.

Charity as a Commandment

Far from merely condemning a series of sins, the Fifth Commandment enjoins on the faithful the obligation of charity towards all. After concluding its teachings on the sins against the Fifth Commandment, the Roman Catechism turns to this positive part of the law:

> The mandatory [positive] part of this Commandment, as Christ our Lord enjoins, requires that we have peace with all men. Interpreting the Commandment, He says: *If therefore thou offer thy gift at the altar, and there thou remember that thy brother hath anything against thee; leave there thy offering before the altar, and go first to be reconciled to thy brother, and then coming thou shalt offer thy gift* [Mt. v. 23-24], etc.

Naturally, the command to love follows from the prohibition of hating one's neighbor: *For since hatred is clearly forbidden by this Commandment, as* whosoever hateth his brother is a murderer [I Jn. iii. 15], it follows, as an evident consequence, that the Commandment also inculcates charity and love." This Commandment applies to all our neighbors, friends and enemies alike, as Our Lord taught. We must do good to all and bear our wrongs and injuries with patience and resignation to the will of God. Forgiving our enemies of wrongs done to us is the highest expression of the positive part of the Fifth Commandment:

> "Finally, if we consider the law of charity, which is kind, we shall be convinced that to practice the good offices of mildness, clemency, and other kindred virtues, is a duty prescribed by that law.
>
> But the most important duty of all, and that which is the fullest expression of charity, and to the practice of which we should most habituate ourselves, is to pardon and forgive from the heart the injuries which we may have received from others. The Sacred Scriptures, as we have

already observed, frequently admonish and exhort us to a full compliance with this duty. Not only do they pronounce *blessed* those who do this, but they also declare that God grants pardon to those who really fulfil this duty, while He refuses pardon to those who neglect it, or refuse to obey it.

Despite our inclination to sin and resort to vengeance, Our Lord desires us to forgive as He forgave even His executioners from the Cross. And the Catechism concludes its discussion on the Fifth Commandment by affirming two key advantages for us if we can forgive those who harm us:

> ...there are two advantages, which are the special rewards of those, who, influenced by a holy desire to please God, freely forgive injuries. In the first place, God has promised that he who forgives, shall himself obtain forgiveness of sins, a promise which clearly shows how acceptable to God is this duty of piety. In the next place, the forgiveness of injuries ennobles and perfects our nature; for by it man is in some degree made like to God, *Who maketh his sun to shine on the good and the bad, and raineth upon the just and the unjust* [Mt. v. 45].

Should we feel angry for either small or serious injuries done to us, it is highly recommended to take a few minutes to pause, gaze on a crucifix, and ask Our Lord for help. If He who is sinless could forgive His murderers, how can we not forgive others when we ourselves are sinners? As the Roman Catechism wisely counsels, "Reflect frequently and again and again that you must soon die, and since at death there will be nothing you desire or need more than great mercy from God, that now you should keep that mercy always before your mind."

XXVI

The Sixth Commandment

Thou shalt not commit adultery (Ex. xx. 14). Adultery is a serious sin against the institution of marriage, which God established in the Garden of Eden. Owing to the seriousness of this crime, the Roman Catechism begins its consideration of the Sixth Commandment by explaining the profound significance of its placement immediately after the prohibition against murder:

> The bond between man and wife is one of the closest, and nothing can be more gratifying to both than to know that they are objects of mutual and special affection. On the other hand, nothing inflicts deeper anguish than to feel that the legitimate love which one owes the other has been transferred elsewhere. Rightly, then, and in its natural order, is the Commandment which protects human life against the hand of the murderer, followed by that which forbids adultery, which aims to prevent anyone from injuring or destroying by such a crime the holy and honorable union of marriage -- a union which is generally the source of ardent affection and love.

Sins Against the Sixth Commandment

Adultery is "the defilement of the marriage bed, whether it be one's own or another's. If a married man has intercourse with an unmarried woman, he violates the integrity of his marriage bed; and if an unmarried man has intercourse with a married woman, he defiles the sanctity of the marriage bed of another." Adultery, therefore, occurs by means of "sexual sin with another's wife or husband, or of a single person with a married person."[155] Consequently, it is entirely possible for a single person to be guilty of the sin of adultery.

---

[155] Canon Francis Ripley, *This Is the Faith* (Gracewing Publishing, 1973), 88.

However, far from merely forbidding adultery, the Sixth Commandment forbids all sins of impurity. The Baltimore Catechism similarly notes the all-encompassing nature of this Commandment: "The sixth Commandment forbids all unchaste freedom with another's wife or husband; also all immodesty with ourselves or others in looks, dress, words, and actions."[156] On this point, the Roman Catechism, uniquely among the Church's catechisms, explains that even in the Old Testament the Sixth Commandment was applied to a variety of sins:

> But that every species of immodesty and impurity are included in this prohibition of adultery, is proved by the testimonies of St. Augustine and St. Ambrose; and that such is the meaning of the Commandment is borne out by the Old, as well as the New Testament. In the writings of Moses, besides adultery, other sins against chastity are said to have been punished. Thus the book of Genesis records the judgment of Judah against his daughter-in-law [cf. Gen. xxxviii. 14]. In Deuteronomy is found the excellent law of Moses, *that there should be no harlot amongst the daughters of Israel* [Dt. xxiii. 17]. *Take heed to keep thyself, my son, from all fornication* [Tob. iv. 13], is the exhortation of Tobias to his son; and in Ecclesiasticus we read: *Be ashamed [...] of looking upon a harlot* [Ecclus. xli. 21, 25].

The New Testament likewise condemns adultery and related sins of impurity, as St. Paul warned that those who had these sins on their soul at the moment of death would not enter Heaven: *Do not err: neither fornicators, nor idolaters, nor adulterers, nor the effeminate, nor liars with mankind, nor thieves, nor covetous, nor drunkards, nor railers, nor extortioners, shall possess the kingdom of God* (I Cor. vi. 9-10).

Consequently, the Sixth Commandment condemns *incest* (sexual relations with a relative or in-law), *fornication* (sexual relations with someone of the opposite sex when neither of is in the state of marriage), *homosexual relations* (sexual activity with someone of the same sex), *masturbation* (the stimulation of one's own sexual organs for pleasure), rape, and other similar offenses. Prostitution, artificial insemination, pornography, seducing others, sexually abusing children, dressing immodestly, reading impure literature, listening to impure jokes, songs, or movies, or using artificial contraception are likewise all condemned.

---

[156] Baltimore Catechism No. 3, Q. 1284.

The Evil of Artificial Contraception

Artificial contraception is contrary to the will of God. In 1968, Pope Paul VI issued the Encyclical *Humanae Vitae* in which he reemphasized the Church's constant teaching that it is always intrinsically evil to use contraception to prevent the conception of human life. As defined in *Humanae Vitae*, contraception is "any action which either before, at the moment of, or after sexual intercourse, is specifically intended to prevent procreation."[157] This would include sterilization, condoms and other barrier methods, spermicides, the birth control pill, onanism (cf. Gen. xxxviii. 9-10), and all other such methods.

Artificial contraception is wrong because it is opposed to the natural law of God. St. Thomas Aquinas, considered the greatest theologian in the history of the Church, ranks the evil of contraception immediately after that of homicide, in that the first destroys human nature and the second prevents it from coming into being.[158]

Artificial Insemination is likewise categorically forbidden, for the reasons which Pope Pius XII enumerated in 1949:

> Artificial fertilization, outside of marriage, is to be condemned outright as immoral. Such is indeed the natural law and the positive divine law, that the procreation of a new life can only be the fruit of marriage. Marriage alone safeguards the dignity of the spouses (mainly the woman in this case), their personal property. By itself, only it provides for the good and education of the child. Consequently, on the condemnation of artificial fertilization outside the conjugal union, no difference of opinion is possible between Catholics. A child conceived under these conditions would, by the very fact, be illegitimate.

> Artificial fertilization in marriage but produced by the active element of a third party, is also immoral and, as such, to be condemned without appeal. Only the spouses have a reciprocal right over their body to engender a new

---

[157] Paul VI, Encyclical *Humanae Vitae* (July 25, 1968), n. 14 (http://www.vatican.va/content/paul-vi/en/encyclicals/documents/hf_p-vi_enc_25071968_humanae-vitae.html).

[158] Cf. Aquinas, *Summa Contra Gentiles* 1.3, c. 122.

life, an exclusive, non-transferable, inalienable right. And that must also be taken into consideration of the child.[159]

As shown by both Sacred Scripture and through the Church's magisterial teachings, a variety of sins directly violate this Commandment. But, if this is the case, why were so many various manifestations of sin like fornication not written explicitly on the Tablets of the Law when they were commonplace even in ancient times? On this point, the Roman Catechism illuminates:

> ...the reason why adultery is expressly forbidden is because in addition to the turpitude which it shares with other kinds of incontinence, it adds the sin of injustice, not only against our neighbor, but also against civil society.
>
> Again, it is certain that he who abstains not from other sins against chastity, will easily fall into the crime of adultery. By the prohibition of adultery, therefore, we at once see that every sort of immodesty and impurity by which the body is defiled is prohibited.

Consequently, we would do well to immediately flee from all temptations against the Sixth Commandment, whether they be suggestions to commit sins by looks, words, or actions. Only by fleeing from these sins repeatedly can we hope to conquer them, lest we fall into mortal sin and run the risk of committing graver sins, including adultery.

The Grievousness of These Sins

On the gravity of these sins, the Roman Catechism sternly warns of the consequences God inflicted on those guilty of sexual sins:

> The grievousness of the sin of adultery may be easily inferred from the severity of its punishment. According to the law promulgated by God in the Old Testament, the adulterer was stoned to death [cf. Lev. xx. 10]. Nay more, because of the criminal passion of one man, not only the perpetrator of the crime, but a whole city was destroyed, as we read with regard to the Sichemites [cf. Gen. xxxiv. 25]. The Sacred Scriptures abound with

---

[159] Speech of Pope Pius XII to Catholic Doctors in Rome for their 4th International Congress (Sept. 29, 1949), *Acta Apostolicae Sedis* 49.

examples of the divine vengeance, such as the destruction of Sodom and of the neighboring cities [cf. Gen. xix. 24], the punishment of the Israelites who committed fornication in the wilderness with the daughters of Moab [cf. Num. xxv. 4], and the slaughter of the Benjamites [cf. Jdg. XX].

In similarly strong words, the Catechism further explains the perversity of these sins in light of the New Testament:

...the Christian who shamefully sins with a harlot makes the members of Christ the members of a harlot, according to these words of St. Paul: *Know you not that your bodies are the members of Christ? Shall I then take the members of Christ and make them the members of a harlot? God forbid. Or know you not, that he who is joined to a harlot is made one body?* [I Cor. vi. 15-16] Moreover, a Christian, as St. Paul testifies is *the temple of the Holy Ghost* [I Cor. vi. 19]; and to violate this temple is nothing else than to expel the Holy Ghost.

Deliberate sins against the Sixth Commandment, when committed with full consent of the will and knowledge of the sin's gravity are always mortal sins. As a result, if someone were to commit impure sins while hypnotized or while drugged, these would not be mortal sins. However, to commit sins against the Sixth Commandment where pleasure is expected but is not the primary motive is still mortally sinful. The Roman Catechism is clear that such sins are surely mortal when it affirms:

Now the evil of this crime we may learn from the fact that, on account of it, man is banished and excluded from the kingdom of God, which is the greatest of all evils.

However, Canon Francis Ripley does clarify a few circumstances which may make a sin along these lines to be venial:

There is venial sin when what we do is something which of its nature is *not likely* to produce sexual pleasure, even if at the same time we act out of no good motive, but merely, e.g., out of levity, imprudence, curiosity, bravado, vanity or the like. For example, deliberate but only passing glances at a naked body, a passing glance at immodest pictures... these would be venial.[160]

---

[160] Ripley, *op. cit.*, 92.

And furthermore, to glance at art where figures are depicted naked (e.g., Renaissance-era artwork) would be no offense, as Canon Ripley explains:

> There is no sin at all when what we do is quite innocent or decent in itself, or even if it is something which of its very nature is likely to arouse sexual pleasure, provided that we have an adequate and just reason for doing it and there is no real danger of our consenting to the pleasure aroused.[161]

As a result, those who struggle against these sins may need to take more caution than others who are not as prone to falling into these temptations.

Blessed Are the Pure in Heart

For many, the struggle against sins of the flesh will be present to stronger or lesser degrees all of one's life. But to those who frequently continue to fall into these sins, they run the risk of developing a blindness to these sins and a hardness of heart, as the Catechism warns:

> But even though the adulterer may escape the punishment of death, he does not escape the great pains and torments that often overtake such sins as his. He becomes afflicted with blindness of mind, a most severe punishment; he is lost to all regard for God, for reputation, for honor, for family, and even for life; and thus, utterly abandoned and worthless, he is undeserving of confidence in any matter of moment and becomes unfitted to discharge any kind of duty.

Life, however, is not merely a continuous battle to avoid sin – it is an opportunity to practice virtue and grow in God's grace. We do this by advancing in purity, which is also enjoined by virtue of the Sixth Commandment as the Roman Catechism affirms:

> We now come to explain the positive part of the precept. The faithful are to be taught and earnestly exhorted to cultivate continence and chastity with all care, to cleanse themselves *from all defilement of the flesh and of the spirit, perfecting sanctification in the fear of God* [II Cor. viii. 1].

---

[161] Ibid.

The strongest motivation of all for why we should do so is Our Lord's own words: *Blessed are the pure of heart: for they shall see God* (Mt. v. 8). As St. John Chrysostom reminds us, "Those who love chastity, whose consciences are completely clear, keep their hearts pure. No other virtue is so necessary in order to see God."[162] Among the disciples, Our Lord's purity was most imitated by St. John the Evangelist, who was a perpetual virgin. Fr. Alban Butler in his *Lives of the Saints* recounts three primary reasons why he was especially loved by Our Lord and the third of which, his virginal purity, should instill in us a great desire to persevere in purity for the rest of our lives if we too hope to see the Lord:

> Our divine Redeemer had a particular affection for him above the rest of the apostles; insomuch that when St. John speaks of himself, he saith that he was *The disciple whom Jesus loved*; and frequently he mentions himself by this only characteristic; which he did not out of pride to distinguish himself, but out of gratitude and tender love for his blessed Master. If we inquire into the causes of this particular love of Christ towards him, which was not blind or unreasonable, the first was doubtless, as St. Austin observes, the love which this disciple bore Him; secondly, his meekness and peaceable disposition by which he was extremely like Christ Himself; thirdly, his virginal purity.[163]

Remedies Against Impurity

St. Bernard used to say, "Ambition was the sin of the Angels, avarice the sin of men, impurity the sin of the beast." In commenting on this line, Canon Francis Ripley remarks, "The great Saints of God went to extraordinary lengths to preserve their purity. St. Benedict rolled in the briars; St. Francis of Assisi rolled in the snow; St. Bernard plunged into a pool."[164] Yet, what does the average Catholic do to conquer such sins when the amount of impure content and suggestions has proliferated in society?

St. Philip Neri remarked that any remedies against impurity must be above all rooted in humility:

> Humility is the safeguard of chastity. In the matter of purity, there is no greater danger than not fearing the danger. For my part, when I find a man secure of himself

---

[162] Quoted from *The Way* by Josemaría Escrivá, 119.
[163] Butler, *The Lives of the Fathers, Martyrs, and Other Principal Saints*, Vol. 12.
[164] Ripley, *op. cit.*, 89.

and without fear, I give him up for lost. I am less alarmed for one who is tempted and who resists by avoiding the occasions, than for one who is not tempted and is not careful to avoid occasions. When a person puts himself in an occasion, saying, *I shall not fall*, it is an almost infallible sign that he will fall, and with great injury to his soul.

With humility as the foundation of our spiritual life – and especially for combat against sins of the flesh – the Roman Catechism enumerates seven chief means of practicing purity: (1) avoidance of idleness, (2) temperance, (3) custody of the eyes, (4) avoidance of immodest dress, (5) avoidance of impure conversations or literature, (6) frequenting the Sacraments, and (7) mortification. In fact, these remedies address the six primary causes of impurity mentioned by Canon Ripley: pride; idleness; bad books, entertainment, and company; immodest dress; excess in eating and drinking; and failure of watchfulness over the senses.

Regarding avoidance of idleness and temperance, the Roman Catechism states:

> We now come to the remedies which consist in action. The first is studiously to avoid idleness; for, according to Ezechiel, it was by yielding to the enervating influence of idleness that the Sodomites plunged into the most shameful crime of criminal lust [cf. Ez. xvi. 49].

> In the next place, intemperance is carefully to be avoided. *I fed them to the full*, says the Prophet, *and they committed adultery* [Jer. v. 7]. An overloaded stomach begets impurity. This our Lord intimates in these words: *Take heed to yourselves, lest perhaps your hearts be overcharged with surfeiting and drunkenness* [Lk. xxi. 34]. *Be not drunk with wine*, says the Apostle, *wherein is luxury* [Eph. v. 18].

To truly advance in purity, a soul must have recourse to fasting. St. Thomas Aquinas, when explaining the three-fold purpose of fasting, mentions its role in restraining lust:

> First, in order to bridle the lusts of the flesh, wherefore the Apostle says (II Cor. vi. 5-6): *In fasting, in chastity*, since fasting is the guardian of chastity. For, according to Jerome, '*Venus is cold when Ceres and Bacchus are*

261

not there,' that is to say, lust is cooled by abstinence in meat and drink (II-II q147 a1).

Likewise, dressing modestly and refraining from visiting places where people are prone to dress immodestly is a further defense against sexual temptations. Both the Blessed Virgin Mary and St. John the Apostle provide worthy models to imitate. Regarding immodest books or entertainment, the Baltimore Catechism provides concrete practical considerations on how we should act regarding them:

> Immodest books and newspapers should be destroyed as soon as possible, and if we cannot destroy them ourselves, we should induce their owners to do so... The Church considers bad all books containing teaching contrary to faith or morals, or that willfully misrepresent Catholic doctrine and practice... Indecent theaters and similar places of amusement are dangerous to the virtue of purity, because their entertainments are frequently intended to suggest immodest things.[165]

Above all, however, prayer and the Sacraments must be frequently employed to conquer temptations of the flesh. Without these means, no one can safely persist in a life of purity. The Roman Catechism concludes its explanation of the Sixth Commandment by wisely explaining the role of the Sacraments in conquering impurity:

> If the occasions of sin which we have just enumerated be carefully avoided, almost every excitement to lust will be removed. But the most efficacious means for subduing its violence are frequent use of confession and Communion, as also unceasing and devout prayer to God, accompanied by fasting and almsdeeds. Chastity is a gift of God. To those who ask it aright He does not deny it; nor does He suffer us to be tempted beyond our strength.

There are several practical actions we can take in our own spiritual lives to combat these sins. Receiving Holy Communion – even daily – if someone is in the state of grace, making daily spiritual Communions, praying three Hail Marys each morning on our knees for the virtue of purity, wearing the Brown Scapular, calling immediately on the assistance of Our Lady when we are tempted, and finding a regular confessor are all effective means we

---

[165] Baltimore Catechism No. 3, Q. 1287 – 1289.

have at our disposal. Similarly, meditating on the Four Last Things (especially the eternal pains of hell), as well as practicing fifteen minutes of daily mental prayer, can also help against impure temptations.

Finally, as a pragmatic suggestion, since so many temptations to commit sins of the flesh come by way of modern technology, put accountability software on all your devices and have a trusted friend or family member keep the password to help keep you from looking at impure websites. In so doing, may we truly advance in purity and avoid these sins so that we may one day truly be worthy to see Our Lord, since nothing defiled will enter Heaven (cf. Apoc. xxi. 27).

Conclusion

Conscious of the importance of observing the Sixth Commandment as well as the need to immerse ourselves in the liturgical life of the Church, write a note on your calendar to make special reparation on the Sunday after the Immaculate Conception and on the feast days of St. Thomas More and St. Maria Goretti for sins against this Commandment. At a meeting in Washington in 1938, the American bishops requested all Ordinaries to have the Pledge of the Legion of Decency taken by all the Faithful at all Masses, in all churches and chapels throughout the United States, on the Sunday within the Octave of the Feast of the Immaculate Conception. We can continue to make such a pledge in our own families.[166]

---

[166] https://acatholiclife.blogspot.com/2008/12/pledge-against-indecent-and-immoral.html.

XXVII

The Seventh Commandment

Thou shalt not steal (Ex. xx. 15). Like the Commandments which precede it, the prohibition against theft is ultimately rooted in the love of God Who seeks our protection, as the Roman Catechism wisely explains in its opening remarks on the Seventh Commandment of the Decalogue:

> In the first place the pastor should exercise care and industry in declaring the infinite love of God for man. Not satisfied with having fenced round, so to say, our lives, our persons and our reputation, by means of the two Commandments, *Thou shalt not kill, Thou shalt not commit adultery*, God defends and places a guard over our property and possessions, by adding the prohibition, *Thou shalt not steal.* These words can have no other meaning than that which we indicated above when speaking of the other Commandments. They declare that God forbids our worldly goods, which are placed under His protection, to be taken away or injured by anyone.
>
> Our gratitude to God, the author of this law, should be in proportion to the greatness of the benefit the law confers upon us. Now since the truest test of gratitude and the best means of returning thanks, consists not only in lending a willing ear to His precepts, but also in obeying them, the faithful are to be animated and encouraged to an observance of this Commandment.

Continuing, the Roman Catechism explains that like the preceding Commandments, the Seventh Commandment enjoins both a negative and a positive precept: "Like the preceding Commandments, this one also is divided into two parts. The first, which prohibits theft, is mentioned expressly; while the spirit and force of the second, which enforces kindliness and liberality towards our neighbor, are implied in the first part."

Sins Against the Seventh Commandment

The Seventh Commandment requires us to abstain from a wide range of activities that violate another person's personal property. As stated by Canon Francis Ripley, "In the Fifth and Sixth Commandments, God protects our life and honor; in the Seventh, He places our property and wealth in security."[167] Chief among these sins is theft, as the Catechism explains:

> We shall begin with the prohibitory part of the Commandment, *Thou shalt not steal.* It is to be observed, that by the word *steal* is understood not only the taking away of anything from its rightful owner, privately and without his consent, but also the possession of that which belongs to another, contrary to the will, although not without the knowledge, of the true owner; else we are prepared to say that He who prohibits theft does not also prohibit robbery, which is accomplished by violence and injustice, whereas, according to St. Paul, *extortioners shall not possess the kingdom of God* [I Cor. vi. 10], and their very company and ways should be shunned, as the same Apostle writes.

Through the eloquence of the Roman Catechism, the Church explains the distinction between theft and robbery:

> But though robbery is a greater sin than theft, inasmuch as it not only deprives another of his property, but also offers violence and insult to him; yet it cannot be a matter of surprise that the divine prohibition is expressed under the milder word, *steal*, instead of *rob*. There was good reason for this, since theft is more general and of wider extent than robbery, a crime which only they can commit who are superior to their neighbor in brute force and power. Furthermore, it is obvious that when lesser crimes are forbidden, greater enormities of the same sort are also prohibited.

The Catechism wisely states "that when lesser crimes are forbidden, greater enormities of the same sort are also prohibited," which indicates that as the centuries have evolved and commerce has changed, the same principles apply today. As a result, as enumerated by Canon Francis Ripley, some of the many offenses against the Seventh Commandment include theft, borrowing without the intention of repaying, accepting bribes, not paying

---

[167] Canon Francis Ripley, *This Is the Faith* (Gracewing Publishing, 1973), 94.

just wages in a reasonable time, producing and using counterfeit money, forgery, usury, wasting time at work, engaging in unlawful strikes, gambling away the family savings, cheating, plagiarism, and violation of copyright laws.[168] However, such a list is not exhaustive since the Roman Catechism even in its time acknowledged that "[t]o enumerate the various other modes of theft, invented by the ingenuity of avarice, which is versed in all the arts of making money, would be a tedious and, as already said, a most difficult task."

Indeed, rather than merely condemning the act of stealing, the desire or intention to steal from another is also sinful:

> But, besides actual theft, that is, the outward commission, the will and desire are also forbidden by the law of God. The law is spiritual and concerns the soul, the source of our thoughts and designs. *From the heart*, says our Lord in St. Matthew, *come forth evil thoughts, murders, adulteries, fornications, thefts, false testimonies* [Mt. xv. 19].

Among the various sins which violate the Seventh Commandment, usury and sacrilege are deserving of special treatment due to their gravity and the ignorance of modern man concerning them.

Usury

On Nov. 1, 1745, Pope Benedict XIV promulgated the Encyclical *Vix Perveni* (On Usury and Other Dishonest Profit) to the Italian Bishops, which unambiguously and authoritatively condemned usury:

> The nature of the sin called usury has its proper place and origin in a loan contract. This financial contract between consenting parties demands, by its very nature, that one return to another only as much as he has received. The sin rests on the fact that sometimes the creditor desires more than he has given. Therefore, he contends some gain is owed him beyond that which he loaned, but any gain which exceeds the amount he gave is illicit and usurious.

In striking terms, the Roman Catechism echoes the Church's longstanding condemnation of usury by likening it not only to robbery but also murder:

---

[168] Ibid., 95.

266

Among those who are guilty of robbery are also included persons who do not pay, or who turn to other uses or appropriate to themselves, customs, taxes, tithes and such revenues, which are owed to the Church or civil authorities.

To this class also belong usurers, the most cruel and relentless of extortioners, who by their exorbitant rates of interest, plunder and destroy the poor. Whatever is received above the capital and principal, be it money, or anything else that may be purchased or estimated by money, is usury; for it is written in Ezechiel: *He hath not lent upon usury, nor taken an increase* [Ez. xviii. 8, xxii. 12]; and in Luke our Lord says: *Lend, hoping for nothing thereby.* [Lk. vi. 33] Even among the pagans, usury was always considered a most grievous and odious crime. Hence the question, 'What is usury?' was answered: 'What is murder?' And, indeed, he who lends at usury sells the same thing twice or sells that which has no real existence.

The condemnation of usury in *Vix Perveni*, like the previous condemnations issued by the First Council of Nicaea, rejected interest of any amounts – even modest interest rates. In fact, the encyclical went further than mere loan contracts and condemned those who "falsely and rashly persuade themselves" that "other just contracts exist, for which it is permissible to receive a moderate amount of interest. Should anyone think like this, he will oppose not only the judgment of the Catholic Church on usury, but also common human sense and natural reason."[169]

Yet, Benedict XIV clarified that "entirely just and legitimate reasons arise to demand something over and above the amount due on the contract. Nor is it denied that it is very often possible for someone, by means of contracts differing entirely from loans, to spend and invest money legitimately either to provide oneself with an annual income or to engage in legitimate trade and business. From these types of contracts honest gain may be made."[170] In so doing, the Church underscores the virtue of justice and restitution. Usury, far from making a transaction balanced, harms the good of another by robbing him and taking more than one's fair share.

Sacrilege

---

[169] *Vix Perveni*, n. 3.V.
[170] Ibid., n. 3.III.

Also worthy of special mention is the grievous sin of stealing from God. Addressing the seriousness of sacrilege, the Roman Catechism explains, "To steal anything sacred is called *sacrilege* — a crime most enormous and sinful, yet so common in our days that what piety and wisdom had set aside for the necessary expenses of divine worship...."

More specifically, the Catholic Encyclopedia indicates that sacrilege is always incurred when a consecrated person or a consecrated object (e.g., chalice, altar, church) is profaned. However, sacrilege does not necessarily always apply to blessed objects – indicating the distinction between blessed and consecrated objects: "...the profanation of a consecrated person or thing carries with it a new species of sin, namely sacrilege, which the profanation of a blessed person or thing does not always do." In the context of the Seventh Commandment, sacrilege is incurred by those who steal from churches or those who steal any consecrated vessels.

The Gravity of Theft

Far from being small offenses, sins of theft offend Almighty God and must be eschewed completely:

> The grievousness of the sin of theft is sufficiently seen by the light of natural reason alone, for it is a violation of justice which gives to every man his own. The distribution and allotment of property, fixed from the beginning by the law of nations and confirmed by human and divine laws, must be considered as inviolable, and each one must be allowed secure possession of what justly belongs to him, unless we wish the overthrow of human society. Hence these words of the Apostle: *Neither thieves, nor covetous, nor drunkards, nor railers, nor extortioners, shall possess the kingdom of God* [I Cor. vi. 10].

Canon Francis Ripley notes three conditions that affect whether theft is a mortal sin: the value of the thing stolen, the person from whom it was stolen, and the time over which the theft occurred. The value of the thing stolen may be absolutely grave or relatively grave. Moral theologians "are united in fixing this sum as the equivalent of the weekly wages earned by a person of the middle class of society." For relative grave value, "theologians fix this amount as the average day's pay of the victim of the injustice."[171] Should either of these conditions be satisfied, the amount constitutes matter for a mortal sin.

He continues by further clarifying that "if the thief has the intention to accumulate a large sum by such [smaller] thefts," it nevertheless is a mortal sin. And likewise, "if several people conspire to a theft, even if the individual thief obtains only a small amount, but the aggregate sum is large, each one would commit a mortal sin."[172]

Socialism and Private Property

The greatest attack on the Seventh Commandment in modern times comes not from individuals but from governments under the influence of Socialism, which rejects private property rights. The Catholic Church has condemned Socialism in all its forms without exception. Among its many errors, Socialism advances that private property is not a human right but can be taken away from individuals by the State and given to others.

In 1891, Pope Leo XIII issued his landmark Encyclical *Rerum Novarum* (On Capitol and Labor) in which he states:

> Hence, it is clear that the main tenet of socialism, community of goods, must be utterly rejected, since it only injures those whom it would seem meant to benefit, is directly contrary to the natural rights of mankind, and would introduce confusion and disorder into the commonweal. The first and most fundamental principle, therefore, if one would undertake to alleviate the condition of the masses, must be the inviolability of private property.[173]

Some people make the erroneous claim that the Apostles practiced Socialism. They base this on the fact that the early Christians *had all things in common. Their possessions and goods they sold, and divided them to all, according as everyone had need* (Acts ii. 44-45). Yet, this sharing in common was done entirely by free will. It was not mandated by any government authority. Thus, no early Christian denied he had a right to private property, nor was he stripped of any natural rights by another. Similarly, those who enter religious life freely choose to take a vow of poverty, and a monastery communally owns all property for the good of its members.

---

[171] Ripley, *op. cit.*, 97.
[172] Ibid.
[173] Pope Leo XIII, *Rerum Novarum* (On Capital and Labor), n. 15.

The State has no authority to abolish all private property "because that would be to abolish what is natural to man," as Canon Ripley asserts. And to those who claim that stealing from the rich to give to the poor is praiseworthy or at least permissible, the Church unequivocally condemns such a falsity: "But do we not sometimes hear the thief contend that he is not guilty of sin, because he steals from the rich and the wealthy, who, in his mind, not only suffer no injury, but do not even feel the loss? Such an excuse is as wretched as it is baneful."

Restitution Required for Forgiveness

As with all sins, forgiveness is possible by virtue of Our Lord's death on the Cross and through His established means of the Sacrament of Confession. We know from our study of this sacrament that it involves three integral parts: (1) *contrition* (sorrow for sin), (2) *confession* (telling our sins to a priest), and (3) *satisfaction* (some form of reparation). For sins against the Seventh Commandment, satisfaction takes the form of *restitution* (restoring what was stolen to its rightful owner): "We now come to the positive part of this Commandment, in which the first thing to be considered is satisfaction or restitution; for without restitution the sin is not forgiven."

In similar sentiments, Canon Francis Ripley writes: "We are bound to restore ill-gotten goods if we are able, or else our sin will not be forgiven. When the theft was a mortal sin, neglect of restitution is also a mortal sin. The obligation is binding until it is fulfilled, and the greater the willful delay, the greater is the sin. Restitution must be made to the owner, if possible, or to his heirs, if he be dead. If neither is possible, it should be given in alms in the name of the owner. Not only must the stolen property be returned, but also the loss resulting from the thief's actual injustice must be made good."[174]

Beyond the thief, those who associated with the theft are bound to make restitution. The Catechism notes seven classes of individuals who are bound by this requirement:

> The first consists of those who order others to steal, and who are not only the authors and accomplices of theft, but also the most criminal among thieves.
>
> Another class embraces those, who, when they cannot command others to commit theft persuade and encourage

---

[174] Ripley, *op. cit.*, 96.

it. These, since they are like the first class in intention, though unlike them in power, are equally guilty of theft.

A third class is composed of those who consent to the theft committed by others.

The fourth class is that of those who are accomplices in and derive gain from theft; if that can be called gain, which, unless they repent, consigns them to everlasting torments. Of them David says: *If thou didst see a thief, thou didst run with him.* [Ps. xlix. 18]

The fifth class of thieves are those who, having it in their power to prohibit theft, so far from opposing or preventing it, fully and freely suffer and sanction its commission.

The sixth class is constituted of those who are well aware that the theft was committed, and when it was committed; and yet, far from mentioning it, pretend they know nothing about it.

The last class comprises all who assist in the accomplishment of theft, who guard, defend, receive or harbor thieves.

All these are bound to make restitution to those from whom anything has been stolen and are to be earnestly exhorted to the discharge of so necessary a duty.

Everyone who is guilty of these sins is bound to perform restitution with one exception, as Canon Francis Ripley notes: "If it is physically or morally impossible for us to make restitution, the obligation ceases to bind us. But apart from such cases, the sin of theft is not really repented of until restitution has been made, and so it cannot be forgiven."[175]

Almsgiving as a Commandment

Turning to the positive precept of the Seventh Commandment, the Catechism begins by affirming the need for the faithful to engage in almsgiving:

---

[175] Ripley, *op. cit.*, 96.

This Commandment also implies an obligation to sympathize with the poor and needy, and to relieve their difficulties and distresses by our means and good offices.
...

The pastor, therefore, should encourage the faithful to be willing and anxious to assist those who have to depend on charity, and should make them realize the great necessity of giving alms and of being really and practically liberal to the poor, by reminding them that on the last day God will condemn and consign to eternal fires those who have omitted and neglected the duty of almsgiving, while on the contrary He will praise and introduce into His heavenly country those who have exercised mercy towards the poor.

By giving to the poor, we make reparation for sins as we see in the poor the Person of Christ Himself. And although it is not strictly almsgiving, the giving of our time to visit the sick, the elderly, or those in prison also makes reparation for sin.

Conclusion

In many respects, wealth can be a hindrance to our eternal salvation. Yet, it is possible to become a saint even while possessing what is far more than the average person, as indicated by the life of St. Casimir of Poland, St. Louis IX of France, and others. Conversely, it is possible for a poor person to become so greedy over the few items that he does own that he loses his salvation because of it.

In all things, we must practice detachment. Whether God blesses us with many earthly possessions or few, we must be detached from earthly things. All things, whether in large or small quantity, are only means to help us achieve our eternal salvation. In the words of St. Ignatius of Loyola in his *Spiritual Exercises*: "Therefore, we must make ourselves indifferent to all created things, as far as we are allowed by free choice and are not under any prohibition. Consequently, as far as we are concerned, we should not prefer health to sickness, riches to poverty, honor to dishonor, a long life to a short."[176]

---

[176] St. Ignatius of Loyola, *The Spiritual Exercises of St. Ignatius: A New Translation Based on Studies in the Language of the Autograph Edited by Translated by Father Louis J. Puhl, S.J.* (The Newman Press, 1951), 12.

XXVIII

The Eighth Commandment

Thou shalt not bear false witness against thy neighbor (Ex. xx. 16). Drawing on the wisdom found in Holy Scripture, the Roman Catechism begins its explanation of the Eighth Commandment by expounding upon two basic truths concerning the use of speech:

> The great utility, nay the necessity, of carefully explaining this Commandment, and of emphasizing its obligation, we learn from these words of St. James: *If any man offend not in word, the same is a perfect man*; and again, *The tongue is indeed a little member, and boasteth great things. Behold how small a fire, what a great wood it kindleth* [Ja. iii. 2, 5]; and so on, to the same effect.
>
> From these words we learn two truths. The first is that sins of the tongue are very prevalent, which is confirmed by these words of the Prophet: *Every man is a liar* [Ps. cxv. 11], so that it would almost seem as if this were the only sin which extends to all mankind. The other truth is that the tongue is the source of innumerable evils. Through the fault of the evil speaker are often lost the property, the reputation, the life, and the salvation of the injured person, or of him who inflicts the injury.

As has been demonstrated by the Church through her explanations of the preceding Commandments, this Commandment obliges both a negative and a positive precept: "The first forbids us to bear false witness. The other commands us to lay aside all dissimulation and deceit, and to measure our words and actions by the standard of truth, a duty of which the Apostle admonishes the Ephesians in these words: *Doing the truth in charity, let us grow up in all things in Him* [Eph. iv. 15]."

Who is Our Neighbor?

In the context of this and all of God's Commandments, our neighbor does not refer only to those alongside whom we live. It does not refer only to friends or family, either. Our neighbor refers to all of humanity – even our enemies – and we may not bear false witness against any of them:

> According to the interpretation of Christ the Lord, our neighbor is he who needs our assistance, whether bound to us by ties of kindred or not, whether a fellow citizen or a stranger, a friend or an enemy. It is wrong to think that one may give false evidence against an enemy, since by the command of God and of our Lord we are bound to love him.

Sins Against the Eighth Commandment

The Eighth Commandment is ultimately ordered toward the good of Truth and, far from being minor offenses against God, our misuse of speech can lead to a host of evils which Canon Francis Ripley notes when he observes, "The right use of the power of speech is necessary for the welfare of society. Untold evils are caused by its abuse in lying, propaganda, defamations of character, libel, calumnies and so forth."[177] Chief among these sins is taking false oaths by which the guilty call God as a witness to a lie, as the Roman Catechism explains:

> With regard to the prohibitory part of this Commandment, although by false testimony is understood whatever is positively but falsely affirmed of anyone, be it for or against him, be it in a public court or elsewhere; yet the Commandment specially prohibits that species of false testimony which is given on oath in a court of justice. For a witness swears by the Deity, because the words of a man thus giving evidence and using the divine name, have very great weight and possess the strongest claim to credit. Such testimony, therefore, because it is dangerous, is specially prohibited; for even the judge himself cannot reject the testimony of sworn witnesses, unless they be excluded by exceptions made in the law, or unless their dishonesty and malice are notorious. This is especially true since it is commanded by divine authority that *in the mouth of*

---

[177] Canon Francis Ripley, *This Is the Faith* (Gracewing Publishing, 1973), 98.

two or three every word shall stand [Mt. xviii. 16; Dt. xix. 15].

Consequently, both false testimony against our neighbor and false testimony in his favor are to be condemned. The Eighth Commandment, however, forbids more than false oaths. It abjures all attacks on truth including false testimony (i.e., perjury), rash judgment, lies, calumny, slander, detraction, libel, talebearing, backbiting, and betraying secrets. On this universal prohibition against falsehood, the clarity of the Roman Catechism shines:

> ...God prohibits all testimony which may inflict injury or injustice, whether it be a matter of legal evidence or not. In the passage of Leviticus where the Commandments are repeated, we read: *Thou shalt not steal; thou shalt not lie; neither shall any man deceive his neighbor.* [Lev. xix. 11] To none, therefore, can it be a matter of doubt, that this Commandment condemns lies of every sort, as these words of David explicitly declare: *Thou wilt destroy all that speak a lie* [Ps. v. 7].

Perjury

Throughout Holy Scripture and particularly in the story of Susanna (cf. Daniel XIII), perjury is condemned as mortal sin. Perjury is never permittable and must always be condemned, as the Roman Catechism unwaveringly declares:

> But if we are forbidden to injure our neighbor by false testimony, let it not be inferred that the contrary is lawful, and that we may help by perjury those who are bound to us by ties of kinship or religion. It is never allowed to have recourse to lies or deception, much less to perjury. Hence St. Augustine in his book to Crescentius *On Lying* teaches from the words of the Apostle that a lie, although uttered in false praise of anyone, is to be numbered among false testimonies.

Rash Judgment

The Law of Charity forbids rash judgment against others, which, like all offenses against our fellow man, calls to mind the requirement to *love thy neighbor as thyself* (Mt. xxii. 39) which Our Lord calls the second greatest of the Commandments. Instead of focusing on the apparent faults of others, we must remember to improve our own lives through the practice of virtue and the avoidance of vice. To those who neglect their own improvement in favor of condemning others, Our Lord says most sternly: *Thou hypocrite, cast out first the beam in thy own eye, and then shalt thou see to cast out the mote out of thy brother's eye* (Mt. vii. 5).

Lies

As stated by Canon Francis Ripley, "The intention to deceive is not necessary for a lie. Merely to employ our God-given faculty of speech in order to manifest as the thought of one's mind what is not the thought of one's mind is contrary to the primary object of speech. In itself, a lie is never more than a venial sin, but the act of telling a lie may be gravely sinful because of some other factor, for example, injury to a person's character."[178] Regardless of the moral gravity of a particular lie, the Roman Catechism strongly denounces lies of all kinds without exception:

> In a word, lies of every sort are prohibited, especially those that cause grave injury to anyone, while most impious of all is a lie uttered against or regarding religion.

> God is also grievously offended by those attacks and slanders which are termed lampoons, and other defamatory publications of this kind.

> To deceive by a jocose or officious lie, even though it helps or harms no one, is, notwithstanding, altogether unworthy; for thus the Apostle admonishes us: *Putting away lying, speak ye the truth.* [Eph. iv. 25] This practice begets a strong tendency to frequent and serious lying, and from jocose lying men contract the habit of lying, lose all reputation for truth, and ultimately find it necessary, in order to gain belief, to have recourse to continual swearing.

An important distinction exists, however, between lies and mental reservations. Canon Ripley explains:

> Here we must distinguish between strict and broad mental reservations. Strict mental reservations are always a lie and therefore sinful. The reason is that there is no clue given in the person's answer as to the true meaning the speaker is intending, because the mental

---

[178] Ripley, *op. cit.*, 98.

reservation is kept *strictly* in the speaker's mind, and there is no outward indication as to the limited meaning. For example: You ask a person 'Did you leave town yesterday,' and he answers 'No' meaning, 'I did not leave town yesterday in a car.'[179]

Canon Ripley then distinguishes these strict mental reservations, which are always lies, from broad mental reservations:

Broad mental reservations are not sinful so long as the broad mental reservation is used only as a refuge to guard a secret from prying questioners who have no right to the information we seek. In a broad mental reservation there is a clue to the correct meaning of the answer, e.g., when a child under instruction from his mother tells a salesman, 'My mother is not at home.' The meaning is, 'Not at home to you.' The salesman did not have a right to know. Our Lord Himself used the broad mental reservation for a serious reason (cf. John 7:8-10)."[180]

We are not obligated to disclose all known facts to everyone we encounter. As such, a broad mental reservation used to guard a secret from someone who has no right to the information is not sinful, and such a reservation is not a lie.

Calumny and Libel

Calumny (i.e., slander) is a serious offense against both truth and charity toward our neighbor. Through this offense, we impute crimes to others and exaggerate their malice while downplaying any goodness done by the person. Whereas slander refers to defamation in speech, libel refers to similar defamation done through written means. These sins are to be condemned without exception. Calumny and libel are forms of detraction, and the Roman Catechism admonishes the faithful on such sins:

This Commandment forbids not only false testimony, but also the detestable vice and practice of detraction — a pestilence, which is the source of innumerable and calamitous evils. This vicious habit of secretly reviling and calumniating character is frequently reprobated in the Sacred Scriptures. *With him*, says David, *I would not*

---

[179] Ripley, *op. cit.*, 99.
[180] Ibid.

eat [Ps. c. 5]; and St. James: *Detract not one another, my brethren.* [Ja. iv. 11]

Holy Writ abounds not only with precepts on the subject, but also with examples which reveal the enormity of the crime. Aman, by a crime of his own invention, had so incensed Assuerus against the Jews that he ordered the destruction of the entire race. Sacred history contains many other examples of the same kind, which priests should recall in order to deter the people from such iniquity.

Talebearing and Backbiting

Talebearing consists in repeating to anyone what others have said about him. It is a source of fighting and arguments; therefore, it is against the Law of Charity, even if we do not lie.

Backbiting occurs when one speaks of another person's faults, thereby exhibiting a lack of charity. Sincere criticism is not condemned because it seeks to improve others, but backbiting does not have this goal as its focus.

Flattery and Hypocrisy

The final general category of prohibited speech is flattery and hypocrisy. On these sins, the Roman Catechism counsels:

> Among the transgressors of this Commandment are to be numbered those fawners and sycophants who, by flattery and insincere praise, gain the hearing and good will of those whose favor, money, and honors they seek, *calling good evil, and evil good,* as the Prophet says [Is. v. 20]. Such characters David admonishes us to repel and banish from our society. *The just man,* he says, *shall correct me in mercy, and shall reprove me; but let not the oil of the sinner fatten my head* [Ps. cxl. 5]. This class of persons do not, it is true, speak ill of their neighbor; but they greatly injure him, since by praising his sins they cause him to continue in vice to the end of his life.

> ...Finally, the first part of this Commandment prohibits dissimulation. It is sinful not only to speak, but to act deceitfully. Actions, as well as words, are signs of what is in our mind; and hence our Lord, rebuking the Pharisees, frequently calls them hypocrites.

While committing any of these is sinful, even listening to any of the above-mentioned offenses is also sinful, unless one is doing so for a just cause.

Restitution Required for Forgiveness

As with sins against the Seventh Commandment, the Eighth Commandment obliges restitution. In its usual brevity, the Baltimore Catechism states: "They who have lied about their neighbor and seriously injured his character must repair the injury done as far as they are able, otherwise they will not be forgiven."[181] Similar sentiments are stated by Fr. Dominic Prümmer in his *Handbook of Moral Theology*, from which Canon Ripley draws when he writes:

> Restitution of another's good name is obligatory for sins of the tongue: One who has injured another by misuse of speech is strictly bound to make satisfaction as far as possible and without delay. This is a positive obligation which binds gravely if the injury done has been grave. This satisfaction usually entails speaking highly of a person's good qualities.[182]

Safeguarding Truth as a Commandment

Turning to the positive precept of the Eighth Commandment, the Baltimore Catechism succinctly affirms, "We are commanded by the eighth Commandment to speak the truth in all things and to be careful of the honor and reputation of everyone."[183] Likewise, the Roman Catechism affirms the need for the faithful to safeguard the truth at all times:

> To all conscientious persons is addressed the divine command that in all their intercourse with society, in every conversation, they should speak the truth at all times from the sincerity of their hearts; that they should utter nothing injurious to the reputation of another, not even of those by whom they know they have been injured and persecuted. For they should always remember that between them and others there exists such a close social bond that they are all members of the same body.

---

[181] Baltimore Catechism No. 2, Q. 381.
[182] Ripley, *op. cit.*, 101.
[183] Baltimore Catechism No. 2, Q. 379.

Predicated on this positive precept, the Catechism affirms that judges must pass sentences according to law and justice, witnesses must give testimony truthfully, lawyers and plaintiffs must be guided by love of justice, and everyone, in short, must be truthful and pursue charity as the goal. While error has no right to exist or spread, truth has an obligation to flourish and disseminate:

> The spirit of the precept not only prohibits false testimony, but also commands the truth to be told. In human affairs, to bear testimony to the truth is a matter of the highest importance, because there are innumerable things of which we must be ignorant unless we arrive at a knowledge of them on the faith of witnesses. In matters with which we are not personally acquainted and which we need to know, there is nothing so important as true evidence. Hence the words of St. Augustine: *He who conceals the truth and he who utters falsehood are both guilty; the one, because he is unwilling to render a service; the other, because he has the will to do an injury.*

Consequently, we are obligated to speak the truth in all things, although this does not include disclosing private or unnecessary matters. Our right to the truth does not generally extend so far as to open the private correspondence of others, as Fr. Prümmer clarifies:

> It is grievously sinful to read the secret letters or writings of another without the consent of either the sender or recipient or without legitimate authority or without just cause, because in so doing a person is deprived of secrets which he has a perfect right to preserve. Just as theft is committed by secretly removing the goods of another, so it is theft to pry into secrets contained in letters. In practice, however, grievous sin is often not committed either because such letters contain nothing that is secret, or because their readers arc acting with an erroneous conscience, since many people think that no grave sin is involved in reading another's letters.[184]

---

[184] Fr. Dominic Prümmer, O.P., *Handbook of Moral Theology* (The Mercier Press, 1956), 136.

Every Idle Word Will Be Judged

After expounding upon both the negative and the positive precepts of the Eighth Commandment, the Roman Catechism concludes with a practical admonition against vain speech: "The pastor should also teach that loquacity is to be avoided. By avoiding loquacity other evils will be obviated, and a great preventive opposed to lying, from which loquacious [i.e., talkative] persons can scarcely abstain."

Fr. Athanasius Iskander in *Practical Spirituality* elaborates on the merits of avoiding loquaciousness:

> That talkativeness is a sin is obvious from what the Bible tells us. Here are some verses from the Old Testament about talkativeness: 'In the multitude of words there wanteth not sin: but he that refraineth his lips is wise' (Prov. x. 19). 'He that hath knowledge spareth his words' (Prov. xvii. 27). 'A fool's voice is known by multitude of words' (Eccles. v. 3).
>
> But the most stern warning about talkativeness comes from the Lord of Glory Himself, in Matthew XII. 36-37: 'But I say unto you, that every idle word that men shall speak, they shall give account thereof in the day of judgment. For by thy words thou shalt be justified, and by thy words thou shalt be condemned.' That means that every word said unnecessarily, we will have to account for on the day of judgment. That is scary!
>
> The Fathers tell us that talkativeness is a sign of pride. A talkative person feels that he has lots of wisdom that he feels obliged to share with the world! Talkativeness is the mother of gossip and backbiting and ruining of people's reputation. It is the root of arguments and boasting. A talkative person usually embellishes his stories with exaggerations and half-truths to attract the admiration of the hearers.[185]

Conclusion

The Eighth Commandment requires us to condemn and refrain from all attacks against the Truth. In the words of the first moral relativist, Pontius

---

[185] Fr. Athanasius Iskander, *Practical Spirituality According to the Desert Fathers* (St. Shenouda Press, 2011).

Pilate, *What is Truth?* (Jn. xviii. 38). And it is Our Lord Who gave the answer in advance: *I am the way, and the truth, and the life. No man cometh to the Father, but by Me* (Jn. xiv. 6). Our Lord is the Truth, the pearl of great price (cf. Mt. xiii. 45-46), and if we love Him, we will keep His commandments (cf. Jn. xiv. 15).

Let us examine ourselves to discern if we have violated the Eighth Commandment so that we might confess our sins in the Sacrament of Confession, receive absolution, and perform fitting penance.

XXIX

The Ninth and Tenth Commandments

Thou shalt not covet thy neighbor's house: neither shalt thou desire his wife, nor his servant, nor his handmaid, nor his ox, nor his ass, nor any thing that is his (Ex. xx. 17). Contained in this single line of Sacred Scripture are the Ninth and Tenth Commandments of the Decalogue. The Roman Catechism, in its opening remarks on these closely related Commandments, underscores their importance, even though they appear last among the ten:

> It is to be observed, in the first place, that these two precepts, which were delivered last in order, furnish a general principle for the observance of all the rest. What is commanded in these two amounts to this, that if we wish to observe the preceding precepts of the law, we must be particularly careful not to covet. For he who does not covet, being content with what he has, will not desire what belongs to others, but will rejoice in their prosperity, will give glory to the immortal God, will render Him boundless thanks, and will observe the Sabbath, that is, will enjoy perpetual repose, and will respect his superiors. In fine, he will injure no man in word or deed or otherwise; for the root of all evil is concupiscence, which hurries its unhappy victims into every species of crime and wickedness. Keeping these considerations in mind, the pastor should be more diligent in explaining this Commandment, and the faithful more ready to hear (his instruction).

Both Commandments require us to fight various vices and to grow in the contrary virtues. The Ninth Commandment forbids coveting another human being (e.g., another's wife or husband). In order to avoid such sins, one must especially fight against the vice of lust. As stated by Canon Francis Ripley, "The Ninth Commandment forbids all willful consent to impure thoughts and desires and all willful pleasure in the irregular sexual promptings or motions of the flesh. That is, it forbids interior sins of thought and desire against the Sixth Commandment."[186] Similarly, the Tenth Commandment forbids coveting the possessions of others; hence, curbing the vice of envy is pivotal in the observance of the Tenth Commandment. Canon Francis Ripley writes, "The Tenth Commandment forbids all envious and covetous thoughts and unjust desires for our neighbor's goods and profits. By this commandment, God wants to protect us against the evil inclinations of our own hearts and to blunt the sting of the unlawful desires which make us yearn for things that belong to others."[187]

But why did the Roman Catechism choose to unite these distinct Commandments under a joint explanation? Rather than affirming the error of the Protestants, who consider them both as the Tenth Commandment, the Roman Catechism affirms that each of these Commandments remains separate. Yet, due to their related subject matter, they may wisely be explained under a joint heading:

> We have united these two Commandments because, since their subject matter is similar, they may be treated together. However, the pastor may explain them either together or separately, according as he may deem it more effective for his exhortations and admonitions. If, however, he has undertaken the exposition of the Decalogue, he should point out in what these two Commandments are dissimilar; how one covetousness differs from another — a difference noticed by St. Augustine, in his book of *Questions on Exodus*. The one covetousness looks only to utility and interest, the other to unlawful desire and criminal pleasure. He, for instance, who covets a field or house, pursues profit rather than pleasure, while he who covets another man's wife yields to a desire of pleasure, not of profit.

The Ninth and Tenth Commandments Are Necessary

At first glance, these Commandments seem to repeat the prohibitions already contained in the Sixth and Seventh Commandments. However, as the wisdom of the Roman Catechism explains, they go further and, as such, their promulgation was necessary for two reasons:

> The first is to explain the sixth and seventh Commandments. Reason alone shows that to prohibit

---

[186] Canon Francis Ripley, *This Is the Faith* (Gracewing Publishing, 1973), p. 90.
[187] Ibid., 96.

adultery is also to prohibit the desire of another man's wife, because, were the desire lawful, its indulgence must be so too; nevertheless, many of the Jews, blinded by sin, could not be induced to believe that such desires were prohibited by God. Nay, even after the Law had been promulgated and become known, many who professed themselves its interpreters, continued in the same error, as we learn from these words of our Lord recorded in St. Matthew: *You have heard that it was said to them of old: 'Thou shalt not commit adultery,' but I say to you, etc.*

The second reason (for the promulgation) of these two Commandments is that they distinctly and in express terms prohibit some things of which the sixth and seventh Commandments do not contain an explicit prohibition. The seventh Commandment, for instance, forbids an unjust desire or endeavor to take what belongs to another; but this Commandment further prohibits even to covet it in any way, even though it could be acquired justly and lawfully, if we foresee that by such acquisition our neighbor would suffer some loss.

Both Commandments ultimately teach us both God's love for us and our need for Him, as the Catechism poignantly observes:

"But before we come to the exposition of the Commandments, the faithful are first to be informed that by this law we are taught not only to restrain our inordinate desires, but also to know the boundless love of God towards us.

By the preceding Commandments God had, as it were, fenced us round with safeguards, securing us and ours against injury of every sort; but by the addition of these two Commandments, He intended chiefly to provide against the injuries which we might inflict on ourselves by the indulgence of inordinate desires, as would easily happen were we at liberty to covet all things indiscriminately. By this law, then, which forbids to covet, God has blunted in some degree the keenness of desire, which excites to every kind of evil, so that by reason of His command these desires are to some extent diminished, and we ourselves, freed from the annoying importunity of the passions, are enabled to devote more time to the performance of the numerous and important duties of piety and religion which we owe to God.

As has been demonstrated for each of the preceding Commandments, these two Commandments oblige both a negative and a positive precept, which in this instance takes the form of both a prohibition against coveting and a desire for heavenly goods.

Thou Shalt Not Covet *Sometimes*

Turning to the simplicity and clarity of the Baltimore Catechism, the Church summarizes both of these Commandments as follows:

> The ninth Commandment is: *Thou shalt not covet thy neighbor's wife.* We are commanded by the ninth Commandment to keep ourselves pure in thought and desire. Impure thoughts and desires are always sins, unless they displease us and we try to banish them. The tenth Commandment is: *Thou shalt not covet thy neighbor's goods.* By the tenth Commandment we are commanded to be content with what we have and to rejoice in our neighbor's welfare. The tenth Commandment forbids all desires to take or keep wrongfully what belongs to another.[188]

Coveting underpins both Commandments, but, going further than the Baltimore Catechism, the Roman Catechism distinguishes between the concupiscence (i.e., desire) that is permitted and that which is forbidden. The desire for what we do not possess is not always sinful, as the Roman Catechism clarifies:

> Concupiscence, then, is a certain commotion and impulse of the soul, urging men to the desire of pleasures, which they do not actually enjoy. As the other propensities of the soul are not always sinful, neither is the impulse of concupiscence always vicious. It is not, for instance, sinful to desire food and drink; when cold, to wish for warmth; when warm, to wish to become cool. This lawful species of concupiscence was implanted in us by the Author of nature; but in consequence of the sin of our first parents it passed the limits prescribed by nature and became so depraved that it frequently excites

---

[188] Baltimore Catechism No. 2, Q. 382 - 388.

to the desire of those things which conflict with the spirit and reason.

Furthermore, by clarifying the meaning of St. Paul in Sacred Scripture, the Roman Catechism affirms that certain desires — including the desire for Heaven, of course — are not sinful:

> If then it is sometimes lawful to covet, it must be conceded that not every species of concupiscence is forbidden. St. Paul, it is true, says that *concupiscence is sin* [Rom. vii. 20]; but his words are to be understood in the same sense as those of Moses, whom he cites, as the Apostle himself declares when, in his Epistle to the Galatians, he calls it the concupiscence of the flesh for he says: *Walk in the spirit, and you shall not fulfil the lusts of the flesh*. [Gal. v. 16] Hence that natural, well-regulated concupiscence, which does not go beyond its proper limits, is not prohibited; still less do these Commandments forbid that spiritual desire of the virtuous mind, which prompts us to long for those things that war against the flesh, for the Sacred Scriptures themselves exhort us to such a desire: *Covet ye my words,* [Wis. vi. 12] *Come over to me all ye that desire me* [Ecclus. xxiv. 26].

Two Kinds of Sinful Concupiscence

After clarifying the existence of permittable and even praiseworthy desires, the Roman Catechism next considers which desires are ultimately inordinate and sinful. These evil desires are termed as "concupiscence of the flesh" and are directly contrary to the Commandments of God:

> It is not, then, the mere power of desire, which can move either to a good or a bad object, that is prohibited by these Commandments; it is the indulgence of evil desire, which is called *the concupiscence of the flesh*, and *the fuel of sin*, and which, when accompanied by the consent of the will, is always sinful. Therefore, only that covetousness is forbidden which the Apostle calls *the concupiscence of the flesh*, that is to say, those motions of desire which are contrary to the dictates of reason and outstep the limits prescribed by God.

The Roman Catechism distinguishes two primary kinds of sinful concupiscence, explaining the reasons why each are in themselves contrary to God's law:

> [The first] kind of covetousness is condemned, either because it desires what is evil, such as adultery, drunkenness, murder, and such heinous crimes, of which the Apostle says: *Let us not covet evil things, as they also coveted* [I Cor. x. 6]; or because, although the objects may not be bad in themselves, yet there is some other reason which makes it wrong to desire them, as when, for instance, God or His Church prohibit their possession; for it is not permitted us to desire these things which it is altogether unlawful to possess. Such were, in the Old Law, the gold and silver from which idols were made, and which the Lord in Deuteronomy forbade anyone to covet [cf. Dt. vii. 25-26].
>
> Another reason why this sort of vicious desire is condemned is that it has for its object that which belongs to another, such as a house, maid-servant, field, wife, ox, ass and many other things, all of which the law of God forbids us to covet, simply because they belong to another. The desire of such things, when consented to, is criminal, and is numbered among the most grievous sins.

Envy is often used in connection with the Tenth Commandment as it expresses our unjust desire to possess that which belongs to another. Fr. John A. Hardon, S.J. defines envy in his *Modern Catholic Dictionary* as "sadness or discontent at the excellence, good fortune, or success of another person. It implies that one considers oneself somehow deprived by what one envies in another or even that an injustice has been done. Essential to envy is this sense of deprivation."[189] The Curé of Ars, writing on the sin of envy, adamantly ties envy back to the sin of Lucifer:

> Envy, my children, follows pride; whoever is envious is proud. See, envy comes to us from Hell; the devils having sinned through pride, sinned also through envy, envying our glory, our happiness. Why do we envy the happiness and the goods of others? Because we are proud; we should like to be the sole possessors of talents, riches, of the esteem and love of all the world! We hate

---

[189] Fr. John Hardon, *Modern Catholic Dictionary*, "Envy" (accessed via https://www.catholicculture.org/culture/library/dictionary/index.cfm?id=33338).

our equals, because they are our equals; our inferiors, from the fear that they may equal us; our superiors, because they are above us. In the same way, my children, that the devil after his fall felt, and still feels, extreme anger at seeing us the heirs of the glory of the good God, so the envious man feels sadness at seeing the spiritual and temporal prosperity of his neighbor.[190]

A distinction must however be made between our just desires to find a spouse, a better employment situation, or a new home and the unjust desires prohibited by God's command. As the Roman Catechism notes, the sinful coveting that underpins each of these Commandments is rooted in an insatiable desire and one which often expresses anger at the prosperity of others:

When, therefore, the Law says: *Thou shalt not covet*, it means that we are not to desire those things which belong to others. A thirst for what belongs to others is intense and insatiable; for it is written: *A covetous man shall not be satisfied with money* [Eccles. v. 9]; and of such a one Isaias says: *Woe to you that join house to house, and lay field to field* [Is. v. 8].

What We May Not Covet

After enumerating the various kinds of desires which are sinful, the Roman Catechism next uses the language of the Commandments to explicitly teach what is prohibited by the Lord:

The pastor, therefore, should teach that by the word *house* is to be understood not only the habitation in which we dwell, but all our property, as we know from the usage and custom of the sacred writers. ...

The words that follow, *nor his ox, nor his ass*, teach us that not only is it unlawful to desire things of greater value, such as a house, rank, glory, because they belong to others; but also things of little value, whatever they may be, animate or inanimate.

---

[190] St. John Vianney "On Envy" (accessed via https://catholicsaints.info/on-envy-by-saint-john-vianney/).

The words, *nor his servant*, come next, and include captives as well as other slaves whom it is no more lawful to covet than the other property of our neighbor.

The word *neighbor* is mentioned in this Commandment to mark the wickedness of those who habitually covet the lands, houses and the like, which lie in their immediate vicinity; for neighborhood, which should make for friendship, is transformed by covetousness from a source of love into a cause of hatred.

Likewise, the Roman Catechism affirms that to covet another's wife is explicitly prohibited, but so too is it to covet a wife who is separated from her husband, one who is betrothed, or one who has taken a vow of virginity. Everyone, especially due to the influence of modern fashion and media, must have a serious effort to avoid sins against purity. Resources like *True Knights: Combat Training Daily Prayers for Purity*[191] could be an invaluable aid in overcoming sins against the Ninth Commandment. Through prayer and reflection, we must work earnestly to remove all such sins and occasions of sin from our lives. Remember, temptation is not a sin, but "the sin occurs when the thoughts are deliberately encouraged," as Canon Francis Ripley reminds us.[192]

The Rise of Materialism

Like the Ninth Commandment, the Tenth Commandment has become widely violated as the modern world's love of materialism. Seeing such a proliferation in materialism, Pope Pius XII in 1957 issued *Le Pèlerinage de Lourdes* which warned against materialism:

> But the world, which today affords so many justifiable reasons for pride and hope, is also undergoing a terrible temptation to materialism which has been denounced by Our Predecessors and Ourselves on many occasions. This materialism is not confined to that condemned philosophy which dictates the policies and economy of a large segment of mankind. It rages also in a love of money which creates ever greater havoc as modern enterprises expand, and which, unfortunately, determines many of the decisions which weigh heavy on

---

[191] Kenneth Henderson and Jesse Romero, *True Knights: Combat Training Daily Prayers for Purity* (R.A.G.E. Media, 2006).
[192] Ripley, *op. cit.*, 90.

the life of the people. It finds expression in the cult of the body, in excessive desire for comforts, and in flight from all the austerities of life. It encourages scorn for human life, even for life which is destroyed before seeing the light of day.[193]

In an unmistakable reference to the Ninth Commandment, the Holy Father continues:

This materialism is present in the unrestrained search for pleasure, which flaunts itself shamelessly and tries, through reading matter and entertainments, to seduce souls which are still pure. It shows itself in lack of interest in one's brother, in selfishness which crushes him, in justice which deprives him of his rights — in a word, in that concept of life which regulates everything exclusively in terms of material prosperity and earthly satisfactions.[194]

And to this, he adds a sobering admonition, in reference to the centenary of the Blessed Virgin Mary's apparitions in Lourdes, France:

To a society which in its public life often contests the supreme rights of God, to a society which would gain the whole world at the expense of its own soul and thus hasten to its own destruction, the Virgin Mother has sent a cry of alarm. May priests be attentive to her appeal and have the courage to preach the great truths of salvation fearlessly. The only lasting renewal, in fact, will be one based on the changeless principles of faith, and it is the duty of priests to form the consciences of Christian people.[195]

The Desire for Heavenly Things

After carefully studying the negative precepts of the Ninth and Tenth Commandments, the Roman Catechism turns to the positive part of this Commandment, which is expressed in the lawful desire for heavenly things:

---

[193] Pius XII, *Le Pèlerinage de Lourdes*, para. 45-46.
[194] Ibid., para. 47.
[195] Ibid., para. 49-50.

Likewise, this Commandment requires us to desire, with all the ardor and all the earnestness of our souls, the consummation, not of our own wishes, but of the holy will of God, as it is expressed in the Lord's Prayer. Now it is His will that we be made eminent in holiness; that we preserve our souls pure and undefiled; that we practice those duties of mind and spirit which are opposed to sensuality; that we subdue our unruly appetites, and enter, under the guidance of reason and of the spirit, upon a virtuous course of life; and finally, that we hold under restraint those senses in particular which supply matter to the passions.

Incorporating prayers of gratitude and thanksgiving to God into our daily lives can help us resist the lure of envy. Similarly, actively working for the propagation of the Faith, the extirpation of heresy, the advance of the rights of the Church, the protection of the human person, and by offering reparation for sin, we properly focus on lasting treasures rather than fleeting ones which will one day come to an end.

Conclusion of the Ten Commandments

As the Catechism illustrated, rather than merely following the Commandments at face value, the faithful have an obligation to understand the various modern-day manifestations against each of them.

The Ten Commandments are not a burden but a joy. Our Lord has given them to us to set us apart *because thou art a holy people to the Lord thy God. The Lord thy God hath chosen thee, to be His peculiar people of all peoples that are upon the earth* (Dt. vii. 6). How can we be set apart as people of God if we behave like the heathens who do not know God? *We are the children of saints, and we must not be joined together like heathens that know not God* (Tob. viii. 5). Pope Benedict XVI voiced similar sentiments:

> Help them to recognize the inability of the secular, materialist culture to bring true satisfaction and joy. Be bold in speaking to them of the joy that comes from following Christ and living according to His commandments. Remind them that our hearts were made for the Lord and that they find no peace until they rest in Him.[196]

---

[196] Benedict XVI, Address to the Bishops of Ireland on their *Ad Limina* Visit (Oct. 28, 2006).

XXX

The Lord's Prayer

Our Father, Who Art in Heaven

After having systematically studied the articles of the Creed, the theology of the Sacraments, and the Ten Commandments, we now turn to the Catechism's fourth and final part on the quintessential prayer unpinning Catholic life — the prayer which our Divine Redeemer taught us while He walked this earth. Known as "The Lord's Prayer" or the "Our Father," this is a prayer which all Catholics must know and should pray devoutly daily, as St. Francis de Sales observed: "One Our Father said devoutly is worth more than many prayers hurried over."[197]

Before considering the first words of this venerable prayer, the Roman Catechism begins with a short consideration on the merits, necessity, and qualities of prayer in general. Since prayer is such an important topic, the Catechism begins by expounding upon this necessary activity which is all too often neglected by modern man. It reiterates the importance for priests to instruct the faithful in developing an authentic prayer life:

> Whatever is necessary to the performance of the duty of prayer is comprised in that divine formula which Christ the Lord deigned to make known to His Apostles, and through them and their successors to all Christians. Its thoughts and words should be so deeply impressed on the mind and memory as to be ever in readiness.

On the Necessity of Prayer

Always rejoice. Pray without ceasing. In all things give thanks; for this is the will of God in Christ Jesus concerning you all (I Thess. v. 16-18).

---

[197] St. Francis de Sales, *Introduction to the Devout Life* (Image Books, 1989), 82.

The goal of prayer is based on our foundational purpose in life to know, love, and serve God. When we meditate deeply on the wonder of creation, the great gift of the Incarnation, and the powerful guidance of our Blessed Lord's life, we come to know God more fully. Prayer is our forum for communicating with and listening to Him. Prayer is our opportunity to show reverence and return love. And when we intercede for others, asking for goodness in the world, we serve Him. Far from being only a time for asking for favors, we have a duty to pray every day to honor, praise, worship, and glorify God. Along with prayers of adoration and petition, prayers of thanksgiving and contrition should likewise be offered on a regular basis. As such, prayer may take the form of adoration, thanksgiving, confession, or supplication.

Since prayer is essential for preserving and increasing the life of grace in our souls, we can rightly affirm that it is "necessary to the Christian," as the Roman Catechism explains:

> In the first place the necessity of prayer should be insisted upon. Prayer is a duty not only recommended by way of counsel, but also commanded by obligatory precept. Christ the Lord declared this when He said: *We should pray always.* [Lk. xviii. 1] This necessity of prayer the Church points out in the prelude, if we may so call it, which she prefixes to the Lord's Prayer: *Admonished by salutary precepts, and taught by divine instruction, we presume to say*, etc.

> Therefore, since prayer is necessary to the Christian, the Son of God, yielding to the request of the disciples, *Lord, teach us to pray*, [Lk. xi. 1] gave them a prescribed form of prayer, and encouraged them to hope that the objects of their petitions would be granted. He Himself was to them a model of prayer; He not only prayed assiduously but watched whole nights in prayer [cf. Lk. vi. 12].

On this point, St. Alphonsus Liguori, among many other Saints and theologians, affirms the necessity of prayer for salvation:

> If then we would be saved, we must pray, and this too with humility, confidence, and above all with perseverance. And hence it is that meditation is of so

much use; because by it we are reminded to pray; we should otherwise forget it, and thus should be lost.[198]

The Fruits of Prayer

After affirming the necessity of prayer, the Catechism connects this necessity to the many spiritual fruits which spring forth from prayer. Indeed, prayer is not a mere requirement imposed on man by a demanding God but a true means of conversing with Him and the primary means by which we preserve and increase the divine life of grace we receive through the Sacraments:

> Moreover, this necessity of prayer is also productive of the greatest delight and usefulness, since it bears most abundant fruits. …
>
> The first fruit which we receive is that by praying we honor God, since prayer is a certain act of religion, which is compared in Scripture to a sweet perfume. …
>
> Another most pleasing and invaluable fruit of prayer is that it is heard by God. *Prayer is the key of heaven*, says St. Augustine; *prayer ascends, and the mercy of God descends.* …
>
> Nor can we, for a moment, doubt that God in His goodness awaits and is at all times ready to hear our petitions — a truth to which the Sacred Scriptures bear ample testimony.

It is important to recall that prayer is not a mechanical activity. Whether our prayer is mental prayer, vocal prayer, liturgical prayer, or any other form, it must be from the heart. The use of specific written prayers is quite useful and meritorious, and many are enriched by the Church with indulgences, but any prayer must above all come from the heart. Therefore, the Catechism warns that prayer said without devotion is unheard:

> *God*, says St. Augustine, *denies some things in His mercy which He grants in His wrath.* …
>
> Sometimes, also, such is the remissness and negligence with which we pray, that we ourselves do not attend to

---

[198] St. Alphonsus Liguori, *The Way of Salvation: Meditations for Everyday of the Year*, (Keating & Brown, 1836), 302.

what we say. Since prayer is an elevation of the soul to God, if, while we pray, the mind, instead of being fixed upon God, is distracted, and the tongue slurs over the words at random, without attention, without devotion, with what propriety can we give to such empty sounds the name of Christian prayer?

We should not, therefore, be at all surprised, if God does not comply with our requests; either because by our negligence and indifference we almost show that we do not really desire what we ask, or because we ask those things, which, if granted, would be prejudicial to our interests.

In similar words, the Catechism of St. Pius X reminds us, "Many times our prayers are not heard, either because we ask things not conducive to our eternal salvation, or because we do not ask properly."[199] Indeed, the Roman Catechism affirms that for the devout, our prayers are answered in abundance should they be in accordance of God's will:

On the other hand, to those who pray with devout attention, God grants more than they ask. This the Apostle declares in his Epistle to the Ephesians [cf. Eph. iii. 20], and the same truth is unfolded in the parable of the prodigal son, who would have deemed it a kindness to be admitted into the number of his father's servants [cf. Lk. xv. 11-32].

Nay, God heaps His favors not only on those who seek them, but also on those who are rightly disposed; and this, not only with abundance, but also with readiness. This is shown by the words of Scripture: *The Lord hath heard the desire of the poor.* [Ps. x. 17] For God hastens to grant the inner and hidden desires of the needy without awaiting their utterance.

The Catechism also affirms that prayer increases faith, strengthens our hope, increases charity, disposes the soul for divine blessings, makes us realize our needfulness, protects against the devil, and promotes a virtuous life. The final fruit of prayer, as mentioned by the Roman Catechism, is its ability to disarm divine vengeance:

---

[199] Fr. Marshall Roberts, *Catechism of St. Pius X* (St. Michael's Press, 2010), 59.

> Finally, as St. Jerome observes, prayer disarms the anger of God. ... Nothing is so efficacious in appeasing God, when His wrath is kindled; nothing so effectually delays or averts the punishments prepared for the wicked as the prayers of men.

Consequently, one of the primary responsibilities of parents is certainly to teach their children how to pray devoutly. This is achieved not only by words and instruction in the Faith but also (and perhaps even more so) by example and practice. The same applies to teachers, catechists, government officials, lawyers, priests, godparents, and anyone else who has the responsibility to inspire others.

"Our" Father

In just 56 words, the Our Father summarizes how we are to approach God. It combines praise and petition. It calls for surrender and understanding. This prayer puts us into a relationship with God, Who reaches down to us as a loving Father. It also unites us with all those who are of the true Faith, as we do not address God as "my" Father but "our" Father:

> When we invoke the Father and when each one of us calls Him *our* Father, we are to understand thereby that from the privilege and gift of divine adoption it necessarily follows that all the faithful are brethren and should love each other as such: *You are all brethren for one is your Father who is in heaven.* [Mt. xxiii. 8] This is why the Apostles in their Epistles address all the faithful as *brethren.*

The word "our" also obliges us to work toward the salvation of our fellow man. On this point, and the fraternal charity which it induces, the Roman Catechism further explains:

> How sincere should be the manner in which we ought to utter the word *our*, we learn from St. Chrysostom. *God*, he says, *listens willingly to the Christian who prays not only for himself but for others; because to pray for ourselves is an inspiration of nature; but to pray for others is an inspiration of grace; necessity compels us to pray for ourselves, whereas fraternal charity calls on us to pray for others.* And he adds: *That prayer which is inspired by fraternal charity is more agreeable to God than that which is dictated by necessity.*

Indeed, the fraternal spirit which must animate this prayer is so important that the Catechism further reminds priests:

> In connection with the important subject of salutary prayer, the pastor should be careful to remind and exhort all the faithful of every age, condition and rank, never to forget the bonds of universal brotherhood that bind them, and consequently ever to treat each other as friends and brothers, and never to seek arrogantly to raise themselves above their neighbors.

The Fatherly Care of God

By praying the Lord's Prayer, we affirm the truth of our divine sonship: *For you are all the children of God by faith in Christ Jesus* (Gal. iii. 26). The Catechism of St. Pius X concisely affirms the same sentiments: "In the beginning of the Lord's Prayer we call God Our Father, to foster confidence in His infinite goodness by the remembrance that we are His children."[200]

Both Scripture and Tradition teach us that through faith and Baptism, we receive *the spirit of adoption* (Rom. viii. 15) and become true children of God. This awesome reality of divine sonship permits us to pray to God as our "Father." The Roman Catechism explains the importance of the word "Father" at the beginning of the Lord's Prayer by stating:

> The first word, which, by the order and institution of God we employ in this prayer, is *Father*. Our Savior could, indeed, have commenced this divine prayer with some other word, conveying more the idea of majesty, such, for instance, as *Lord* or *Creator*. Yet He omitted all such expressions because they might rather inspire fear, and instead of them He has chosen a term inspiring confidence and love in those who pray and ask anything of God; for what is sweeter than the name *Father*, conveying, as it does, the idea of indulgence and tenderness? The reasons why this name *Father* is applicable to God, can be easily explained to the faithful by speaking to them on the subjects of creation, providence, and redemption.

The Catechism next specifies three primary reasons why we refer to God as "Father": first, because He created us; secondly, because He provides

---

[200] Fr. Marshall Roberts *op. cit.*, p. 63.

for us; and finally, because He cares for us. Regarding the third point, the Catechism cites the appointment of guardian angels over each soul as a proof of God's fatherly care:

> By God's providence, Angels have been entrusted with the office of guarding the human race and of accompanying every human being so as to preserve him from any serious dangers. Just as parents, whose children are about to travel a dangerous and infested road, appoint guardians and helpers for them, so also in the journey we are making towards our heavenly country our heavenly Father has placed over each of us an Angel under whose protection and vigilance we may be enabled to escape the snares secretly prepared by our enemy, repel the dreadful attacks he makes on us, and under his guiding hand keep the right road, and thus be secure against all false steps which the wiles of the evil one might cause us to make in order to draw us aside from the path that leads to heaven.

Far from being an invention of the Church, early Christians were devoted to angels. Origen, the famous Christian scholar and theologian, wrote in A.D. 225: "Every believer — although the humblest in the Church — is said to be attended by an angel, who the Savior declares always beholds the face of God the Father. Now, this angel has the purpose of being his guardian."[201]

Beyond creating us and caring for us in His Providence, Almighty God has shown us His fatherly love above all in Christ's act of redemption accomplished on the Cross and made present again at every Holy Sacrifice of the Mass:

> The creation of the world and God's providence are, then, of great weight in bringing into relief the singular love of God for the human race and the special care He takes of man. But far above these two shines the work of redemption, so much so indeed that our most bountiful God and Father has crowned His infinite goodness towards us by granting us this third favor.
>
> Accordingly, the pastor should instruct his spiritual children and constantly recall to their minds the surpassing love of God for us, so that they may be fully

---

[201] Origen, *De Principiis*, Bk. II, chap. 10, par. 7

alive to the fact that having been redeemed in a wonderful manner they are thereby made the sons of God. To them, says St. John, *He gave power to be made the sons of God* ... and *they are born of God* [Jn. i. 12, 13].

This is why Baptism, the first pledge and token of our redemption, is called the Sacrament of regeneration; for it is by Baptism that we are born children of God: *That which is born of the Spirit*, says our Lord, *is spirit*; and: *You must be born again* [Jn. iii. 6]. In the same way we have the words of St. Peter: *Being born again, not of corruptible seed, but incorruptible, by the word of God who liveth* [I Pet. i. 23].

By reason of this redemption, we have received the Holy Ghost and have been made worthy of the grace of God.

Good Fathers Discipline Their Children

God is our Creator, our Provider and Defender, and our Redeemer. And the awareness of this sublime reality necessarily obliges us to the duties of love, piety, obedience, and respect. Even if God chastises us, we must see in trials the wisdom of a truly loving Father Who orders all things for our ultimate good while respecting our free will. On this crucial point, the Roman Catechism saliently reminds us:

> The faithful, therefore, should be recommended to recognize in such chastisements the fatherly love of God, and ever to have in their hearts and on their lips the saying of Job, the most patient of men: *He woundeth and cureth; He striketh and His hands shall heal* [Job v. 18]; as well as to repeat frequently the words written by Jeremias in the name of the people of Israel: *Thou hast chastised me and I was instructed, as a young bullock unaccustomed to the yoke: convert me and I shall be converted; for Thou art the Lord my God* [Jer. xxxi. 18]; and to keep before their eyes the example of Tobias who, recognizing in the loss of his sight the paternal hand of God raised against him, cried out: *I bless thee, O Lord God of Israel, because Thou hast chastised me and Thou hast saved me* [Tob. xi. 17].

> In this connection the faithful should be particularly on their guard against believing that any calamity or

affliction that befalls them can take place without the knowledge of God; for we have His own words: *A hair of your heads shall not perish* [Lk. xxi. 18]. Let them rather find consolation in that divine oracle read in the Apocalypse: *Those whom I love I rebuke and chastise* [Apoc. iii. 19]....

Who Art in Heaven

As we know from both reason and revelation, God is *omnipotent*, *omniscient*, and *omnipresent* — that is, present everywhere. Why, then, did Our Lord teach us to say, "Who art in Heaven"? The Roman Catechism explains:

> But though God is present in all places and in all things, without being bound by any limits, as has been already said, yet in Sacred Scripture it is frequently said that He has His dwelling in heaven. And the reason is because the heavens which we see above our heads are the noblest part of the world, remain ever incorruptible, surpass all other bodies in power, grandeur and beauty, and are endowed with fixed and regular motion.
>
> God, then, in order to lift up the minds of men to contemplate His infinite power and majesty, which are so preeminently visible in the work of the heavens, declares in Sacred Scripture that heaven is His dwelling place. Yet at the same time He often affirms, what indeed is most true, that there is no part of the universe to which He is not present intimately by His nature and His power.

And as the Catechism does so many other times, it connects this truth with a spiritual reality which all of us may take to heart:

> In connection with this consideration, however, let the faithful keep before their minds not only the image of the common Father of all, but also of a God reigning in heaven; and hence when about to pray, let them remember that they should raise heart and soul to heaven, and that the more the name of Father inspires them with hope and trust, the more should the sublime nature and divine majesty of our Father who is in heaven inspire them with sentiments of Christian humility and respect.

Conclusion

The Roman Catechism, unlike so many others, insightfully and thoroughly instructs on the meaning of the Lord's Prayer and various practical considerations related to it. The next time we pray this all-holy prayer, let us pause and reflect on the words "Our Father, Who art in Heaven" and give thanks that we, mere creatures, are able to call the God of the universe by the name of *Father*.

XXXI

Hallowed Be Thy Name

The first petition of the Lord's Prayer begins with sentiments of praise and adoration for the most adorable Name of God. In so doing, our Savior, the true Author of this prayer, has shown us the primary importance of giving honor and glory to God from Whom all things come. With the clarity and depth we have come to expect from the Roman Catechism, the Church opens her explanation of this petition and explains why it appropriately ranks first among the seven petitions:

> What we are to ask of God and in what order, the Master and Lord of all has Himself taught and commanded. For prayer is the ambassador and interpreter of our thoughts and desires; and consequently, we pray well and properly when the order of our petitions follows the order in which the things sought are desirable.

> Now, genuine charity tells us to direct our whole soul and all our affections to God, for He alone being the one supreme Good, it is but reasonable that we love Him with superior and singular love. On the other hand, God cannot be loved from the heart and above all things else, unless we prefer His honor and glory to all things created. For all the good that we or others possess, all that in any way bears the name of good, comes from Him, and is therefore inferior to Him, the sovereign Good.

> Hence, that our prayers may be made with due order, our Savior has placed this Petition regarding the sovereign Good at the head of all the other Petitions of the Lord's Prayer, thus showing us that before asking the things necessary for ourselves or for others, we ought to ask those that appertain to God's honor, and to manifest and make known to Him the affections and desires of our hearts in this regard.

The Catechism further elaborates by tying this petition back to the greatest of the Commandments, namely, to love God above all else: "Acting thus, we shall be faithful to the claims and rules of charity, which teaches us to love God more than ourselves and to ask, in the first place, those things we desire on His account, and next, those things we desire on our own."

In a similar vein, the Catechism of St. Pius X asks, "Why do we first of all ask that the Name of God may be sanctified?" The answer: "We first of all ask that the Name of God may be sanctified, because the glory of God should be nearer our hearts than all other goods and interests."[202]

Can We Add to An All-Powerful God's Honor?

It is fitting that our Lord and God — He Who is our Creator, Redeemer, and Sanctifier — is honored and praised at the beginning of the Our Father. However, God is infinitely perfect in Himself and needs nothing from us, a truth that can be ascribed to the aseity of God (He exists in and of Himself). Consequently, one may conclude that God gains nothing from our praise and, taken to its extreme, condemns all prayers of adoration since He cannot benefit from them. In unwavering terms, the Roman Catechism denounces this error:

> But as our desires and petitions concern such things only as are needed, and as nothing can be added to God; that is to say, to the Divine Nature, nor can His Divine Substance, which is ineffably rich in all perfection, be in any way increased, we must remember that the things we ask of God on God's own account are extrinsic and concern His exterior glory.

> Thus, we desire and beg that His Name may be more and better known in the world, that His kingdom may be extended, and that each day new servants may come to obey His holy will. These three things, His Name, His kingdom, and obedience (to His will), do not appertain to the intrinsic nature and perfection of God, but are extrinsic thereto.

> To enable the faithful to understand still more clearly the force and bearing of these Petitions, the pastor should take care to point out to them that the words, *On earth as it is in heaven*, may be understood of each of the first three Petitions, as follows: *Hallowed be Thy Name on*

---

[202] Fr. Marshall Roberts, Catechism of St. Pius X (St. Michael's Press, 2010), 64.

earth as it is in heaven; Thy kingdom come on earth as it is in heaven; and, Thy will be done on earth as it is in heaven.

The Catechism next adds, "In praying that the Name of God may be hallowed, our meaning is that the sanctity and glory of the divine name may be increased." As a result, our prayer that God's Name will be honored is prayed in part to help us recall our own duty to spread His adorable Name far and wide. St. Augustine, the illustrious Doctor of the Church (A.D. 354–430), concluded the same in a letter to Proba, more than a millennium before the Roman Catechism was written:

> We need to use words so that we may remind ourselves to consider carefully what we are asking, not so that we may think we can instruct the Lord or prevail on Him. Thus, when we say: *Hallowed be Thy Name*, we are reminding ourselves to desire that His Name, which in fact is always holy, should also be considered holy among men. I mean that it should not be held in contempt. But this is a help for men, not for God.[203]

The Five Sanctifications of God's Name

After establishing the importance of this petition, the Roman Catechism next enumerates and explains the five sanctifications of God's Name for which we should pray: that the faithful may glorify Him, that unbelievers may be converted, that sinners may be converted, that God may be thanked for His favors, and that the Church may be recognized by all.

First and foremost, we pray that the faithful — those of us who are united in the *one Lord, one faith, [and] one baptism* (Eph. iv. 5) — may glorify God. How do we do so in accordance with this first petition? The Roman Catechism teaches:

> In other words, we pray that our minds, our souls and our lips may be so devoted to the honor and worship of God as to glorify Him with all veneration both interior and exterior, and, after the model of the heavenly citizens, to celebrate with all our might the greatness, the glory and the holiness of the Name of God.

---

[203] As quoted in the *Liturgy of the Hours*, Office of Readings (Tuesday, 29th week *Tempus Per Annum*).

While we can and must work for the salvation of our neighbor, our chief responsibility is always our own salvation. No one is saved or lost for all eternity by accident. This is why the Catechism of St. Pius X further adds the importance of our adherence to the greatest of the Commandments: "In the First Petition, *Hallowed be Thy Name*, we ask that God may be known, loved, honored and served by the whole world and by ourselves in particular."[204]

The next two sanctifications concern the conversion of unbelievers and sinners, a cause which should be close to all our hearts. As our Lord lamented the fate of the inhabitants of Jerusalem who would reject salvation (cf. Luke 19:41-44), the death of souls in the state of mortal sin should cause us great lament. Outside of the Church there is no salvation, and we must pray that our Lord helps bring about the conversion of all erring souls. On this point of true charity, the Roman Catechism elaborates:

> Thus, then, as the heavenly spirits with perfect unanimity exalt and glorify God, so do we pray that the same be done over all the earth; that all nations may come to know, worship, and reverence God; that all without a single exception may embrace the Christian religion, may devote themselves wholly to the service of God, and may be convinced that in Him is the source of all sanctity and that there is nothing pure, nothing holy, that does not proceed from the sanctity of His divine name. According to the testimony of the Apostle, *The Church is cleansed by the laver of water in the word of life* [Eph. v. 26]: and the *word of life* signifies the Name of the Father and of the Son and of the Holy Ghost in which we are baptized and sanctified.

Thoughtfully praying this petition of the Lord's Prayer is a spiritual act of mercy as we hope to bring about the conversion of sinners and greater honor to God through His one true Church. The Catechism of St. Pius X in addressing this petition further emphasizes the sentiments which should animate our souls when we recite these holy words, by tying them to the conversion of infidels, heretics, and schismatics:

> We intend to beg that infidels may come to the knowledge of the Lord God, that heretics may recognize their errors, that schismatics may return to the unity of

---

[204] Roberts *op. cit.*

the Church, that sinners may repent, and that the just may persevere in well-doing.[205]

The phrase, *Hallowed be Thy Name*, is also a means for us to praise and thank God for all of His manifold blessings, both spiritual and temporal, and to recognize ever more deeply that God our Father is the true Source of all that is good:

> …we pray that God may make His light to shine on the minds of all, so as to enable them to see that *every best gift and every perfect gift coming from the Father of lights* [Ja. i. 17], is conferred on us by Him, and consequently that temperance, justice, life, health, in a word, all goods of soul, body and possessions, all goods both natural and supernatural, must be recognized as gifts given by Him from whom, as the Church proclaims, proceed all blessings. If the sun by its light, if the stars by their motion and revolutions, are of any advantage to man; if the air with which we are surrounded serves to sustain us; if the earth with its abundance of produce and its fruits furnishes the means of subsistence to all men; if our rulers by their vigilance enable us to enjoy peace and tranquility, it is to the infinite goodness of God that we owe these and innumerable blessings of a similar kind….

Sadly, the fifth sanctification of God's Name — that the Church may be recognized by all — is often forgotten in an era which promotes religious liberty and indifferentism to such an extent that many souls consider all religions equal. However, the divinely revealed truth is that the Catholic Faith alone is the true Faith, and it is necessary for salvation. With this in mind, the wisdom of the Roman Catechism provides us ample material for meditation as it explains:

> But what we most particularly ask in this Petition is that all may acknowledge and revere the spouse of Jesus Christ, our most holy mother the Church, in which alone is to be found the copious and inexhaustible fountain that cleanses and effaces all the stains of sin, and from which are drawn all the Sacraments of salvation and sanctification, those Sacraments through which, like so many sacred channels, is diffused over us by the hand of God the dew, of sanctity. To that Church alone and to those whom she embraces in her bosom and holds in her

---

[205] Roberts *op. cit.*

arms, appertains the invocation of that divine name, outside of which *there is no other name under heaven given to men whereby we must be saved* [Acts iv. 12].

Living A Holy Life

From this, it follows that by praying the Lord's Prayer we affirm our own desire and intention to live a holy life. On this essential point, the Roman Catechism admonishes:

> The pastor should be careful to insist particularly on the fact that it is the duty of a good son not only to pray to God his Father in words, but also to endeavor by his conduct and actions to promote the sanctification of the divine name. And would to God there were none who, though continually praying for the sanctification of God's Name, yet, as far as in them lies, violate and profane it by their deeds, and by whose fault God Himself is sometimes blasphemed. It was of such as these that the Apostle said: *The name of God through you is blasphemed among the Gentiles* [Rom. ii. 24]; and in Ezechiel we read: *They entered among the nations whither they went, and profaned My holy Name, when it was said of them: 'This is the people of the Lord, and they are come forth out of His land'* [Ez. xxxvi. 20]; for according to the sort of life and conduct led by those professing a particular religion, so precisely in the eyes of the unlettered multitude will be the opinion held of that religion and of its author.

We must be uncompromising in our fidelity to Catholic doctrine while also maintaining the utmost charity towards God and neighbor. Souls will only be converted after great labor by our work with apologetics. But souls will be lost in only a few moments if they see us living a hypocritical life at odds with the Faith we verbally profess. Keep this in mind in all your actions, no matter how small: souls can be lost by scandal. As a reminder of this reality, the Roman Catechism concludes its exposition on the first petition thus:

> Those, therefore, who live according to the dictates of the Christian religion which they have embraced, and who regulate their prayers and actions by its precepts, furnish others with a powerful motive for greatly praising, honoring and glorifying the name of our heavenly Father. As for us, it is a duty which the Lord

has imposed on us, to lead others by shining deeds of virtue to praise and glorify the name of God. This is how He addresses us in the Gospel: *Let your light so shine before men, that they may see your good works and glorify your Father who is in heaven* [Matt. v. 16]; and the Prince of the Apostles says: *Having your conversation good among the Gentiles, that they may, by the good works which they shall behold in you, glorify God* [I Pet. ii. 12].

Padre Pio once remarked, "Holiness means loving our neighbor as our self for love of God. In this connection holiness means loving those who curse us, who hate and persecute us and even doing good to them. Holiness means living humbly, being disinterested, prudent, just, patient, kind, chaste, meek, diligent, carrying out one's duties for no other reason than that of pleasing God and receiving from Him alone the reward one deserves." Thus, to truly pray, "Hallowed be Thy Name," we must be serious about pursuing and practicing these characteristics of a holy life.

Conclusion

It is all too common to hastily pray the Lord's Prayer and, in the process, forget the immense wisdom and meaning behind each of the petitions — precious words given to by our Savior Himself. We would do well to take a minute right now to slowly pray the Our Father and, as we do so, to recall the five sanctifications of God's Name for which we should earnestly pray. May our Lord's Name truly be honored and praised and may those who are separated from the true Faith convert so that we may all be united under the one true God.

XXXII

Thy Kingdom Come

The second petition in the Lord's Prayer is often glossed over. What is the Kingdom of God? Where is it? What do we mean when we ask for it to "come" and how does that impact our lives here on earth? The three simple words of this petition are of great importance for the faithful and priests are admonished in this section of the Roman Catechism to explain them with great attention:

> The kingdom of heaven which we pray for in this second Petition is the great end to which is referred, and in which terminates all the preaching of the Gospel; for from it St. John the Baptist commenced his exhortation to penance: *Do penance, for the kingdom of heaven is at hand* [Mt. iii. 2] With it also the Savior of the world opened His preaching [cf. Mt. iv. 17]. In that admirable discourse on the mount in which He points out to His disciples the way to happiness, having proposed, as it were, the subject matter of His discourse, our Lord commences with the kingdom of heaven: *Blessed are the poor in spirit, for theirs is the kingdom of heaven* [Mt. vi. 3]. Again, to those who would detain Him with them, He assigns as the necessary cause of His departure: *To other cities, also, I must preach the kingdom of God; therefore, am I sent* [Lk. iv. 43]. This kingdom He afterwards commanded the Apostles to preach [cf. Mt. x. 7]. And to him who expressed a wish to go and bury his father, He replied: *Go thou, and preach the kingdom of God* [Lk ix. 60]. And after He had risen from the dead, during those forty days in which He appeared to the Apostles, He spoke of *the kingdom of God* [Acts i. 3].

> This second Petition, therefore, the pastor should treat with the greatest attention, in order to impress on the minds of his faithful hearers its great importance and necessity.

Seek First the Kingdom of God

The Roman Catechism concludes its opening remarks on this petition with a reminder for priests:

> In the first place pastors will be greatly assisted towards an accurate and careful explanation of this Petition by the thought that the Redeemer Himself commanded this Petition, although united to the others, to be also offered separately, in order that we may seek with the greatest earnestness that for which we pray; for He says: *Seek first the kingdom of God and his justice, and all these things shall be added unto you* [Mt. vi. 33].

Our Redeemer Himself, the Author of the Lord's Prayer, said as part of His sermon on the Mount: *Seek ye therefore first the kingdom of God, and His justice, and all these things shall be added unto you. Be not therefore solicitous for tomorrow; for the morrow will be solicitous for itself. Sufficient for the day is the evil thereof* (Mt. vi. 33-34).

The Kingdom of God is referenced over 150 times in the New Testament and even the last verse of the Acts of the Apostles describes St. Paul as *preaching the kingdom of God, and teaching the things which concern the Lord Jesus Christ, with all confidence, without prohibition* (Acts xxviii. 31). Yet far from referencing an earthly military kingdom, Our Lord affirmed multiple times — to the confusion of even His disciples — that His Kingdom *is not of this world* (Jn. xviii. 36).

To what, then, does the Kingdom of God refer? Turning to the Catechism of St. Pius X, we find the answer: "By the Kingdom of God we mean a threefold spiritual Kingdom; that is, the reign of God in us, or the reign of grace; the reign of God on earth, or the Holy Catholic Church; and the reign of God in heaven, or Paradise."[206] The Kingdom of God therefore refers chiefly to all things necessary for our salvation. On this salient point, the Roman Catechism shines in wisdom:

> We compress, therefore, within the small compass of this Petition for God's kingdom all that we stand in need of in our present pilgrimage, or rather exile, and all this God graciously promises to grant us; for He immediately subjoins: *All these things shall be added unto you.* Thus, does He declare that He is that king who with bountiful hand bestows upon man an abundance of all things, whose infinite goodness enraptured David when he sang:

---

[206] *Catechism of St. Pius X*, 65.

The Lord ruleth me, and I shall want nothing [Ps. xxii. 1].

The Kingdom of Nature, of Grace, and of Glory

Expanding further than the Catechism of St. Pius X, the Roman Catechism next expounds upon the Kingdom of God as a three-fold kingdom of nature, grace, and glory. First and foremost, while the Kingdom of God is concerned with our own souls, it nevertheless also includes all created things since God, Who is the Author of all things, possesses them as His own creation. This, says the Roman Catechism, refers to the Kingdom of Nature:

> In their ordinary sense, which is frequently employed by Scripture, the words, *kingdom of God*, signify not only that power which God possesses over all men and over the entire universe, but, also, His providence which rules and governs all things. *In His hands*, says the Prophet, *are all the ends of the earth* [Ps. xciv. 4]. The word *ends* includes those things also which lie buried in the depths of the earth and are concealed in the most hidden recesses of creation. In this sense Mardochaeus exclaims: *O Lord, Lord, almighty king, for all things are in Thy power, and there is none that can resist Thy will: Thou art God of all, and there is none that can resist Thy majesty* [Esth. xiii. 9].

The Church's annual celebration of the Kingship of Christ commemorates in a tangible manner the Kingdom of God over all individuals, institutions, and nations. There is no part of the world that is not under God's domain, regardless of whether or not leaders, citizens, or nations choose to recognize Christ the King. Thus, even pagan lands are truly the possession of Christ by nature, and it is our earnest prayer that all of society publicly honor and adore Our Lord as the true Ruler of our world and Master of our souls. Msgr. Rudolph G. Bandas connects these sentiments with the reasons why Pope Pius XI instituted the Feast of the Kingship of Christ in 1925:

> The Feast of Christ the King was established by Pope Pius XI in 1925 as an antidote to secularism, a way of life which leaves God out of man's thinking and living and organizes his life as if God did not exist. The feast is intended to proclaim in a striking and effective manner Christ's royalty over individuals, families, society, governments, and nations... [This] Mass also describes

the qualities of Christ's kingdom. This kingdom is: 1) supreme, extending not only to all peoples but also to their princes and kings; 2) universal, extending to all nations and to all places; 3) eternal, for 'The Lord shall sit a King forever'; 4) spiritual, Christ's kingdom is not of this world.

The Kingdom of God is also a Kingdom of Grace, as the Roman Catechism explains:

> By *the kingdom of God* is also understood that special and singular providence by which God protects and watches over pious and holy men. It is of this peculiar and admirable care that David speaks when he says: *The Lord rules me, I shall want nothing*, and Isaias: *The Lord our king He will save us* [Is. xxxiii. 22].

> But although, even in this life, the pious and holy are placed, in a special manner, under this kingly power of God; yet our Lord Himself informed Pilate that His kingdom was not of this world, that is to say, had not its origin in this world, which was created and is doomed to perish. In this perishable way power is exercised by kings, emperors, commonwealths, rulers, and all whose titles to the government of states and provinces is founded upon the desire or election of men, or who have intruded themselves, by violent and unjust usurpation, into sovereign power.

There is no greater treasure worth protecting on this earth than the state of sanctifying grace in our souls, as its presence will ultimately win for us Heaven — while its absence will damn us to hell. This is a dogmatic reality. Thus, regarding Kingdom of Grace, we beg Our Lord to keep us and preserve us in grace, as the Catechism of St. Pius X similarly states:

> With regard to grace we beg that God may reign in us by His sanctifying grace, by which He deigns to dwell within us as a king in his palace; and that He may keep us ever united to Himself by the virtues of faith, hope and charity, through which He reigns over our intellect, our heart and our will.[207]

---

[207] Roberts, *op. cit.*

Lastly, the Kingdom of God refers to the Kingdom of Glory which is rightfully preceded by the Kingdom of Grace:

> By the words *kingdom of God* is also meant that kingdom of His glory, of which Christ our Lord says in St. Matthew: *Come ye blessed of My Father, possess the kingdom which was prepared for you from the beginning of the world* [Mt. xxv. 34]. This kingdom the thief, when he had admirably acknowledged his crimes, begged of Christ in the words related by St. Luke: *Lord, remember me, when Thou comest into Thy kingdom* [Lk. xxiii. 42]...

> But the kingdom of grace must precede that of glory; for God's glory cannot reign in anyone in whom His grace does not already reign. Grace, according to the Redeemer, is a *fountain of water springing up to eternal life* [Jn. iii. 5]; while as regards glory, what can we call it except a certain perfect and absolute grace? As long as we are clothed with this frail mortal flesh, as long as we wander in this gloomy pilgrimage and exile, weak and far away from God, we often stumble and fall, because we rejected the aid of the kingdom of grace, by which we were supported. But when the light of the kingdom of glory, which is perfect, shall have shone upon us, we shall stand forever firm and secure. Then shall all that is defective and unsuitable be utterly removed; then shall every infirmity be strengthened and invigorated; in a word, God Himself will then reign in our souls and bodies.

Thy Kingdom *Come*

After systematically explaining the meaning and importance of the word "kingdom," the Roman Catechism next turns to explaining all of the sentiments encapsulated in the word "come." When the Lord's Prayer is said quickly and in haste, so many spiritual realities are ignored. Yet in one simple word are contained multiple sentiments integral to the Christian life.

First, by praying for the Kingdom of God to "come," we pray for the conversion of all those who are outside the Barque of Peter:

> In this Petition we ask God that the kingdom of Christ, that is, His Church, may be enlarged; that Jews and infidels may embrace the faith of Christ and the

knowledge of the true God; that schismatics and heretics may return to soundness of mind, and to the communion of the Church of God which they have deserted; and that thus may be fulfilled and realized the words of the Lord, spoken by the mouth of Isaias: *Enlarge the place of thy tent, and stretch out the skins of thy tabernacles; lengthen thy cords, and strengthen thy stakes, for thou shalt pass on to the right hand and to the left, for He that made thee shall rule over thee* [Is. liv. 2-3, 5]. And again: *The Gentiles shall walk in thy light, and kings in the brightness of thy rising; lift up thy eyes round about and see; all these are gathered together, they are come to thee; thy sons shall come from afar, and thy daughters shall rise up at thy side* [Is. lx. 3].

Similarly, we pray through these words for the conversion of sinners — that is, for Catholics who persist in grave sin:

But in the Church there are to be found those who profess they know God, but in their works deny Him [cf. Tit. i. 16]; whose conduct shows that they have only a deformed faith; who, by sinning, become the dwelling place of the devil, where the demon exercises uncontrolled dominion. Therefore do we pray that the kingdom of God may also come to them so that the darkness of sin being dispelled from around them, and their minds being illumined by the rays of the divine light, they may be restored to their lost dignity of children of God; that heresy and schism being removed, and all offences and causes of sins being eradicated from His kingdom, our heavenly Father may cleanse the floor of His Church; and that, worshipping God in piety and holiness, she may enjoy undisturbed peace and tranquility.

The final object of our petition is that Our Lord, the vanquisher of death, will reign over all of us: "Finally, we pray that God alone may live, alone may reign within us; that death may no longer exist, but may be absorbed in the victory achieved by Christ our Lord, who, having broken and scattered the power of all His enemies, may, in His might, subject all things to His dominion." The Catechism of St. Pius X concurs: "In the words: *Thy Kingdom come*, what do we ask regarding Heaven? Regarding Heaven, we beg to be one day admitted into that Paradise for which we were created and where we shall be perfectly happy."[208]

This is our ultimate destiny as Christ has already won (cf. Jn. xvi. 33), and we pray that the day will soon arrive when Christ will return in glory and reward those who are faithful to Him. St. Augustine, in commenting on the petitions of the Lord's Prayer, wisely reminds us: "And as for our saying: *Your kingdom come*, it will surely come whether we will it or not. But we are stirring up our desires for the kingdom so that it can come to us and we can deserve to reign there."[209] For we will deserve to reign with Christ only if we die in the state of sanctifying grace, as Our Lord Himself affirmed with the words: *Not every one that saith to me, Lord, Lord, shall enter into the kingdom of heaven: but he that doth the will of My Father Who is in heaven, he shall enter into the kingdom of heaven* (Mt. vii. 21).

Three Dispositions in This Petition

Before concluding its commentary on the second petition, the Roman Catechism enumerates three dispositions which should accompany this petition. First and foremost, the Roman Catechism reminds us that we must prize the Kingdom of God above all earthly things:

> He [the parish priest] should exhort them [his parishioners], in the first place, to consider the force and import of that similitude of the Redeemer: *The kingdom of heaven is like a treasure hidden in a field: which when a man hath found he hideth, and for joy thereof goeth and selleth all that he hath, and buyeth that field* [Mt. xiii. 44]. He who knows the riches of Christ the Lord will despise all things when compared to them; to him wealth, riches, power, will appear as dross. Nothing can be compared to or stand in competition with that inestimable treasure. Whoever, then, is blessed with this knowledge will say with the Apostle: *I esteem all things to be but loss, and count them but as dung, that I may gain Christ* [Philip. iii. 8]. This is that precious jewel of the Gospel, and he who sells all his earthly goods to purchase it shall enjoy an eternity of bliss [cf. Mt. xiii. 45].

---

[208] Roberts, *op. cit.*

[209] As quoted in the *Liturgy of the Hours*, Office of Readings (Tuesday, 29th week *Tempus Per Annum*).

The second disposition reminds us that we are all exiles on this earth working out our salvation in "fear and trembling":

> To obtain the object of our prayers it will be found most helpful to reflect within ourselves who we are — namely, children of Adam, exiled from Paradise by a just sentence of banishment, and deserving, by our unworthiness and perversity, to become the objects of God's supreme hatred, and to be doomed to eternal punishment.
>
> This consideration should excite in us humility and lowliness. Thus, our prayers will be full of Christian humility; and wholly distrusting ourselves, like the publican, we will fly to the mercy of God. Attributing all to His bounty we will render immortal thanks to Him who has imparted to us that Holy Spirit, relying on whom we are emboldened to say: *Abba* (*Father*) [Rom. viii. 15].

And the final disposition, building on the previous, affirms our need to labor for the coming of the Kingdom:

> We should also be careful to consider what is to be done, what avoided, in order to arrive at the kingdom of heaven. For we are not called by God to lead lives of ease and indolence. On the contrary, He declares that *the kingdom of God suffereth violence, and the violent bear it away* [Mt. xi. 12]; and, *If thou wilt enter into life, keep the commandments* [Mt. xix. 17]. It is not enough, therefore, that we pray for the kingdom of God; we must also use our best exertions. It is a duty incumbent on US to cooperate with the grace of God, to use it in pursuing the path that leads to heaven. God never abandons us; He has promised to be with us at all times. We have therefore only this to see to, that we forsake not God, or abandon ourselves.

These sentiments are those of a man firmly rooted in the virtue of hope, as Fr. Pius Parsch (1884-1954), the renown liturgical scholar of the first half of the 20th century, explains:

> The man who is wholly rooted in temporal things, and desires nor awaits anything beyond them, is without hope. He is not a Christian, since he puts his entire trust

in an earthly reward. The more a man sees through the emptiness of this life and prepares himself for the coming of the Lord, the more hope there is in him. Hence we see that hope is one of the foundation stones of the Christian life, and without it there is no such thing as Christianity.[210]

Thus, a life rooted in the three theological virtues naturally seeks the fulfillment of Christ's Kingdom in earnest, both now and hereafter. There is no earthly utopia; our homeland is Heaven. As Pope Pius XI reminds us in *Quas Primas*: "Men must look for the peace of Christ in the Kingdom of Christ."[211]

Conclusion

The Roman Catechism concludes its reflections on the second petition of the Lord's prayer with the following words:

> To conclude, let us then earnestly implore the Spirit of God that He may command us to do all things in accordance with His holy will; that He may so overthrow the empire of Satan that it shall have no power over us on the great accounting day; that Christ may be victorious and triumphant; that the divine influence of His law may be spread throughout the world; that His ordinances may be observed; that there be found no traitor, no deserter; and that all may so conduct themselves, as to come with joy into the presence of God their King, and may reach the possession of the celestial kingdom, prepared for them from all eternity, in the fruition of endless bliss with Christ Jesus.

Far from a mere intellectual exercise, these reflections should cultivate a greater desire in our own souls to pray the Lord's Prayer well. Fr. Parsch remarked: "Let us pray the Our Father with the greatest reverence and devotion. It would be well at times to preface it with the introduction given in the Mass: 'Admonished by Thy saving precepts and encouraged by divine instruction, we make body to say.' Let us often pray just one Our Father very slowly and without adding the Hail Mary, not because we in

---

[210] Fr. Pius Parsch, *Sermons on the Liturgy* (The Bruce Publishing Company, 1953), 271.

[211] Pius XI, Encyclical *Quas Primas* on the Feast of Christ the King (Dec. 11, 1925), n. 1.

any way wish to disparage devotion to our Lady, but because the Lord's prayer is so sublime and in a class all by itself."[212]

---

[212] Parsch, *op. cit.*, 265–266.

XXXIII

Thy Will Be Done on Earth as It Is in Heaven

Heaven Depends on Fidelity to God's Will

Continuing its systematic explanation of this most venerable prayer, the Roman Catechism begins by highlighting the connection of this petition to the previous one:

> Whoever desires to enter into the kingdom of heaven should ask of God that His will may be done. For Christ the Lord has said: *Not everyone that says to me, Lord, Lord, shall enter into the kingdom of heaven; but he that doth the will of my Father who is in heaven, he shall enter into the kingdom of heaven* [Mt. vii. 21]. Consequently, this Petition follows immediately after the one which prays for the kingdom of heaven.

St. John Chrysostom echoes these sentiments by connecting whether we will ultimately enter the Kingdom of God to our fidelity to God's holy will, illustrating how this petition logically follows from the preceding one:

> Those who desire to arrive at the kingdom of heaven must endeavor so to order their life and conversation as if they were already conversing in heaven. This petition is also to be understood for the accomplishment of the divine will in every part of the world, for the extirpation of error, and explosion of vice, that truth and virtue may everywhere obtain, and heaven and earth differ no more in honoring the supreme majesty of God.[213]

While most of mankind at least passively hopes for a blessed and peaceful eternity, it is no surprise that man is often rebellious to the will of God and often neglects the means made readily available for his salvation. As the

---

[213] St. Chrysostom, Homily XX, Accessed via the Haydock's Catholic Bible Commentary.

Catechism of St. Pius X reminds us with clarity, our salvation depends on our fidelity to the will of God: "It is as necessary to do the will of God as it is to work out our salvation, because Jesus Christ has said that they alone who have done the will of His Father shall enter into the Kingdom of Heaven."[214]

Man Rebels Against God's Will

Appropriately, before addressing the meaning of God's holy will, the Roman Catechism next describes man's inclinations to act against God's will, blindness concerning His will, and weakness in ultimately fulfilling it:

> From the beginning God implanted in all creatures an inborn desire of pursuing their own happiness that, by a sort of natural impulse, they may seek and desire their own end, from which they never deviate, unless impeded by some external obstacle. This impulse of seeking God, the author and father of his happiness, was in the beginning all the more noble and exalted in man because of the fact that he was endowed with reason and judgment. But, while irrational creatures, which, at their creation were by nature good, continued, and still continue in that original state and condition, unhappy man went astray, and lost not only original justice, with which he had been supernaturally gifted and adorned by God, but also obscured that singular inclination toward virtue which had been implanted in his soul. ...
>
> Although man is continually beset by these evils, yet his greatest misery is that many of these appear to him not to be evils at all. It is a proof of the most calamitous condition of man, that he is so blinded by passion and cupidity as not to see that what he deems salutary generally contains a deadly poison, that he rushes headlong after those pernicious evils as if they were good and desirable, while those things which are really good and virtuous are shunned as the contrary. Of this false estimate and corrupt judgment of man God thus expresses His detestation: *Woe to you that call evil good, and good evil; that put darkness for light and light for darkness; that put bitter for sweet, and sweet for bitter* [Is. v. 20].

---

[214] *Catechism of St. Pius X*, 66.

Despite such a condition, man is not without hope. On this essential point, the Roman Catechism continues by connecting our fallen nature with the hope available through this petition:

> Now this is what we ask when we address to God these words: *Thy will be done.* We fell into this state of misery by disobeying and despising the divine will. God vouchsafes to propose to us, as the sole corrective of such great evils, a conformity to His will, which by sinning we despised; He commands us to regulate all our thoughts and actions by this standard. Now it is precisely His help to accomplish this that we ask when we suppliantly address to God the prayer, *Thy will be done.*

Far from excluding those already numbered among the children of God, we too must earnestly pray for continued fidelity to God's holy will and for our eventual salvation, since our salvation is not assured. The Roman Catechism does not fail to remind us of this truth:

> The same should also be the fervent prayer of those in whose souls God already reigns; who have been already illumined with the divine light, which enables them to obey the will of God. Although thus prepared, they have still to struggle against their own passions on account of the tendency to evil implanted in man's sensual appetite. Hence even though we are of the number of the just, we are still exposed to great danger from our own frailty, and should always fear lest, drawn aside and allured by our concupiscences, *which war in our members* [cf. Rom. vii. 22-25], we should again stray from the path of salvation. Of this danger Christ the Lord admonishes us in these words: *Watch ye and pray that ye enter not into temptation; the spirit indeed is willing but the flesh is weak* [Mt. xxvi. 41].

The Six Ways We Pray for God's Will to Be Done

"Thy will be done." When we pray these words, what do we ask God to accomplish? To what does His will refer, specifically? Foreseeing the need for the faithful to understand this petition, the Roman Catechism insightfully teaches what few other catechisms do:

> ...we shall content ourselves with saying that by the will of God is here meant that will which is commonly called

the will of sign; that is to say, whatever God has commanded or counselled us to do or to avoid.

What do we mean though when we pray that God's will be done? How can we do anything to bring about the accomplishment of the will of God, Who is the Creator and Master of all of creation? First and foremost, we ask that we may fulfill what God desires of us:

> When, therefore, we pray, *Thy will be done*, we first of all ask our heavenly Father to give us the strength to obey His Commandments, and to serve Him *in holiness and justice all our days* [Lk. i. 75]; to do all things according to His will and pleasure; to discharge all the duties prescribed for us in Sacred Scripture; under His guidance and assistance to perform all that becomes those who are born, *not of the will of the flesh but of God* [Jn. i. 13], thus following the example of Christ the Lord *Who was made obedient unto death, even unto the death of the cross* [Philip. ii. 8]; finally, to be ready to bear all things rather than depart from His holy will in even the slightest degree.

The Catechism of St. Pius X further explains, in a pithier manner, the various ways in which the faithful are called to accomplish the will of God in day-to-day life:

> We can know the will of God especially by means of the Church and of the spiritual superiors appointed by God to guide us along the way of salvation; we may also learn His most holy will from the divine inspirations that come to us and from the very surroundings in which the Lord has placed us.[215]

Through the example of the Saints who have gone before us and who now reign in the Kingdom of Heaven, their fidelity to this petition — even to death — assuredly serves as a profound inspiration for us. Regarding their example, the Roman Catechism further elaborates:

> Assuredly there is no one who burns with a more ardent desire and anxiety to obtain (the effect of this Petition) than he who has been so blessed as to be able to understand the sublime dignity attaching to those who obey God. For such a one thoroughly understands how

---

[215] Fr. Marshall Roberts *op. cit.*

true it is to say that to serve God and obey Him is to reign. *Whoever*, says the Lord, *shall do the will of My Father Who is in heaven, he is My brother and sister and mother* [Mt. xii. 50]; that is to say, to him am I attached by the closest bonds of good will and love.

The Saints, with scarcely a single exception, failed not to make the principal gift contemplated by this Petition the object of their fervent prayers to God. All, indeed, have in substance made use of this admirable prayer, but not unfrequently in different words.

Secondly, we ask through this petition that we not yield to any inordinate desires and thus remain steadfast against the works of the flesh:

In the second place, when we say, *Thy will be done*, we express our detestation of the works of the flesh, of which the Apostle writes: *The works of the flesh are manifest, which are fornication, uncleanness immodesty, lust, etc* [Gal. v. 19]; *if you live according to the flesh you shall die* [Rom. viii. 13]. We also beg of God not to suffer us to yield to the suggestions of sensual appetite, of our lusts, of our infirmities, but to govern our will by His will. ...

We are not easily induced to entreat God not to satisfy our inordinate desires. This disposition of soul is difficult of attainment, and by offering such a prayer we seem in some sort to hate ourselves. To those who are slaves to the flesh such conduct appears folly; but be it ours cheerfully to incur the imputation of folly for the sake of Christ who has said: *If any man will come after Me, let him deny himself* [Mt. xvi. 24; Lk. ix. 23]. This is especially so since we know that it is much better to desire what is right and just, than to obtain what is opposed to reason and religion and to the laws of God. Unquestionably the condition of the man who attains the gratification of his rash and inordinate desires is less enviable than that of him who does not obtain the object of his pious prayers.

Thirdly, and rather profoundly, the petition that God's will "be done" asks Almighty God to not grant our mistaken requests:

Our prayers, however, have not solely for object that God should deny us what accords with our desires, when it is clear that they are depraved; but also that He would not grant us those things for which, under the persuasion and impulse of the devil, who *transforms himself into an Angel of light* [II Cor. xi. 14], we sometimes pray, believing them to be good.

The desire of the Prince of the Apostles to dissuade the Lord from His determination to meet death, appeared not less reasonable than religious; yet the Lord severely rebuked him, because he was led, not by supernatural motives, but by natural feeling.

What stronger proof of love towards the Lord than that shown by the request of St. James and St. John, who, filled with indignation against the Samaritans for refusing to entertain their Master, besought Him to command fire to descend from heaven and consume those hard-hearted and inhuman men? Yet they were reproved by Christ the Lord in these words: *You know not of what spirit you are; the Son of man came not to destroy souls but to save them* [Lk. ix. 55-56].

Lastly, and naturally following from the previous three, we also ask that our good requests be granted only when they are according to God's will, that God may perfect in us what His grace has begun, and that the whole world may know and obey God's will. The Catechism of St. Pius X again concisely summarizes the Church's teaching in the Roman Catechism by affirming: "Both in prosperity and adversity we should always recognize the will of God, Who directs or permits all things for our good."[216]

On Earth as It Is in Heaven

Our Lord inserted the words "as it is in Heaven" for a real purpose, and yet, few pause to reflect on how our Father's will is done in Heaven. What does this mean and what can we learn from these holy words to bring about the accomplishment of God's will on earth? Once again, the singular spiritual wisdom of the Roman Catechism shines for the edification of the faithful:

We also pray for the standard and model of this obedience, that our conformity to the will of God be regulated according to the rule observed in heaven by the

---

[216] Fr. Marshall Roberts *op. cit.*

blessed Angels and choirs of heavenly spirits, that, as they willingly and with supreme joy obey God, we too may yield a cheerful obedience to His will in the manner most acceptable to Him.

God requires that in serving Him we be actuated by the greatest love and by the most exalted charity; that although we devote ourselves entirely to Him with the hope of receiving heaven as reward, yet the reason we look forward to that reward should be that the Divine Majesty has commanded us to cherish that hope. Let all our hopes, therefore, be based on the love of God, Who promises to reward our love with eternal happiness.

There are some who serve another with love, but who do so solely with a view to some recompense, which is the end and aim of their love; while others, influenced by love and loyalty alone, look to nothing else in the services which they render than the goodness and worth of him whom they serve, and, knowing and admiring his qualities consider themselves happy in being able to render him these services. This is the meaning of the clause *on earth as it is in heaven* appended (to the Petition).

At the heart of this phrase is the virtue of obedience, which the Roman Catechism does not fail to highlight immediate thereafter:

It is, then, our duty to endeavor to the best of our ability to be obedient to God, as we have said the blessed spirits are, whose profound obedience is praised by David in the Psalm in which he sings*: Bless the Lord, all ye hosts; ye ministers of His that do His will* [Ps. cii. 21].

Should anyone, adopting the interpretation of St. Cyprian, understand the words *in heaven* to mean in the good and the pious, and the words *on earth*, in the wicked and the impious, we do not disapprove of the interpretation, by the word *heaven* understanding *the spirit*, and by the word *earth*, *the flesh*, that every person and every creature may in all things obey the will of God.

Similarly, St. Augustine remarked for our edification that these words should stir up the virtue of obedience in our own wills: "When we say: *Your will be done on earth as it is in heaven*, we are asking Him to make

326

us obedient so that His will may be done in us as it is done in heaven by His angels."[217] With a clear conscience we should pray this petition, affirming our own desire to remain obedient to the Church's enduring and unalterable teaching on faith and morals while also asking our own guardian angel to guard and guide us each and every day towards eternity.

And lastly, the final sentiment expressed by the phrase "on earth as it is in heaven" expresses a subtle but real act of thanksgiving. Turning again to the unique wisdom of the Roman Catechism:

> This Petition also includes thanksgiving. We revere the most holy will of God, and in transports of joy celebrate all His works with the highest praise and acknowledgment, being assured that He has done all things well. It is certain that God is omnipotent; and the consequence necessarily forces itself on the mind that all things were created at His command. We also confess the truth that He is the supreme Good. We must, therefore, confess that all His works are good, for to all He imparted His own goodness. But if we cannot fathom in everything the divine plan, let us in all things banish every doubt and hesitation from the mind, and with the Apostle declare that His ways are unsearchable.
>
> But the most powerful incentive to revere the will of God is that He has deigned to illumine by His heavenly light; for, *He hath delivered us from the power of darkness, and hath translated us into the kingdom of the Son of His love* [Col. i. 13].

The Three Dispositions Necessary for This Petition

Before turning to the fourth petition of the Our Father, the Roman Catechism concludes its section on the third petition by briefly summarizing the three dispositions that should accompany anyone praying. First, we should pray that God's holy will be done with a sense of our own weakness of will:

> It is that the faithful in uttering this Petition should be humble and lowly in spirit: keeping in view the violence of their inborn passions which revolt against the will of God; recollecting that in this duty (of obedience) man is excelled by all other creatures, of whom it is written: *All*

---

[217] St. Augustine, *op. cit.*

things serve thee [Ps. 118:91]; and reflecting, that he who is unable without divine help to undertake, not to say, perform, anything acceptable to God, must be very weak indeed.

Secondly, we must have an appreciation for the dignity that comes from participating in God's work:

> But as there is nothing greater, nothing more exalted, as we have already said, than to serve God and live in obedience to His law and Commandments, what more desirable to a Christian than to walk in the ways of the Lord, to think nothing, to undertake nothing, at variance with His will? In order that the faithful may adopt this rule of life, and adhere to it with greater fidelity, (the pastor) should borrow from Scripture examples of individuals, who, by not referring their views to the will of God, have failed in all their undertakings.

And lastly, we must have a trusting resignation to the will of God so that we may truly say, "Thy will be done," regardless of what transpires:

> Finally, the faithful are to be admonished to acquiesce in the simple and absolute will of God. Let him, who thinks that he occupies a place in society inferior to his deserts, bear his lot with patient resignation; let him not abandon his proper sphere, but abide in the vocation to which he has been called. Let him subject his own judgment to the will of God, Who provides better for our interests than we can even desire ourselves. If troubled by poverty, by sickness, by persecution, or afflictions and anxieties of any sort, let us be convinced that none of these things can happen to us without the permission of God, Who is the supreme Arbiter of all things. We should, therefore, not suffer our minds to be too much disturbed by them, but bear up against them with fortitude, having always on our lips the words: *The will of the Lord be done* [Acts xxi. 4]; and also those of holy Job, *As it hath pleased the Lord, so it is done: blessed be the Name of the Lord* [Job i. 21].

The next time you pray the Lord's Prayer, pause to reflect on these sentiments, acts, and dispositions all contained in the simple words, "Thy will be done on earth and as it in heaven."

XXXIV

Give Us This Day Our Daily Bread

Ask And You Shall Receive

The Roman Catechism begins its explanation of this petition by reinforcing its connection with the ones that preceded it:

> The fourth and following Petitions, in which we particularly and expressly pray for the needs of soul and body, are subordinate to those which preceded. According to the order of the Lord's Prayer we ask for what regards the body and the preservation of life after we have prayed for the things which pertain to God. For since man has God as his last end, the goods of human life should be subordinated to those that are divine. These goods should be desired and prayed for, either because the divine order so requires, or because we need them to obtain divine blessings, that being assisted by these temporal things we may reach our destined end, the kingdom and glory of our heavenly Father, and the reverential observance of those commands which we know to emanate from His holy will. In this Petition, therefore, we should refer all to God and His glory.

It is only after adoring and thanking God and praying for His Kingdom to envelope the entire world that we turn to our own temporal needs. Whereas many are prone to pray only when they need or want something, true children of God will pray not only for our earthly needs but first and foremost for God's glory. On the other hand, we should not neglect to ask God in prayer for our earthly needs, as if such trifling matters were a bother to Him. This opposite extreme is equally to be avoided, as the Roman Catechism reminds us to pray for our everyday needs:

> Those, therefore, who say that it is unlawful for Christians to ask from God the earthly goods of this life, are by no means to be listened to; for not only the

unanimous teaching of the Fathers, but also very many examples, both in the Old and New Testaments, are opposed to this error.

Thus Jacob, making a vow, prayed as follows: *If God shall be with me, and shall keep me in the way, by which I walk, and shall give me bread to eat, and raiment to put on, and I shall return prosperously to my father's house, the Lord shall be my God, and this stone, which I have set up for a title, shall be called the house of God; and of all things Thou shalt give to me, I will offer up tithes to Thee* [Gen. xxviii. 20-22]. Solomon also asked a certain means of subsistence in this life, when he prayed: *Give me neither beggary nor riches: give me only the necessaries of life* [Prov. xxx. 8].

Nay, the Savior of mankind Himself commands us to pray for those things which no one will dare deny appertain to the benefit of the body. *Pray*, He says, *that your flight be not in the winter, or on the sabbath.* [Mt. xxiv. 20] St. James also says: *Is any one of you sad? Let him pray. Is he cheerful in mind? Let him, sing.* [Ja. v. 13] And the Apostle thus addressed himself to the Romans: *I beseech you, brethren, through our Lord Jesus Christ, and by the charity of the Holy Ghost, that you assist me in your prayers for me to God, that l may be delivered front the unbelievers that are in Judea.* [Rom. xv. 30] As, then, the faithful are divinely permitted to ask these temporal succors, and as this perfect form of prayer was given us by Christ the Lord, there remains no doubt that such a request constitutes one of the seven Petitions.

In even more clear terms, the Roman Catechism reminds us that unless the Lord blesses our endeavors, they will ultimately fail, illustrating the need to pray for success in anything we do:

Pastors, therefore, should apply themselves earnestly to the treatment of this subject, in order that the faithful may know that men fall into these perplexities and miseries through their own fault; that they may understand that while they must sweat and toil to procure the necessaries of life, unless God bless their labors, their hope must prove fallacious, and all their exertions unavailing. *For neither he that planteth is anything, nor he that watereth but God who giveth the increase* [I Cor. iii. 7]; *unless the Lord build the house, they labor in vain that build it* [Ps. cxxvi. 1].

The Needs of Body and Soul

The Catechism of St. Pius X echoes these sentiments by affirming that this petition concerns the needs for both man's soul as well as his body: "In the Fourth Petition we beg of God all that is daily necessary for soul and body."[218] Whether our petitions concern body or soul, the Roman Catechism explains the paramount importance of purity of intention underscoring all of our prayers. This salient point cannot be emphasized enough:

> In the discharge of his duty towards the faithful the pastor, therefore, should endeavor to make them understand that, in praying for the use and enjoyment of temporal blessings, our minds and our desires are to be directed in conformity with the law of God, from which we are not to swerve in the least. ...

> A sure standard for judging what petition is good, and what bad, is the purpose and intention of the petitioner. Thus, if a person prays for temporal blessings under the impression that they constitute the sovereign good, and rests in them as the ultimate end of his desires, wishing nothing else, he unquestionably does not pray as he ought. As St. Augustine observes, *we ask not these temporal things as our goods, but as our necessaries.* The Apostle also in his Epistle to the Corinthians teaches that whatever regards the necessary purposes of life is to be referred to the glory of God: *Whether you eat or drink, or whatever else you do, do all to the glory of God* [I Cor. x. 31].

Concerning which needs of soul or body we should bring before the Lord in prayer, the Catechism of St. Pius X counsels:

> For our soul we ask of God the sustenance of our spiritual life, that is, we pray the Lord to give us His grace of which we stand in continual need. The life of

---

[218] Fr. Marshall Roberts, Catechism of St. Pius X (St. Michael's Press, 2010), p. 67.

the soul is nourished principally by the food of the word of God and by the Most Holy Sacrament of the Altar. For the body we ask all that is necessary for the sustainment of our temporal life.[219]

The Roman Catechism elaborates:

> Parish priests, therefore, should point out that the things necessary to human existence, or, at least, to its comfort, are almost innumerable; for by this knowledge of our wants and weaknesses, Christians will be compelled to have recourse to their heavenly Father, and humbly to ask of Him both earthly and spiritual blessings.
>
> They will imitate the prodigal son, who, when he began to suffer want in a far distant country and could find no one to give him even husks in his hunger, at length entering into himself, perceived that from the evils by which he was oppressed, he could expect relief from no one but from his father.
>
> Here the faithful will also have recourse more confidently to prayer, if, in reflecting on the goodness of God, they recollect that His paternal ears are ever open to the cries of His children. When He exhorts us to ask for bread, He promises to bestow it on us abundantly, if we ask it as we ought; for, by teaching us how to ask, He exhorts; by exhorting, He urges; by urging, He promises; by promising, He puts us in hope of most certainly obtaining our request.

All things necessary for life may be brought to God in prayer. But whether we receive many earthly blessings and possessions or not, we must practice detachment, which is necessary for our souls.

In All Things, Detachment

The foundation of *The Spiritual Exercises*, which pious tradition teaches was given to St. Ignatius of Loyola by the Mother of God herself, affirms that earthly goods are sinful in themselves; rather, we must practice detachment in relation to them, whether we are rich or poor. Everything we receive from God is a gift, and while we may pray for money, new

---

[219] Fr. Marshall Roberts *op. cit.*

possessions, a new job, or even good health, ultimately our prayer must always be, *Thy will be done.*

> Man is created to praise, reverence, and serve God our Lord, and by this means to save his soul. And the other things on the face of the earth are created for man and that they may help him in prosecuting the end for which he is created. From this it follows that man is to use them as much as they help him on to his end, and ought to rid himself of them so far as they hinder him as to it. For this it is necessary to make ourselves indifferent to all created things in all that is allowed to the choice of our free will and is not prohibited to it; so that, on our part, we want not health rather than sickness, riches rather than poverty, honor rather than dishonor, long rather than short life, and so in all the rest; desiring and choosing only what is most conducive for us to the end for which we are created.[220]

The Two Meanings of "Bread"

While we are reminded of our obligation to bring before God in prayer all of our needs, the Lord specifically taught us to pray for "bread." Why bread? What does this word truly signify? In its characteristic insight, the Roman Catechism explains:

> It should then be known that, in the Sacred Scriptures, by the word *bread*, are signified many things, but especially two: first, whatever we use for food and for other corporal wants; secondly, whatever the divine bounty has bestowed on us for the life and salvation of the soul.

> In this Petition, then, according to the interpretation and authority of the holy Fathers, we ask those helps of which we stand in need in this life on earth.

Similarly, St. Augustine teaches: "Here we ask for a sufficiency by specifying the most important part of it; that is, we use the word *bread* to stand for everything. Or else we are asking for the sacrament of the faithful, which is necessary in this world, not to gain temporal happiness but to gain the happiness that is everlasting."[221]

---

[220] St. Ignatius of Loyola, *The Spiritual Exercises*, First Week — Principle and Foundation.
[221] St. Augustine of Hippo, *op. cit.*

The Roman Catechism further clarifies that our daily "bread" should not be interpreted as praying for the luxurious of the world:

> We also ask *our daily bread*; that is, the things necessary for sustenance, understanding by the word *bread*, what is sufficient for raiment and for food, whether that food be bread, or flesh, or fish, or anything else. In this sense we find Eliseus to have used the word when admonishing the king to provide bread for the Assyrian soldiers, to whom was then given a large quantity of various kinds of food [cf. IV Kngs. vi. 22]. We also know that of Christ the Lord it is written that *He went into the house of a certain prince of the Pharisees on the sabbath day to eat bread* [Lk. xiv. 1], by which words we see are signified the things that constitute food and drink.

> To comprehend the full signification of this Petition, it is, moreover, to be observed that by this word bread ought not to be understood an abundant and exquisite profusion of food and clothing, but what is necessary and simple, as the Apostle has written: *Having food and wherewith to he covered, with these we are content*; and Solomon, as said above: *Give me only the necessaries of life*.

"Our" Bread

The Roman Catechism similarly remarks on the word "our", a simple word on which few pause to reflect. Why do we pray for "our" bread rather than "my" bread? The Roman Catechism explains:

> Of this frugality and moderation, we are admonished in the next word; for when we say *our*, we ask for bread sufficient to satisfy our necessities, not to gratify luxury.

> We do not say *our* in the sense that we are able of ourselves, and independently of God, to procure bread; for we read in David: *All expect of Thee that Thou give them food in season: when Thou givest to them they shall gather up: when Thou openest Thy hand they shall all be filled with good* [Ps. ciii. 27]; and in another place, *The eyes of all hope in Thee, O Lord, and Thou givest them meat in due season* [Ps. cxliv. 15].

334

The Roman Catechism further teaches: "But why say *give us*, in the plural number, and not *give me*? Because it is the duty of Christian charity that each individual be not solicitous for himself alone, but that he be also active in the cause of his neighbor; and that, while he attends to his own interests, he forgets not the interests of others."

Stated another way, the Catechism of St. Pius X succinctly explains: "We say: *Give us this day our daily bread*, rather than: *Give us bread this day*, to exclude all desire of what is another's; and hence we beg the Lord to help us in acquiring just and lawful gains, so that we may procure our maintenance by our own toil and without theft or fraud."[222] Consequently, we are reminded of our obligation toward Christian charity every time we pray the Lord's Prayer.

"Daily" Bread

Every time we pray the Lord's Prayer, which we as Catholics should pray at least once a day, we ask for "daily" bread. Like "our," the word "daily" has an important meaning which does not escape the attention of the Roman Catechism:

> By the word *daily* also is suggested the idea of frugality and moderation, to which we referred a short time ago; for we pray not for variety or delicacy of food, but for that which may satisfy the wants of nature. This should bring the blush of shame to those who, disdaining ordinary food and drink, look for the rarest viands and wines. …
>
> Indeed, the cupidity of such men is insatiable, and it is of them that Solomon has written: *A covetous man shall not be satisfied with money* [Eccles. v. 9]. To them also applies that saying of the Apostle: *They who would become rich fall into temptation, and into the snare of the devil* [I Tim. vi. 9].
>
> We also call it our *daily* bread, because we use it to recruit the vital power that is daily consumed by the natural heat of the system.
>
> Finally, another reason for the use of the word *daily* is the necessity of continually praying to God, in order that we may be kept in the practice of loving and serving

---

[222] Fr. Marshall Roberts, *op. cit.*, pp. 67-68.

Him, and that we may be thoroughly convinced of the
fact that on Him depend our life and salvation.

The word "daily" helps to reinforce our concern for the present day. We
cannot change the past and we should not be overly anxious about the
future. As the following daily meditation attributed to St. Augustine
reminds us: "Remember, Christian soul, that thou hast *this day*, and every
day of thy life: God to glorify, Jesus to imitate, the Blessed Virgin and
Saints to venerate, the Angels to invoke, a soul to save, a body to mortify,
sins to expiate, virtues to acquire, hell to avoid, Heaven to gain, eternity to
prepare for, time to profit by, neighbors to edify, the world to despise,
devils to combat, passions to subdue, death perhaps to suffer, and Judgment
to undergo."[223]

We need not be concerned with tomorrow as today's problems and
opportunities are sufficient for themselves (cf. Mt. vi. 34). And in its
characteristically succinct manner, the Catechism of St. Pius X concurs:
"The word *daily* signifies that we should not be too solicitous regarding the
future, but that we should simply ask what we need at present."[224]

As for the words "this day," the Roman Catechism insightfully observes:

> The words *this day* remind us of our common infirmity.
> For who is there that, although he does not expect to be
> able by his own individual exertions to provide for his
> maintenance during a considerable time does not feel
> confident of having it in his power to procure necessary
> food for the day? Yet even this confidence God will not
> permit us to entertain but has commanded us to ask Him
> for the food even of each successive day; and the
> necessary reason is, that as we all stand in need of daily
> bread, each should also make daily use of the Lord's
> Prayer.

The Bread of Life

We have thus far summarized the Roman Catechism's teaching on what it
calls "the bread which we eat and which nourishes and supports the body,"
and in what manner we should pray for our temporal needs in general. "It
remains," says the venerable text, "to speak of the spiritual bread which we
also ask in this Petition, by which are meant all things whatever that are

---

[223] Subjects for Daily Meditation. English Translation taken from the *Manual of
Prayers*, Third Plenary Council of Baltimore, 1888.
[224] Fr. Marshall Roberts *op. cit.,* 68.

required in this life for the health and safety of the spirit and soul," most especially the Word of God and the Sacraments:

> For as the food by which the body is nourished and supported is of various sorts, so is the food which preserves the life of the spirit and soul not of one kind.

> The Word of God is the food of the soul, as Wisdom says: *Come, eat my bread, and drink the wine which I have mingled for you* [Prov. ix. 5]. And when God deprives men of the means of hearing His Word, which He is wont to do when grievously provoked by our crimes, He is said to visit the human race with famine; for we thus read in Amos: *I will send forth a famine into the land, not a famine of bread, or a thirst of water, but of hearing the word of the Lord* [Amos viii. 11].

> And as an incapability of taking food, or of retaining it when taken, is a sure sign of approaching death, so is it a strong argument for their hopelessness of salvation, when men either seek not the Word of God, or, having it, endure it not, but utter against God the impious cry, *Depart from us, We desire not the knowledge of Thy ways* [Job xxi. 14]. This is the spiritual folly and mental blindness of those who, disregarding their lawful pastors, the Catholic Bishops and priests, and, abandoning the Holy Roman Church, have transferred themselves to the direction of heretics that corrupt the Word of God.

But chief among all the spiritual food given to us by God is certainly the Holy Eucharist — the true Body, Blood, Soul, and Divinity of the Incarnate Word. As the Roman Catechism emphasizes:

> Now Christ the Lord is that bread which is the food of the soul. *I am,* He says of Himself, *the living bread which came down from heaven* [Jn. vi. 41]. It is incredible with what pleasure and delight this bread fills devout souls, even when they must contend with earthly troubles and disasters. Of this we have an example in the Apostles, of whom it is written: *They, indeed, went into the presence of the council rejoicing* [Acts v. 41]. The lives of the Saints are full of similar examples; and of these inward joys of the good, God thus speaks: *To him that overcometh, I will give the hidden manna* [Apoc. ii. 17].

But Christ the Lord is especially our bread in the Sacrament of the Eucharist, in which He is substantially contained. This ineffable pledge of His love He gave us when about to return to the Father, and of it He said: *He that eateth my flesh, and drinketh my blood, abideth in me, and I in him* [Jn. vi. 56]; *Take ye and eat: this is My Body* [Mt. xxvi. 26; I Cor. xi. 24]. ...

The Eucharist is called *our bread*, because it is the food of the faithful only, that is to say, of those who, uniting charity to faith, wash away the defilement of their sins in the Sacrament of Penance, and mindful that they are the children of God, receive and adore this divine Sacrament with all possible holiness and veneration.

Concluding its commentary on how the Holy Eucharist is our "daily bread," the Roman Catechism states:

The Eucharist is called *daily* bread for two reasons. The first is that it is daily offered to God in the sacred mysteries of the Christian Church and is given to those who seek it piously and holily. The second is that it should be received daily, or, at least, that we should so live as to be worthy, as far as possible, to receive it daily. Let those who hold the contrary, and who say that we should not partake of this salutary banquet of the soul but at distant intervals, hear what St. Ambrose says: *If it is daily bread, why do you receive it yearly?*

Conclusion

The Roman Catechism's exposition of the fourth petition concludes with the following instruction:

In the explanation of this Petition the faithful are emphatically to be exhorted that when they have honestly used their best judgment and industry to procure the necessary means of subsistence, they leave the issue to God and submit their own wish to the will of Him Who *shall not suffer the just to waver forever* [Ps. liv. 23]. For God will either grant what is asked, and thus they will obtain their wishes; or He will not grant it, and that will be a most certain proof that what is denied the good by Him is not conducive either to their interest or their salvation, since He is more desirous of their eternal welfare than they themselves.

Rather than hurrying through the Lord's prayer, pause and reflect on the sublime beauty and insights in each of the words of this prayer. It was our Lord Himself who by His own mouth taught us this prayer. May we never let a day pass without saying it piously and with gratitude for all His manifold blessings.

XXXV

Forgive Our Trespasses, As We Forgive Others

The God of Forgiveness

In the fifth petition of the Lord's Prayer, we ask for forgiveness from the very Author of forgiveness. The Roman Catechism, in its opening words on the fifth petition of the "Our Father," highlights the forgiveness of God in the Scriptures and chiefly in the Passion of our Redeemer:

> So many are the things which display at once God's infinite power and His equally infinite wisdom and goodness, that wheresoever we turn our eyes or direct our thoughts, we meet with the most certain signs of omnipotence and benignity. And yet there is truly nothing that more eloquently proclaims His supreme love and admirable charity towards us, than the inexplicable mystery of the Passion of Jesus Christ, whence springs that never failing fountain to wash away the defilements of sin. (It is this fountain) in which, under the guidance and bounty of God, we desire to be merged and purified, when we beg of Him to forgive us our debts.

> This Petition contains a sort of summary of those benefits with which the human race has been enriched through Jesus Christ. This Isaias taught when he said: *The iniquity of the house of Jacob shall be forgiven; and this is all the fruit, that the sin thereof should be taken away.* David also shows this, proclaiming those blessed who could partake of that salutary fruit: *Blessed are they whose iniquities are forgiven.*

> The pastor, therefore, should study and explain accurately and diligently the meaning of this Petition,

which, we perceive, is so important to the attainment of salvation.

Yet the Catechism distinguishes this petition from those which precede it on a rather significant point:

> In this Petition we enter on a new manner of praying. For hitherto we asked of God not only eternal and spiritual goods, but also transient and temporal advantages; whereas we now ask to be freed from the evils of the soul and of the body, of this life and of the life to come.

The Two Dispositions Necessary

The Roman Catechism continues by explaining the two dispositions which must accompany this petition: acknowledgment of sin and sorrow for sin. On the first disposition, the Catechism examples in detail:

> The pastor, then, should admonish the faithful, that he who comes to offer this Petition must first acknowledge, and next feel sorrow and compunction for his sins. He must also be firmly convinced that to sinners, thus disposed and prepared, God is willing to grant pardon. This confidence is necessary to sinners, lest perhaps the bitter remembrance and acknowledgment of their sins should be followed by that despair of pardon, which of old seized the mind of Cain and of Judas, both of whom looked on God solely as an avenger and punisher, forgetting that He is also mild and merciful.

> In this Petition, therefore, we ought to be so disposed, that, acknowledging our sins in the bitterness of our souls, we may fly to God as to a Father, not as to a Judge, imploring Him to deal with us not according to His justice, but according to His mercy.

However, we must do more than merely call to mind our sins since true sorrow must accompany this petition, just as sorrow for sin is required for the Sacrament of Confession. The Catechism elaborates:

> In making this necessary acknowledgment of our sins, it is not enough to call them to mind lightly; for it is necessary that the recollection of them be bitter, that it touch the heart, pierce the soul, and imprint sorrow. Wherefore, the pastor should treat this point diligently,

that his pious hearers may not only recollect their sins, and iniquities, but recollect them with pain and sorrow; so that with true interior contrition they may betake themselves to God their Father, humbly imploring Him to pluck from the soul the piercing stings of sin.

But far from merely considering the horror of sin which may lead to despair, we should have unbridled hope in our Redeemer, as the Catechism does not fail to remind us:

But lest the faithful, terrified by the grievousness of their sins, despair of being able to obtain pardon, the pastor ought to encourage them to hope by the following considerations.

As is declared in an Article of the Creed, Christ the Lord has given power to the Church to remit sins.

Furthermore, in this Petition, our Lord has taught how great is the goodness and bounty of God towards mankind; for if God were not ready and prepared to pardon penitents their sins, never would He have prescribed this formula of prayer: *Forgive us our trespass*es. Wherefore we ought to be firmly convinced, that since He commands us in this Petition to implore His paternal mercy, He will not fail to bestow it on us. For this Petition assuredly implies that God is so disposed towards us as willingly to pardon those who are truly penitent.

Debts

After explaining the motives and dispositions that should be at the forefront of our minds during this petition in prayer, the Roman Catechism next explains the meaning of the words of this petition, beginning with "debts." We ask of Almighty God: "forgive us our debts." What debts? As shown in the Catechism, they refer to the debt owed to God from our sins:

First, then, we are to know, that we by no means ask for exemption from the debt we owe to God on so many accounts, the payment of which is essential to salvation, namely, that of loving Him with our whole heart, our whole soul, and our whole mind; neither do we ask to be in future exempt from the duties of obedience, worship,

THE LORD'S PRAYER

veneration, or any other similar obligation, comprised also under the word *debts*.

What we do ask is that He may deliver us from sins. This is the interpretation of St. Luke, who, instead of debts, makes use of the word *sins*, because by their commission we become guilty before God and incur a debt of punishment, which we must pay either by satisfaction or by suffering. It was of this debt that Christ the Lord spoke by the mouth of His Prophet: *Then did I pay that which I took not away* [Ps. lxviii. 5]. From these words of God, we may understand that we are not only debtors, but also unequal to the payment of our debt, the sinner being of himself utterly incapable of making satisfaction.

Furthermore, the Catechism does not fail to explain that the pardon we seek applies to both venial and mortal sins, while acknowledging the need for the Sacrament of Confession to removal the latter:

Here we ask pardon not only for our venial offences, for which pardon may most easily be obtained, but also for grievous and mortal sins. With regard to grave sins, however, this Petition cannot procure forgiveness unless it derives that efficacy from the Sacrament of Penance, received, as we have already said, either actually or at least in desire.

The Catechism of St. Pius X likewise recognizes our debts to be sins on account of the justice owed to God for them: "Our sins are called debts, because we must satisfy God's justice for them either in this life or in the next."[225]

"Our" Debts

In usual fashion, the Roman Catechism does not fail to explain even the word "our", showing how "our debts" differs from "our daily bread" and the moral implication of this simple word:

The words *our debts* are used here in a sense entirely different from that in which we said *our bread*. That bread is ours, because it is given us by the munificence of God; whereas sins are ours, because with us rests their

---

[225] *Catechism of St. Pius X*, 68.

343

guilt. They are our voluntary acts, otherwise they would not have the character of sin.

Admitting, therefore, and confessing the guilt of our sins, we implore the clemency of God, which is necessary for their expiation. In this we make use of no palliation whatever, nor do we transfer the blame to others, as did our first parents Adam and Eve. We judge ourselves, employing, if we are wise, the prayer of the Prophet: *Incline not my heart to evil words, to make excuses in sins.*

"Forgive Us"

While we hope for Heaven and work to satisfy the temporal punishment due to sins already forgiven, we do not neglect in praying for our fellow man. For this reason of charity, our Divine Redeemer especially taught us to pray "forgive us" instead of "forgive me":

> Nor do we say, *forgive me*, but *forgive us*; because the fraternal relationship and charity which subsist between all men, demand of each of us that, being solicitous for the salvation of all our neighbors, we pray also for them while offering prayers for ourselves.

> This manner of praying, taught by Christ the Lord, and subsequently received and always retained by the Church of God, the Apostles most strictly observed themselves and taught others to observe.

> Of this ardent zeal and earnestness in praying for the salvation of our neighbors, we have the splendid example of Moses in the Old and of St. Paul in the New Testament. The former besought God thus: *Either forgive them this trespass; or, if Thou dost not, strike me out of the book that Thou hast written* [Ex. xxxii. 32]; while the latter prayed after this manner: *I wished myself to be anathema from Christ for my brethren* [Rom. ix. 3].

Charity demands that we seek the salvation of souls by praying and working for their conversion (whether or initial or ongoing).

Conditional Forgiveness

We would be remiss if we did not reflect upon the condition which Our Lord Himself attached to this petition: "…as we forgive those who trespass against us." Our forgiveness is predicated on the forgiveness of our fellow man, as the Catechism of St. Pius X admonishes: "Those who do not forgive their neighbor have no reason to hope that God will pardon them; especially since they condemn themselves when they ask God to forgive them as they forgive their neighbor."[226]

The Roman Catechism, commenting on the two senses of these words, shows the same inevitable conclusion:

> The word *as* may be understood in two senses. It may be taken as having the force of a comparison, meaning that we beg of God to pardon us our sins, just as we pardon the wrongs and contumelies which we receive from those by whom we have been injured. It may also be understood as denoting a condition, and in this sense Christ the Lord interprets that formula. *If,* He says, *you forgive men their offences, your heavenly Father will also forgive you your offences; but if you will not forgive men, neither will your Father forgive you your sins* [Mt. vi. 14-15].

> Either sense, however, equally contains the necessity of forgiveness, intimating, as it does that, if we desire that God should grant us the pardon of our offences, we ourselves must pardon those from whom we have received injury; for so rigorously does God exact from us forgetfulness of injuries and mutual affection and love, that He rejects and despises the gifts and sacrifices of those who are not reconciled to one another.

Fr. Pius Parsch in "Sermons on the Liturgy" reflects on this petition in the context of the 21st Sunday after Pentecost while teaching:

> It is the only time in the prayer that we promise something in return for all the favors that we ask of God. God has forgiven us so many trespasses that we cannot even number them. Compared to these, how little are the offenses we have to forgive our neighbor. But we are bound to forgive our brethren from our heart, if we

---

[226] Fr. Marshall Roberts, *op. cit.*

expect God to forgive the enormity of our sins. But who of us can honestly say that he fully forgives his fellow man, not retaining the least feeling of bitterness? Let us admit that we do not find it easy.[227]

Similarly, St. Augustine concisely teaches: "When we say: *Forgive us our trespasses as we forgive those who trespass against us*, we are reminding ourselves of what we must ask and what we must do in order to be worthy in turn to receive."[228]

Even human obliges us to forgive as the Roman Catechism adds:

> Even the law of nature requires that we conduct ourselves towards others as we would have them conduct themselves towards us; hence he would be most impudent who would ask of God the pardon of his own offences while he continued to cherish enmity against his neighbor.

The Difficulty in Forgiving Others

The writer C.S. Lewis once wrote: "Forgiveness is a beautiful word, until you have something to forgive." And this reality is often the case in the lives of even the most devout Catholics. Fr. Scott Haynes of the Archdiocese of Chicago comments on the extraordinary difficulty we often experience in forgiving others on account of our own desire for vindication:

> Why is forgiveness so hard for us? As Christians, we are to forgive just as Jesus forgave. Because of our sinful nature, forgiveness is unnatural. It seems we prefer revenge to forgiveness. Forgiveness is hard because it is not fair. It offends our sense of justice. We want vindication. Yet, Christ told us more than once, 'Forgive, and ye shall be forgiven.' He established the forgiveness of our neighbor as the indispensable condition for obtaining forgiveness from God.[229]

Father Haynes continues:

---

[227] Fr. Pius Parsch, Sermons on the Liturgy (The Bruce Publishing Company, 1965), p. 303.

[228] As quoted in the *Liturgy of the Hours*, Office of Readings (Tuesday in the 29th week *Tempus Per Annum*).

[229] Rev. Scott Haynes, "Mystical Theology of the Mass," <https://www.mysticaltheologyofthemass.com>, accessed October 22, 2022.

Imagine an old-fashioned country church with a bell in the steeple. To ring that bell, you have to tug on the rope for a while. Once it has begun to ring, you merely maintain the momentum. As long as you keep pulling the bell keeps ringing. Forgiveness is letting go of the rope. It is just that simple. But when you do so, the bell keeps ringing. Momentum is at work. However, if you keep your hands off the rope, the bell will begin to slow and eventually stop. Forgiveness is like that. When you decide to forgive, the old feelings of unforgiveness may continue to assert themselves. They have momentum. But if we steadfastly imitate Christ and make a firm decision from the heart to forgive in the Name of Jesus, that unforgiving spirit will begin to slow and will eventually be still. Forgiveness is not something you feel, it is something you do. It is an act of the will— letting go of the rope of retribution.[230]

Similarly, the Roman Catechism acknowledges the same difficulty for some in forgiving others who injure us by counseling:

There are those who, aware that they ought to bury injuries in voluntary oblivion and ought to love those that injure them, desire to do so, and do so as far as they are able, but feel that they cannot efface from their mind all recollection of injuries. For there lurk in the mind some remains of private grudge, in consequence of which such persons are disturbed by misgivings of conscience, fearing that they have not in simplicity and frankness laid aside their enmities and consequently do not obey the command of God.

Here, therefore, the pastor should explain the contrary desires of the flesh and of the spirit; that the former is prone to revenge, the latter ready to pardon; that hence a continual struggle and conflict goes on between them. Wherefore he should point out that although the appetites of corrupt nature are ever opposing and rebelling against reason, we are not on this account to be uneasy regarding salvation, provided the spirit persevere in the duty and disposition of forgiving injuries and of loving our neighbor.

---

[230] Ibid.

Yet even those who continue to struggle, or outright fail, to forgive others are reminded of the obligation to nevertheless pray this petition of the "Our Father" for two chief reasons:

> (In the first place), whoever belongs to the number of the faithful, offers this prayer in the name of the entire Church, in which there must necessarily be some pious persons who have forgiven their debtors the debts here mentioned.

> Secondly, when we ask this favor from God, we also ask for whatever cooperation with the Petition is necessary on our part in order to obtain the object of our prayer. Thus, we ask the pardon of our sins and the gift of true repentance; we pray for the grace of inward sorrow; we beg that we may be able to abhor our sins and confess them truly and piously to the priest. Since then, it is necessary for us to forgive those who have inflicted on us any loss or injury, when we ask pardon of God, we beg of Him at the same time to grant us grace to be reconciled to those against whom we harbor hatred.

Praying this Petition Fervently

The Roman Catechism concludes its reflection on the fifth petition of the Lord's Prayer by reminding the faithful of the various means whereby we make this petition fruitful. In so doing, the Catechism mentions six points including the penitential dispositions which must accompany this petition, the need to avoid the dangers of sin in the future, and the merit of initiating fervent penitents. On this third point, the Catechism references both the penitent St. Mary Magdalene and the Prince of the Apostles himself:

> Let each one also call to mind the ardent love of prayer of those who obtained from God through their entreaties the pardon of their sins. Such was the publican, who, standing afar off through shame and grief, and with eyes fixed on the ground, only smote his breast, crying: *O God, be merciful to me, a sinner* [Lk. xviii. 13]. Such was also the woman, *a sinner*, who, standing behind Christ the Lord, washed His feet, wiped them with her hair, and kissed them [cf. Lk. vii. 38]. Lastly, there is the example of Peter, the Prince of the Apostles, who *going forth wept bitterly* [Mt. xxvi. 75].

Furthermore, the frequent use of the Sacraments (especially Penance and the Holy Eucharist), in addition to almsgiving, prepare our souls for this heavenly command. Regarding almsgiving, which few priests regularly address in their preaching, the Catechism greatly encourages thus:

> Next almsdeeds, as the Sacred Scriptures declare, are a medicine suited to heal the wounds of the soul. Wherefore, let those who desire to make pious use of this prayer act kindly to the poor according to their means. Of the great efficacy of alms in effacing the stains of sin, the Angel of the Lord in Tobias, holy Raphael, is a witness, who says: *Alms deliver from death, and the same is that which purgeth away sins, and maketh to find mercy and life everlasting* [Tob. xii. 9]. Daniel is another witness, who thus admonished King Nabuchodonosor: *Redeem thou thy sins with alms, and thy iniquities with works of mercy to the poor* [Dan. iv. 24].

Almsgiving refers to giving to the poor. By giving to the poor, we make reparation for sins as we see in the poor the person of Christ Himself (cf. Mt. xxv. 31-40). Though, while not strictly almsgiving, the giving of our time to visit the sick, the elderly, or those in prison also makes reparation for sin.

The Roman Catechism concludes its explanation of the fifth petition with the sixth point:

> The best alms and the most excellent act of mercy is forgetfulness of injuries, and good will towards those who have injured us or ours, in person, in property, or in character. Whoever, therefore, desires to experience in a special manner the mercy of God, should make an offering to God Himself of all his enmities, remit every offence, and pray for his enemies with the greatest good will, seizing every opportunity of doing them good. But as this subject was explained when we treated of murder, we refer the pastor to that place.

> The pastor ought to conclude his explanation of this Petition with this final reflection, that nothing is, or can be conceived, more unjust than that he who is so rigorous towards men as to extend indulgence to no one, should himself demand that God be mild and kind towards him.

Conclusion

We should pray for our enemies each day. This is one chief means of forgiving everyone who injures us, no matter how small or large. While it is undoubtedly an extremely difficult thing to do in the moment when we feel violated, it is nonetheless essential. God commands us to forgive others. While we may in prudence not trust someone again with a secret, seek out a friendship, or associate in business, we must nevertheless in prayer forgive those who injure us. God wills it and subordinates our own forgiveness to it. After all, if God, Who is infinitely offended by the least sin, died for our sins, we can surely forgive fellow sinners.

XXXVI

Lead Us Not into Temptation

Deliver Us, O Lord

In the sixth petition of the Lord's Prayer, we pray for deliverance from temptation. After commenting at length on how we should seek forgiveness of our own sins, the Roman Catechism transitions to the sentiments which should inflame souls who ask for deliverance from temptation:

> When the children of God, having obtained the pardon of their sins, are inflamed with the desire of giving to God worship and veneration; when they long for the kingdom of heaven; when they engage in the performance of all the duties of piety towards the Deity, relying entirely on His paternal will and providence — then it is that the enemy of mankind employs the more actively all his artifices, and prepares all his resources to attack them so violently as to justify the fear that, wavering and altered in their sentiments, they may relapse into sin, and thus become far worse than they had been before. To such as these may justly be applied the saying of the Prince of the Apostles: *It had been better for them not to have known the way of justice, than, after they have known it, to turn back from that holy commandment which was delivered to them* [II Pet. ii. 21]

> Hence, Christ the Lord has commanded us to offer this Petition so that we may commend ourselves daily to God, and implore His paternal care and assistance, being assured that, if we be deserted by the divine protection, we shall soon fall into the snares of our most crafty enemy.

Referring as well to the words of our Blessed Redeemer immediately before His Passion, the Catechism in its opening remarks on the sixth petition underscores that on multiple occasions Our Lord commanded us to pray for deliverance from temptation:

> Nor is it in the Lord's Prayer alone that He has commanded us to beg of God not to suffer us to be led into temptation. In His address to the holy Apostles also, on the very eve of His death, after He had declared them *clean* [Jn. xiii. 10], He admonished them of this duty in these words: *Pray that ye enter not into temptation* [Mt. xxvi. 41].

> This admonition, reiterated by Christ the Lord, imposes on the pastor the weighty obligation of exciting the faithful to a frequent use of this prayer, so that, beset as men constantly are by the great dangers which the devil prepares, they may ever address to God, Who alone can repel those dangers, the prayer, *Lead us not into temptation.*

Human Frailty and the Assaults of the Devil

The Catechism of St. Pius X defines temptation as "an incitement to sin that comes from the devil, or from the wicked, or from our own evil passions."[231] Hence, temptations may result from our own human frailty or from the assaults of demons. Concerning the frailty of our own human nature, the Roman Catechism presents the example of the Apostles, the chosen band of Our Lord, who succumbed to temptation brought about by their own weakness:

> The faithful will understand how very much they stand in need of this divine assistance, if they remember their own weakness and ignorance, if they recollect this saying of Christ the Lord: *The spirit indeed is willing, but the flesh is weak* [Mt. xxvi. 41]; if they call to mind how grievous and destructive are the misfortunes of men brought on through the instigation of the devil, unless they be upheld and assisted by the right hand of the Most High.

> What more striking example can there be of human infirmity, than the holy band of the Apostles, who, though they had just before felt very courageous, at the first sight of danger, abandoned the Savior and fled.

---

[231] *Catechism of St. Pius X*, 69.

Similarly, temptations also come from the assaults of the flesh because of the effects of original sin on human nature:

> How few are there who are not compelled to experience at their great cost what anger, what concupiscence can do in us? Who is not annoyed by these stings? Who does not feel these goads? Who does not burn with these smoldering fires? And, indeed, so various are these assaults, so diversified these attacks, that it is extremely difficult not to receive some grievous wound.

The Roman Catechism does not refrain from also acknowledging demons as source of temptation. While all temptation does not come from demons, some temptations undoubtedly come from their hellish suggestions, which they place in our imagination:

> And besides these enemies that dwell and live with us, there are, moreover, those most bitter foes, of whom it is written: *Our wrestling is not against, flesh and blood; but against principalities and powers, against the rulers of the world of this darkness, against the spirits of wickedness in the high places* [Eph. vi. 12] For to our inward conflicts are added the external assaults and attacks of the demons, who both assail us openly, and also insinuate themselves by stratagem into our souls, so much so that it is only with great difficulty that we can escape them.

While not seeking to drive us to despair, the Roman Catechism does not shy away from further commenting on both the audacity and multitude of evil spirits who seek our damnation:

> How great is their audacity is evidenced by the words of Satan, recorded by the Prophet: *I will ascend into heaven* [Is. xiv. 13]. He attacked our first parents in Paradise; he assailed the Prophets; he beset the Apostles in order, as the Lord says in the Gospel, that he might sift them as wheat [cf. Lk. xxii. 31]. Nor was he abashed even by the presence of Christ the Lord Himself. His insatiable desire and unwearied diligence St. Peter therefore expressed when he said: *Your adversary, the devil, as a roaring lion goeth about, seeking whom he may devour* [I Pet. v. 8]. But it is not Satan alone that tempts men, for sometimes a host of demons combine to attack an

individual. This that evil spirit confessed, who, having been asked his name by Christ the Lord, replied, *My name is legion* [Mk. v. 9; Lk. viii. 30]; that is to say, a multitude of demons, tormented their unhappy victim. And of another demon it is written: *He taketh with him seven other spirits more wicked than himself, and they enter in and dwell there* [Mt. xii. 45].

This reality should lead us to greater reliance on the Holy Rosary, the St. Michael Prayer, daily prayer to our guardian angel, and the frequent and devout reception of the Sacraments of Penance and the Holy Eucharist. The Catechism of St. Pius X echoes these sentiments when it counsels: "To avoid temptation we should fly dangerous occasions, guard our senses, receive the sacraments frequently, and have recourse to the practice of prayer."[232]

Our Lord Will Not Leave Us Orphans

Temptations are part of human life as a consequence of original sin, and even Our Lord Himself, who is sinless in every way, was tempted in His human nature while dwelling among us during His 33 years of life on earth. While temptation will always exist, the Roman Catechism reminds us that prayer protects man against temptations:

> Who, then, can deem himself sufficiently secure in his own resources? Hence the necessity of offering to God pure and pious prayer, that He suffer us not to be tempted above our strength, but make issue with temptation, that we may be able to bear it [cf. I Cor. x. 13].

> But should any of the faithful, through weakness or ignorance, feel terrified at the power of the demons, they are to be encouraged, when tossed by the waves of temptation, to take refuge in this harbor of prayer. For however great the power and pertinacity of Satan, he cannot, in his deadly hatred of our race, tempt or torment us as much, or as long as he pleases; but all his power is governed by the control and permission of God.

St. John Vianney likewise asserts that while temptations will always exist, they can be conquered by those who are serious about overcoming them:

---

[232] Fr. Marshall Roberts, *op. cit.*

We are all inclined to sin, my children; we are idle, greedy, sensual, given to the pleasures of the flesh. We want to know everything, to learn everything, to see everything; we must watch over our mind, over our heart, and over our senses, for these are the gates by which the devil penetrates. See, he prowls round us incessantly; his only occupation in this world is to seek companions for himself. All our life he will lay snares for us, he will try to make us yield to temptations; we must, on our side, do all we can to defeat and resist him. We can do nothing by ourselves, my children; but we can do everything with the help of the good God; let us pray Him to deliver us from this enemy of our salvation, or to give strength to fight against him. With the Name of Jesus, we shall overthrow the demons; we shall put them to flight. With this Name, if they sometimes dare to attack us, our battles will be victories, and our victories will be crowns for Heaven, all brilliant with precious stones.[233]

All Temptation is Not Evil

Before addressing the words of the sixth petition of the Lord's Prayer, the Roman Catechism wisely notes that while temptation is often understood in a negative sense, there are forms of temptation (or testing) which come from God and ultimately work for our good. Concerning these forms, the Catechism observes:

> Temptation has a good purpose, when someone's worth is tried, in order that when it has been tested and proved he may be rewarded and honored, his example proposed to others for imitation, and all may be incited thereby to the praises of God. This is the only kind of tempting that can be found in God. Of it there is an example in Deuteronomy: *The Lord your God tries you, that it may appear whether you love him or not* [Dt. viii. 3].

> In this manner God is also said to tempt His own, when He visits them with want, disease and other sorts of calamities. This He does to try their patience, and to make them an example of Christian virtue. Thus, we read that Abraham was tempted to immolate his son, by which fact he became a singular example of obedience and

---

[233] St. John Vianney, "Sermon on Temptations."

patience to all succeeding times [cf. Gen. xxii. 1]. Thus, also is it written of Tobias: *Because thou wast acceptable to God, it was necessary that temptation should prove thee* [Tob. xii. 13].

The Catechism of St. Pius X further reminds us that giving in to temptation is a sin but experiencing temptation is not: "It is no sin to have temptations; but it is a sin to consent to them, or voluntarily to expose oneself to the danger of consenting to them."[234] There is no need to confess having been tempted if we do not sin as a result of being tempted.

Lead Us Not into Temptation

Since temptations may come from evil sources or from God, what do we pray for when we ask Almighty God to "lead us not into temptation"? The Roman Catechism explains the two ways in which souls are led into temptation:

> We are said to be *led into temptation* when we yield to temptations. Now this happens in two ways. First, we are led into temptation when, yielding to suggestion, we rush into that evil to which some one tempts us. No one is thus led into temptation by God; for to no one is God the author of sin, nay, *He hates all who work iniquity* [Ps. v. 5]; and accordingly, we also read in St. James: *Let no man, when he is tempted, say that he is tempted of God; for God is not a tempter of evils* [Ja. i. 13].

> Secondly, we are said to be led into temptation by him who, although he himself does not tempt us nor cooperate in tempting us, yet is said to tempt because he does not prevent us from being tempted or from being overcome by temptations when he is able to prevent these things. In this manner God, indeed, suffers the good and the pious to be tempted, but does not leave them unsupported by His grace. Sometimes, however, we fall, being left to ourselves by the just and secret judgment of God, in punishment of our sins.

Since all temptation does not come from evil, it is important to note that by this petition of the Lord's Prayer, we do not ask to be exempt from all temptation in this life. Since even Our Lord was tempted, it would be

---

[234] Fr. Marshall Roberts, op. cit.

presumptuous on our part to pray for total immunity from temptation? The Roman Catechism likewise teaches:

> We do not ask to be totally exempt from temptation, for human life is one continued temptation. This, however, is useful and advantageous to man. Temptation teaches us to know ourselves, that is, our own weakness, and to humble ourselves *under the powerful hand of God*; and by fighting manfully, we expect to receive a *never-fading crown of glory* [I Pet. iv. 6]. *For he that striveth for the mastery is not crowned, except he strive lawfully* [II Tim. ii. 5]. *Blessed is the man*, says St. James, *that endureth temptation; for when he hath been proved, he shall receive the crown of life, which God hath promised to them that love Him* [Ja. i. 12]. If we are sometimes hard pressed by the temptation of the enemy, it will also cheer us to reflect, that we have *a high priest* to help us, *Who can have compassion on our infirmities*, having been tempted Himself *in all things* [Heb. iv. 15].

Consequently, in this petition we ask God, above all, to not forsake us and allow us to fall prey to evil desires:

> We pray that the divine assistance may not forsake us, lest having been deceived, or worsted, we should yield to temptation; and that the grace of God may be at hand to succor us when our strength fails, to refresh and invigorate us in our trials.

> We should, therefore, implore the divine assistance, in general, against all temptations, and especially when assailed by any particular temptation. This we find to have been the conduct of David, under almost every species of temptation. Against lying, he prays in these words: *Take not Thou the word of truth utterly out of my mouth* [Ps. cxviii. 43]; against covetousness: *Incline my heart unto Thy testimonies, and not to covetousness* [Ps. cxviii. 36]; and against the vanities of this life and the allurements of concupiscence, he prays thus: *Turn away my eyes, that they may not behold vanity* [Ps. cxviii. 37].

> We pray, therefore, that we yield not to evil desires, and be not wearied in enduring temptation; that we *deviate not from the way of the Lord* [Dt. xxxi. 29]; that in adversity, as in prosperity, we preserve equanimity and

fortitude; and that God may never deprive us of His protection. Finally, we pray that God may *crush Satan beneath our feet* [Rom. xvi. 20].

St. Augustine echoes these sentiments when he writes, "When we say: *Lead us not into temptation,* we are reminding ourselves to ask that His help may not depart from us; otherwise, we could be seduced and consent to some temptation, or despair and yield to it."[235]

Dispositions Which Should Accompany the Sixth Petition

Having established what temptation is, its sources, and the object for which we pray in the sixth petition, the Roman Catechism concludes by explaining the three primary dispositions which should accompany this prayer: distrust of self and confidence in God, remembrance of the victory of Christ and the Saints, and watchfulness.

The first disposition which should animate our souls is confidence in God and distrust of our own abilities since we know that *every perfect gift is from above* (Ja. i. 17) and not from ourselves. The Roman Catechism further explains:

> It will, then, be found most efficacious, when offering this Petition that, remembering our weakness, we distrust our own strength; and that, placing all our hopes of safety in the divine goodness and relying on the divine protection, we encounter the greatest dangers with undaunted courage, calling to mind particularly the many persons, animated with such hope and resolution, who were delivered by God from the very jaws of Satan.

And far from being a mere theory, the Catechism places before our eyes the victory won by both Our Lord and His Saints, who conquered temptation:

> The faithful should also reflect who is their leader against the temptations of the enemy; namely, Christ the Lord, Who was victorious in the same combat. He overcame the devil; He is that *stronger man* who, *coming upon the strong-armed man,* overcame him, deprived him of his arms, and stripped him of his spoils [Lk. xi. 22]. Of Christ's victory over the world, we read in St. John: *Have confidence: I have overcome the world* [Jn.

---

[235] St. Augustine, *op. cit.*

xvi. 33]; and in the Apocalypse, He is called *the conquering lion* [Apoc. v. 5]; and it is said of Him that He went forth conquering that He might conquer, because by His victory He has given power to others to conquer.

The Epistle of St. Paul to the Hebrews abounds with the victories of holy men, *who by faith conquered kingdoms, stopped the mouths of lions*, etc [Heb. xi. 33].

Similarly, watchfulness must underpin a life grounded in prayer and penance:

Satan, however, is overcome not by indolence, sleep, wine, reveling, or lust; but by prayer, labor, watching, fasting, continence and chastity. *Watch ye and pray, that ye enter not into temptation* [Mt. xxvi. 41], as we have already said, is the admonition of our Lord. They who make use of these weapons in the conflict put the enemy to flight; for the devil flees from those who resist him [cf. Ja. iv. 7].

Victory Over Temptation Comes from God

Rather than congratulating ourselves when temptation is overcome, the Roman Catechism reminds the faithful that all victory comes ultimately from God, highlighting again the importance we must place on praying (especially the Lord's Prayer) every day, since victory only comes from God:

The strength by which we lay prostrate the satellites of Satan comes from God, *who maketh our arms as a bow of brass*; by whose aid *the bow of the mighty is overcome, and the weak are girt with strength*; who giveth us *the protection of salvation, whose right hand upholdeth us: who teacheth our hands to war, and our fingers to battle* [Ps. xvii. 35; I Kngs. ii. 4; Ps. xvii. 36, cxliii. 1]. Hence to God alone must thanks be given for victory, since it is only through His guidance and help that we are able to conquer. This the Apostle did; for he said: *Thanks to God, who hath given us the victory, through our Lord Jesus Christ* [I Cor. xv. 57].

This is a battle worth fighting, as St. Paul reminds us in the Epistle appointed to be read each year on Septuagesima Sunday: *Know you not*

that they that run in the race, all run indeed, but one receiveth the prize.
So run that you may obtain (I Cor ix. 24). On this final point, the Roman
Catechism concludes its exposition on the sixth petition of the Lord's
Prayer with wise words directed to priests:

> When these things have been explained, the pastor
> should instruct the faithful concerning the crowns
> prepared by God, and the eternal and superabundant
> rewards reserved for those who conquer. He should
> quote from the Apocalypse the following divine
> promises: *He that shall overcome shall not be hurt by the*
> *second death* [Apoc. ii. 11]; and in another place: *He that*
> *shall overcome, shall thus be clothed in white garments,*
> *and I will not blot out his name out of the book of life,*
> *and I will confess his name before My Father, and before*
> *His angels* [Apoc. iii. 5]. A little after, our divine Lord
> Himself thus addresses John: *He that shall overcome, I*
> *will make him a pillar in the temple of My God: and he*
> *shall go out no more* [Apoc. iii. 12]: and again: *To him*
> *that shall overcome, I will give to sit with Me in My*
> *throne; as I also have overcome and am set down with*
> *My Father in His throne* [Apoc. iii. 21]. Finally, having
> unveiled the glory of the Saints, and the never-ending
> bliss which they shall enjoy in heaven, He adds, *He that*
> *shall overcome shall possess these things* [Apoc. xxi. 7].

Conclusion

St. Paul wrote that *the Spirit also helpeth our infirmity. For we know not*
what we should pray for as we ought; but the Spirit himself asketh for us
with unspeakable groanings (Rom. viii. 26-27). While temptations will
always be a part of human life, we have a responsibility to grow in virtue
and persevere in the state of sanctifying grace, which we can do with the
help of God. We must likewise resist the enemy's temptations by having
recourse to prayer, fasting, and almsgiving.

XXXVII

But Deliver Us from Evil

In the seventh and final petition of the Lord's Prayer, after having prayed for deliverance from temptation, we pray for deliverance from evil. The Roman Catechism highlights the appropriateness of this petition as the final, crowning petition of the *Pater Noster*:

> This Petition with which the Son of God concludes this divine prayer embodies the substance of all the other Petitions. To show its force and importance our Lord made use of this Petition when, on the eve of His Passion, He prayed to God His Father for the salvation of mankind. *I pray*, He said, *that Thou keep them from evil* [Jn. xvii. 15] In this Petition, then, which He not only commanded us to use, but made use of Himself, He has epitomized, as it were, the meaning and spirit of all the other Petitions. For if we obtain what this Petition asks, that is, *the protection of God against evil, which enables us to stand secure and safe against the machinations of the world and the devil, then,* as St. Cyprian remarks, *nothing more remains to be asked.*

The Necessity of This Petition

Evils are undoubtedly part of human life, even for the baptized, due to the effects of original sin. According to St. Thomas Aquinas, evil is defined as the absence of what should be there. This especially applies to the presence of God in our lives. We have evil in our world because people have free will and some freely choose to reject God and His Commandments and embrace evil. Yet, like all things, free will was created to be good. It is naturally good for a creature to be rational and make its own decisions. If we happen to suffer because of another, it does not mean that we are not loved by God. God is with us through the sufferings of life. He, too, came and suffered by being betrayed by His friends, denied by Peter, mocked and crowned with thorns, stripped of His garments, commanded to carry the Cross, and crucified. The God of Heaven and earth was put to death by our sins so that we might have eternal life, thus drawing unfathomable good out of the most horrific evil possible.

Scripture confirms that the source of all the evil is ultimately the sin of Adam (original sin): "Wherefore, as by one man sin entered into the world, and death by sin; and so death passed upon all men, for that all have sinned" (Rom. v. 12). Death and destruction do not come from God (cf. Wis. i. 13), but rather from the evil one who seeks to damn us all (cf. Wis. ii. 24).

The Roman Catechism thus acknowledges the necessity of the petition, "But deliver us from evil," by referencing the Holy Scriptures as well as the manifold evils which threaten souls in this world:

> It cannot be necessary to remind the faithful of the numerous evils and calamities to which we are exposed, and how much we stand in need of the divine assistance. The many and serious miseries of human life have been fully described by sacred and profane writers, and there is hardly anyone who has not observed them either in his own life or in that of others.

> We are all convinced of the truth of these words of Job, that model of patience: *Man, born of woman, and living for a short time, is filled with many miseries. He cometh forth like a flower, and is destroyed, and fleeth as a shadow, and never continueth in the same state* [Job xiv. 1-2]. That no day passes without its own trouble or annoyance is proved by these words of Christ the Lord: *Sufficient for the day is the evil thereof* [Mt. vi. 34] Indeed, the condition of human life is pointed out by the Lord Himself, when He admonishes us that we are to take up our cross daily and follow Him [cf. Luke ix. 23].

> Since, therefore, everyone must realize the trials and dangers inseparable from this life, it will not be difficult to convince the faithful that they ought to implore of God deliverance from evil, since no inducement to prayer exercises a more powerful influence over men than a desire and hope of deliverance from those evils which oppress or threaten them. There is in the heart of everyone a natural inclination to have instant recourse to God in the face of danger, as it is written: *Fill their faces with shame, and they shall seek thy name, Lord* [Ps. lxxxii. 17].

We cannot blame God for the evils present in the world. Rather, it is our duty to bear them and carry our own crosses throughout this life. Pope Benedict XVI expressed a similar message when he wrote: "Jesus, whose divine love alone can redeem all humanity, wants us to share His Cross so that we can complete what is still lacking in His suffering (cf. Col. i. 24). Whenever we show kindness to the suffering, the persecuted, and defenseless, and share in their sufferings, we help to carry that same Cross of Jesus. In this way, we obtain salvation and help contribute to the salvation of the world."[236]

How to Pray This Final Petition

Rather than turning to God in prayer only in times of distress, Christians must "[p]ray without ceasing" (1 Thess. 5:17), as St. Paul says, and not simply when evils threaten us. Considering the order of the petitions in the Lord's Prayer, we know that we must first seek to honor and praise God before asking for our own needs. And the Roman Catechism, under the heading, "We Should Seek First the Glory of God," does not shy away from emphasizing this proper hierarchy:

> For there are some who, contrary to the command of Christ, reverse the order of this prayer. He who commands us to have recourse to Him in the day of tribulation [cf. Ps. xlix. 15], has also prescribed to us the order in which we should pray. It is His will that, before we pray to be delivered from evil, we ask that the Name of God be sanctified, that His kingdom come, and so on through the other Petitions, which are, as it were, so many steps by which we reach this last Petition.

> Yet there are those who, if their head, their side, or their foot, ache; if they suffer loss of property; if menaces or dangers from an enemy alarm them; if famine, war or pestilence afflict them, omit all the other Petitions of the Lord's Prayer and ask only to be delivered from these evils. This practice is at variance with the command of Christ the Lord: *Seek first the kingdom of God* [Mt. vi. 33].

Furthermore, we affirm in our prayer that God is the ultimate Author of all healing and deliverance, even through the medium of modern medicine. All healing ultimately comes from God and we must place our hope in Him.

---

[236] Robert Moynihan (ed.), *Let God's Light Shine Forth: The Spiritual Vision of Pope Benedict XVI* (New York: Image Books, 2005), 99.

Yet, the use of modern medicine, which is subordinate to the will of God, is certainly permissible:

> When visited by sickness, or other adversity, [the true Christian] flies to God as his supreme refuge and defense. Acknowledging and revering God alone as the author of all his good and his deliverer, he ascribes to Him whatever healing virtue resides in medicines, convinced that they help the sick only in so far as God wills it. For it is God Who has given medicines to man to heal his corporal infirmities; and hence these words of Ecclesiasticus: *The Most High hath created medicines out of the earth, and a wise man will not abhor them.* [Ecclus. xxxviii. 4] He, therefore, who has pledged his fidelity to Jesus Christ, does not place his principal hope of recovery in such remedies; he places it in God, the author of these medicines.

At the same time, the Roman Catechism does not fail to condemn the use of medicines prepared by pagans using "charms, spells, or other diabolical arts":

> Hence the Sacred Scriptures condemn the conduct of those who, confiding in the power of medicine, seek no assistance from God [cf. II Para. xvi. 12]. Nay more, those who regulate their lives by the laws of God, abstain from the use of all medicines which are not evidently intended by God to be medicinal; and, were there even a certain hope of recovery by using any other, they abstain from them as so many charms and diabolical artifices.

What We Pray for In This Petition

Turning to the Catechism of St. Pius X, we read: "In the Seventh Petition: *But deliver us from evil*, we ask God to free us from evils, past, present, and future, and particularly from the greatest of all evils which is sin, and from eternal damnation, which is its penalty."[237] We should not expect to be spared from all trials and temptations, of course, since they help us grow in virtue and ultimately win *the crown of life* (Ja. i. 12) prepared for those who *persevere to the end* (Mt. x. 22, xxiv. 13). The Catechism of St. Pius X therefore adds: "We say: *Deliver us from evil,* and not, *from evils,* because we should not desire to be exempt from all the evils of this life,

---

[237] *Catechism of St. Pius X*, 70.

but only from those which are not good for our souls; and hence we beg liberation from evil in general, that is, from whatever God sees would be bad for us."[238]

The Roman Catechism likewise acknowledges that we do not pray for deliverance from all evils in this petition:

> There are some things which are commonly considered evils, and which, notwithstanding, are of advantage to those who endure them. Such was the sting of the flesh to which the Apostle was subjected in order that, by the aid of divine grace, power might be perfected in infirmity [cf. II Cor. xii. 17]. When the pious man learns the salutary influence of such things, far from praying for their removal, he rejoices in them exceedingly. We pray, therefore, against those evils only, which do not conduce to our spiritual interests; not against such as are profitable to our salvation.

From what evils do we pray for deliverance? First and foremost, they include the evils inherent in our broken world: disaster, famine, disease, war, and sin:

> The full meaning of this Petition, therefore, is, that having been freed from sin and from the danger of temptation, we may be delivered from internal and external evils; that we may be protected from floods, fire and lightning; that the fruits of the earth be not destroyed by hail; that we be not visited by famine, sedition, or war. We ask that God may banish disease, pestilence, and disaster from us; that He may keep us from slavery, imprisonment, exile, betrayals, treachery, and from all other evils which fill mankind with terror and misery. Finally, we pray that God would remove all occasions of sin and iniquity.

Yet our petition goes further by also asking God to deliver us from the riches, honors, and other temporal goods that could potentially endanger our souls:

> We do not, however, pray to be delivered only from those things which all look upon as evils, but also from those things which almost all consider to be good, such

---

[238] Ibid.

as riches, honors, health, strength and even life itself; that is, we ask that these things be not detrimental or ruinous to our soul's welfare.

And chief of all, we ask for deliverance from everlasting suffering in hell:

We also beg of God that we be not cut off by a sudden death; that we provoke not His anger against us; that we be not condemned to suffer the punishments reserved for the wicked; that we be not sentenced to endure the fire of purgatory, from which we piously and devoutly implore that others may be liberated.

St. Augustine reminds us that the final petition of the Lord's Prayer affirms that we do not yet possess the Beatific Vision of God in Heaven, and that attaining heavenly glory is not a given. On the contrary, we must *with fear and trembling work out [our] salvation* (Philip. ii. 12) on a daily basis:

When we say: *Deliver us from evil*, we are reminding ourselves to reflect on the fact that we do not yet enjoy the state of blessedness in which we shall suffer no evil. This is the final petition contained in the Lord's Prayer, and it has a wide application. In this petition Christians can utter cries of sorrow, in it they can shed tears, and through it they can begin, continue and conclude their prayers, whatever the distress in which they find themselves.

While God, in His omniscience, ultimately knows the final destination of each soul (including those who will be lost), He wants *all men to be saved and to come to the knowledge of the truth* (I Tim. ii. 4). As such, He calls each of us to cooperate with His grace, rooted in Baptism, and to persevere in the *faith that worketh by charity* (Gal. v. 6) so as to *reap life everlasting* (Gal. vi. 8). If we die in the state of sanctifying grace, we will one day enter Heaven (likely after some time in purgatory). If we die in the state of mortal sin, we will go to hell for all eternity. These points are dogmatically defined by the Church. And since it is possible for a Catholic to mortally sin at the end of his life and die before receiving sacramental absolution or making a perfect act of contrition, it is certainly possible for any human soul on earth to lose Heaven. Thus, it is necessary for us to keep in mind our ultimate goal of Heaven at all times and to pray for final perseverance.

How Does God Deliver Us from Evil?

In its usual style of complementing Sacred Scriptures with beautiful commentary, the Roman Catechism explains:

> The goodness of God delivers us from evil in a variety of ways. He prevents impending evils, as we read with regard to the Patriarch Jacob, whom He delivered from the enemies that were stirred up against him on account of the slaughter of the Sichimites. For we read: *The terror of God fell upon all the cities round about, and they durst not pursue after them as they went away* [Gen. xxxv. 5].
>
> The blessed who reign with Christ the Lord in Heaven have been delivered by the divine assistance from all evil; but, as for us, although the Almighty delivers us from some evils, it is not His will that, while journeying in this, our mortal pilgrimage, we should be entirely exempt from all. The consolations with which God sometimes refreshes those who labor under adversity are, however, equivalent to an exemption from all evil; and with these the Prophet consoled himself when he said: *According to the multitude of my sorrows in my heart, thy consolations have rejoiced my soul* [Ps. xciii. 19].
>
> God, moreover, delivers men from evil when he preserves them unhurt in the midst of extreme danger, as He did in the case of the children thrown into the fiery furnace [cf. Dan. vi. 22], whom the fire did not burn; and of Daniel, whom the lions did not injure [cf. Dan. iii. 50].

Concerning various tribulations which God permits us to endure for our own ultimate good, the Catechism of St. Pius X further adds: "Tribulations help us to do penance for our sins, to practice virtue, and above all to imitate Jesus Christ, our Head, to whom it is fitting we should conform ourselves in our sufferings, if we wish to have a share in His glory." As Our Lord has asked us to carry our crosses after Him, we cannot expect to be immune from all evils in a world hurt by the effects of sin — both original sin and our actual sins.

The Importance of Penance

Our Lord tells us, *Unless you shall do penance, you shall all likewise perish* (Lk. xiii. 3). And St. John the Baptist announced the coming of the Savior with the admonition, *Do penance: for the kingdom of Heaven is at hand* (Mt. iii. 2). When we do penance, we make satisfaction to God for our sins. When we sin, we incur both guilt and a debt of punishment. The eternal guilt that would sentence a soul to hell for mortal sin is removed by the Sacrament of Confession (or, in rare circumstances, by an act of perfect contrition). The debt, however, remains and must be satisfied before a soul can be admitted to Heaven. We share a responsibility to make restitution to God for our debts and those of our family, friends, fellow citizens, and the whole of humanity. Every sin on earth wounds all of us since it is an offense of our race against the one true God.

The debt we owe to God may be paid in the form of indulgences, which are various holy works or prayers that the Church possesses by virtue of the authority granted by Christ to bind and loose (cf. Mt. xvi. 19, xviii. 18), or by our own sufferings. Those sufferings, if they are borne with patience and resignation while in the state of sanctifying grace, help to pay the debt to Almighty God. Thus, we do not just offer up abstinence from meat or dessert during Lent. We can offer up everything — our prayers, sufferings, good works, disappointments, joys, and our entire lives. Hence, it is appropriate that some trials and temptations must remain part of life for our own spiritual good.

Deliverance from Satan

Before concluding, the Roman Catechism adds an important point that of the many evils for which we pray for deliverance, one of the chief among them is deliverance from the devil, who, day and night, seeks our eternal damnation:

> According to the interpretation of St. Basil the Great, St. Chrysostom, and St. Augustine, the devil is specially called the evil one, because he was the author of man's transgression, that is, of his sin and iniquity, and also because God makes use of him as an instrument to chastise sinful and impious men. For the evils which mankind endures in punishment of sin are appointed by God; and this is the meaning of these words of Holy Writ: *Shall there be evil in a city which the Lord hath not done?* [Amos iii. 6] and: *I am the Lord and there is none else: I form the light and create darkness: I make peace and create evil* [Is. xlv. 7].
>
> The devil is also called evil, because, although we have never injured him, he wages perpetual war against us, and pursues us with mortal hatred. If we put on the armor

of faith and the shield of innocence, he can have no power to hurt us; nevertheless, he unceasingly tempts us by external evils and every other means of annoyance within his reach. Wherefore we beseech God to deliver us from the evil one.

The devil was once an angel, even one of the greatest of the angels, whose name is Lucifer, which means "light bearer." Yet, before the creation of man, roughly one-third of the angels fell from Heaven and became demons, sentenced to an eternity in hell away from God. The Baltimore Catechism teaches clearly: "Before he fell, Satan, or the devil, was called Lucifer, or light-bearer, a name which indicates great beauty. He was cast out of Heaven because through pride he rebelled against God."[239]

The demons fell from grace because they refused to accept that God would become a man to share with man the life of the Blessed Trinity in a unique way unavailable to them. They chose to be condemned to hell and spend all eternity away from God when He revealed to them His plan regarding the creation of man. And for this reason, the demons seek day and night to bring about our own damnation. The Baltimore Catechism again clearly teaches: "The devil tempts us because he hates goodness and does not wish us to enjoy the happiness which he himself has lost."[240] They are lost forever, and they want us to be lost, as well. And one of the greatest tricks of the devil is to convince man into believing his diabolical suggestion that he does not exist. From these evils, we especially pray deliverance.

Conclusion

Rather than concluding with words of despair, the Roman Catechism reminds us of the treasures that God has in store for those who persevere to the end. This time of trial will end one day, and then, we pray to see God "face to face" and enjoy His presence forever in Heaven, where no evils may threaten us:

> If to prayer we bring with us these reflections and these dispositions, although surrounded by menaces and encompassed by evils on every side, we shall, like the three children who passed unhurt amidst the flames, be preserved uninjured; or at least, like the Maccabees, we shall bear up against adverse fortune with firmness and fortitude.

---

[239] Baltimore Catechism No. 3, Q. 229.
[240] Ibid., Q. 231.

In the midst of contumelies and tortures we should imitate the blessed Apostles, who, after they had been scourged, rejoiced exceedingly that they were accounted worthy to suffer reproach for Christ Jesus [cf. Acts v. 40]. Filled with such sentiments, we shall sing in transports of joy: *Princes have persecuted me without cause; and my heart hath been in awe of Thy words; I will rejoice at Thy words, as one that hath found great spoil* [Ps. cxviii. 161-162].

XXXVIII

Amen

The Seal of the Lord's Prayer

After having studied the seven petitions of the Lord's Prayer, we come to the conclusion not only of the Our Father but also of the Roman Catechism itself. It is most fitting that the crowning word "Amen" completes the Lord's Prayer and our study of the Faith as presented with clarity, precision, and timeless beauty in the Roman Catechism, which opens its final chapter by calling "Amen" the "seal of the Lord's Prayer":

> St. Jerome in his commentary on St. Matthew rightly calls this word what it really is, *the seal of the Lord's Prayer*. As then we have already admonished the faithful with regard to the preparation to be made before this holy prayer, so we deem it necessary that they should also know why we close our prayers with this word, and what it signifies; for devotion in concluding our prayers is not less important than attention in beginning them.

The Fruits of Prayer

Before explaining the meaning of the Hebrew word "Amen," which we say so often but rarely reflect upon, the Roman Catechism first sets before us the spiritual fruits that come to the soul at the conclusion of prayer. The first such fruit is truly sublime — that the God of the universe hears our lowly prayers:

> The faithful, then, should be taught that the fruits, which we gather from the conclusion of the Lord's Prayer are numerous and abundant, the greatest and most joyful of them being the attainment of what we ask. On this point enough has already been said.

Fervor and illumination also are obtained by those who pray the Our Father with devotion:

By this concluding word, not only do we obtain a propitious hearing from God, but also receive other blessings of a higher order still, the excellence of which surpasses all powers of description.

For since, as St. Cyprian remarks, *by prayer man converses with God*, it happens in a wonderful manner that the divine Majesty is brought nearer to those who are engaged in prayer than to others and enriches them with singular gifts. Those, therefore, who pray devoutly, may not be inaptly compared to persons who approach a glowing fire; if cold, they derive warmth; if warm, they derive heat. Thus, also, those who approach God (in prayer) depart with a warmth proportioned to their faith and fervor; the heart is inflamed with zeal for the glory of God, the mind is illumined after an admirable manner, and they are enriched exceedingly with divine gifts, as it is written: *Thou hast prevented him with blessings of sweetness* [Ps. xx. 4].[241]

An example for all is that great man Moses. By intercourse and converse with God he so shone with the reflected splendors of the Divinity, that the Israelites could not look upon his eyes or countenance [cf. Ex. xxxiv. 35].

Likewise, sweetness, confidence, and gratitude are granted to souls as God sees fit:

The more familiar these truths are to the mind, the more piously do we venerate, and the more fervently do we worship God, and the more delightfully do we taste *how sweet is the Lord* [Ps. xxxiii. 9], and how truly blessed are all who hope in Him.

Encircled by the most clear light from above we also discover our own lowliness and how exalted is the majesty of God, according to the saying of St. Augustine: *Give me to know Thee: give me to know myself.* Distrusting our own strength, we thus throw ourselves

---

[241] "Prevent", in the Douay Rheims, bears the sense of "to come or go before ...", and not the sense of "to hinder" which we often associate with "to prevent."

unreservedly upon the goodness of God, not doubting that He, Who cherishes us in the bosom of His paternal wondrous love, will afford us in abundance whatever is necessary for life and salvation. Thus, we shall turn to God with the warmest gratitude our hearts can conceive and our lips express. This we read that holy David did, who commenced by praying: *Save me from all them that persecute me*, and concluded with these words, *I will give glory to the Lord according to His justice, and will sing to the Name of the Lord the Most High* [Ps. vii. 2, 18].

Regarding the fruits of prayer, the Roman Catechism concludes: "Let him, therefore, who has recourse to holy prayer approach God his Father, fortified by faith and animated by hope, not doubting that he will obtain those blessings of which he stands in need." At the same time, the Catechism of St. Pius X importantly cautions that it is not enough to merely recite the words of the Our Father. We must truly pray them: "To obtain the graces asked in the *Our Father* we must recite it without haste and with attention; and we must put our heart into it."[242]

It must also be stated that Our Lord Himself repeatedly taught us by His holy example to pray this word. As the Catholic Encyclopedia remarks, "St. Matthew attributes it to Our Lord twenty-eight times, and St. John in its doubled form twenty-six times."[243]

Amen: So Be It!

Regarding this capstone to the Lord's Prayer, the Catechism of St. Pius X concisely teaches that "Amen means: So be it; So I do desire; Thus do I pray the Lord; Thus do I hope"[244] all the same time, illustrating the difficulty in translating this Hebrew word into the vernacular. The Roman Catechism discusses this translation difficulty by way of example:

> By many, the word *amen* is differently interpreted. The Septuagint interprets it, *So be it*; others translate it, *Verily*: Aquila renders it, *Faithfully*. Which of these versions we adopt is a matter of little importance, provided we understand the word to have the sense already mentioned, namely, that when the priest

---

[242] *Catechism of St. Pius X*, 71.
[243] Fr. Herbert Thurston. "Amen." *The Catholic Encyclopedia*. Vol. 1. (New York: Robert Appleton Company, 1907).
[244] *Catechism of St. Pius X*, 70.

(pronounces *Amen*), it signifies the concession of what
has been prayed for. This interpretation is supported by
St. Paul in his Epistle to the Corinthians [cf. II Cor. i.
20]....

The Roman Catechism, in its characteristic manner, insightfully teaches
one peculiarity of the meaning of the word "Amen," as it is prayed by the
priest during the Holy Sacrifice of the Mass:

> The word *amen*, with which the Lord's Prayer concludes,
> contains, as it were, the germs of many of these thoughts
> and reflections which we have just considered. Indeed,
> so frequent was this Hebrew word in the mouth of the
> Savior, that it pleased the Holy Ghost to have it retained
> in the Church of God. Its meaning may be said to be:
> *Know that thy prayers are heard.* It has the force of a
> response, as if God answers the suppliant, and graciously
> dismisses him, after having favorably heard his prayers.
>
> This interpretation has been approved by the constant
> usage of the Church of God. In the Sacrifice of the Mass,
> when the Lord's Prayer is said she does not assign the
> word *amen* to the server who answers: *But deliver us
> front evil.* She reserves it as appropriate to the priest
> himself, who, as mediator between God and man,
> answers *Amen*, thus intimating that God has heard the
> prayers of His people.
>
> This practice, however, is not common to all the prayers,
> but is peculiar to the Lord's Prayer. To the other prayers
> the server answers *Amen*, because in every other this
> word only expresses assent and desire. In the Lord's
> Prayer it is an answer, intimating that God has heard the
> petition of His suppliant.

In *The Holy Sacrifice of the Mass: Dogmatically, Liturgically, and
Ascetically Explained* (1908), Fr. Nicholas Gihr explains this uniqueness
as such:

> This last petition is here made in the name of the faithful
> by the acolyte or choir, after which the priest concludes
> the Our Father by saying, in a low voice, *Amen.*
> This *Amen* from the lips of the priest, who is mediator
> between God and man, has in this place a peculiar
> significance. It expresses not as at other times consent

374

and desire, but is, so to speak, the answer that God has received and heard the petition of the people. The Our Father is recited aloud, or sung, in order that all present may join in the prayer with devout hearts and in childlike confidence, to which they are also incited by the *Oremus*, previously said.

The priest has seen the Lord and spoken to Him. We ask for deliverance from evil and the priest says it is done. God has heard our prayer.

The Our Father as Prayed by the Priest

The Our Father has been prayed during the Holy Sacrifice of the Mass since time immemorial. Surviving written records from the 4th century indicate it was normative in the Mass, but there is no reason to doubt it has always been part of the Church's liturgical prayer since the Apostles received this prayer from Christ precisely when they asked Him to *teach us how to pray* (Lk. xi. 1).

We know further that around the year A.D. 600, Pope St. Gregory the Great confirmed the *Pater Noster*'s place in the liturgy immediately before the fracturing of the Host and Holy Communion. As the Angelus Press Hand Missal observes, "In the ancient Church it was considered the only preparation worthy of Holy Communion."

Those familiar with the Traditional Latin Mass will be aware that every action of the priest at the altar — and his every word — is legislated by the Church and delineated in the Missal. Hence, it does not matter which ordained priest is offering the Mass, as an individual's own personal characteristics (e.g., manner of speaking or personality) fade away through the rubrics. Even his facial expression is shielded from us since he faces east (*ad orientem*) as he addresses God the Father *in persona Christi* and on our behalf.

Despite all the rubrics (e.g., look here, do this, say this while making the Sign of the Cross, etc.), the rubrics for how the priest prays the *Pater Noster* are very simple. The Church prescribes for him that he is to speak these most sacred words to the Sacred Host. The priest, who offers the Holy Sacrifice as an *alter Christus*, speaks to Our Lord the words which He Himself taught: "Our Father, Who art in Heaven...." We thus see how the Sacred Liturgy brings to life the words of Christ: *I and the Father are one* (Jn. x. 30). The priest is looking on the very Face of God when he pronounces those venerable words to the Consecrated Host and when he answers the server with the word "Amen."

The Rubrics Regarding Amen in the Liturgical Life of the Church

Commenting on the various times at which *amen* is used in the Church's traditional rituals, the Catholic Encyclopedia article on the topic illustrates some liturgical oddities. While we may be accustomed to always add *amen* to the end of our prayers, some prayers — like the form of Baptism — do not and, per the Holy See, should not include "Amen" at the end. Concerning these interesting liturgical differences, Fr. Herbert Thurston writes:

> General as was the use of the Amen as a conclusion, there were for a long time certain liturgical formulas to which it was not added. It does not for the most part occur at the end of the early creeds, and a Decree of the Congregation of Rites (n. 3014, 9 June, 1853) has decided that it should not be spoken at the end of the form for the administration of baptism, where indeed it would be meaningless. On the other hand, in the Churches of the East, Amen is still commonly said after the form of baptism, sometimes by the bystanders, sometimes by the priest himself.

> In the prayers of exorcism, it is the person exorcised who is expected to say 'Amen,' and in the conferring of sacred orders, when the vestments are given to the candidate by the bishop with some prayer of benediction, it is again the candidate who responds, just as in the solemn blessing of the Mass the people answer in the person of the server. Still, we cannot say that any uniform principle governs liturgical usage in this matter, for when at a High Mass the celebrant blesses the deacon before the latter goes to read the Gospel, it is the priest himself who says Amen.

> Similarly in the Sacrament of Penance and in the Sacrament of Extreme Unction it is the priest who adds Amen after the essential words of the sacramental form, although in the Sacrament of Confirmation this is done by the assistants. Further, it may be noticed that in past centuries certain local rites seem to have shown an extraordinary predilection for the use of the word Amen. In the Mozarabic ritual, for example, not only is it inserted after each clause of the long episcopal

benediction, but it was repeated after each petition of the *Pater Noster*. A similar exaggeration may be found in various portions of the Coptic Liturgy.[245]

The Capstone to All Prayers

But in our own lives, we know that most prayers are ordinarily concluded with this sublime word, even the prayers we say in our daily lives outside of the Sacred Liturgy. And the Roman Catechism, in its very last remarks, demonstrates the advantages of this holy word and counsels us to prayer it always:

> To us also this word is very appropriate, containing, as it does, some confirmation of the Petitions which we have already offered up. It also fixes our attention when we are engaged in holy prayer; for it frequently happens that in prayer a variety of distracting thoughts divert the mind to other objects. Nay, more, by this word we most earnestly beg of God that all our preceding Petitions may be granted; or rather, understanding that they have been all granted, and feeling the divine assistance powerfully present with us, we cry out together with the Prophet: *Behold God is my helper; and the Lord is the protector of my soul* [Ps. liii. 6].

> Nor can anyone doubt that God is moved by the Name of His Son, and by a word so often uttered by Him Who, as the Apostle says, *was always heard for His reverence* [Heb. v. 7].

Like the Creed and the Hail Mary, the Our Father should be prayed by all the Christian faithful each and every day, as the Catechism of St. Pius X teaches, "because every day we have need of God's help."[246]

Conclusion

May the Good Lord inflame all of our souls with His love, and may we, who have learned the Faith through the wisdom of the Fathers of the Council of Trent, share this wisdom with others!

In an era when the Faith is under constant assault from both within and without the Church, and when so few Catholics can explain and defend the

---

[245] Fr. Herbert Thurston, *op. cit.*
[246] Fr. Marshall Roberts, *op. cit.*, 71.

Faith, may the great saints who preceded us in this battle pray for us to emerge victorious. God will win. The Immaculate Heart of Mary will triumph. And until that day, may we labor for His reign, for the exaltation of the true Faith, and for the conquest of as many souls for His Kingdom as possible.

St. Charles Borromeo, pray for us!